Mathnawi Ma'navi

OF
Rumi

مثنوی معنوی مولانا

The Mysteries of Attainment to the Truth and Certainty

Translated By:
Reynold Alleyne Nicholson

Compiled by:
Hamid Eslamian

Persian - English

Book One

The Mathnawi Ma'navi of Rumi Book-1

Published by Persian Learning Center

Web: www.persianbell.com

Email: info@persianbell.com

Copyright © 2021 by the Persian Learning Center. All rights reserved. No part of this publication may be reproduced, stored in a retrieval system, or transmitted in any form or by any means, electronic, mechanical, photocopying, recording, scanning, or otherwise, except as permitted under Section 107 or 108 of the 1976 United States Copyright Ac, without permission of the author.

All inquiries should be addressed to the Persian Learning Center.

ISBN: 978-1-63620-903-6

One of the Greatest Persian Classic Book

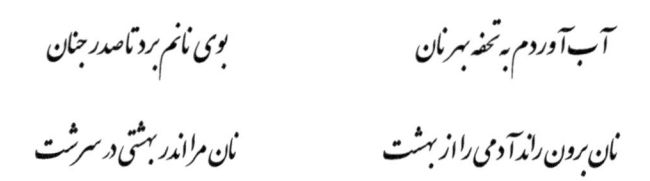

آب آوردم به تحفه بهر نان   بوی نانم برد تا صدر جنان

نان برون راندآدمی را از بهشت   نان مرا اندر بهشتی در سرشت

I brought water as a gift for the sake of (getting) bread:
the hope of bread led me to the highest place in Paradise.

Bread drove an Adam forth from Paradise:
bread caused me to mix with those who belong to Paradise.

Mathnawi Ma'navi (also known as Masnavi or "Spiritual Couplets of Maulana") is one of the most influential works of both Sufism and Persian literature. The Masnavi, written by Jalal al-Din Muhammad, Rumi is a series of six books of poetry containing more than 25,000 verses. This spiritual writing teaches Sufis how to reach their goal of being in true love with God.

Rumi is one of the best Persian poets and the Mathnawi is his masterpiece. Rumi used Persian and Arabic in his poetry. By the end of the 20th century, Rumi's popularity had become a global phenomenon, with his poetry achieving a wide circulation in the United States and western Europe.

His poems have been translated into many different languages including Turkish, Urdu, French, Turkmen, Spanish, English, Arabic, German, Italian, Albanian, Swedish, etc.

Reynold Alleyne Nicholson's translation of Mathnawi is based on the oldest known manuscripts. The prose translation, similarly, is intended to be an exact and faithful guide to the Persian.

In Book, the first of six volumes, Rumi opens the spiritual path towards higher spiritual understanding.

**We are very happy that
the Mathnawi Ma'navi of Rumi has found its way to you!**

WWW.PERSIANBELL.COM

... So Much More Online!

- ✓ FREE Farsi Lessons
- ✓ More Farsi Learning Books!
- ✓ Persian Lessons
- ✓ Online Farsi Tutors

For a PDF Version of This Book

Please Visit www.persianbell.com

Contents

سرآغاز	17
Proem	17
عاشق شدن پادشاه بر کنیزک رنجور و تدبیر کردن در صحت او	21
The story of the king's falling in love with a handmaiden and buying her	21
ظاهر شدن عجز حکیمان از معالجه کنیز	23
How it became manifest to the king that the physicians were unable to cure the handmaiden,	23
از خداوند ولی التوفیق درخواست رعایت توفیق ادب در همه حال ها	26
Beseeching the Lord, who is our Helper, to help us to observe self-control in all circumstances,	26
ملاقات پادشاه با آن ولی که در خوابش نمودند	28
The meeting of the king with the divine physician whose coming had been announced to him in a dream.	28
بردن پادشاه آن طبیب را بر سر بیمار تا حال او را ببیند	29
How the king led the physician to the bedside of the sick girl, that he might see her condition.	29
خلوت طلبیدن آن ولی از پادشاه جهت دریافتن رنج کنیزک	34
How that saint demanded of the king to be alone with the handmaiden for the purpose of discovering her malady	34
دریافتن آن ولی رنج را و عرض کردن رنج او پیش پادشاه را	38
How the saint, having discovered the (cause of) the illness, laid it before the king	38
فرستادن پادشاه رسولان به سمرقند به آوردن زرگر	39
How the king sent messengers to Samarcand to fetch the goldsmith	39
بیان آن که کشتن و زهر دادن مرد زرگر به اشارت الهی بود نه به هوای نفس و تامل فاسد	43
Setting forth how the slaying and poisoning of the goldsmith was (prompted) by Divine suggestion, not by sensual desire and wicked meditation.	43
حکایت بقال و طوطی و روغن ریختن طوطی در دکان	46
The story of the greengrocer and the parrot and the parrot's spilling the oil in the shop	46
داستان آن پادشاه جهود کی نصرانیان را می کشت از بهر تعصب	54
Story of the Jewish king who for bigotry's sake used to slay the Christians	54
آموختن وزیر مکر پادشاه را	56
How the vizier instructed the king to plot	56
تلبیس وزیر با نصارا	57
How the vizier brought the Christians into doubt and perplexity	57

قبول کردن نصارا مکر وزیر را	59
How the Christians let themselves be duped by the vizier	59
متابعت نصارا وزیر را	60
How the Christians followed the vizier	60
قصهٔ دیدن خلیفه لیلی را	64
Story of the Caliph's seeing Laylá.	64
بیان حسد وزیر	68
Explanation of the envy of the vizier.	68
فهم کردن حاذقان نصاری مکر وزیر را	69
How the sagacious among the Christians perceived the guile of the vizier	69
پیغام شاه پنهان با وزیر	70
How the king sent messages in secret to the vizier.	70
بیان دوازده سبط از نصارا	70
Explanation of the twelve tribes of the Christians	70
تخلیط وزیر در احکام آن چهیل	71
How the vizier confused the ordinances of the Gospel.	71
بیان این که این اختلافات در صورت روش است نه در حقیقت راه	75
Showing how this difference lies in the form of the doctrine not the real of the way	75
بیان خسارت وزیر در این مکر	78
Setting forth how the vizier incurred perdition (by engaging in this plot)	78
مکر دیگر انگیختن وزیر در اضلال قوم	81
How the vizier started another plan to mislead the) folk.	81
دفع گفتن وزیر مریدان را	83
How the vizier refused the request of the disciples.	83
مکر کردن مریدان کی خلوت را بشکن	84
How the disciples repeated their request that he should interrupt his seclusion	84
جواب گفتن وزیر کی خلوت را نمی شکنم	86
The refusal of the vizier to interrupt his seclusion	86
اعتراض مریدان در خلوت مدیر	86
How the disciples raised objections against the vizier's secluding himself.	86
نومید کردن وزیر مریدان را از رفض خلوت	92
How the vizier made the disciples lose hope of his abandoning seclusion.	92
ولی عهد ساختن وزیر هر یک امیر را جدا جدا	93
How the vizier appointed each one of the amírs separately as his successor	93
کشتن وزیر خویشتن را در خلوت	94
How the vizier killed himself in seclusion.	94
طلب کردن امت عیسی علیه السلام از امرا کی ولی عهد از شما کدامست	95
How the people of Jesus on him be peace! asked the amírs, "Which one of you is the successor?"	95

منازعت امرا در ولی عهدی	98
The quarrel of the amírs concerning the succession.	98
تعظیم نعت مصطفی صلی الله علیه وسلم کی مذکور بود در آن چهیل	102
How honour was paid to the description of Mustafá (Mohammed), on whom be peace, which was mentioned in the Gospel.	102
حکایت پادشاه جهود دیگر کی در هلاک دین عیسی سعی نمود	103
The story of another Jewish king who endeavored to destroy the religion of Jesus.	103
آتش کردن پادشاه جهود و بت نهادن پهلوی آتش که هر که این بت را سجود کند از آتش برست	107
How the Jewish king made a fire and placed an idol beside it, saying, "Whoever bows down to this idol shall escape the fire"	107
به سخن آمدن طفل در میان آتش و تحریض کردن خلق را در افتادن آتش	108
How a child began to speak amidst the fire and urged the people to throw themselves into the fire	108
کج ماندن دهان آن مرد که نام محمد صلی الله علیه را به تسخر خواند	112
How the mouth remained awry of a man who pronounced the name of Mohammed, on whom be peace, derisively	112
عتاب کردن آتش را آن پادشاه جهود	113
How the fire reproached the Jewish king	113
قصه باد که در عهد هود علیه السلام قوم عاد را هلاک کرد	117
The story of the wind which destroyed the people of 'Ád in the time of (the prophet) Húd, on whom be peace	117
طنز و انکار پادشاهان جهود و قبول تکردن نصیحت خاصان خویش	118
How the Jewish king scoffed and denied and would not accept the counsel of his intimates.	118
بیان توکل و ترک جهد گفتن نخچیران بشیر	122
Setting forth how the beasts of chase told the lion to trust in God and cease from exerting himself.	122
جواب گفتن شیر نخچیران را و فایده جهد گفتن	123
How the lion answered the beasts and explained the advantage of exertion	123
ترجیح دادن نخچیران توکل را بر جحد و اکتساب	123
How the beasts asserted the superiority of trust in God to exertion and acquisition	123
ترجیح نهادن شیر جحد و اکتساب بر توکل و تسلیم	124
How the lion upheld the superiority of exertion and acquisition to trust in God and resignation.	124
ترجیح نهادن نخچیران توکل را بر اجتهاد	124
How the beasts preferred trust in God to exertion.	124
ترجیح نهادن شیر جهد را بر توکل باز	126
How the lion again pronounce d exertion to be superior to trust in God	126
باز ترجیح نهادن نخچیران توکل را بر جهد	128
How the beasts once more asserted the superiority of trust in God to exertion	128

نگریستن عزرائیل بر مردی..129	
How 'Azrá'íl (Azrael) looked at a certain man,..129	
باز ترجیح نهادن شیر جهد را بر توکل و فواید جهد را بیان کردن.....................................131	
How the lion again declared exertion to be superior to trust in God and expounded the advantages of exertion..131	
مقرر شدن ترجیح جهد بر توکل...134	
How the superiority of exertion to trust in God was established...........................134	
انکار کردن نخجیران بر خرگوش در تاخیر رفتن بر شیر...134	
How the beasts of chase blamed the hare for his delay in going to the lion........134	
جواب گفتن خرگوش ایشان را..135	
How the hare answered the beasts...135	
اعتراض نخجیران بر سخن خرگوش..136	
How the beasts objected to the proposal of the hare...136	
جواب خرگوش نخجیران را..136	
How the hare again answered the beasts..136	
ذکر دانش خرگوش و بیان فضیلت و منافع دانستن..139	
An account of the knowledge of the hare and an explanation of the excellence and advantages of knowledge...139	
باز طلبیدن نخجیران از خرگوش سر اندیشه او را..140	
How the beasts requested the hare to tell the secret of his thought...................140	
منع کردن خرگوش از راز ایشان را...141	
How the hare withheld the secret from them..141	
قصه مکر خرگوش..143	
The story of the hare's stratagem...143	
زیافت تاویل رکیک مگس..146	
The baseness of the foul interpretation given by the fly.....................................146	
تولیدن شیر از دیر آمدن خرگوش...147	
How the lion roared wrathfully because the hare was late in coming..................147	
هم در بیان مکر خرگوش...149	
Further setting forth the stratagem of the hare...149	
رسیدن خرگوش به شیر...154	
The hare's coming to the lion and the lion's anger with him................................154	
عذر گفتن خرگوش...155	
The hare's apology..155	
جواب گفتن شیر خرگوش را و روان شدن با او...158	
How the lion answered the hare and set off with him...158	
قصه هد هد و سلیمان در بیان اینکه چون قضا آید چشم های روشن بسته شود............161	
Story of the hoopoe and Solomon, showing that when the Divine destiny comes to pass, clear eyes are sealed...161	

طعنه زاغ در دعوی هدهد	163
How the crow impugned the claim of the hoopoe	163
جواب گفتن هد هد طعنه زاغ.	164
The hoopoe's answer to the attack of the crow.	164
قصه ادم علیه السلام	165
The story of Adam, on whom be peace,	165
پا واپس کشیدن خرگوش از شیر چون نزدیک چاه رسید	169
How the hare drew back from the lion when he approached the well.	169
پرسیدن شیر از سبب پای واپس کشیدن خرگوش	173
How the lion asked the reason of the hare's drawing back	173
نظر کردن شیر در چاه و دیدن عکس خود را و آن خرگوش را.	174
How the lion looked into the well and saw the reflexion of himself and the hare in the water	174
مژده بردن خرگوش سوی نخجیران که شیر در چاه افتاد	178
How the hare brought to the beasts of chase the news that the lion had fallen into the well	178
جمع شدن نخجیران گرد خرگوش و ثنا گفتن او را.	180
How the beasts gathered round the hare and spoke in praise of him.	180
پند دادن خرگوش نخجیران را که بدین شاد مشوید	181
Advise of Nabbit Nakhjiran: Do Not Be Happy with this	181
تفسیر رجعنا من الجهادالاصغر الی الجهاد الاکبر	182
Commentary on (the Tradition) "We have returned from the lesser Jihád to the greater Jihád."	182
آمدن رسول روم تا نزد عمر و دیدن کرامات او	184
How the ambassador of Rúm came to the Commander of the Faithful, 'Umar, and witnessed the gifts of grace with which 'Umar, was endowed	184
یافتن رسول روم عمر را خفته در زیر درخت.	187
How the ambassador of Rúm found the Commander of the Faithful, 'Umar, may God be well-pleased with him, sleeping under the palm-tree.	187
سلام کردن رسول روم بر عمر	188
How the ambassador of Rúm saluted the Commander of the Faithful, may God be well pleased with him.	188
سوال کردن رسول روم از عمر	191
How the ambassador of Rúm questioned the Commander of the Faithful, may God be well-pleased with him.	191
اضافت کردن آدم علیه‌السلام آن زلت را به خویشتن	195
How Adam imputed that fault (which he had committed) to himself,	195
تفسیر و هو معکم این ما کنتم	198
Commentary on "And He is with you wheresoever ye be."	198
سؤال کردن رسول روم از عمر رضی‌الله عنه از سبب ابتلای ارواح با این آب وگل جسم.	199

How the ambassador asked 'Umar, may God be well-pleased with him, concerning the cause of the tribulation suffered by spirits in these bodies of clay. 199

در معنی آنک من اراد ان یجلس مع الله فلیجلس مع اهل التصوف 201
On the inner sense of "Let him who desires to sit with God sit with the Súfis." 201

قصهٔ بازرگان کی طوطی محبوس او را پیغام داد به طوطیان هندوستان هنگام رفتن به تجارت 203
The story of the merchant to whom the parrot gave a message for the parrots of India on the occasion of his going (thither) to trade. 203

صفت اجنحهٔ طیور عقول الهی 206
Description of the wings of the birds that are Divine Intelligences. 206

دیدن خواجه طوطیان هندوستان را در دشت و پیغام رسانیدن از آن طوطی 208
How the merchant saw the parrots of India in the plain and delivered the parrot's message. 208

تفسیر قول فریدالدین عطار قدس الله روحه 210
Commentary on the saying of Farídu'ddín 'Attár, -may God sanctify his spirit- 210

تعظیم ساحران مر موسی را علیه‌السلام کی چه می‌فرمایی اول تو اندازی عصا 211
How the magicians paid respect to Moses, on whom be peace, saying, "What dost thou command? Wilt thou cast down thy rod first, or shall we?" 211

باز گفتن بازرگان با طوطی آنچه دید از طوطیان هندوستان 215
How the merchant related to the parrot what he had witnessed on the part of the parrots of India. 215

چون فراموشی خلق با یادشان و بیست و او رسد فریادشان 219
Inasmuch as the forgetfulness and recollection of (God's) creatures are with him (depend on the perfect saint), and he comes at their call for help, ...219

شنیدن آن طوطی حرکت آن طوطیان و مردن آن طوطی در قفص و نوحهٔ خواجه بر وی 220
How the parrot heard what those parrots had done, and died in the cage, and how the merchant made lament for her. 220

تفسیر قول حکیم 228
Commentary on the saying of the Hakím (Saná'í): 228

رجوع به حکایت خواجهٔ تاجر 234
Reverting to the tale of the merchant who went to trade (in India). 234

برون انداختن مرد تاجر طوطی را از قفص و پریدن طوطی مرده 235
How the merchant cast the parrot out of the cage and how the dead parrot flew away. 235

وداع کردن طوطی خواجه را و پریدن 238
How the parrot bade farewell to the merchant and flew away. 238

مضرت تعظیم خلق و انگشت‌نمای شدن 238
The harmfulness of being honoured by the people and of becoming conspicuous. 238

تفسیر ما شاء الله کان 242
Explanation of (the Tradition) "Whatsoever God wills cometh to pass." 242

داستان پیر چنگی 246
The story of the old harper 246

11

در بیان این حدیث کی ان لربکم فی ایام دهرکم نفحات الا فتعر ضوا لها	250
Explanation of the Tradition, "Verily, your Lord hath, during the days of your time, certain breathings: oh, address yourselves to (receive) them."	250
قصهٔ سوال کردن عایشه رضی الله عنها از مصطفی صلی‌الله علیه و سلم	257
The story of 'Á'isha, may God be well-pleased with her, how she asked Mustafá (Mohammed), on whom be peace, saying,	257
تفسیر بیت حکم رضی‌الله عنه	260
Commentary on the verse of Hakím (Saná'í):	260
در معنی این حدیث کی اغتنموا برد الربیع الی آخره	261
On the meaning of the Tradition, "Take advantage of the coolness of the spring season, etc."	261
پرسیدن صدیقه رضی‌الله عنها از مصطفی صلی‌الله علیه و سلم کی سر باران امروزینه چه بود	263
How the Siddíqa ('Á'isha), may God be well-pleased with her, asked Mustafá, God bless him and give him peace, saying, "What was the inner meaning of to-day's rain?"	263
بقیهٔ قصهٔ پیر چنگی و بیان مخلص آن	264
The remainder of the story of the old harper and the explanation of its issue (moral)	264
خواب گفتن هاتف مر عمر را رضی الله عنه	268
How the heavenly voice spoke to 'Umar, may God be well-pleased with him, while he was asleep, saying,	268
نالیدن ستون حنانه چون برای پیغامبر صلی الله علیه و سلم منبر ساختند	269
How the moaning pillar complained when they made a pulpit for the Prophet, on whom be peace	269
اظهار معجزهٔ پیغمبر صلی الله علیه و سلم	274
How the Prophet, on whom be peace, manifested a miracle	274
بقیهٔ قصهٔ مطرب	275
The rest of the story of the minstrel,	275
گردانیدن عمر رضی الله عنه نظر او را از مقام گریه	280
How 'Umar, may God be well-pleased with him, bade him (the harper) turn his gaze from the stage of weeping,	280
تفسیر دعای آن دو فرشته	283
Commentary on the prayer of the two angels	283
قصهٔ خلیفه	286
The story of the Caliph	286
قصهٔ اعرابی درویش و ماجرای زن با او به سبب قلت و درویشی	287
Story of the poor Arab of the desert and his wife's altercation with him because of (their) penury and poverty.	287
مغرور شدن مریدان محتاج به مدعیان مزور	288
How disciples (novices in Súfism) are beguiled in their need by false impostors	288
در بیان آنک نادر افتد کی مریدی در مدعی مزور اعتقاد بصدق ببندد	291

Explaining how it may happen, (though) rarely, that a disciple sincerely puts his faith in a false impostor 291

صبر فرمودن اعرابی زن خود را و فضیلت صبر و فقر بیان کردن با زن 292
How the Bedouin bade his wife be patient and declared to her the excellence of patience and poverty. 292

نصیحت کردن زن مر شوی را 295
How the wife counselled her husband, saying, ... 295

نصیحت کردن مرد مر زن را 298
How the man counselled his wife, saying, ... 298

در بیان آنک جنبیدن هر کسی از آنجا 301
Explaining how every one's movement (action) proceeds from the place 301

مراعات کردن زن شوهر را و استغفار کردن از گفتهٔ خویش 304
How the wife paid regard to her husband and begged God to forgive her for what she had said. 304

در بیان این خبر ک انهن یغلبن العاقل و یغلبهن الجاهل 309
Explanation of the Tradition, "Verily, they (women) prevail over the wise man, and the ignorant man prevails over them." 309

تسلیم کردن مرد خود را بآنچه التماس زن بود 309
How the man yielded to his wife's request 309

در بیان آنک موسی و فرعون هر دو مسخر مشیت‌اند 311
Explaining that both Moses and Pharaoh are subject to the Divine Will, ... 311

سبب حرمان اشقیا از دو جهان 315
The reason why the unblest are disappointed of both worlds, ... 315

حقیر و بی‌خصم دیدن دیده‌های حس صالح و ناقهٔ صالح علیه‌السلام را 318
How the eyes of (external) sense regarded Sálih and his she-camel as despicable and without a champion; 318

در معنی آنک مرج البحرین یلتقیان بینهما برزخ لا یبغیان 325
On the meaning of "He let the two seas go to meet one another: between them is a barrier which they do not seek 325

در معنی آنک آنچه ولی کند مرید را نشاید گستاخی کردن 329
Concerning the impropriety of the disciple's (muríd) presuming to do the same things as are done by the saint (walí), ... 329

مخلص ماجرای عرب و جفت او 331
The moral of the altercation of the Arab and his wife. 331

دل نهادن عرب بر التماس دلبر خویش و سوگند خوردن 334
How the Arab set his heart on (complying with) his beloved's request and swore 334

تعیین کردن زن طریق طلب روزی کدخدای خود را و قبول کردن او 338
How the wife specified to her husband the way to earn daily bread and how he accepted (her proposal). 338

هدیه بردن عرب سبوی آب باران از میان بادیه 341

341	How the Arab carried a jug of rain-water from the midst of the desert as a gift
343	در نمد دوختن زن عرب سبوی آب باران را
343	How the Arab's wife sewed the jug of rain-water in a felt cloth
346	در بیان آنک چنانک گدا عاشق کرمست
346	Showing that, as the beggar is in love with bounty
347	فرق میان آنک درویش است به خدا و تشنهٔ خدا
347	The difference between one that is poor for (desirous of) God and thirsting for Him
349	پیش آمدن نقیبان و دربانان خلیفه از بهر اکرام اعرابی و پذیرفتن هدیهٔ او را
349	How the Caliph's officers and chamberlains came forward to pay their respects to the Bedouin and to receive his gift.
353	در بیان آنک عاشق دنیا بر مثال عاشق دیواریست
353	Showing that the lover of this world is like the lover of a wall
353	مثل عرب اذا زنیت فازن بالحرة و اذا سرقت فاسرق الدرة
353	The Arabic proverb, "If you commit fornication, commit it with a free woman, and if you steal, steal a pearl."
355	سپردن عرب هدیه را یعنی سبو را به غلامان خلیفه
355	How the Arab delivered the gift, that is, the jug to the Caliph's servants
357	حکایت ماجرای نحوی و کشتیبان
357	The story of what passed between the grammarian and the boatman.
359	قبول کردن خلیفه هدیه را
359	How the Caliph accepted the gift
368	در صفت پیر و مطاوعت وی
368	Concerning the qualities of the Pír (Spiritual Guide) and (the duty of) obedience to him.
371	وصیت کردن رسول صلی الله علیه و سلم مر علی را کرم الله وجهه
371	How the Prophet, on whom be peace, enjoined 'Alí—may God make his person honoured—saying,
374	کبودی زدن قزوینی بر شانه گاه صورت شیر
374	How the man of Qazwín was tattooing the figure of a lion in blue on his shoulders,
378	رفتن گرگ و روباه در خدمت شیر به شکار
378	How the wolf and fox went to hunt in attendance on the lion.
381	امتحان کردن شیر گرگ را
381	How the lion made trial of the wolf
383	قصه آنکس کی در یاری بکوفت از درون
383	The story of the person who knocked at a friend's door:
385	صفت توحید
385	Description of Unification.
388	ادب کردن شیر گرگ را کی در قسمت بی ادبی کرده بود
388	How the lion punished the wolf who had shown disrespect in dividing (the prey).

تهدید کردن نوح علیه‌السلام مر قوم را 391	
How Noah, on whom be peace, threatened his people, saying, ... 391	
نشاندن پادشاه صوفیان عارف را پیش روی خویش تا چشمشان بدیشان روشن شود 394	
How kings seat in front of them the Súfís who know God, in order that their eyes may be illumined by (seeing) them. 394	
آمدن مهمان پیش یوسف علیه‌السلام 395	
How the guest came to Joseph, on whom be peace, ... 395	
گفتن مهمان یوسف علیه‌السلام کی آینه‌ای آوردمت 399	
How the guest said to Joseph, "I have brought thee the gift of a mirror, ... 399	
مرتد شدن کاتب وحی 403	
How the writer of the (Qur'ánic) Revelation fell into apostasy 403	
دعا کردن بلعم با عور 411	
How Bal'am son of Bá'úr prayed (to God), saying, ... 411	
اعتماد کردن هاروت و ماروت بر عصمت خویش 414	
How Hárút and Márút relied upon their immaculateness 414	
باقی قصهٔ هاروت و ماروت 417	
The rest of the story of Hárút and Márút, ... 417	
به عیادت رفتن کر بر همسایهٔ رنجور خویش 419	
How the deaf man went to visit his sick neighbour. 419	
اول کسی کی در مقابلهٔ نص قیاس آورد ابلیس بود 423	
The first to bring analogical reasoning to bear against the Revealed Text was Iblís. .. 423	
در بیان آنک حال خود و مستی خود پنهان باید داشت از جاهلان 426	
Explaining that one must keep one's own (spiritual) state and (mystical) intoxication hidden from the ignorant 426	
قصهٔ مری کردن رومیان و چینیان در علم نقاشی و صورت‌گری. 431	
The story of the contention between the Greeks and the Chinese in the art of painting and picturing 431	
پرسیدن پیغمبر صلی الله علیه و سلم مر زید را 435	
How the Prophet, on whom be peace, asked Zayd, ... 435	
متهم کردن غلامان و خواجه‌تاشان مر لقمان را 445	
How suspicion was thrown upon Luqmán by the slaves and fellow-servants 445	
بقیهٔ قصه زید در جواب رسول صلی الله علیه و سلم 448	
The remainder of the story of Zayd (and what he said) in answer to the Prophet, on whom be peace. 448	
گفتن پیغامبر صلی الله علیه و سلم مر زید را 453	
How the Prophet, on whom be peace, said to Zayd, ... 453	
رجوع به حکایت زید 455	
The (author's) return to the story of Zayd. 455	
آتش افتادن در شهر بایام عمر رضی الله عنه 459	

How a conflagration occurred in the city (Medina) in the days of 'Umar, may God be well-pleased with him. 459

خدو انداختن خصم در روی امیر المؤمنین علی کرم الله وجهه 461
How an enemy spat in the face of the Prince of the Faithful, Alí, may God honour his person, ... 461

سؤال کردن آن کافر از علی کرم الله وجهه 467
How that infidel asked 'Alí, may God honour his person, saying, ... 467

جواب گفتن امیر المؤمنین. 469
How the Prince of the Faithful made answer (and explained) 469

گفتن پیغامبر صلی الله علیه و سلم به گوش رکابدار امیر المومنین علی کرم الله وجهه 475
How the Prophet, on whom be peace, said in the ear of the stirrup-holder of the Prince of the Faithful ('Ali), may God honour his person, ... 475

تعجب کردن آدم علیه‌السلام از ضلالت ابلیس لعین و عجب آوردن 481
How Adam, on whom be peace, marvelled at the perdition of Iblís and showed vanity. 481

بازگشتن به حکایت علی کرم الله وجهه 485
Returning to the story of the Prince of the Faithful, 'Alí -may God honour his person! 485

افتادن رکابدار هر باری پیش امیر المؤمنین علی کرم الله وجهه 487
How the stirrup-holder of 'Alí, may God honour his person, came (to him), saying, ... 487

بیان آنک فتح طلبیدن مصطفی صلی الله علیه و سلم مکه را و غیر مکه را 488
Explaining that the motive of the Prophet, on whom be peace, in seeking to conquer Mecca and other (places) than Mecca 488

گفتن امیر المؤمنین علی کرم الله وجهه با قرین خود. 491
How the Prince of the Faithful, 'Ali-may God honour his person! said to his antagonist, 491

سرآغاز
Proem

بشنو از نی چون حکایت می‌کند
Listen to the reed how it tells a tale
از جدایی‌ها شکایت می‌کند
complaining of separations

کز نیستان تا مرا ببریده‌اند
Saying, "Ever since I was parted from the reed-bed,
در نفیرم مرد و زن نالیده‌اند
My lament hath caused man and woman to moan

سینه خواهم شرحه شرحه از فراق
I want a bosom torn by severance,
تا بگویم شرح درد اشتیاق
that I may unfold (to such a one) the pain of love-desire.

هر کسی کو دور ماند از اصل خویش
Everyone who is left far from his source
باز جوید روزگار وصل خویش
wishes back the time when he was united with it

من به هر جمعیتی نالان شدم
In every company I uttered my wailful notes
جفت بدحالان و خوش‌حالان شدم
I consorted with the unhappy and with them that rejoice

هرکسی از ظن خود شد یار من
Every one became my friend from his own opinion
از درون من نجست اسرار من
none sought out my secrets from within me

سر من از نالهٔ من دور نیست
My secret is not far from my plaint
لیک چشم و گوش را آن نور نیست
but ear and eye lack the light (whereby it should be apprehended)

تن ز جان و جان ز تن مستور نیست
Body is not veiled from soul
لیک کس را دید جان دستور نیست
nor soul from body, yet none is permitted to see the soul

آتشست این بانگ نای و نیست باد
This noise of the reed is fire
هر که این آتش ندارد، نیست باد
it is not wind: whoso hath not this fire, may he be naught!

17

آتش عشقست کاندر نی فتاد
Tis the fire of Love that is in the reed

جوشش عشقست کاندر می فتاد
tis the fervour of Love that is in the wine

نی حریف هرکه از یاری برید
The reed is the comrade of every one who has been parted from a friend

پرده هایش پرده های ما درید
its strains pierced our hearts

همچو نی زهری و تریاقی کی دید
Who ever saw a poison and antidote like the reed?

همچو نی دمساز و مشتاقی کی دید
Who ever saw a sympathiser and a longing lover like the reed?

نی حدیث راه پر خون می‌کند
The reed tells of the Way full of blood

قصه‌های عشق مجنون می‌کند
and recounts stories of the passion of Majnún

محرم این هوش جز بیهوش نیست
Only to the senseless is this sense confided

مر زبان را مشتری جز گوش نیست
the tongue hath no customer save the ear

در غم ما روزها بیگاه شد
In our woe the days (of life) have become untimely

روزها با سوزها همراه شد
Our days travel hand in hand with burning griefs.

روزها گر رفت گو رو باک نیست
If our days are gone, let them go! —'tis no matter

تو بمان ای آنک چون تو پاک نیست
Do Thou remain, for none is holy as Thou art!

هر که جز ماهی ز آبش سیر شد
Whoever is not a fish becomes sated with His water

هرکه بی روزیست روزش دیر شد
whoever is without daily bread finds the day long

در نیابد حال پخته هیچ خام
None that is raw understands the state of the ripe

پس سخن کوتاه باید والسلام
therefore my words must be brief. Farewell!

بند بگسل باش آزاد ای پسر
O son, burst thy chains and be free!
چند باشی بند سیم و بند زر
How long wilt thou be a bondsman to silver and gold?

گر بریزی بحر را در کوزه‌ای
If thou pour the sea into a pitcher,
چند گنجد قسمت یک روزه‌ای
how much will it hold?

کوزهٔ چشم حریصان پر نشد
The pitcher, the eye of the covetous, never becomes full
تا صدف قانع نشد پر در نشد
the oyster-shell is not filled with pearls until it is contented.

هر که را جامه ز عشقی چاک شد
He (alone) whose garment is rent by a (mighty)
او ز حرص و عیب کلی پاک شد
love is purged of covetousness and all defect

شاد باش ای عشق خوش سودای ما
Hail, O Love that bringest us good gain
ای طبیب جمله علتهای ما
thou that art the physician of all our ills,

ای دوای نخوت و ناموس ما
The remedy of our pride and vainglory
ای تو افلاطون و جالینوس ما
our Plato and our Galen!

جسم خاک از عشق بر افلاک شد
Through Love the earthly body soared to the skies
کوه در رقص آمد و چالاک شد
the mountain began to dance and became

عشق جان طور آمد عاشقا
Love inspired Mount Sinai, O lover
طور مست و خر موسی صاعقا
(so that) Sinai (was made) drunken and Moses fell in a swoon

با لب دمساز خود گر جفتمی
Were I joined to the lip of one in accord with me
همچو نی من گفتنی‌ها گفتمی
I too, like the reed, would tell all that may be told

هر که او از هم زبانی شد جدا
(But) whoever is parted from one who speaks his language
بی زبان شد گرچه دارد صد نوا
becomes dumb, though he have a hundred songs

چونک گل رفت و گلستان درگذشت
When the rose is gone and the garden faded
نشنوی زان پس ز بلبل سرگذشت
thou wilt hear no more the nightingale's story.

جمله معشوقست و عاشق پرده‌ای
The Beloved is all and the lover (but) a veil
زنده معشوقست و عاشق مرده‌ای
the Beloved is living and the lover a dead thing.

چون نباشد عشق را پروای او
When Love hath no care for him
او چو مرغی ماند بی پر وای او
he is left as a bird without wings. Alas for him then!

من چگونه هوش دارم پیش و پس
How should I have consciousness (of aught) before or behind
چون نباشد نور یارم پیش و پس
when the light of my Beloved is not before me and behind?

عشق خواهد کین سخن بیرون بود
Love wills that this Word should be shown forth:
آینه غماز نبود چون بود
if the mirror does not reflect, how is that?

آینت دانی چرا غماز نیست
Dost thou know why the mirror (of thy soul) reflects nothing?
زانک زنگار از رخش ممتاز نیست
Because the rust is not cleared from its face.

◆◉◆◆◉◆

عاشق شدن پادشاه بر کنیزک رنجور و تدبیر کردن در صحت او
The story of the king's falling in love with a handmaiden and buying her

بشنوید ای دوستان این داستان
O my friends, hearken to this tale

خود حقیقت نقد حال ماست آن
in truth it is the very marrow of our inward state.

بود شاهی در زمانی پیش ازین
In olden time there was a king

ملک دنیا بودش و هم ملک دین
to whom belonged the power temporal and also the power spiritual.

اتفاقا شاه روزی شد سوار
It chanced that one day he rode

با خواص خویش از بهر شکار
with his courtiers to the chase.

یک کنیزک دید شه بر شاه راه
On the king's highway the king espied a handmaiden

شد غلام آن کنیزک پادشاه
the soul of the king was enthralled by her.

مرغ جانش در قفس چون می‌طپید
Forasmuch as the bird, his soul was fluttering in its cage

داد مال و آن کنیزک را خرید
he gave money and bought the handmaiden.

چون خرید او را و برخوردار شد
After he had bought her and won to his desire,

آن کنیزک از قضا بیمار شد
by Divine destiny she sickened.

آن یکی خر داشت و پالانش نبود
A certain man had an ass but no pack-saddle: (as soon as)

یافت پالان گرگ خر را در ربود
he got a saddle, the wolf carried away his ass.

کوزه بودش آب می‌نامد بدست
He had a pitcher but no water could be obtained:

آب را چون یافت خود کوزه شکست
when he found water, the pitcher broke.

شه طبیبان جمع کرد از چپ و راست
The king gathered the physicians together from left and right

گفت جان هر دو در دست شماست
and said to them, "The life of us both is in your hands.

جان من سهلست جان جانم اوست
My life is of no account, (but) she is the life of my life.
دردمند و خسته‌ام درمانم اوست
I am in pain and wounded: she is my remedy.

هر که درمان کرد مر جان مرا
Whoever heals her that is my life
برد گنج و در و مرجان مرا
will bear away with him my treasure and pearls, large and small."

جمله گفتندش که جانبازی کنیم
They all answered him, saying, "We will hazard our lives
فهم گرد آریم و انبازی کنیم
and summon all our intelligence and put it into the common stock.

هر یکی از ما مسیح عالمیست
Each one of us is the Messiah of a world (of people):
هر الم را در کف ما مرهمیست
in our hands is a medicine for every pain."

گر خدا خواهد نگفتند از بطر
In their arrogance they did not say,
پس خدا بنمودشان عجز بشر
"If God will"; therefore God showed unto them the weakness of Man.

ترک استثنا مرادم قسوتیست
I mean (a case in which) omission of the saving clause is (due to) a hardness of heart;
نه همین گفتن که عارض حالتیست
not the mere saying of these words, for that is a superficial circumstance.

ای بسا ناورده استثنا بگفت
How many a one has not pronounced the saving clause,
جان او با جان استثناست جفت
and yet his soul is in harmony with the soul of it!

هرچه کردند از علاج و از دوا
The more cures and remedies they applied,
گشت رنج افزون و حاجت ناروا
the more did the illness increase, and the need was not fulfilled.

آن کنیزک از مرض چون موی شد
The sick girl became (thin) as a hair,
چشم شه از اشک خون چون جوی شد
(while) the eyes of the king flowed with tears of blood, like a river.

از قضا سرکنگبین صفرا فزود
By Divine destiny, oxymel produced bile,
روغن بادام خشکی می‌نمود
and oil of almonds was increasing the dryness.
از هلیله قبض شد اطلاق رفت
From (giving) myrobalan constipation resulted,
آب آتش را مدد شد همچو نفت
relaxation ceased; and water fed the flames, like naphtha

❁◉❁◉❁

ظاهر شدن عجز حکیمان ازمعالجه کنیز
How it became manifest to the king that the physicians were unable to cure the handmaiden,
و روی آوردن پادشاه به درگاه خدا و در خواب دیدن او و ولی او را
and how he turned his face towards God and dreamed of a holy man

شه چو عجز آن حکیمان را بدید
When the king saw the powerlessness of those physicians
پا برهنه جانب مسجد دوید
he ran bare-footed to the mosque.

رفت در مسجد سوی محراب شد
He entered the mosque and advanced to the mihráb (to pray)
سجده‌گاه از اشک شه پر آب شد
the prayer-carpet was bathed in the king's tears.

چون به خویش آمد ز غرقاب فنا
On coming to himself out of the flood of ecstasy (faná)
خوش زبان بگشاد در مدح و دعا
he opened his lips in goodly praise and laud,

کای کمینه بخششت ملک جهان
Saying, "O Thou whose least gift is the empire of the world
من چه گویم چون تو می‌دانی نهان
what shall I say, in as much as Thou knowest the hidden thing?

ای همیشه حاجت ما را پناه
O Thou with whom we always take refuge in our need,
بار دیگر ما غلط کردیم راه
once again we have missed the way.

23

لیک گفتی گرچه می‌دانم سرت
But Thou hast said, 'Albeit I know thy secret
زود هم پیدا کنش بر ظاهرت
nevertheless, declare it forthwith in thine outward act.'"

چون برآورد از میان جان خروش
When from the depths of his soul he raised a cry (of supplication)
اندر آمد بحر بخشایش به جوش
the sea of Bounty began to surge.

درمیان گریه خوابش در ربود
Slumber overtook him in the midst of weeping
دید در خواب او که پیری رو نمود
he dreamed that an old man appeared

گفت ای شه مژده حاجاتت رواست
And said, "Good tidings, O king! Thy prayers are granted.
گر غریبی آیدت فردا ز ماست
If to-morrow a stranger come for thee, he is from me.

چونک آید او حکیمی حاذقست
When he comes, he is the skilled physician
صادقش دان کو امین و صادقست
deem him veracious, for he is trusty and true.

در علاجش سحر مطلق را ببین
In his remedy behold absolute magic,
در مزاجش قدرت حق را ببین
in his temperament behold the might of God!"

چون رسید آن وعده‌گاه و روز شد
When the promised hour arrived and day broke and the sun,
آفتاب از شرق اخترسوز شد
(rising) from the east, began to burn the stars,

بود اندر منظره شه منتظر
The king was in the belvedere,
تا ببیند آنچه بنمودند سر
expecting to see that which had been shown mysteriously.

دید شخصی فاضلی پر مایه‌ای
He saw a person excellent and worshipful,
آفتابی درمیان سایه‌ای
a sun amidst a shadow,

می‌رسید از دور ماند هلال
Coming from afar, like the new moon (in slenderness and radiance):
نیست بود و هست بر شکل خیال
he was nonexistent, though existent in the form of phantasy.

نیست وش باشد خیال اندر روان
In the spirit phantasy is as naught,
تو جهانی بر خیالی بین روان
(yet) behold a world(turning) on a phantasy!

بر خیالی صلحشان و جنگشان
Their peace and their war (turn) on a phantasy,
وز خیالی فخرشان و ننگشان
and their pride and their shame spring from a phantasy;

آن خیالاتی که دام اولیاست
(But) those phantasies which ensnare the saints are
عکس مه‌رویان بستان خداست
the reflexion of the fair ones of the garden of God.

آن خیالی که شه اندر خواب دید
that phantasy which the king beheld in his dream.
در رخ مهمان همی آمد پدید
In the countenance of the stranger-guest was appearing

شه به جای حاجبان فا پیش رفت
The king himself, instead of the chamberlains,
پیش آن مهمان غیب خویش رفت
ent forward to meet his guest from the Invisible.

هر دو بحری آشنا آموخته
Both were seamen who had learned to swim,
هر دو جان بی دوختن بر دوخته
the souls of both were knit together without sewing

گفت معشوقم تو بودستی نه آن
The king said, "Thou wert my Beloved (in reality),
لیک کار از کار خیزد در جهان
not she; but in this world deed issues from deed.

ای مرا تو مصطفی من چو عمر
O thou who art to me (as) Mustafá (Mohammed),
از برای خدمتت بندم کمر
while I am like unto 'Umar—I will gird my loins to do thee service."

25

از خداوند ولی التوفیق درخواست رعایت توفیق ادب در همه حال ها
Beseeching the Lord, who is our Helper, to help us to observe self-control in all circumstances,

و بیان کردن وخامت ضررهای بی ادبی
and explaining the harmful and pernicious consequences of indiscipline

از خدا جوییم توفیق ادب
Let us implore God to help us to self-control

بی‌ادب محروم گشت از لطف رب
one who lacks self-control is deprived of the grace of the Lord.

بی‌ادب تنها نه خود را داشت بد
The undisciplined man does not maltreat himself alone,

بلک آتش در همه آفاق زد
but he sets the whole world on fire.

مایده از آسمان در می‌رسید
A table (of food) was coming down from heaven

بی‌شری و بیع و بی‌گفت و شنید
without headache (trouble) and without selling and buying,

درمیان قوم موسی چند کس
(When) some of the people of Moses

بی‌ادب گفتند کو سیر و عدس
cried disrespectfully, "Where is garlic and lentils?"

منقطع شد خوان و نان از آسمان
(Straightway) the heavenly bread and dishes (of food) were cut off:

ماند رنج زرع و بیل و داس مان
there remained (for all of them) the toil of sowing and (labouring with) mattock and scythe.

باز عیسی چون شفاعت کرد حق
Again, when Jesus made intercession,

خوان فرستاد و غنیمت بر طبق
God sent food and bounty (from heaven) on trays,

مائده از آسمان شد عائده
But once more the insolent fellows omitted to show respect

چون که گفت انزل علینا مائده
and, like beggars, snatched away the viands.

باز گستاخان ادب بگذاشتند
But once more the insolent fellows omitted to show respect and,

چون گدایان زله‌ها برداشتند
like beggars, snatched away the viands.

لابه کرده عیسی ایشان را که این
Although) Jesus entreated them, saying,
دایمست و کم نگردد از زمین
"This is lasting and will not fail from off the earth."

بدگمانی کردن و حرص‌آوری
To show suspicion and greed
کفر باشد پیش خوان مهتری
at the table of Majesty is ingratitude.

زان گدارویان نادیده ز آز
Because of those impudent wretches who were blinded by greed,
آن در رحمت بریشان شد فراز
that gate of mercy was closed upon them.

ابر بر ناید پی منع زکات
On account of withholding the poor-tax no rain-clouds arise,
وز زنا افتد وبا اندر جهات
and in consequence of fornication the plague spreads in all directions

هر چه بر تو آید از ظلمات و غم
Whatever befalls thee of gloom and sorrow
آن ز بی‌باکی و گستاخیست هم
is the result of irreverence and insolence withal.

هر که بی‌باکی کند در راه دوست
Any one behaving with irreverence in the path of the Friend
رهزن مردان شد و نامرد اوست
is a brigand who robs men, and he is no man

از ادب پرنور گشته ست این فلک
Through discipline this Heaven has been filled with light,
وز ادب معصوم و پاک آمد ملک
and through discipline the angels became immaculate and holy.

بد ز گستاخی کسوف آفتاب
By reason of irreverence the sun was eclipsed,
شد عزازیلی ز جرات رد باب
and insolence caused an 'Azázíl to be turned back from the door.

◈◉◈◉◈

ملاقات پادشاه با آن ولی که در خوابش نمودند

The meeting of the king with the divine physician whose coming had been announced to him in a dream.

دست بگشاد و کنارانش گرفت
He (the king) opened his hands and clasped him to his breast

همچو عشق اندر دل و جانش گرفت
and received him like love, into his heart and soul,

دست و پیشانیش بوسیدن گرفت
And began to kiss his hand and brow

وز مقام و راه پرسیدن گرفت
and inquire concerning his home and journey.

پرس پرسان می‌کشیدش تا بصدر
(So) with many a question he led him to the dais.

گفت گنجی یافتم آخر بصبر
"At last," said he, "I have found a treasure by being patient."

گفت ای نور حق و دفع حرج
He said (also), "O gift from God and defence against trouble,

معنی‌الصبر مفتاح الفرج
(O thou who art) the meaning of 'Patience is the key of joy'!

ای لقای تو جواب هر سئوال
O thou whose countenance is the answer to every question,

مشکل از تو حل شود بی‌قیل و قال
by thee hard knots are loosed without discussion.

ترجمانی هرچه ما را در دلست
Thou interpretest all that is in our hearts,

دستگیری هر که پایش در گلست
thou givest a helping hand to every one whose foot is in the mire

مرحبا یا مجتبی یا مرتضی
Welcome, O chosen one, O approved one!

ان تغب جاء القضا ضاق الفضا
If thou vanish, Destiny will come (upon us) and the wide room will be straitened

انت مولی‌القوم من لا یشتهی
Thou art the protector of the people.

قد ردی کلا لئن لم ینته
He that desires(thee) not hath gone to perdition. Nay, verily, if he do not refrain...!"

چون گذشت آن مجلس و خوان کرم
When that meeting and bounteous (spiritual) repast was over,

دست او بگرفت و برد اندر حرم
he took his hand and conducted him to the harem.

◆◉◆◉◆

بردن پادشاه آن طبیب را بر سر بیمار تا حال او را ببیند
How the king led the physician to the bedside of the sick girl, that he might see her condition.

قصهٔ رنجور و رنجوری بخواند
He rehearsed the tale of the invalid and her illness,

بعد از آن در پیش رنجورش نشاند
and then seated him beside the sick (girl).

رنگ روی و نبض و قاروره بدید
The physician observed the colour of her face, (felt) her pulse, and (inspected) her urine;

هم علاماتش هم اسبابش شنید
he heard both the symptoms and the (secondary) causes of her malady.

گفت هر دارو که ایشان کرده‌اند
He said, "None of the remedies which they have applied builds up (health)

آن عمارت نیست ویران کرده‌اند
they (the false physicians) have wrought destruction.

بی‌خبر بودند از حال درون
They were ignorant of the inward state.

استعیذ الله مما یفترون
I seek refuge with God from that which they invent."

دید رنج و کشف شد بر وی نهفت
He saw the pain, and the secret became open to him,

لیک پنهان کرد و با سلطان نگفت
but he concealed it and did not tell the king.

رنجش از صفرا و از سودا نبود
Her pain was not from black or yellow bile

بوی هر هیزم پدید آید ز دود
the smell of every firewood appears from the smoke.

دید از زاریش کو زار دلست
From her sore grief he perceived that she was heart-sore

تن خوشست و او گرفتار دلست
well in body, but stricken in heart.

عاشقی پیداست از زاری دل
Being in love is made manifest by soreness of heart
نیست بیماری چو بیماری دل
there is no sickness like heartsickness.

علت عاشق ز علتها جداست
The lover's ailment is separate from all other ailments
عشق اصطرلاب اسرار خداست
love is the astrolabe of the mysteries of God.

عاشقی گر زین سر و گر زان سرست
Whether love be from this (earthly) side or from that (heavenly) side,
عاقبت ما را بدان سر رهبرست
in the end it leads us yonder

هرچه گویم عشق را شرح و بیان
Whatsoever I say in exposition and explanation of Love,
چون به عشق آیم خجل باشم از آن
when I come to Love (itself) I am ashamed of that (explanation).

گرچه تفسیر زبان روشنگرست
Although the commentary of the tongue makes (all) clear,
لیک عشق بی‌زبان روشنترست
yet tongueless love is clearer.

چون قلم اندر نوشتن می‌شتافت
Whilst the pen was making haste in writing,
چون به عشق آمد قلم بر خود شکافت
it split upon itself as soon as it came to Love.

عقل در شرحش چو خر در گل بخفت
In expounding it, the intellect lay down (helplessly) like an ass in the mire
شرح عشق و عاشقی هم عشق گفت
it was Love (alone) that uttered the explanation of love and loverhood.

آفتاب آمد دلیل آفتاب
The proof of the sun is the sun (himself)
گر دلیلت باید از وی رو متاب
if thou require the proof, do not avert thy face from him!

از وی ار سایه نشانی می‌دهد
If the shadow gives an indication of him,
شمس هر دم نور جانی می‌دهد
the sun (himself) gives spiritual light every moment.

سایه خواب آرد ترا همچون سمر
The shadow, like chat in the night-hours, brings sleep to thee
چون برآید شمس انشق القمر
when the sun rises the moon is cloven asunder.

خود غریبی در جهان چون شمس نیست
There is nothing in the world so wondrous strange as the sun,
شمس جان باقیست کاو را امس نیست
(but) the Sun of the spirit is everlasting: it hath no yesterday.

شمس جان باقیست کاو را امس نیست
Although the external sun is unique,
می‌توان هم مثل او تصویر کرد
still it is possible to imagine one resembling it;

شمس جان کو خارج آمد از اثیر
The spiritual Sun, which is beyond the aether,
نبودش در ذهن و در خارج نظیر
hath no peer in the mind or externally.

در تصور ذات او را گنج کو
Where is room in the imagination for His essence,
تا در آید در تصور مثل او
that the like of Him should come into the imagination?

چون حدیث روی شمس الدین رسید
When news arrived of the face of Shamsu'ddín (the Sun of the Religion),
شمس چارم آسمان سر در کشید
the sun of the fourth heaven drew in its head (hid itself for shame).

واجب آید چونک آمد نام او
Since his name has come (to my lips),
شرح کردن رمزی از انعام او
it behoves me to set forth some hint of his bounty.

این نفس جان دامنم بر تافتست
At this moment my Soul has plucked my skirt
بوی پیراهان یوسف یافتست
he has caught the perfume of Joseph's vest.

کز برای حق صحبت سالها
(He said): "For the sake of our years of companionship,
بازگو حالی از آن خوش حالها
recount one of those sweet ecstasies,

تا زمین و آسمان خندان شود
That earth and heaven may laugh (with joy),
عقل و روح و دیده صد چندان شود
that intellect and spirit and eye may increase a hundredfold."
لاتکلفنی فانی فی الفنا
(I said): "Do not lay tasks on me, for I have passed away from myself (faná);
کلت افهامی فلا احصی ثنا
my apprehensions are blunted and I know not how to praise.
کل شیء قاله غیرالمفیق
Everything that is said by one who has not returned to consciousness,
ان تکلف او تصلف لا یلیق
if he constrains himself or boastfully exaggerates, is unseemly.
من چه گویم یک رگم هشیار نیست
How should I not a vein of mine is sensible
شرح آن یاری که او را یار نیست
describe that Friend who hath no peer?
شرح این هجران و این خون جگر
The description of this severance and this heart's blood
این زمان بگذار تا وقت دگر
do thou at present leave over till another time."
قال اطعمنی فانی جائع
He said: "Feed me, for I am hungry,
واعتجل فالوقت سیف قاطع
and make haste, for Time is a cutting sword.
صوفی ابن الوقت باشد ای رفیق
The Súfí is the son of the (present) time,
نیست فردا گفتن از شرط طریق
O comrade: it is not the rule of the Way to say 'To-morrow.'
تو مگر خود مرد صوفی نیستی
Art not thou indeed a Súfí, then?
هست را از نسیه خیزد نیستی
That which is (in hand) is reduced to naught by postponing the payment
گفتمش پوشیده خوشتر سر یار
I said to him: "It is better that the secret of the Friend should be disguised"
خود تو در ضمن حکایت گوش دار
do thou hearken (to it as implied) in the contents of the tale

32

خوشتر آن باشد که سر دلبران
It is better that the lovers' secret
گفته آید در حدیث دیگران
should be told in the talk of others

گفت مکشوف و برهنه بی‌غلول
He said: "Tell it forth openly and nakedly and without unfaithfulness"
بازگو دفعم مده ای بوالفضول
do not put me off, O trifler!

پرده بردار و برهنه گو که من
Lift the veil and speak nakedly,
می‌نخسپم با صنم با پیرهن
for I do not wear a shirt when I sleep with the Adored One."

گفتم ار عریان شود او در عیان
I said: "If He should become naked in (thy) vision,
نه تو مانی نه کنارت نه میان
neither wilt thou remain nor thy bosom nor thy waist.

آرزو می‌خواه لیک اندازه خواه
Ask thy wish, but ask with measure:
بر نتابد کوه را یک برگ کاه
a blade of straw will not support the mountain.

آفتابی کز وی این عالم فروخت
If the Sun, by whom this world is illumined,
اندکی گر پیش آید جمله سوخت
should approach a little (nearer), all will be burned.

فتنه و آشوب و خون‌ریزی مجوی
Do not seek trouble and turmoil and bloodshed:
بیش ازین از شمس تبریزی مگوی
say no more concerning the Sun of Tabriz!"

این ندارد آخر از آغاز گوی
This (mystery) hath no end
رو تمام این حکایت بازگوی
tell of the beginning. Go, relate the conclusion of this tale.

◆◉◆◆◉◆

خلوت طلبیدن آن ولی از پادشاه جهت دریافتن رنج کنیزک
How that saint demanded of the king to be alone with the handmaiden for the purpose of discovering her malady

گفت ای شه خلوتی کن خانه را
He said: "O king, make the house empty

دور کن هم خویش و هم بیگانه را
send away both kinsfolk and strangers.

کس ندارد گوش در دهلیزها
Let no one listen in the entrance-halls,

تا بپرسم زین کنیزک چیزها
that I may ask certain things of this handmaiden."

خانه خالی ماند و یک دیار نه
The house was left empty, and not one inhabitant (remained):

جز طبیب و جز همان بیمار نه
nobody save the physician and that sick girl.

نرم نرمک گفت شهر تو کجاست
Very gently he said (to her), "Where is thy native town?

که علاج اهل هر شهری جداست
for the treatment suitable to the people of each town is separate.

و اندر آن شهر از قرابت کیست
And in that town who is related to thee?

خویشی و پیوستگی با چیست
With what hast thou kinship and affinity?

دست بر نبضش نهاد و یک بیک
He laid his hand on her pulse and put questions,

باز می‌پرسید از جور فلک
one by one, about the injustice of Heaven.

چون کسی را خار در پایش جهد
When a thorn darts into any one's foot,

پای خود را بر سر زانو نهد
he sets his foot upon his knee,

وز سر سوزن همی جوید سرش
And keeps searching for its head with the point of a needle,

ور نیابد می‌کند با لب ترش
and if he does not find it, he keeps moistening it (the place) with his lip

خار در پا شد چنین دشواریاب
A thorn in the foot is so hard to find
خار در دل چون بود واده جواب
how (then) is it with a thorn in the heart? Answer (that)!

خار در دل گر بدیدی هر خسی
If every base fellow had seen the thorn in the heart,
دست کی بودی غمان را بر کسی
when would sorrows gain the upper hand over any one?

کس به زیر دم خر خاری نهد
Somebody sticks a thorn under a donkey's tail
خر نداند دفع آن بر می‌جهد
the donkey does not know how to get rid of it: he starts jumping.

برجهد وان خار محکم تر زند
He jumps, and the thorn strikes more firmly (pierces deeper):
عاقلی باید که خاری برکند
it needs an intelligent person to extract a thorn

خر ز بهر دفع خار از سوز و درد
In order to get rid of the thorn, the donkey from irritation and pain went on kicking
جفته می‌انداخت صد جا زخم کرد
and dealing blows in a hundred places

آن حکیم خارچین استاد بود
(But) that thorn-removing physician was an expert
دست می‌زد جابجا می‌آزمود
putting his hand on one spot after another, he tested (it)

زان کنیزک بر طریق داستان
He inquired of the girl concerning
باز می‌پرسید حال دوستان
her friends, by way of narrative,

با حکیم او قصه‌ها می‌گفت فاش
And she disclosed to the physician (many) circumstances
از مقام و خواجگان و شهر و باش
touching her home and (former) masters and fellowtownsmen.

سوی قصه گفتنش می‌داشت گوش
He listened to her story (while)
سوی نبض و جستنش می‌داشت هوش
he continued to observe her pulse and its beating,

تا که نبض از نام کی گردد جهان
So that at whosoever's name her pulse should begin to throb,
او بود مقصود جانش در جهان
(he might know that) that person is the object of her soul's desire in the world

دوستان و شهر او را برشمرد
He counted up the friends in her native town;
بعد از آن شهری دگر را نام برد
then he mentioned another town by name.

گفت چون بیرون شدی از شهر خویش
He said: "When you went forth from your own town,
در کدامین شهر بودستی تو بیش
in which town did you live mostly?"

نام شهری گفت و زان هم در گذشت
She mentioned the name of a certain town and from that too she passed on (to speak of another,
رنگ روی و نبض او دیگر نگشت
and meanwhile) there was no change in the colour of her face or in her pulse.

خواجگان و شهرها را یک به یک
Masters and towns, one by one,
باز گفت از جای و از نان و نمک
she told of, and about dwelling-place and bread and salt.

شهر شهر و خانه خانه قصه کرد
She told stories of many a town and many a house,
نه رگش جنبید و نه رخ گشت زرد
no vein of her quivered nor did her cheek grow pale.

نبض او بر حال خود بد بی‌گزند
Her pulse remained in its normal state, unimpaired,
تا بپرسید از سمرقند چو قند
till he asked about Samarcand, the (city) sweet as candy.

نبض جست و روی سرخ و زرد شد
(Thereat) her pulse jumped and her face went red and pale (by turns),
کز سمرقندی زرگر فرد شد
for she had been parted from a man of Samarcand, a goldsmith.

چون ز رنجور آن حکیم این راز یافت
When the physician found out this secret from the sick (girl),
اصل آن درد و بلا را باز یافت
he discerned the source of that grief and woe.

گفت کوی او کدامست در گذر
He said: "Which is his quarter in passing (through the town)?"
او سر پل گفت و کوی غاتفر
"Sar-i Pul (Bridgehead)," she replied, "and Ghátafar street."

گفت دانستم که رنجت چیست زود
Said he: "I know what your illness is
در خلاصت سحرها خواهم نمود
and I will at once display the arts of magic in delivering you.

شاد باش و فارغ و آمن که من
Be glad and care-free and have no fear,
آن کنم با تو که باران با چمن
for I will do to you that which rain does to the meadow.

من غم تو می‌خورم تو غم مخور
I will be anxious for you, be not you anxious
بر تو من مشفق‌ترم از صد پدر
I am kinder to you than a hundred fathers

هان و هان این راز را با کس مگو
Beware! tell not this secret to any one
گرچه از تو شه کند بس جست و جو
not though the king should make much inquiry from you.

خانهٔ اسرار تو چون دل شود
When your heart becomes the grave of your secret
آن مرادت زودتر حاصل شود
that desire of yours will be gained more quickly

گفت پیغامبر که هر که سر نهفت
The Prophet said that anyone who hides
زود گردد با مراد خویش جفت
his inmost thought will soon attain to the object of his desire.

دانه چون اندر زمین پنهان شود
When seeds are hidden in the earth
سر او سرسبزی بستان شود
their inward secret becomes the verdure of the garden.

زر و نقره گر نبودندی نهان
If gold and silver were not hidden
پرورش کی یافتندی زیر کان
how would they get nourishment (grow and ripen) in the mine?

وعده‌ها و لطفهای آن حکیم
The promises and soothing words of the physician made

کرد آن رنجور را آمن ز بیم
made the sick (girl) safe (free) from fear

وعده‌ها باشد حقیقی دل‌پذیر
There are true promises,

وعده‌ها باشد مجازی تا سه گیر
grateful to the heart; there are false promises, fraught with disquietude

وعدهٔ اهل کرم گنج روان
The promise of the noble is current (sterling) coin;

وعدهٔ نا اهل شد رنج روان
the promise of the unworthy becomes anguish of soul.

◈◉◈◉◈

دریافتن آن ولی رنج را و عرض کردن رنج او پیش پادشاه را
How the saint, having discovered the (cause of) the illness, laid it before the king

بعد از آن برخاست و عزم شاه کرد
Then he arose and went to see the king

شاه را زان شمه‌ای آگاه کرد
and acquainted him with a portion of that matter.

گفت تدبیر آن بود کان مرد را
"The (best) plan," said he, "is that we should

حاضر آریم از پی این درد را
bring the man here for the sake of (curing) this malady

مرد زرگر را بخوان زان شهر دور
Summon the goldsmith from that far country;

با زر و خلعت بده او را غرور
beguile him with gold and robes of honour."

◈◉◈◉◈

فرستادن پادشاه رسولان به سمرقند به آوردن زرگر
How the king sent messengers to Samarcand to fetch the goldsmith

شه فرستاد آن طرف یک دو رسول
The king sent thither one or two messengers,

حاذقان و کافیان بس عدول
clever men and competent and very just.

تا سمرقند آمدند آن دو امیر
To Samarcand came the two messengers

پیش آن زرگر ز شاهنشه بشیر
thou whose quality (of perfection in thy craft) is famous in (all) the lands

کای لطیف استاد کامل معرفت
Saying, "O fine master, perfect in knowledge,

فاش اندر شهرها از تو صفت
the goldsmith's craft, because thou art eminent.

نک فلان شه از برای زرگری
Lo, such-and-such a king hath chosen thee for (thy skill in)

اختیارت کرد زیرا مهتری
when thou comest (to the king), thou wilt be a favourite and

اینک این خلعت بگیر و زر و سیم
Look now, receive this robe of honour and gold and silver;

چون بیایی خاص باشی و ندیم
when thou comest (to the king), thou wilt be a favourite and boon-companion"

مرد مال و خلعت بسیار دید
The man saw the much wealth and the many robes

غره شد از شهر و فرزندان برید
he was beguiled, he parted from his town and children

اندر آمد شادمان در راه مرد
Blithely the man came into the road,

بی‌خبر کان شاه قصد جانش کرد
unaware that the king had formed a design against his life.

اسپ تازی برنشست و شاد تاخت
He mounted an Arab horse and sped on joyously:

خونبهای خویش را خلعت شناخت
(what really was) the price of his blood he deemed a robe of honour

ای شده اندر سفر با صد رضا
O (fool), who with a hundred consents thyself

خود به پای خویش تا سؤ القضا
with thine own foot didst enter on the journey to the fated ill!

39

در خیالش ملک و عز و مهتری
In his fancy (were dreams of) riches, power, and lordship.

گفت عزرائیل رو آری بری
Said 'Azrá'íl (the Angel of Death), "Go (thy way). Yes, thou wilt get (them)!"

چون رسید از راه آن مرد غریب
When the stranger arrived (and turned) from the road,

اندر آوردش به پیش شه طبیب
the physician brought him into the presence of the king.

سوی شاهنشاه بردندش بناز
Proudly and delicately they conducted him to the king of kings,

تا بسوزد بر سر شمع طراز
that he might burn (like a moth) on that candle of Tiráz.

شاه دید او را بسی تعظیم کرد
The king beheld him, showed great regard (for him),

مخزن زر را بدو تسلیم کرد
and entrusted to him the treasure house (full) of gold

پس حکیمش گفت کای سلطان مه
Then the physician said to him: "O mighty Sultan,

آن کنیزک را بدین خواجه بده
give the handmaiden to this lord,

تا کنیزک در وصالش خوش شود
In order that the handmaiden may be happy in union with him,

آب وصلش دفع آن آتش شود
and that the water of union with him may put out the fire (of passion)."

شه بدو بخشید آن مه روی را
The king bestowed on him that moon-faced

جفت کرد آن هر دو صحبت جوی را
one andwedded those twain (who were) craving (each other's) company.

مدت شش ماه می راندند کام
During the space of six months they were satisfying their desire,

تا به صحت آمد آن دختر تمام
till the girl was wholly restored to health.

بعد از آن از بهر او شربتی بساخت
Thereafter he prepared for him a potion,

تا بخورد و پیش دختر می گداخت
so that when he drank it he began to dwindle away before her.

40

چون ز رنجوری جمال او نماند
When because of sickness his beauty remained not,
جان دختر در وبال او نماند
the soul of the girl remained not in his pestilence (deadly toils).

چونک زشت و ناخوش و رخ زرد شد
Since he became ugly and ill-favoured and sallow-cheeked,
اندک‌اندک در دل او سرد شد
little by little he became cold (irksome and unpleasing) in her heart.

عشقهایی کز پی بی رنگی بود
Those loves which are for the sake of a colour (outward beauty)
عشق نبود عاقبت ننگی بود
are not love: in the end they are a disgrace.

کاش کان هم ننگ بودی یکسری
Would that he too had been disgrace (deformity) altogether,
تا نرفتی بر وی آن بد داوری
so that that evil judgement might not have come to pass upon him!

خون دوید از چشم همچون جوی او
Blood ran from his eye (that flowed with tears) like a river;
دشمن جان وی آمد روی او
his (handsome) face became the enemy of his life.

دشمن طاووس آمد پر او
The peacock's plumage is its enemy:
ای بسی شه را بکشته فر او
O many the king who hath been slain by his magnificence!

گفت من آن آهوم کز ناف من
He said, "I am the muskdeer on account of whose gland
ریخت این صیاد خون صاف من
that hunter shed my pure (innocent) blood.

ای من آن روباه صحرا کز کمین
Oh, I am the fox of the field whose head they (the hunters springing forth) from the covert
سر بریدندش برای پوستین
cut off for the sake of the fur.

ای من آن پیلی که زخم پیلبان
Oh, I am the elephant whose blood was
ریخت خونم از برای استخوان
shed by the blow of the mahout for the sake of the bone (ivory).

آنک کشتستم پی مادون من
He who hath slain me for that which is other than I,
می‌نداند که نخسپد خون من
does not he know that my blood sleepeth not (will not rest unavenged)?

بر منست امروز و فردا بر ویست
To-day it lies on me and to-morrow it lies on him:
خون چون من کس چنین ضایع کیست
when does the blood of one such as I am go to waste like this?

گر چه دیوار افکند سایهٔ دراز
Although the wall casts a long shadow,
باز گردد سوی او آن سایه باز
(yet at last) the shadow turns back again towards it.

این جهان کوهست و فعل ما ندا
This world is the mountain, and our action the shout:
سوی ما آید نداها را صدا
the echo of the shouts comes (back) to us."

این بگفت و رفت در دم زیر خاک
He said this and at the (same) moment went under the earth (gave up the ghost)
آن کنیزک شد ز عشق و رنج پاک
The handmaiden was purged of pain and love,

زانک عشق مردگان پاینده نیست
Because love of the dead is not enduring,
زانک مرده سوی ما آینده نیست
because the dead one is never coming (back) to us;

عشق زنده در روان و در بصر
But) love of the living is in the spirit and in the sight.
هر دمی باشد ز غنچه تازه‌تر
is every moment fresherthan a bud

عشق آن زنده گزین کو باقیست
Choose the love of that Living One who is everlasting,
کز شراب جان‌فزایت ساقیست
who gives thee to drink of the wine that increases life.

عشق آن بگزین که جمله انبیا
Choose the love of Him from whose love all the prophets
یافتند از عشق او کار و کیا
gained power and glory.

42

تو مگو ما را بدان شه بار نیست
Do not say, "We have no admission to that King."
با کریمان کارها دشوار نیست
Dealings with the generous are not difficult.

※※※

بیان آن که کشتن و زهر دادن مرد زرگر به اشارت الهی بود نه به هوای نفس و تامل فاسد
Setting forth how the slaying and poisoning of the goldsmith was (prompted) by Divine suggestion, not by sensual desire and wicked meditation.

کشتن آن مرد بر دست حکیم
The slaying of this man by the hand of the physician
نه پی امید بود و نه ز بیم
was not(done) on account of hope or fear.

او نکشتش از برای طبع شاه
He did not slay him to humour the king,
تا نیامد امر و الهام اله
(he did not slay him) until the Divine command and inspiration came

آن پسر را کش خضر ببرید حلق
As for the boy whose throat was cut by Khadir,
سر آن را در نیابد عام خلق
the vulgar do not comprehend the mystery thereof

آنک از حق یابد او وحی و جواب
He that receives from God inspiration and answer (to his prayer),
هرچه فرماید بود عین صواب
whatsoever he may command is the essence of right.

آنک جان بخشد اگر بکشد رواست
If one who bestows (spiritual) life should slay, it is allowable
نایبست و دست او دست خداست
he is the (Divine) vicegerent, and his hand is the hand of God.

همچو اسمعیل پیشش سر بنه
Like Ismá'íl (Ishmael), lay your head before him;
شاد و خندان پیش تیغش جان بده
gladly and laughingly give up your soul before his dagger,

تا بماند جانت خندان تا ابد
In order that your soul may remain laughing unto eternity,
همچو جان پاک احمد با احد
like the pure soul of Ahmad (Mohammed) with the One(God).

عاشقان آنگه شراب جان کشند
Lovers drain the cup of joy at the moment
که به دست خویش خوبانشان کشند
when the fair ones slay them with their own hand

شاه آن خون از پی شهوت نکرد
The king did not commit that bloodshed because of lust
تو رها کن بدگمانی و نبرد
cease from thinking evil and disputing.

تو گمان بردی که کرد آلودگی
You thought that he committed a foul crime, (but) in (the state of)
در صفا غش کی هلد پالودگی
purity how should the sublimation leave (any) alloy (behind)?

بهر آنست این ریاضت وین جفا
The purpose of this (severe) discipline and this rough treatment is
تا بر آرد کوره از نقره جفا
that the furnace may extract the dross from the silver.

بهر آنست امتحان نیک و بد
The testing of good and bad is in order that
تا بجوشد بر سر آرد زر زبد
the gold may boil and bring the scum to the top.

گر نبودی کارش الهام اله
If his act were not the inspiration of God,
او سگی بودی دراننده نه شاه
he would have been a dog that rends (its prey), not a king

پاک بود از شهوت و حرص و هوا
He was unstained by lust and covetousness and passion:
نیک کرد او لیک نیک بد نما
(what) he did (was) good, but good that wore the aspect of evil.

گر خضر در بحر کشتی را شکست
If Khadir stove the boat in the sea,
صد درستی در شکست خضر هست
(yet) in Khadir's staving there are a hundred rightnesses

وهم موسی با همه نور و هنر
The imagination of Moses, notwithstanding his (spiritual) illumination and excellence
شد از آن محجوب تو بی پر مپر
was screened from (the comprehension of) that (act of Khadir). Do not thou fly without wings!

آن گل سرخست تو خونش مخوان
That (deed of the king) is a red rose (worthy of praise); do not call it blood (murder)
مست عقلست او تو مجنونش مخوان
He is intoxicated with Reason; do not call him a madman.

گر بدی خون مسلمان کام او
Had it been his desire to shed the blood of a Moslem,
کافرم گر بردمی من نام او
I am an infidel if I would have mentioned his name (with praise).

می‌بلرزد عرش از مدح شقی
The highest heaven trembles at praise of the wicked,
بدگمان گردد ز مدحش متقی
and by praise of him the devout man is moved to think evil.

شاه بود و شاه بس آگاه بود
He was a king and a very heedful king;
خاص بود و خاصهٔ الله بود
he was elect and the elect (favourite) of God

آن کسی را کش چنین شاهی کشد
One who is slain by a king like this,
سوی بخت و بهترین جاهی کشد
he (the king) leads him to fortune and to the best (most honourable) estate

گر ندیدی سود او در قهر او
Unless he (the king) had seen advantage to him (the goldsmith) in doing violence to him,
کی شدی آن لطف مطلق قهرجو
how should that absolute Mercy have sought to do violence?

بچه می‌لرزد از آن نیش حجام
The child trembles at the barber's scalpel
مادر مشفق در آن دم شادکام
(but) the fond mother is happy in that pain (of her child).

نیم جان بستاند و صد جان دهد
He takes half a life and gives a hundred lives (in exchange):
آنچه در وهمت نیاید آن دهد
he gives that which enters not into your imagination.

تو قیاس از خویش می‌گیری ولیک
You are judging (his actions) from (the analogy of) yourself,
دور دور افتاده‌ای بنگر تو نیک
but you have fallen far, far (away from the truth). Consider well!

حکایت بقال و طوطی و روغن ریختن طوطی در دکان
The story of the greengrocer and the parrot and the parrot's spilling the oil in the shop

بود بقالی و وی را طوطیی
There was a greengrocer who had a parrot,
خوش‌نوایی سبز و گویا طوطیی
a sweet-voiced green talking parrot.

بر دکان بودی نگهبان دکان
(Perched) on the bench, it would watch over the shop (in the owner's absence)
نکته گفتی با همه سوداگران
and talk finely to all the traders.

در خطاب آدمی ناطق بدی
In addressing human beings it would speak (like them);
در نوای طوطیان حاذق بدی
it was (also) skilled in the song of parrots

جست از سوی دکان سویی گریخت
Once) it sprang from the bench and flew away
شیشه‌های روغن گل را بریخت
it spilled the bottles of rose-oil

از سوی خانه بیامد خواجه‌اش
Its master came from the direction of his house
بر دکان بنشست فارغ خواجه وش
and seated himself on the bench at his ease as a merchant does.

دید پر روغن دکان و جامه چرب
Then) he saw the bench was full of oil and his clothes greasy;
بر سرش زد گشت طوطی کل ز ضرب
he smote the parrot on the head: it was made bald by the blow.

روزکی چندی سخن کوتاه کرد
For some few days it refrained from speech;
مرد بقال از ندامت آه کرد
the greengrocer, in repentance, heaved deep sighs,

ریش بر می‌کند و می‌گفت ای دریغ
Tearing his beard and saying, "Alas!
کافتاب نعمتم شد زیر میغ
the sun of my prosperity has gone under the clouds.

دست من بشکسته بودی آن زمان
Would that my hand had been broken (powerless) at that moment!
که زدم من بر سر آن خوش زبان
How (ever) did I strike (such a blow) on the head of that sweet-tongued one?"

هدیه‌ها می‌داد هر درویش را
He was giving presents to every dervish,
تا بیابد نطق مرغ خویش را
that he might get back the speech of his bird.

بعد سه روز و سه شب حیران و زار
After three days and three nights,
بر دکان بنشسته بد نومیدوار
he was seated on the bench, distraught and sorrowful, like a man in despair

می‌نمود آن مرغ را هر گون نهفت
Showing the bird every sort of marvel (in the hope)
تا که باشد اندر آید او بگفت
that maybe it would begin to speak.

جولقیی سر برهنه می‌گذشت
Meanwhile a bare-headed dervish, clad in a jawlaq (coarse woollen frock)
با سر بی مو چو پشت طاس و طشت
passed by, with a head hairless as the outside of bowl and basin.

آمد اندر گفت طوطی آن زمان
Thereupon the parrot began to talk,
بانگ بر درویش زد چون عاقلان
screeched at the dervish and said, "Hey, fellow!

کز چه ای کل با کلان آمیختی
How were you mixed up with the bald, O baldpate?
تو مگر از شیشه روغن ریختی
Did you, then, spill oil from the bottle?"

از قیاسش خنده آمد خلق را
The bystanders laughed at the parrot's inference,
کو چو خود پنداشت صاحب دلق را
because it deemed the wearer of the frock to be like itself.

کار پاکان را قیاس از خود مگیر
Do not measure the actions of holy men by (the analogy of) yourself,
گر چه ماند در نبشتن شیر و شیر
though shér (lion) and shír (milk) are similar in writing.

جمله عالم زین سبب گمراه شد
On this account the whole world is gone astray:
کم کسی ز ابدال حق آگاه شد
scarcely any one is cognisant of God's Abdál (Substitutes).

همسری با انبیا برداشتند
They set up (a claim of) equality with the prophets;
اولیا را همچو خود پنداشتند
they supposed the saints to be like themselves.

گفته اینک ما بشر ایشان بشر
Behold," they said, "we are men, they are men;
ما و ایشان بستهٔ خوابیم و خور
both we and they are in bondage to sleep and food."

این ندانستند ایشان از عمی
In (their) blindness they did not perceive that
هست فرق درمیان بی‌منتهی
there is an infinite difference between (them).

هر دو گون زنبور خوردند از محل
Both species of zanbúr ate and drank from the (same) place,
لیک شد زان نیش و زین دیگر عسل
from that one (the hornet) came a sting, and from this other (the bee) honey

هر دو گون آهو گیا خوردند و آب
Both species of deer ate grass and drank water:
زین یکی سرگین شد و زان مشک ناب
from this one came dung, and from that one pure musk.

هر دو نی خوردند از یک آبخور
Both reeds drank from the same water-source,
این یکی خالی و آن پر از شکر
(but) this one is empty and that one (full of) sugar.

صد هزاران این چنین اشباه بین
Consider hundreds of thousands of such likenesses and
فرقشان هفتاد ساله راه بین
observe that the distance between the two is (as great as) a seventy years' journey.

این خورد گردد پلیدی زو جدا
This one eats, and filth is discharged from him;
آن خورد گردد همه نور خدا
that one eats, and becomes entirely the light of God.

این خورد زاید همه بخل و حسد
This one eats, (and of him) is born nothing but avarice and envy;
وآن خورد زاید همه نور احد
that one eats, (and of him) is born nothing but love of the One (God).

این زمین پاک و آن شوره‌ست و بد
This one is good (fertile) soil and that one brackish and bad;
این فرشتهٔ پاک و آن دیوست و دد
this one is a fair angel and that one a devil and wild beast.

هر دو صورت گر به هم ماند رواست
If both resemble each other in aspect, it may well be(so)
آب تلخ و آب شیرین را صفاست
bitter water and sweet water have (the same) clearness.

جز که صاحب ذوق کی شناسد بیاب
Who knows (the difference) except a man possessed of (spiritual) taste?
او شناسد آب خوش از شوره آب
Find (him): he knows the sweet water from the brine

سحر را با معجزه کرده قیاس
Comparing magic with (prophetic) miracle,
هر دو را بر مکر پندارد اساس
he (the ignorant one) fancies that both are founded on deceit

ساحران موسی از استیزه را
The magicians (in the time) of Moses, for contention's sake,
برگرفته چون عصای او عصا
lifted up (in their hands) a rod like his,

زین عصا تا آن عصا فرقیست ژرف
(But) between this rod and that rod there is a vast difference;
زین عمل تا آن عمل راهی شگرف
from this action (magic) to that action (miracle) is a great way.

لعنة الله این عمل را در قفا
This action is followed by the curse of God,
رحمة الله آن عمل را در وفا
(while) that action receives in payment the mercy (blessing) of God

کافران اندر مری بوزینه طبع
The infidels in contending (for equality with the prophets and saints) have the nature of an ape:
آفتی آمد درون سینه طبع
the (evil) nature is a canker within the breast.

هرچه مردم می‌کند بوزینه هم
Whatever a man does, the ape at every moment does
آن کند کز مرد بیند دم بدم
the same thing that he sees done by the man

او گمان برده که من کردم چو او
He thinks, "I have acted like him"

فرق را کی داند آن استیزه‌رو
how should that quarrelsome-looking one know the difference?

این کند از امر و او بهر ستیز
This one acts by the command (of God), and he for the sake of quarrelling (rivalry).

بر سر استیزه‌رویان خاک ریز
Pour dust on the heads of those who have quarrelsome faces!

آن منافق با موافق در نماز
That (religious) hypocrite joins in ritual prayer with the (sincere) conformist

از پی استیزه آید نه نیاز
(only) for quarrelling's sake, not for supplication.

در نماز و روزه و حج و زکات
In prayer and fasting and pilgrimage and alms-giving

با منافق مؤمنان در برد و مات
the true believers are with the hypocrite in (what brings) victory and defeat.

مؤمنان را برد باشد عاقبت
Victory in the end is to the true believers;

بر منافق مات اندر آخرت
upon the hypocrite (falls) defeat in the state hereafter.

گرچه هر دو بر سر یک بازی‌اند
Although both are intent on one game,

هر دو با هم مروزی و رازی‌اند
in relation to each other they are (as far apart as) the man of Merv and the man of Rayy.

هر یکی سوی مقام خود رود
Each one goes to his (proper) abiding-place;

هر یکی بر وفق نام خود رود
each one fares according to his name.

مؤمنش خوانند جانش خوش شود
If he be called a true believer, his soul rejoices;

ور منافق تیز و پر آتش شود
and if you say "hypocrite," he becomes filled with fire (rage).

نام او محبوب از ذات وی است
His (the true believer's) name is loved on account of its essence (which is true faith);

نام این مبغوض از آفات وی است
this one's (the hypocrite's) name is loathed on account of its pestilent qualities.

میم و واو و میم و نون تشریف نیست

(The four letters) mím and wáw and mím and nún do not confer honour

لطف مؤمن جز پی تعریف نیست

the word múmin (true believer) is only for the sake of denotation

گر منافق خوانیش این نام دون

If you call him (the true believer) hypocrite,

همچو کژدم می‌خلد در اندرون

this vile name is stinging (him) within like a scorpion

گرنه این نام اشتقاق دوزخست

If this name is not derived from Hell,

پس چرا در وی مذاق دوزخست

then why is there the taste of Hell in it?

زشتی آن نام بد از حرف نیست

The foulness of that ill name is not from the letters;

تلخی آن آب بحر از ظرف نیست

the bitterness of that sea-water is not from the vessel (containing it).

حرف ظرف آمد درو معنی چون آب

The letters are the vessel: therein the meaning is (contained) like water;

بحر معنی عنده ام الکتاب

(but) the sea of the meaning is (with God)—with Him is the Ummu 'l-Kitáb

بحر تلخ و بحر شیرین در جهان

In this world the bitter sea and the sweet sea

در میانشان برزخ لا یبغیان

between them is a barrier which they do not seek to cross.

وانگه این هر دو ز یک اصلی روان

Know that both these flow from one origin.

برگذر زین هر دو رو تا اصل آن

Pass on from them both, go (all the way) to their origin!

زر قلب و زر نیکو در عیار

adulterated gold and fine gold by (using your own) judgement

بی محک هرگز ندانی ز اعتبار

Without the touchstone you will never know in the assay

هر که را در جان خدا بنهد محک

Any one in whose soul God shall put the touchstone,

هر یقین را باز داند او ز شک

he will distinguish certainty from doubt.

در دهان زنده خاشاکی جهد
A piece of rubbish jumps into the mouth of a living man,
آنگه آرامد که بیرونش نهد
and only when he ejects it is he at ease.

در هزاران لقمه یک خاشاک خرد
When, amongst thousands of morsels (of food), one little piece of rubbish entered (his mouth),
چون در آمد حس زنده پی ببرد
the living man's sense (of touch or taste) tracked it down.

حس دنیا نردبان این جهان
The worldly sense is the ladder to this world;
حس دینی نردبان آسمان
the religious sense is the ladder to Heaven.

صحت این حس بجویید از طبیب
Seek ye the well-being of the former sense from the physician;
صحت آن حس بخواهید از حبیب
beg ye the well-being of the latter sense from the Beloved.

صحت این حس ز معموری تن
The health of the former arises from the flourishing state of the body;
صحت آن حس ز تخریب بدن
the health of the latter arises from the ruin of the body.

راه جان مر جسم را ویران کند
The spiritual way ruins the body and,
بعد از آن ویرانی آبادان کند
after having ruined it, restores it to prosperity

کرد ویران خانه بهر گنج زر
Ruined the house for the sake of the golden treasure,
وز همان گنجش کند معمورتر
and with that same treasure builds it better (than before);

آب را برید و جو را پاک کرد
Cut off the water and cleansed the river-bed,
بعد از آن در جو روان کرد آب خورد
then caused drinking-water to flow in the river-bed;

پوست را بشکافت و پیکان را کشید
Cleft the skin and drew out the iron point (of the arrow or spear)
پوست تازه بعد از آنش بر دمید
then fresh skin grew over it (the wound);

قلعه ویران کرد و از کافر ستد
Rased the fortress and took it from the infidel,
بعد از آن بر ساختش صد برج و سد
then reared thereon a hundred towers and ramparts.

کار بی‌چون را که کیفیت نهد
Who shall describe the action of Him who hath no like?
اینک گفتم این ضرورت می‌دهد
This that I have said (is only what the present) necessity is affording.

گه چنین بنماید و گه ضد این
Sometimes it (the action of God) appears like this and sometimes the contrary of this:
جز که حیرانی نباشد کار دین
the work of religion is naught but bewilderment

نه چنان حیران که پشتش سوی اوست
(I mean) not one bewildered in such wise that his back is (turned) towards Him;
بل چنان حیران و غرق و مست دوست
nay, but one bewildered (with ecstasy) like this and drowned and intoxicated with the Beloved.

آن یکی را روی او شد سوی دوست
The face of the one is set towards the Beloved,
وان یکی را روی او خود روی اوست
(while) the face of the other is just his own face (he is facing himself).

روی هر یک می‌نگر می‌دار پاس
Look long on the face of every one, keep watch attentively:
بوک گردی تو ز خدمت روشناس
it may be that by doing service (to Súfís) you will come to know the face (of the true saint).

چون بسی ابلیس آدم‌روی هست
Since there is many a devil who hath the face of Adam,
پس بهر دستی نشاید داد دست
it is not well to give your hand to every hand,

زانک صیاد آورد بانگ صفیر
Because the fowler produces a whistling sound
تا فریبد مرغ را آن مرغ‌گیر
in order to decoy the bird,

بشنود آن مرغ بانگ جنس خویش
(So that) the bird may hear the note of its congener and come down
از هوا آید بیاید دام و نیش
from the air and find trap and knife-point.

حرف درویشان بدزدد مرد دون
The vile man will steal the language of dervishes, that he may thereby

تا بخواند بر سلیمی زان فسون
chant a spell over (fascinate and deceive) one who is simple.

کار مردان روشنی و گرمیست
The work of (holy) men is (as) light and heat;

کار دونان حیله و بی‌شرمیست
the work of vile men is trickery and shamelessness.

شیر پشمین از برای کد کنند
They make a woolen lion for the purpose of begging;

بومسیلم را لقب احمد کنند
they give the title of Ahmad (Mohammed) to Bú Musaylim;

بومسیلم را لقب کذاب ماند
(But) to Bú Musaylim remained the title of Kadhdháb (Liar),

مر محمد را اولوا الالباب ماند
to Mohammed remained (the title of) Ulu 'l-albáb (Endowed with understanding).

آن شراب حق ختامش مشک ناب
The wine of God, its seal (last result) is pure musk,

باده را ختمش بود گند و عذاب
(but) as for (the other) wine, its seal is stench and torment

◆◉◆◉◆

داستان آن پادشاه جهود کی نصرانیان را می‌کشت از بهر تعصب
Story of the Jewish king who for bigotry's sake used to slay the Christians

بود شاهی در جهودان ظلم ساز
Amongst the Jews there was a king who wrought oppression,

دشمن عیسی و نصرانی گداز
an enemy of Jesus and a destroyer of Christians.

عهد عیسی بود و نوبت آن او
Twas the epoch of Jesus and the turn was his:

جان موسی او و موسی جان او
he was the soul of Moses, and Moses the soul of him;

شاه احول کرد در راه خدا
(But) the squint-eyed (double-seeing) king separated in the way of God

آن دو دمساز خدایی را جدا
those two Divine (prophets) who were (really) in accord (with each other).

گفت استاد احولی را کاندر آ
The master said to a squint-eyed (pupil), "Come on;
زو برون آر از وثاق آن شیشه را
fetch that bottle out of the room

گفت احول زان دو شیشه من کدام
Said the squint-eyed one: "Which of the two bottles
پیش تو آرم بکن شرح تمام
shall I bring to you? Explain fully

گفت استاد آن دو شیشه نیست رو
There are not two bottles," replied the master;
احولی بگذار و افزون بین مشو
go, leave off squinting and do not be seeing more (than one)."

گفت ای استا مرا طعنه مزن
O master," said he, "don't chide me."
گفت استا زان دو یک را در شکن
Said the master, "Smash one of those two."

چون یک بشکست هر دو شد ز چشم
The bottle was one, though in his eyes it seemed two;
مرد احول گردد از میلان و خشم
when he broke the bottle, there was no other.

شیشه یک بود و به چشمش دو نمود
When one was broken, both vanished from sight:
چون شکست او شیشه را دیگر نبود
a man is made squint-eyed by (evil) propensity and anger.

خشم و شهوت مرد را احول کند
Anger and lust make a man squint-eyed,
ز استقامت روح را مبدل کند
they change the spirit (so that it departs) from rectitude.

چون غرض آمد هنر پوشیده شد
When self-interest appears, virtue becomes hidden:
صد حجاب از دل به سوی دیده شد
a hundred veils rise from the heart to the eye.

چون دهد قاضی به دل رشوت قرار
When the cadi lets bribery gain hold of his heart,
کی شناسد ظالم از مظلوم زار
how should he know the wronger from the wretched victim of wrong?

شاه از حقد جهودانه چنان

The king, from Jewish rancour, became so squint-eyed that (we cry),

گشت احول کالامان یا رب امان

"Mercy, O Lord, mercy (save us from such an affliction)!"

صد هزاران مؤمن مظلوم کشت

He slew hundreds of thousands of wronged (innocent) believers, saying,

که پناهم دین موسی را و پشت

"I am the protection and support of the religion of Moses."

◆◉◆◆◉◆

آموختن وزیر مکر پادشاه را
How the vizier instructed the king to plot

او وزیری داشت گبر و عشوه ده

He had a vizier, a miscreant and ogler (deceiver),

کو بر آب از مکر بر بستی گره

who by reason of (his exceeding) guile would tie knots on water

گفت ترسایان پناه جان کنند

"The Christians," said he, "seek to save their lives;

دین خود را از ملک پنهان کنند

they hide their religion from the king.

کم کش ایشان را که کشتن سود نیست

Slay them not, for slaying (them) is useless:

دین ندارد بوی مشک و عود نیست

religion hath no smell, it is not musk and aloes-wood.

سر پنهانست اندر صد غلاف

The secret is concealed in a hundred coverings:

ظاهرش با تست و باطن بر خلاف

its outward form is (in agreement) with thee, resembling thee, (but) the inward (reality) is (in) disagreement."

شاه گفتش پس بگو تدبیر چیست

The king said to him: "Tell (me), then,

چارهٔ آن مکر و آن تزویر چیست

what is the (best plan? What is the remedy against that deceit and imposture?

تا نماند در جهان نصرانی

So that there may not remain a single Christian in the world,

نی هویدا دین و نه پنهانی

neither one whose religion is manifest nor one who is concealed."

گفت ای شه گوش و دستم را ببر
"O king," said he, "cut off my ears and hands,
بینی‌ام بشکاف و لب در حکم مر
rip my nose by bitter (cruel) decree;

بعد از آن در زیر دار آور مرا
Then bring me under the gallows,
تا بخواهد یک شفاعت گر مرا
that an intercessor may plead for me.

بر منادی گاه کن این کار تو
Do this deed in the place for (public) proclamation,
بر سر راهی که باشد چارسو
on a highway where roads run in four directions.

آنگهم از خود بران تا شهر دور
Then banish me from thy presence to a distant land,
تا در اندازم در ایشان شر و شور
that I may cast mischief and confusion amongst them.

❖◉❖◉❖

تلبیس وزیر با نصارا
How the vizier brought the Christians into doubt and perplexity

پس بگویم من بسر نصرانیم
Then I will say (to them), 'I am secretly a Christian.
ای خدای رازدان می‌دانیم
O God who knowest (all) things hidden, Thou knowest me.

شاه واقف گشت از ایمان من
The king was informed of my (Christian) faith
وز تعصب کرد قصد جان من
and from bigotry sought to take my life.

خواستم تا دین ز شه پنهان کنم
I wished to hide my religion from the king
آنک دین اوست ظاهر آن کنم
and profess his religion,

شاه بویی برد از اسرار من
(But) the king got a scent of my inmost beliefs,
متهم شد پیش شه گفتار من
and my words were suspected (when I stood) before the king.

گفت گفت تو چو در نان سوزنست
He said, "Your words are like a needle in bread (specious but pernicious)
از دل من تا دل تو روزنست
there is a window between my heart and yours.

من از آن روزن بدیدم حال تو
Through that window I have seen your (real) state:
حال تو دیدم ننوشم قال تو
I see your state and will not heed your words."

گر نبودی جان عیسی چاره‌ام
Had not the spirit of Jesus been my aid,
او جهودانه بکردی پاره‌ام
he would in Jewish fashion have torn me to pieces

بهر عیسی جان سپارم سر دهم
For Jesus' sake I would yield my life and give my head
صد هزاران منتش بر خود نهم
and lay on myself (confess) myriads of obligations to him.

جان دریغم نیست از عیسی ولیک
I do not grudge Jesus my life
واقفم بر علم دینش نیک نیک
but full well am I versed in the knowledge of his religion.

حیف می‌آمد مرا کان دین پاک
Grief was coming over me (it seemed to me a pity) that that holy religion
درمیان جاهلان گردد هلاک
should perish amongst those who are ignorant (of it).

شکر ایزد را و عیسی را که ما
Thanks be to God and to Jesus that
گشته‌ایم آن کیش حق را رهنما
I have become a guide to the true faith.

از جهود و از جهودی رسته‌ایم
I have escaped from Jews and Judaism so (entirely) that
تا به زناری میان را بسته‌ایم
I have bound my waist with a (Christian) girdle.

دور دور عیسیست ای مردمان
The (present) epoch is the epoch of Jesus.
بشنوید اسرار کیش او بجان
O men, hearken with your souls unto the mysteries of his religion!'"

کرد با وی شاه آن کاری که گفت
The king did to him that deed (mutilation) which he had proposed
خلق حیران مانده زان مکر نهفت
the people remained in amazement at his deed.

راند او را جانب نصرانیان
He (the king) drove him away to the Christians.
کرد در دعوت شروع او بعد از آن
After that, he (the vizier) began to proselytise.

قبول کردن نصارا مکر وزیر را
How the Christians let themselves be duped by the vizier

صد هزاران مرد ترسا سوی او
Myriads of Christian men gathered round him,
اندک‌اندک جمع شد در کوی او
little by little, in his abode,

او بیان می‌کرد با ایشان براز
(While) he secretly expounded to them
سر انگلیون و زنار و نماز
the mysteries of Gospel and girdle and prayer.

او به ظاهر واعظ احکام بود
Outwardly he was a preacher of (religious) ordinances,
لیک در باطن صفیر و دام بود
but inwardly he was (as) the whistle and snare (of the fowler).

بهر این بعضی صحابه از رسول
On this account some Companions (of Mohammed) begged of the Prophet
ملتمس بودند مکر نفس غول
the deceitfulness of the ghoul-like soul,

کو چه آمیزد ز اغراض نهان
Saying, "What of hidden selfish interests does it mingle in
در عبادتها و در اخلاص جان
acts of worship and in pure spiritual devotion?"

فضل طاعت را نجستندی ازو
They were not seeking from him excellence of piety;
عیب ظاهر را بجستندی که کو
they were not inquiring where lay the outward defect

مو به مو و ذره ذره مکر نفس
Hair by hair, speck by speck, they were recognising the deceitfulness
می‌شناسیدند چون گل از کرفس
of the fleshly soul as (plainly as the difference of) the rose from parsley.

موشکافان صحابه هم در آن
Even the hair-splitters (the most scrupulous) of the Companions
وعظ ایشان خیره گشتندی بجان
used to become distraught in spirit at the (Prophet's) admonition to them (the inquirers).

❖◉❖◉❖

متابعت نصارا وزیر را
How the Christians followed the vizier

دل بدو دادند ترسایان تمام
The Christians all gave their hearts to him:
خود چه باشد قوت تقلید عام
what (how great), indeed, is the strength of the (blind) conformity of the vulgar

در درون سینه مهرش کاشتند
They planted love of him within their breasts,
نایب عیسیش می‌پنداشتند
they were regarding him as the vicar of Jesus.

او بسر دجال یک چشم لعین
He inwardly (in reality) was the accursed one-eyed Antichrist.
ای خدا فریاد رس نعم المعین
O God, do Thou (hear and) answer the cry (of those in trouble) —what a good helper art Thou!

صد هزاران دام و دانه ست ای خدا
O God, there are myriads of snares and baits,
ما چو مرغان حریص بی‌نوا
and we are as greedy foodless birds

دم بدم ما بستهٔ دام نویم
From moment to moment we are caught in a fresh snare,
هر یکی گر باز و سیمرغی شویم
though we become, each one, (like) a falcon or a Símurgh.

می‌رهانی هر دمی ما را و باز
Every moment Thou art delivering us, and again we are going to a snare,
سوی دامی می‌رویم ای بی‌نیاز
O Thou who art without want!

ما درین انبار گندم می‌کنیم
We are putting corn in this barn,
گندم جمع آمده گم می‌کنیم
(and then) we are losing the corn that has been garnered

می‌نیندیشیم آخر ما بهوش
(Why), after all do not we consider with intelligent mind that
کین خلل در گندمست از مکر موش
this damage to the corn arises from the deceitfulness of the mouse?

موش تا انبار ما حفره زدست
Since the mouse has made a hole in our barn,
و از فنش انبار ما ویران شدست
and our barn has been ravaged by its guile,

اول ای جان دفع شر موش کن
O soul, in the first place avert the mischief of the mouse,
وانگهان در جمع گندم جوش کن
and then show fervour (zeal) in garnering the corn.

بشنو از اخبار آن صدر الصدور
Hear (one) of the sayings related from the Chiefest of the Chief (the Prophet)
لا صلوة تم الا بالحضور
"No prayer is complete without 'presence' (concentration of the mind on God)"

گر نه موشی دزد در انبار ماست
If there is no thievish mouse in our barn,
گندم اعمال چل ساله کجاست
where is the corn of forty years' works (of devotion)?

ریزه‌ریزه صدق هر روزه چرا
Why is the daily sincerity (of our devotions) not being stored,
جمع می‌ناید درین انبار ما
bit by bit, in this barn of ours?

بس ستارهٔ آتش از آهن جهید
Many a star (spark) of fire shot forth from the iron (of good works),
وان دل سوزیده پذرفت و کشید
and that burning heart received (it) and drew (it) in

لیک در ظلمت یکی دزدی نهان
But in the darkness a hidden thief
می‌نهد انگشت بر استارگان
is laying his finger upon the stars,

61

می‌کشد استارگان را یک به یک
Extinguishing the stars one by one,
تا که نفروزد چراغی از فلک
that no lamp may shine from the (spiritual) sky

گر هزاران دام باشد در قدم
Though there be thousands of snares at our feet,
چون تو با مایی نباشد هیچ غم
when Thou art with us there is not any trouble.

هر شبی از دام تن ارواح را
Every night Thou freest the spirits from the body's snare,
می‌رهانی می‌کنی الواح را
and dost erase (the impressions on) the tablets (of the mind).

می‌رهند ارواح هر شب زین قفس
The spirits are set free every night from this cage,
فارغان نه حاکم و محکوم کس
(they are) done with ordinance and talk and tale.

شب ز زندان بی‌خبر زندانیان
At night prisoners are unconscious of their prison,
شب ز دولت بی‌خبر سلطانیان
at night governors are unconscious of their power.

نه غم و اندیشهٔ سود و زیان
There is no sorrow, no thought of gain or loss,
نه خیال این فلان و آن فلان
no fancy of this person or that person

حال عارف این بود بی‌خواب هم
This is the state of the 'árif (gnostic), even without sleep:
گفت ایزد هم رقود زین مرم
God said, (Thou wouldst deem them awake) whilst they slept. Shy not at this.

خفته از احوال دنیا روز و شب
He is asleep, day and night, to the affairs of the world,
چون قلم در پنجهٔ تقلیب رب
like a pen in the hand of the Lord's control

آنک او پنجه نبیند در رقم
One who sees not the hand in the writing thinks (that)
فعل پندارد بجنبش از قلم
the act (of writing proceeds) from the pen by means of movement

62

شمه‌ای زین حال عارف وا نمود
He (God) hath shown forth some part of this state of the ʿárif,
عقل را هم خواب حسی در ربود
(inasmuch as) the vulgar too are carried off (overtaken by sleep of the senses)

رفته در صحرای بی‌چون جانشان
Their souls are gone into the desert that is without description:
روحشان آسوده و ابدانشان
their spirits and bodies are at rest;

وز صفیری باز دام اندر کشی
And with a whistle thou leadest them back to the snare,
جمله را در داد و در داور کشی
leadest them all (back) to justice and to the judge.

فالق الاصباح اسرافیل وار
Like Isráfíl (Seraphiel), He (God) who causes the dawn to
جمله را در صورت آرد زان دیار
break brings them all from those lands (of spirit) into (the world of) form.

روح‌های منبسط را تن کند
He embodies the spirits divested (of body)
هر تنی را باز آبستن کند
He makes each body pregnant (laden) again (with actions and works).

اسپ جانها را کند عاری ز زین
He makes the steed of the souls bare of saddle:
سر النوم اخ الموتست این
this is the inner meaning of "Sleep is the brother of Death";

لیک بهر آنک روز آیند باز
But in order that they may return in the daytime,
بر نهد بر پایشان بند دراز
He puts a long tether on its leg,

تا که روزش واکشد زان مرغزار
So that in the daytime He may lead it back from that meadow
وز چراگاه آردش در زیر بار
and bring it from the pasture (to go) under the load

کاش چون اصحاب کهف این روح را
Would that He had guarded this spirit as the Men of the Cave
حفظ کردی یا چو کشتی نوح را
or as the Ark of Noah,

تا ازین طوفان بیداری و هوش
the Flood of wakefulness and consciousness!
وا رهیدی این ضمیر و چشم و گوش
That this mind and eye and ear might be delivered from

ای بسی اصحاب کهف اندر جهان
Oh, in the world there is many a Man of the Cave
پهلوی تو پیش تو هست این زمان
Beside you, before you, at this time:

یار با او غار با او در سرود
The Cave is with him, the Friend is in converse with him;
مهر بر چشمست و بر گوشت چه سود
but your eyes and ears are sealed, (so) what does it avail?

◆◉◈◉◆

قصهٔ دیدن خلیفه لیلی را
Story of the Caliph's seeing Laylá.

گفت لیلی را خلیفه کان توی
The Caliph said to Laylá:
کز تو مجنون شد پریشان و غوی
Art thou she by whom Majnún was distracted and led astray?

از دگر خوبان تو افزون نیستی
Thou art not superior to other fair ones."
گفت خامش چون تو مجنون نیستی
"Be silent," she replied, "since thou art not Majnún."

هر که بیدارست او در خوابتر
Whosoever is awake (to the material world) is the more asleep (to the spiritual world);
هست بیداریش از خوابش بتر
his wakefulness is worse than his sleep

چون بحق بیدار نبود جان ما
When our soul is not awake to God,
هست بیداری چو در بندان ما
wakefulness is like closing our doors (to Divine influences).

جان همه روز از لگدکوب خیال
All day long, from the buffets of phantasy and from (thoughts of)
وز زیان و سود وز خوف زوال
loss and gain and from fear of decline,

64

نی صفا می‌ماندش نی لطف و فر
There remains to it (the soul) neither joy nor grace and glory

نی بسوی آسمان راه سفر
nor way of journeying to Heaven.

خفته آن باشد که او از هر خیال
The one asleep (to spiritual things) is he who hath

دارد امید و کند با او مقال
hope of every vain fancy and holds parley with it.

دیو را چون حور بیند او به خواب
Diabolum per somnum videt tanquam virginem caelestem,[During sleep, he sees (in a dream) a demon resembling a heavenly maiden (houri);]

پس ز شهوت ریزد او با دیو آب
deinde propter libidinem effundit cum diabolo aquam(seminis).[then he pours forth (seminal) fluid out of lust (in imagined intercourse) with the demon.]

چونک تخم نسل را در شوره ریخت
Postquam semen generationis in terram salsuginosam infudit,[After he had scattered the seed of generation on salty (infertile) ground,]

او به خویش آمد خیال از وی گریخت
ipse ad se rediit, fugit ab eo illa imago.[he came to himself (and) the phantom fled from him.]

ضعف سر بیند از آن و تن پلید
Hinc percipit languorem capitis et (videt) corpus pollutum.[Because of that, he sees (himself as) faint of head and polluted of body.]

آه از آن نقش پدید ناپدید
Proh dolor ob illud simulacrum visum (sed revera) non visum![Alas, because of that visible (but) invisible form!]

مرغ بر بالا و زیر آن سایه‌اش
The bird is flying on high, and its shadow

می‌دود بر خاک پران مرغ وش
is speeding on the earth, flying like a bird:

ابلهی صیاد آن سایه شود
Some fool begins to chase the shadow,

می‌دود چندانک بی‌مایه شود
running (after it) so far that he becomes powerless (exhausted),

بی‌خبر کان عکس آن مرغ هواست
Not knowing that it is the reflexion of that bird in the air,

بی‌خبر که اصل آن سایه کجاست
not knowing where is the origin of the shadow.

تیر اندازد به سوی سایه او
He shoots arrows at the shadow;
ترکشش خالی شود از جست و جو
his quiver is emptied in seeking (to shoot it):

ترکش عمرش تهی شد عمر رفت
The quiver of his life became empty:
از دویدن در شکار سایه تفت
his life passed in running hotly in chase of the shadow.

سایهٔ یزدان چو باشد دایه‌اش
(But) when the shadow of God is his nurse,
وا رهاند از خیال و سایه‌اش
it delivers him from (every) phantom and shadow

سایهٔ یزدان بود بندهٔ خدا
The shadow of God is that servant of God
مرده او زین عالم و زندهٔ خدا
who is dead to this world and living through God

دامن او گیر زوتر بی‌گمان
Lay hold of his skirt most quickly without misgiving,
تا رهی در دامن آخر زمان
that you may be saved in the skirt (end) of the last days (of the world).

کیف مد الظل نقش اولیاست
(The shadow mentioned in the words) How He (God) extended the shadow is the form of the saints,
کو دلیل نور خورشید خداست
which guides to the light of the Divine Sun.

اندرین وادی مرو بی این دلیل
Do not go in this valley without this guide;
لا احب افلین گو چون خلیل
say, like Khalíl(Abraham), "I love not them that set."

رو ز سایه آفتابی را بیاب
Go, from the shadow gain a sun:
دامن شه شمس تبریزی بتاب
pluck the skirt of the(spiritual) king, Shams-i Tabrízí (the Sun of Tabríz)!

ره ندانی جانب این سور و عرس
If you do not know the way to this feast and bridal,
از ضیاء الحق حسام الدین بپرس
ask of Ziyá'u 'l-Haqq (the Radiance of God) Husámu'ddín.

ور حسد گیرد ترا در ره گلو
And if on the way envy seize you by the throat,
در حسد ابلیس را باشد غلو
it belongs to (is characteristic of) Iblís to go beyond bounds in envy;

کو ز آدم ننگ دارد از حسد
For he because of envy hath disdain for Adam,
با سعادت جنگ دارد از حسد
and because of envy is at war with felicity.

عقبه‌ای زین صعب‌تر در راه نیست
In the Way there is no harder pass than this.
ای خنک آنکش حسد همراه نیست
Oh, fortunate he who is not companioned by envy!

این جسد خانهٔ حسد آمد بدان
This body, you must know, is the house of envy,
از حسد آلوده باشد خاندان
for the household are tainted with envy.

گر جسد خانهٔ حسد باشد ولیک
if the body is the house of envy,
آن جسد را پاک کرد الله نیک
yet God made that body very pure.

طهرا بیتی بیان پاکیست
(The text) Cleanse My house, ye twain, is the explanation of (such) purity:
گنج نورست ار طلسمش خاکیست
it (the purified heart) is a treasure of (Divine) light, though its talisman is of earth.

چون کنی بر بی‌حسد مکر و حسد
When you practise deceit and envy against one who is without envy,
زان حسد دل را سیاهیها رسد
from that envy black stain arise in your heart.

خاک شو مردان حق را زیر پا
Become (as) dust under the feet of the men of God;
خاک بر سر کن حسد را همچو ما
throw dust on the head of envy, even as we do.

بیان حسد وزیر
Explanation of the envy of the vizier.

آن وزیرک از حسد بودش نژاد
That petty vizier had his origin from envy,
تا به باطل گوش و بینی باد داد
so that for vanity he gave to the wind (sacrificed) his ears and nose,
بر امید آنک از نیش حسد
In the hope that by the sting of envy
زهر او در جان مسکینان رسد
his venom might enter the souls of the poor (Christians).
هر کسی کو از حسد بینی کند
Anyone who from envy mutilates his nose
خویش را بی‌گوش و بی بینی کند
makes himself without ear and without nose (unable to apprehend spiritual things).
بینی آن باشد که او بویی برد
The nose is that which catches a scent,
بوی او را جانب کویی برد
and which the scent leads towards an abode (of spiritual truth).
هر که بویش نیست بی بینی بود
Whoever hath no scent is without a nose;
بوی آن بویست کان دینی بود
the scent (referred to) is that scent which is religious.
چونک بویی برد و شکر آن نکرد
When he has caught a scent and given no thanks for it,
کفر نعمت آمد و بینیش خورد
(that) ingratitude comes and devours his nose (deprives him of the organ of spiritual perception).
شکر کن مر شاکران را بنده باش
Give thanks (to God) and be a slave to those who give thanks:
پیش ایشان مرده شو پاینده باش
be in their presence (as one) dead, be steadfast.
چون وزیر از رهزنی مایه مساز
Do not, like the vizier, make brigandage your stock-in-trade;
خلق را تو بر میاور از نماز
do not turn the people away from the ritual prayer.

ناصح دین گشته آن کافر وزیر
The miscreant vizier had become (in appearance) a true religious counsellor,
کرده او از مکر در گوزینه سیر
(but) he had craftily put garlic in the almond cake.

◆◉◆◉◆

فهم کردن حاذقان نصاری مکر وزیر را
How the sagacious among the Christians perceived the guile of the vizier

هر که صاحب ذوق بود از گفت او
Whoever was possessed of (spiritual) discernment
لذقی می دید و تلخی جفت او
was feeling a sweet savour in his words and, joined therewith, bitterness.

نکته‌ها می گفت او آمیخته
He (the vizier) was saying fine things mixed (with foul):
در جلاب قند زهری ریخته
he had poured some poison into the sugared julep.

ظاهرش می گفت در ره چست شو
The outward sense of it was saying, "Be diligent in the Way,"
وز اثر می‌گفت جان را سست شو
but in effect it was saying to the soul, "Be slack."

ظاهر نقره گر اسپیدست و نو
If the surface of silver is white and new,
دست و جامه می سیه گردد ازو
(yet) the hands and dress are blackened by it

آتش ار چه سرخ رویست از شرر
Although fire is red-faced (bright and glorious) with sparks,
تو ز فعل او سیه کاری نگر
look at the black behaviour (displayed) in its action

برق اگر نوری نماید در نظر
If the lightning appears luminous to the eye
لیک هست از خاصیت دزد بصر
(yet) from its distinctive property it is the robber of sight (it strikes men blind).

هر که جز آگاه و صاحب ذوق بود
(As for) any (Christian) who was not wary and possessed of discernment,
گفت او در گردن او طوق بود
the words of him (the vizier) were (as) a collar on his neck.

مدتی شش سال در هجران شاه
During six years, in separation from the king,
شد وزیر اتباع عیسی را پناه
the vizier became a refuge for the followers of Jesus.

دین و دل را کل بدو بسپرد خلق
To him the people wholly surrendered their religion and their hearts:
پیش امر و حکم او می‌مرد خلق
at his command and decree they were ready to die.

پیغام شاه پنهان با وزیر
How the king sent messages in secret to the vizier.

در میان شاه و او پیغام‌ها
Messages (passed) between the king and him:
شاه را پنهان بدو آرام‌ها
the king had words of comfort from him in secret

پیش او بنوشت شه کای مقبلم
The king wrote to him, saying, "O my fortunate one
وقت آمد زود فارغ کن دلم
the time is come: quickly set my mind at ease."

گفت اینک اندر آن کارم شها
He replied: "Behold, O king,
کافکنم در دین عیسی فتنه‌ها
I am preparing to cast disorders into the religion of Jesus.

بیان دوازده سبط از نصارا
Explanation of the twelve tribes of the Christians

قوم عیسی را بد اندر دار و گیر
The people of Jesus had twelve amírs
حاکمانشان ده امیر و دو امیر
as rulers in authority over them.

هر فریقی مر امیری را تبع
Each party followed one amír and had become
بنده گشته میر خود را از طمع
devoted to its own amír from desire (of worldly gain).

این ده و این دو امیر و قومشان
These twelve amírs and their followers
گشته بند آن وزیر بد نشان
became the slaves of that vizier of evil sign.

اعتماد جمله بر گفتار او
They all put trust in his words,
اقتدای جمله بر رفتار او
they all took his procedure as a pattern.

پیش او در وقت و ساعت هر امیر
Each amír would have given up his life in his presence at the time and hour (on the spot),
جان بدادی گر بدو گفتی بمیر
if he (the vizier) had bidden him die.

◆◉◈◉◆

تخلیط وزیر در احکام آن چهیل
How the vizier confused the ordinances of the Gospel.

ساخت طوماری به نام هر یکی
He prepared a scroll in the name of (addressed to) each one,
نقش هر طومار دیگر مسلکی
the (written) form of each scroll (of) a different tenor,

حکمهای هر یکی نوعی دگر
The ordinances of each (of) a diverse kind,
این خلاف آن ز پایان تا به سر
this contradicting that from the end to the beginning.

در یکی راه ریاضت را و جوع
In one he made the path of asceticism and hunger
رکن توبه کرده و شرط رجوع
to be the basis of repentance and the condition (necessary) for conversion.

در یکی گفته ریاضت سود نیست
In one he said: "Asceticism profits naught:
اندرین ره مخلصی جز جود نیست
in this Way there is no place (means) of deliverance but generosity."

در یکی گفته که جوع و جود تو
In one he said: "Your hunger and generosity are (imply)
شرک باشد از تو با معبود تو
association on your part (of other objects) with (Him who is the object of your worship.)

جز توکل جز که تسلیم تمام
Excepting trust (in God) and complete resignation
در غم و راحت همه مکرست و دام
in sorrow and joy, all is a deceit and snare."

در یکی گفته که واجب خدمتست
In one he said: "It is incumbent (on you) to serve (God);
ور نه اندیشه توکل تهمتست
else the thought of putting trust (in Him) is (a cause of) suspicion."

در یکی گفته که امر و نهی هاست
In one he said: "There are (Divine) commands and prohibitionsare not for practice
بهر کردن نیست شرح عجز ماست
(but they) are not for practice (observance): they are (only) to show our weakness (inability to fulfil them),

تا که عجز خود بینیم اندر آن
So that we may behold our weakness therein
قدرت او را بدانیم آن زمان
and at that time recognise the power of God."

در یکی گفته که عجز خود مبین
In one he said: "Do not regard your weakness:
کفر نعمت کردنست آن عجز هین
that weakness is an act of ingratitude. Beware!

قدرت خود بین که این قدرت ازوست
Regard your power, for this power is from Him:
قدرت تو نعمت او دان که هوست
know that your power is the gift of Him who is Hú (the Absolute God)."

در یکی گفته کزین دو بر گذر
In one he said: "Leave both these (qualities) behind:
بت بود هر چه بگنجد در نظر
whatsoever is contained in sight (regard for other than God) is an idol (something which involves dualism)."

در یکی گفته مکش این شمع را
In one he said: "Do not put out this candle (of sight),
کین نظر چون شمع آمد جمع را
for this sight is as a candle (lighting the way) to (interior) concentration

از نظر چون بگذری و از خیال
When you relinquish sight and phantasy (too soon),
کشته باشی نیم شب شمع وصال
you will have put out the candle of union at midnight."

در یکی گفته بکش باکی مدار
In one he said: "Put it out—have no fear—
تا عوض بینی نظر را صد هزار
that you may see myriads of sights in exchange;

که ز کشتن شمع جان افزون شود
For by putting it out the candle of the spirit is increased:
لیلی ات از صبر تو مجنون شود
by your self-denial your Laylá (beloved) becomes your Majnún (lover).

ترک دنیا هر که کرد از زهد خویش
If anyone abandons the world by his own (act of) renunciation,
بیش آید پیش او دنیا و بیش
the world comes to him (with homage) more and more."

در یکی گفته که آنچت داد حق
In one he said: "That which God hath given you
بر تو شیرین کرد در ایجاد حق
He made sweet to you in (at the time of) bringing it into existence.

بر تو آسان کرد و خوش آن را بگیر
He made it easy (blessed) to you,
خویشتن را در میفکن در زحیر
and do you take it gladly: do not throw yourself into anguish."

در یکی گفته که بگذار آن خود
In one he said: "Let go all that belongs to self,
کان قبول طبع تو ردست و بد
for it is wrong and bad to comply with your nature."

راههای مختلف آسان شدست
(Many) different roads have become easy (to follow):
هر یکی را ملتی چون جان شدست
every one's religion has become (to him) as (dear) as life.

گر میسر کردن حق ره بدی
If God's making (religion) easy were the (right) road,
هر جهود و گبر ازو آگه بدی
every Jew and Zoroastrian would have knowledge of Him.

در یکی گفته میسر آن بود
In one he said: "That (alone) is made easy (blessed)
که حیات دل غذای جان بود
That (nothing but) spiritual food should be the life of the heart."

هر چه ذوق طبع باشد چون گذشت
When the enjoyments of the (sensual) nature are past,
بر نه آرد همچو شوره ریع و کشت
like brackish soil they raise no produce and crop.

جز پشیمانی نباشد ریع او
The produce thereof is naught but penitence;
جز خسارت پیش نارد بیع او
the sale thereof yields only loss, nothing more

آن میسر نبود اندر عاقبت
That is not "easy" in the end
نام او باشد معسر عاقبت
its (true) name ultimately is "hard."

تو معسر از میسر بازدان
Distinguish the hard from the easy:
عاقبت بنگر جمال این و آن
consider (what is) the goodliness of this and that in the end

در یکی گفته که استادی طلب
In one he said: "Seek a master (teacher):
عاقبت بینی نیابی در حسب
you will not find foresight as to the end among the qualities derived from ancestors."

عاقبت دیدند هر گون ملتی
Every sort of religious sect foresaw the end (according to their own surmise)
لاجرم گشتند اسیر زلتی
of necessity they fell captive to error.

عاقبت دیدن نباشد دست باف
To foresee the end is not (as simple as) a hand-loom;
ورنه کی بودی ز دینها اختلاف
otherwise, how would there have been difference in religions?

در یکی گفته که استا هم توی
In one he said: "You are the master,
زانک استا را شناسا هم توی
because you know the master.

مرد باش و سخره مردان مشو
Be a man and be not subject to men. Go, take your own head (choose your own way),
رو سر خود گیر و سرگردان مشو
and be not one whose head is turning (bewildered in search of a guide)."

در يكي گفته كه اين جمله يكيست
In one he said: "All this (multiplicity) is one:
هر كه او دو بيند احول مردكيست
whoever sees two is a squint-eyed manikin."

در يكي گفته كه صد يك چون بود
In one he said: "How should a hundred be one?
اين كي انديشد مگر مجنون بود
He who thinks this is surely mad."

هر يكي قوليست ضد هم دگر
The doctrines, every one, are contrary to each other:
چون يكي باشد يكي زهر و شكر
how should they be one? Are poison and sugar one?

تا ز زهر و از شكر در نگذري
Until you pass beyond (the difference of) poison and sugar,
كي تو از گلزار وحدت بو بري
and sugar, how will you catch a scent of unity and oneness?

اين نمط وين نوع ده طومار و دو
Twelve books of this style and fashion
بر نوشت آن دين عيسي را عدو
were drawn up in writing by that enemy to the religion of Jesus.

❂❂

بيان اين كه اين اختلافات در صورت روش است نه در حقيقت راه
Showing how this difference lies in the form of the doctrine not the real of the way

او ز يك رنگي عيسي بو نداشت
He had no scent (perception) of the unicolority of Jesus,
وز مزاج خم عيسي خو نداشت
nor had he a disposition from (imbued with) the tincture of the dyeing-vat of Jesus.

جامهٔ صد رنگ از آن خم صفا
From that pure vat a garment of a hundred colours
ساده و يك‌رنگ گشتي چون صبا
would become as simple and one coloured as light.

نيست يك‌رنگي كزو خيزد ملال
(This) is not the unicolority from which weariness ensues;
بل مثال ماهي و آب زلال
nay, it is (a case) like (that of) fishes and clear water:

گرچه در خشکی هزاران رنگهاست
Although there are thousands of colours on dry land,
ماهیان را با یبوست جنگهاست
(yet) fishes are at war with dryness.

کیست ماهی چیست دریا در مثل
Who is the fish and what is the sea in (my) simile,
تا بدان ماند ملک عز و جل
that the King Almighty and Glorious should resemble them?

صد هزاران بحر و ماهی در وجود
In (the world of) existence myriads of seas and fishes
سجده آرد پیش آن اکرام و جود
prostrate themselves in adoration before that Munificence and Bounty.

چند باران عطا باران شده
How many a rain of largesse hath rained,
تا بدان آن بحر در افشان شده
so that the sea was made thereby to scatter pearls!

چند خورشید کرم افروخته
How many a sun of generosity hath shone,
تا که ابر و بحر جود آموخته
so that loud and sea learned to be bountiful!

پرتو دانش زده بر خاک و طین
The sunbeams of Wisdom struck on soil and clay,
تا که شد دانه پذیرنده زمین
so that the earth became receptive of the seed.

خاک امین و هر چه در وی کاشتی
The soil is faithful to its trust, and whatever you have sown in it,
بی خیانت جنس آن برداشتی
you carry away the (equivalent in) kind thereof without fraud (on the part of the soil).

این امانت زان امانت یافتست
It has derived this faithfulness from that (Divine) faithfulness,
کآفتاب عدل بر وی تافتست
inasmuch as the sun of Justice has shone upon it.

تا نشان حق نیارد نوبهار
Until springtide brings the token of God,
خاک سرها را نکرده آشکار
the soil does not reveal its secrets

آن جوادی که جمادی را بداد
The Bounteous One who gave to an inanimate thing
این خبرها وین امانت وین سداد
these information and this faithfulness and this righteousness

مر جمادی را کند فضلش خبیر
His grace makes an inanimate thing informed,
عاقلان را کرده قهر او ضریر
(while) His wrath makes blind the men of understanding.

جان و دل را طاقت آن جوش نیست
Soul and heart cannot endure that ferment:
با که گویم در جهان یک گوش نیست
to whom shall I speak? There is not in the world a single ear

هر کجا گوشی بد از وی چشم گشت
Wherever there was an ear, through Him it became an eye;
هر کجا سنگی بد از وی یشم گشت
wherever there was a stone, through Him it became a jasper

کیمیاسازست چه بود کیمیا
He is an alchemist—what is alchemy (compared with His action)?
معجزه بخش است چه بود سیمیا
He is a giver of miracles (to prophets)—what is magic

این ثنا گفتن ز من ترک ثناست
This uttering of praise is (really) the omission of praise on my part,
کین دلیل هستی و هستی خطاست
for this (praise) is a proof of (my) being, and being is a sin.

پیش هست او بباید نیست بود
It behoves (us) to be not-being in the presence of His Being:
چیست هستی پیش او کور و کبود
in His presence what is (our) being? Blind and blue.

گر نبودی کور زو بگداختی
Were it not blind it would have been melted (consumed) by Him:
گرمی خورشید را بشناختی
it would have known the heat of (the Divine) sun;

ور نبودی او کبود از تعزیت
And were it not blue from mourning,
کی فسردی همچو یخ این ناحیت
how would this region have (remained) frozen like ice

بیان خسارت وزیر در این مکر
Setting forth how the vizier incurred perdition (by engaging in this plot)

همچو شه نادان و غافل بد وزیر
The vizier was ignorant and heedless,
پنجه می‌زد با قدیم ناگزیر
like the (Jewish) king: he was wrestling with the eternal and inevitable

با چنان قادر خدایی کز عدم
With a God so mighty that in a moment
صد چو عالم هست گرداند بدم
He causes a hundred worlds like ours to come into existence from non-existence:

صد چو عالم در نظر پیدا کند
A hundred worlds like ours He displays to the sight,
چونک چشمت را به خود بینا کند
when He makes your eye seeing by (the light of) Himself.

گر جهان پیشت بزرگ و بی‌بنیست
If the world appears to you vast and bottomless,
پیش قدرت ذره‌ای می‌دان که نیست
know that to Omnipotence it is not (so much as) an atom.

این جهان خود حبس جانهای شماست
This world, indeed, is the prison of your souls:
هین روید آن سو که صحرای شماست
oh, go in yonder direction, for there lies your open country

این جهان محدود و آن خود بی‌حدست
This world is finite, and truly that (other) is infinite:
نقش و صورت پیش آن معنی سدست
image and form are a barrier to that Reality.

صد هزاران نیزهٔ فرعون را
The myriads of Pharaoh's lances were shattered
در شکست از موسی با یک عصا
by (the hand of) Moses (armed) with a single staff.

صد هزاران طب جالینوس بود
Myriads were the therapeutic arts of Galen:
پیش عیسی و دمش افسوس بود
before Jesus and his (life-giving) breath they were a laughing-stock

صد هزاران دفتر اشعار بود
Myriads were the books of (pre-Islamic) poems:
پیش حرف امی‌اش عار بود
at the word of an illiterate (prophet) they were (put to) shame.

با چنین غالب خداوندی کسی
(Confronted) with such an all-conquering Lord,
چون نمیرد گر نباشد او خسی
how should anyone not die (to self), unless he be a vile wretch?

بس دل چون کوه را انگیخت او
Many a mind (strong and firm) as a mountain did He uproot;
مرغ زیرک با دو پا آویخت او
the cunning bird He hung up by its two feet.

فهم و خاطر تیز کردن نیست راه
To sharpen the intelligence and wits is not the (right) way:
جز شکسته می‌نگیرد فضل شاه
none but the broken (in spirit) wins the favour of the King.

ای بسا گنج آگنان کنج کاو
Oh, many the amassers of treasure, digging holes treasure)
کان خیال‌اندیش را شد ریش گاو
who became an ox's beard (dupe) to that vain schemer)!

گاو که بود تا تو ریش او شوی
Who is the ox that you should become his beard?
خاک چه بود تا حشیش او شوی
What is earth that you should become its stubble?

چون زنی از کار بد شد روی زرد
When a woman became pale-faced of (her) wickedness,
مسخ کرد او را خدا و زهره کرد
God metamorphosed her and made her Zuhra

عورتی را زهره کردن مسخ بود
To make a woman Zuhra was metamorphosis:
خاک و گل گشتن نه مسخست ای عنود
what (then) is it to become earth and clay, O contumacious one?

روح می‌بردت سوی چرخ برین
Your spirit was bearing you towards the highest sphere
سوی آب و گل شدی در اسفلین
you went towards the water and the clay amongst the lowest

خویشتن را مسخ کردی زین سفول
By this fall you metamorphosed yourself
زان وجودی که بد آن رشک عقول
from that existence which was the envy of the intelligences.

پس ببین کین مسخ کردن چون بود
Consider, then, how is this metamorphosis:
پیش آن مسخ این به غایت دون بود
compared with that metamorphosis this is exceedingly vile.

اسپ همت سوی اختر تاختی
You urged the steed of ambition towards the stars:
آدم مسجود را نشناختی
you did not acknowledge Adam who was worshipped

آخر آدم زاده‌ای ای ناخلف
After all, you are a son of Adam.
چند پنداری تو پستی را شرف
O degenerate! how long will you regard lowness as nobility?

چند گویی من بگیرم عالمی
How long will you say, "I will conquer a whole world,
این جهان را پر کنم از خود همی
I will make this world full of myself"?

گر جهان پر برف گردد سریسر
If the world should be filled with snow from end to end,
تاب خور بگدازدش با یک نظر
the glow of the sun would melt it with a single look.

وزر او و صد وزیر و صدهزار
burden and of a hundred viziers and a hundred thousand.
نیست گرداند خدا از یک شرار
God by a single spark (of His mercy) maketh naught his

عین آن تخییل را حکمت کند
He maketh the essence of that (false) imagination to be wisdom;
عین آن زهراب را شربت کند
He maketh the essence of that poisoned water to be adrink

آن گمان‌انگیز را سازد یقین
That which raises doubt He turneth into certainty;
مهرها رویاند از اسباب کین
He maketh loving kindnesses grow from the causes of hatred.

پرورد در آتش ابراهیم را
He cherisheth Abraham in the fire;
ایمنی روح سازد بیم را
He turneth fear into security of spirit.

از سبب سوزیش من سوداییم
By His burning of secondary causes I am distraught
در خیالاتش چو سوفسطاییم
in (my) fancies of Him I am like a sophist (sceptic or agnostic)

◆◉◆◉

مکر دیگر انگیختن وزیر در اضلال قوم
How the vizier started another plan to mislead the) folk.

مکر دیگر آن وزیر از خود ببست
The vizier formed in his mind another plan:
وعظ را بگذاشت و در خلوت نشست
he abandoned preaching and sat alone in seclusion

در مریدان در فکند از شوق سوز
He inspired ardour in his disciples from (their) longing
بود در خلوت چهل پنجاه روز
he remained in seclusion forty or fifty days.

خلق دیوانه شدند از شوق او
The people became mad from longing for him
از فراق حال و قال و ذوق او
of being separated from his feeling and discourse and intuition.

لابه و زاری همی کردند و او
They were making supplication and lament,
از ریاضت گشته در خلوت دوتو
while he in solitude was bent double by austerities

گفته ایشان نیست ما را بی تو نور
They said, "Without thee we have no light:
بی عصاکش چون بود احوال کور
how (what) is the state of a blind man without a leader?

از سر اکرام و از بهر خدا
By way of showing favour (to us) and for God's sake,
بیش ازین ما را مدار از خود جدا
do not keep us parted from thee any longer.

ما چو طفلانیم و ما را دایه تو
We are as children and thou art our nurse:
بر سر ما گستران آن سایه تو
do thou spread over us that shadow (of thy protection)."

گفت جانم از محبان دور نیست
He said, "My soul is not far from them that love (me),
لیک بیرون آمدن دستور نیست
but there is no permission to come forth."

آن امیران در شفاعت آمدند
Those amírs came for intercession,
وان مریدان در شناعت آمدند
and the disciples came in reproach,

کین چه بدبختیست ما را ای کریم
Saying, "O noble sir, what a misfortune is this for us!
از دل و دین مانده ما بی تو یتیم
Without thee we are left orphaned (deprived) of our hearts and our religion.

تو بهانه می‌کنی و ما ز درد
Thou art making a pretence while we in grief
می‌زنیم از سوز دل دمهای سرد
are heaving cold(fruitless) sighs from the burning heat of our hearts

ما به گفتار خوشت خو کرده‌ایم
We have become accustomed to thy sweet discourse,
ما ز شیر حکمت تو خورده‌ایم
we have drunk of the milk of thy wisdom

الله الله این جفا با ما مکن
Allah! Allah! do not thou (O vizier) treat us with such cruelty:
خیر کن امروز را فردا مکن
show kindness to-day, do not (put off till) to-morrow.

می‌دهد دل مر ترا کین بی دلان
Does thy heart give to thee (consent) that these who have lost their hearts (to thee) should at last
بی تو گردند آخر از بی‌حاصلان
being without thee, become (numbered) amongst them that have nothing left?

جمله در خشکی چو ماهی می‌طپند
They all are writhing like fishes on dry land:
آب را بگشا ز جو بر دار بند
let loose the water, remove the dam from the stream.

ای که چون تو در زمانه نیست کس
O thou like whom there is none in the world,
الله الله خلق را فریاد رس
for God's sake, for God's sake, come to the aid of thy people!"

دفع گفتن وزیر مریدان را
How the vizier refused the request of the disciples.

گفت هان ای سخرگان گفت و گو
He said: "Beware, O ye enslaved by words and talk,

وعظ و گفتار زبان و گوش جو
ye who seek admonition of the speech of the tongue and of the ear.

پنبه اندر گوش حس دون کنید
Put cotton-wool in the ear of the low (physical) sense,

بند حس از چشم خود بیرون کنید
take off the bandage of (that) sense from your eyes!

پنبهٔ آن گوش سر گوش سرست
The ear of the head is the cotton-wool of the ear of the conscience:

تا نگردد این کر آن باطن کرست
until the former becomes deaf, that inward (ear) is deaf.

بی‌حس و بی‌گوش و بی‌فکرت شوید
Become without sense and without ear and without thought,

تا خطاب ارجعی را بشنوید
that ye may hear the call (of God to the soul), 'Return!'"

تا به گفت و گوی بیداری دری
So long as thou art in the conversation of wakefulness,

تو ز گفت خواب بویی کی بری
how wilt thou catch any scent of the conversation of sleep?

سیر بیرونیست قول و فعل ما
Our speech and action is the exterior journey:

سیر باطن هست بالای سما
the interior journey is above the sky.

حس خشکی دید کز خشکی بزاد
(The) sense saw dryness, because it was born of dryness

عیسی جان پای بر دریا نهاد
the Jesus of the spirit set foot on the sea.

سیر جسم خشک بر خشکی فتاد
The journey of the dry body befell on dry land,

سیر جان پا در دل دریا نهاد
(but) the journey of the spirit set foot (took place) in the heart of the sea.

چونک عمر اندر ره خشکی گذشت
Since thy life has passed in travelling on land,

گاه کوه و گاه دریا گاه دشت
now mountain, now river, now desert,

آب حیوان از کجا خواهی تو یافت
Whence wilt thou gain the Water of Life?
موج دریا را کجا خواهی شکافت
Where wilt thou cleave the waves of the Sea?

موج خاکی وهم و فهم و فکر ماست
The waves of earth are our imagination and understanding and thought;
موج آبی محو و سکرست و فناست
the waves of water are (mystical) self-effacement and intoxication and death (faná).

تا درین سکری از آن سکری تو دور
Whilst thou art in this) intoxication, thou art far from that intoxication;
تا ازین مستی از آن جامی نفور
whilst thou art drunken with this thou art blind to that cup.

گفت و گوی ظاهر آمد چون غبار
Outward speech and talk is as dust:
مدتی خاموش خو کن هوش دار
do thou for a time make a habit of silence. Take heed!

◆◉◆◉◆

مکر کردن مریدان کی خلوت را بشکن
How the disciples repeated their request that he should interrupt his seclusion

جمله گفتند ای حکیم رخنه‌جو
They all said: "O sage who seekest a crevice (means of evasion),
این فریب و این جفا با ما مگو
say not to us this (word of) guile and harshness.

چارپا را قدر طاقت بار نه
Lay on the beast a burden in proportion to its endurance,
بر ضعیفان قدر قوت کار نه
lay on the weak a task in proportion to their strength

دانهٔ هر مرغ اندازهٔ ویست
The bait for every bird is according to its measure
طعمهٔ هر مرغ آن چهیری کیست
how should a fig be the food (lure) for every bird?

طفل را اگر نان دهی بر جای شیر
If you give a babe bread instead of milk,
طفل مسکین را از آن نان مرده گیر
take it (for granted) that the poor babe will die of the bread;

چونک دندانها بر آرد بعد از آن
(Yet) afterwards, when it grows teeth,
هم بخود گردد دلش جویای نان
that babe will of its own accord ask for bread.

مرغ پر نارسته چون پران شود
When an unfledged bird begins to fly,
لقمهٔ هر گربهٔ دران شود
it becomes a mouthful for any rapacious cat;

چون بر آرد پر بپرد او بخود
(But) when it grows wings, it will fly of itself without trouble
بی‌تکلف بی‌صفیر نیک و بد
and without whistling (prompting), good or bad

دیو را نطق تو خامش می‌کند
Thy speech makes the Devil silent,
گوش ما را گفت تو هش می‌کند
thy words make our ears (full of) intelligence.

گوش ما هوشست چون گویا توی
Our ears are (full of) intelligence when thou art speaking;
خشک ما بحرست چون دریا توی
our dry land is a river when thou art the ocean.

با تو ما را خاک بهتر از فلک
With thee, earth is better to us than heaven,
ای سماک از تو منور تا سمک
O thou by whom (the world from) Arcturus to the Fish is illumined!

بی تو ما را بر فلک تاریکیست
Without thee, darkness is over heaven for us,
با تو ای ماه این فلک باری کیست
(but) compared with thee, O Moon, who is this heaven at all?

صورت رفعت بود افلاک را
The heavens have the form of sublimity,
معنی رفعت روان پاک را
(but) the essence of sublimity belongs to the pure spirit.

صورت رفعت برای جسمهاست
The form of sublimity is for bodies;
جسمها در پیش معنی اسمهاست
beside the essence(reality) bodies are (mere) names."

جواب گفتن وزیر کی خلوت را نمی شکنم
The refusal of the vizier to interrupt his seclusion

گفت حجتهای خود کوته کنید
He said: "Cut short your arguments,
پند را در جان و در دل ره کنید
let my advice make its way into your souls and hearts.

گر امینم متهم نبود امین
If I am trustworthy, the trustworthy is not doubted,
گر بگویم آسمان را من زمین
even though I should call heaven earth.

گر کمالم با کمال انکار چیست
If I am (endowed with) perfection, why (this) disbelief in my perfection? and if I am not (perfect),
ور نیم این زحمت و آزار چیست
why this molestation and annoyance?

من نخواهم شد ازین خلوت برون
I will not go forth from this seclusion,
زانک مشغولم باحوال درون
because I am occupied with inward experiences."

◈◈

اعتراض مریدان در خلوت مدیر
How the disciples raised objections against the vizier's secluding himself.

جمله گفتند ای وزیر انکار نیست
They all said: "O vizier, it is not disbelief:
گفت ما چون گفتن اغیار نیست
our words are not as the words of strangers.

اشک دیده‌ست از فراق تو دوان
The tears of our eyes are running because of our separation from thee;
آه آهست از میان جان روان
sigh after sigh is going (up) from the midst of our souls.

طفل با دایه نه استیزد ولیک
A babe does not contend with its nurse, but it weeps,
گرید او گر چه نه بد داند نه نیک
although it knows neither evil nor good.

ما چو چنگیم و تو زخمه می‌زنی
We are as the harp and thou art striking (it with) the plectrum (playing on it):
زاری از ما نه تو زاری می‌کنی
the lamentation is not from us, it is thou that art making lamentation.

ما چو ناییم و نوا در ما ز تست
We are as the flute, and the music in us is from thee;
ما چو کوهیم و صدا در ما ز تست
we are as the mountain, and the echo in us is from thee

ما چو شطرنجیم اندر برد و مات
We are as pieces of chess (engaged) in victory and defeat:
برد و مات ما ز تست ای خوش صفات
our victory and defeat is from thee, O thou whose qualities are comely!

ما که باشیم ای تو ما را جان جان
Who are we, O thou soul of our souls,
تا که ما باشیم با تو درمیان
that we should remain in being beside thee?

ما عدمهاییم و هستیهای ما
We and our existences are (really) non-existences:
تو وجود مطلقی فانی‌نما
thou art the absolute Being which manifests the perishable (causes phenomena to appear).

ما همه شیران ولی شیر علم
We all are lions, but lions on a banner:
حمله شان از باد باشد دم بدم
because of the wind they are rushing onward from moment to moment

حمله‌شان پیداست و ناپیداست باد
Their onward rush is visible, and the wind is unseen:
آنک ناپیداست هرگز گم مباد
may that which is unseen not fail from us!

باد ما و بود ما از داد تست
Our wind (that whereby we are moved) and our being are of thy gift;
هستی ما جمله از ایجاد تست
our whole existence is from thy bringing (us) into being.

لذت هستی نمودی نیست را
Thou didst show the delightfulness of Being unto not-being,
عاشق خود کرده بودی نیست را
(after) thou hadst caused not-being to fall in love with thee.

لذت انعام خود را وامگیر
Take not away the delightfulness of thy bounty;
نقل و باده و جام خود را وا مگیر
take not away thy dessert and wine and wine-cup!

ور بگیری کیت جست و جو کند
And if thou take it away, who is there that will make inquiry?
نقش با نقاش چون نیرو کند
How should the picture strive with the painter?

منگر اندر ما مکن در ما نظر
Do not look on us, do not fix thy gaze on us:
اندر اکرام و سخای خود نگر
look on thine own kindness and generosity.

ما نبودیم و تقاضامان نبود
We were not, and there was no demand on our part,
لطف تو ناگفتهٔ ما می‌شنود
thy grace was hearkening to our unspoken prayer (and calling us into existence)."

نقش باشد پیش نقاش و قلم
Before the painter and the brush the picture
عاجز و بسته چو کودک در شکم
is helpless and bound like a child in the womb

پیش قدرت خلق جمله بارگه
Before Omnipotence all the people of the (Divine) court of audience
عاجزان چون پیش سوزن کارگه
are as helpless as the (embroiderer's) fabric before the needle.

گاه نقشش دیو و گه آدم کند
Now He makes the picture thereon (one of) the Devil, now (of) Adam;
گاه نقشش شادی و گه غم کند
now He makes the picture thereon (one of) joy, now (one of) grief.

دست نه تا دست جنباند به دفع
There is no power (to any one) that he should move a hand in defence; no (right of) speech,
نطق نه تا دم زند در ضر و نفع
that he should utter a word concerning injury or benefit.

تو ز قرآن بازخوان تفسیر بیت
Recite from the Qur'án the interpretation of (i.e. a text which interprets) the (preceding) verse:
گفت ایزد ما رمیت اذ رمیت
God said, Thou didst not throw when thou threwest.

گر پرانیم تیر آن نه ز ماست

If we let fly an arrow, that (action) is not from us:

ما کمان و تیراندازش خداست

we are (only) the bow, and the shooter of the arrow is God.

این نه جبر این معنی جباریست

This is not jabr (compulsion); it is the meaning of jabbárí

ذکر جباری برای زاریست

the mention of almightiness is for the sake of (inspiring us with) humility

زاری ما شد دلیل اضطرار

Our humility is evidence of necessity,

خجلت ما شد دلیل اختیار

(but) our sense of guilt is evidence of freewill.

گر نبودی اختیار این شرم چیست

If there were not freewill, what is this shame?

وین دریغ و خجلت و آزرم چیست

And what is this sorrow and guilty confusion and abashment?

زجر شاگردان و استادان چراست

Why is there chiding between masters and pupils?

خاطر از تدبیرها گردان چراست

Why is the mind changing (so as to depart) from plans (already formed)?

ور تو گویی غافلست از جبر او

And if you say that he (the assertor of freewill) takes no heed of His (God's) compulsion,

ماه حق پنهان کند در ابر رو

(and that) God's moon has become hidden in His cloud,

هست این را خوش جواب ار بشنوی

There is a good answer to this; if you hearken,

بگذری از کفر و در دین بگروی

you will relinquish unbelief and incline towards the (true) religion.

حسرت و زاری گه بیماریست

Remorse and humility occur at the time of illness:

وقت بیماری همه بیداریست

the time of illness is wholly wakefulness (of conscience).

آن زمان که می‌شوی بیمار تو

At the time when you are becoming ill,

می کنی از جرم استغفار تو

you pray God to forgive your trespass;

می‌نماید بر تو زشتی گنه
The foulness of your sin is shown to you,
می‌کنی نیت که باز آیم به ره
you resolve to come back to the (right) way;

عهد و پیمان می‌کنی که بعد ازین
You make promises and vows that henceforth your chosen
جز که طاعت نبودم کاری گزین
course (of action) will be nothing but obedience (to God):

پس یقین گشت این که بیماری ترا
Therefore, it has become certain that illness
می‌ببخشد هوش و بیداری ترا
gives to you conscience and wakefulness.

پس بدان این اصل را ای اصل‌جو
Note, then, this principle, O thou that seekest the principle;
هر که را دردست او بردست بو
everyone who suffers pain has caught the scent (thereof):

هر که او بیدارتر پر دردتر
The more wakeful any one is, the more full of suffering he is;
هر که او آگاه تر رخ زردتر
the more aware (of God) he is, the paler he is in countenance.

گر ز جبرش آگهی زاریت کو
If you are aware of His jabr (compulsion), where is your humility?
بینش زنجیر جباریت کو
Where is your feeling of (being loaded with) the chain of His jabbárí (almightiness)?

بسته در زنجیر چون شادی کند
How should one make merry who is bound in chains?
کی اسیر حبس آزادی کند
When does the captive in prison behave like the man who is free?

ور تو می‌بینی که پایت بسته‌اند
And if you consider that your foot is shackled
بر تو سرهنگان شه بنشسته‌اند
the king's officers are sitting (as custodians) over you

پس تو سرهنگی مکن با عاجزان
Then do not act like an officer (tyrannously) towards the helpless,
زانک نبود طبع و خوی عاجز آن
inasmuch as that is not the nature and habit of a helpless man.

چون تو جبر او نمی‌بینی مگو
Since you do not feel His compulsion, do not say (that you are compelled);
ور همی بینی نشان دید کو
and if you feel it, where is the sign of your feeling?

در هر آن کاری که میلستت بدان
In every act for which you have inclination,
قدرت خود را همی بینی عیان
you are clearly conscious of your power (to perform it),

واندر آن کاری که میلت نیست و خواست
(But) in every act for which you have no inclination and desire,
خویش را جبری کنی کین از خداست
in regard to that (act) you have become a necessitarian, saying, "This is from God."

انبیا در کار دنیا جبری‌اند
The prophets are necessitarians in regard to the works of this world,
کافران در کار عقبی جبری‌اند
(while) the infidels are necessitarians in regard to the works of the next world.

انبیا را کار عقبی اختیار
To the prophets the works of the next world are (a matter of) freewill;
جاهلان را کار دنیا اختیار
to the foolish the works of this world are (a matter of) freewill,

زانک هر مرغی بسوی جنس خویش
Because every bird flies to its own congener:
می‌پرد او در پس و جان پیش پیش
it (follows) behind, and its spirit (goes) before, (leading it on).

کافران چون جنس سجین آمدند
Inasmuch as the infidels were congeners of Sijjín (Hell),
سجن دنیا را خوش آیین آمدند
they were well-disposed to the prison (sijn) of this world.

انبیا چون جنس علیین بدند
Inasmuch as the prophets were congeners of 'Illiyyín
سوی علیین جان و دل شدند
they went towards the 'Illiyyín of spirit and heart.

این سخن پایان ندارد لیک ما
This discourse hath no end,
باز گوییم آن تمام قصه را
but let us (now) relate the story to its completion

نومید کردن وزیر مریدان را از رفض خلوت
How the vizier made the disciples lose hope of his abandoning seclusion.

آن وزیر از اندرون آواز داد
The vizier cried out from within,

کای مریدان از من این معلوم باد
"O disciples, be this made known to you from me,

که مرا عیسی چنین پیغام کرد
That Jesus hath given me a such-like message:

کز همه یاران و خویشان باش فرد
'Be separated from all friends and kinsfolk.

روی در دیوار کن تنها نشین
Set thy face to the wall, sit alone,

وز وجود خویش هم خلوت گزین
and choose to be secluded even from thine own existence.'

بعد ازین دستوری گفتار نیست
After this there is no permission (for me) to speak;

بعد ازین با گفت و گویم کار نیست
after this I have nothing to do with talk.

الوداع ای دوستان من مرده‌ام
Farewell, O friends! I am dead:

رخت بر چارم فلک بر برده‌ام
I have carried my belongings up to the Fourth Heaven,

تا به زیر چرخ ناری چون حطب
In order that beneath the fiery sphere

من نسوزم در عنا و در عطب
I may not burn like firewood in woe and perdition,

پهلوی عیسی نشینم بعد ازین
(But) henceforth may sit beside Jesus

بر فراز آسمان چارمین
at the top of the Fourth Heaven."

ولی عهد ساختن ساختن وزیر هر یک امیر را جدا جدا
How the vizier appointed each one of the amírs separately as his successor

وانگهانی آن امیران را بخواند
And then he summoned those amírs

یک بیک تنها بهر یک حرف راند
one by one and conversed with each (of them) alone

گفت هر یک را بدین عیسوی
He said to each one, "In the religion of Jesus

نایب حق و خلیفهٔ من توی
thou art the vicar of God and my khalífa (vicegerent),

وان امیران دگر اتباع تو
And those other amírs are thy followers:

کرد عیسی جمله را اشیاع تو
Jesus hath made all of them thy assistants

هر امیری کو کشد گردن بگیر
Any amír who lifts his neck (in rebellion),

یا بکش یا خود همی دارش اسیر
seize him and either kill him or hold him captive;

لیک تا من زنده‌ام این وا مگو
But do not declare this whilst I am alive:

تا نمیرم این ریاست را مجو
do not seek this supreme authority until I am dead.

تا نمیرم من تو این پیدا مکن
Until I am dead, do not reveal this:

دعوی شاهی و استیلا مکن
do not lay claim to sovereignty and dominion.

اینک این طومار و احکام مسیح
Here is this scroll and the ordinances of the Messiah:

یک بیک بر خوان تو بر امت فصیح
recite them distinctly, one by one, to his people."

هر امیری را چنین گفت او جدا
Thus he spoke to each amír separately, (saying),

نیست نایب جز تو در دین خدا
"There is no vicar in the religion of God except thee."

هر یکی را کرد او یک‌یک عزیز
He honoured each, one by one, (in this way):

هرچه آن را گفت این را گفت نیز
whatever he said to that (amír) he also said to this.

93

هر یکی را او یکی طومار داد
To each he gave one scroll:
هر یکی ضد دگر بود المراد
everyone was purposely the contrary of the other.

متن آن طومارها بد مختلف
All the scrolls were different,
همچو شکل حرفها یا تاالف
like the forms of the letters(of the alphabet) from yá to alif.

حکم این طومار ضد حکم آن
The rule (laid down) in this scroll was contrary to the rule in that:
پیش ازین کردیم این ضد را بیان
we have already explained (the nature of) this contradiction.

◈◉◈◉◈

کشتن وزیر خویشتن را در خلوت
How the vizier killed himself in seclusion.

بعد از آن چل روز دیگر در ببست
After that, he shut the door for other forty days (and then)
خویش کشت و از وجود خود برست
killed himself and escaped from his existence.

چونک خلق از مرگ او آگاه شد
When the people learned of his death,
بر سر گورش قیامتگاه شد
there came to pass at his grave the scene of the Resurrection.

خلق چندان جمع شد بر گور او
So great a multitude gathered at his grave,
موکنان جامه‌دران در شور او
tearing their hair, rending their garments in wild grief for him,

کان عدد را هم خدا داند شمرد
That only God can reckon the number of them
از عرب وز ترک و از رومی و کرد
Arabs and Turks and Greeks and Kurds.

خاک او کردند بر سرهای خویش
They put his (grave's) earth on their heads;
درد او دیدند درمان جای خویش
they deemed anguish for him to be the remedy for themselves.

آن خلایق بر سر گورش مهی
During a month those multitudes over his grave
کرده خون را از دو چشم خود رهی
made a way for blood from their eyes (shed tears of anguish).

◆◉◈◉◆

کی ولی عهد از شما کدامست طلب کردن امت عیسی علیه السلام از امرا
How the people of Jesus on him be peace! asked the amírs, "Which one of you is the successor?"

بعد ماهی خلق گفتند ای مهان
After a month the people said, "O chiefs,
از امیران کیست بر جایش نشان
which of (the) amírs is designated in his place,

تا به جای او شناسیمش امام
That we may acknowledge him as our religious leader instead of him (the vizier),
دست و دامن را به دست او دهیم
and give our hands and skirts into his hand?

چونک شد خورشید و ما را کرد داغ
Since the sun is gone and has branded us (left the brand of sorrow in our hearts),
چاره نبود بر مقامش از چراغ
is not a lamp the (only) resource in his stead?

چونک شد از پیش دیده وصل یار
Since union with the beloved has vanished from before our eyes,
نایی باید ازومان یادگار
we must needs have a vicar as a memorial of him (i.e. one who will recall him to our memory).

چونک گل بگذشت و گلشن شد خراب
Since the rose is past and the garden ravaged,
بوی گل را از که یابیم از گلاب
from whom shall we get the perfume of the rose? From rosewater."

چون خدا اندر نیاید در عیان
Inasmuch as God comes not into sight,
نایب حق اند این پیغامبران
these prophets are the vicars of God.

نه غلط گفتم که نایب با منوب
Nay, I have said (this) wrongly; for if you suppose that the vicar and He who is represented
گر دو پنداری قبیح آید نه خوب
by the vicar are two, it (such a thought) is bad, not good.

نه دو باشد تا توی صورت‌پرست
Nay; they are two so long as you are a worshipper of form,
پیش او یک گشت کز صورت برست
(but) they have become one to him who has escaped from (consciousness of) form

چون به صورت بنگری چشم تو دوست
When you look at the form, your eye is two;
تو به نورش در نگر کز چشم رست
look at its (the eye's) light, which grew from the eye.

نور هر دو چشم نتوان فرق کرد
'Tis impossible to distinguish the light of the two eyes,
چونک در نورش نظر انداخت مرد
when a man has cast his look upon their light.

ده چراغ ار حاضر آید در مکان
If ten lamps are present in (one) place,
هر یکی باشد بصورت غیر آن
each differs in form from another:

فرق نتوان کرد نور هر یکی
To distinguish without any doubt the light of each,
چون به نورش روی آری بی‌شکی
when you turn your face towards their light, is impossible.

گر تو صد سیب و صد آبی بشمری
If you count a hundred apples or a hundred quinces,
صد نماند یک شود چون بفشری
they do not remain a hundred (but) become one, when you crush them (together).

در معانی قسمت و اعداد نیست
In things spiritual there is no division and no numbers;
در معانی تجزیه و افراد نیست
in things spiritual there is no partition and no individuals.

اتحاد یار با یاران خوشست
Sweet is the oneness of the Friend with His friends:
پای معنی‌گیر صورت سرکشست
catch(and cling to) the foot of spirit. Form is headstrong.

صورت سرکش گدازان کن برنج
Make headstrong form waste away with tribulation,
تا ببینی زیر او وحدت چو گنج
that beneath it you may descry unity, like a (buried) treasure

ور تو نگدازی عنایتهای او
And if you waste it not away, His favours

خود گدازد ای دلم مولای او
will waste it—oh, my heart is His vassal

او نماید هم به دلها خویش را
He even showeth Himself to (our) hearts,

او بدوزد خرقهٔ درویش را
He seweth the tattered frock of the dervish

منبسط بودیم یک جوهر همه
Simple were we and all one substance;

بی‌سر و بی‌پا بدیم آن سر همه
we were all without head and without foot yonder.

یک گهر بودیم همچون آفتاب
We were one substance, like the Sun;

بی گره بودیم و صافی همچو آب
we were knotless and pure, like water.

چون بصورت آمد آن نور سره
When that goodly Light took form,

شد عدد چون سایه‌های کنگره
it became (many in) number like the shadows of a battlement.

کنگره ویران کنید از منجنیق
Rase ye the battlement with the manjaníq (mangonel),

تا رود فرق از میان این فریق
that difference may vanish from amidst this company (of shadows).

شرح این را گفتمی من از مری
I would have explained this (matter) with (eager) contention,

لیک ترسم تا نلغزد خاطری
but I fear lest some (weak) mind may stumble.

نکته‌ها چون تیغ پولادست تیز
The points (involved in it) are sharp as a sword of steel;

گر نداری تو سپر وا پس گریز
if you have not the shield (of capacity to understand), turn back and flee!

پیش این الماس بی اسپر میا
Do not come without shield against this adamant

کز بریدن تیغ را نبود حیا
for the sword is not ashamed of cutting.

زین سبب من تیغ کردم در غلاف
For this cause I have put the sword in sheath,
تا که کژخوانی نخواند برخلاف
that none who misreads may read contrariwise

آمدیم اندر تمامی داستان
We come (now) to complete the tale and
وز وفاداری جمع راستان
and (speak) of the loyalty of the multitude of the righteous

کز پس این پیشوا بر خاستند
Who rose up after (the death of) this leader,
بر مقامش نایی می‌خواستند
demanding a vicar in his place.

❧◉❧◉❧

منازعت امرا در ولی عهدی
The quarrel of the amírs concerning the succession.

یک امیری زان امیران پیش رفت
One of those amírs advanced
پیش آن قوم وفا اندیش رفت
and went before that loyalminded people.

گفت اینک نایب آن مرد من
"Behold," said he, "I am that man's vicar:
نایب عیسی منم اندر زمن
I am the vicar of Jesus at the present time.

اینک این طومار برهان منست
Look, this scroll is my proof that
کین نیابت بعد ازو آن منست
after him the vicarate belongs to me."

آن امیر دیگر آمد از کمین
Another amír came forth from ambush:
دعوی او در خلافت بد همین
his pretension regarding the vicegerency was the same;

از بغل او نیز طوماری نمود
He too produced a scroll from under his arm,
تا برآمد هر دو را خشم جهود
so that in both (amírs) there arose the Jewish anger.

آن امیران دگر یک یک قطار
The rest of the amírs, one after another,
برکشیده تیغهای آبدار
drawing swords of keen mettle,

هر یکی را تیغ و طوماری به دست
Each with a sword and a scroll in his hand,
درهم افتادند چون پیلان مست
fell to combat like raging elephants.

صد هزاران مرد ترسا کشته شد
Hundreds of thousands of Christians were slain,
تا ز سرهای بریده پشته شد
so that there were mounds of severed heads;

خون روان شد همچو سیل از چپ و راست
Blood flowed, on left and right, like a torrent;
کوه کوه اندر هوا زین گرد خاست
mountains of this dust (of battle) rose in the air.

تخمهای فتنهها کو کشته بود
The seeds of dissension which he (the vizier) had sown
آفت سرهای ایشان گشته بود
had become a calamity (cause of destruction) to their heads.

جوزها بشکست و آن کان مغز داشت
The walnuts (bodies) were broken, and those which had the kernel had,
بعد کشتن روح پاک نغز داشت
after being slain, a spirit pure and fair.

کشتن و مردن که بر نقش تنست
Slaughter and death which befalls the bodily frame is
چون انار و سیب را بشکستنست
like breaking pomegranates and apples:

آنچه شیرینست او شد ناردانگ
That which is sweet becomes pomegranate-syrup,
وانک پوسیدهست نبود غیر بانگ
and that which is rotten is naught but noise:

آنچه با معنیست خود پیدا شود
That which has reality is made manifest (after death),
وآنچه پوسیدهست او رسوا شود
and that which is rotten is put to shame.

رو بمعنی کوش ای صورت پرست
Go, strive after reality, O worshipper of form,
زانک معنی بر تن صورت پرست
inasmuch as reality is the wing on form's body.

همنشین اهل معنی باش تا
Consort with the followers of reality,
هم عطا یابی و هم باشی فتی
that you may both win the gift and be generous (in giving yourself up to God).

جان بی‌معنی درین تن بی‌خلاف
Beyond dispute, in this body the spirit devoid of reality
هست همچون تیغ چوبین در غلاف
is even as a wooden sword in the sheath:

تا غلاف اندر بود باقیمتست
Whilst it remains in the sheath, it is (apparently) valuable,
چون برون شد سوختن را آلتست
(but) when it has come forth it is an implement (only fit) for burning.

تیغ چوبین را مبر در کارزار
Do not take a wooden sword into the battle! First see
بنگر اول تا نگردد کار زار
in order that your plight may not be wretched.

گر بود چوبین برو دیگر طلب
If it is made of wood, go, seek another;
ور بود الماس پیش آ با طرب
and if it is adamant, march forward joyously.

تیغ در زرادخانهٔ اولیاست
The sword (of reality) is in the armoury of the saints:
دیدن ایشان شما را کیمیاست
to see (and associate with) them is for you (as precious as) the Elixir.

جمله دانایان همین گفته همین
All the wise have said this same thing:
هست دانا رحمة للعالمین
the wise man is a (Divine) mercy to created beings.

گر اناری می‌خری خندان بخر
If you would buy a pomegranate, buy (it when it is) laughing (having its rind cleft open), تا
دهد خنده ز دانهٔ او خبر
so that its laughter (openness) may give information as to its seeds.

ای مبارک خنده‌اش کو از دهان
Oh, blessed is its laughter, for through its mouth it shows the heart,
می‌نماید دل چو در از درج جان
like a pearl from the casket of the spirit.

نامبارک خندهٔ آن لاله بود
Unblest was the laughter (openness) of the red anemone,
کز دهان او سیاهی دل نمود
from whose mouth appeared the blackness of its heart.

نار خندان باغ را خندان کند
The laughing pomegranate makes the garden laughing (gay and blooming):
صحبت مردانت از مردان کند
companionship with (holy) men makes you one of the (holy) men.

گر تو سنگ صخره و مرمر شوی
Though you be rock or marble, you will become a jewel
چون به صاحب دل رسی گوهر شوی
when you reach the man of heart (the saint).

مهر پاکان درمیان جان نشان
Plant the love of the holy ones within your spirit;
دل مده الا به مهر دلخوشان
do not give your heart (to aught) save to the love of them whose hearts are glad.

کوی نومیدی مرو امیدهاست
Go not to the neighbourhood of despair:
سوی تاریکی مرو خورشیدهاست
there are hopes. Go not in the direction of darkness: there are suns

دل ترا در کوی اهل دل کشد
The heart leads you into the neighbourhood of the men of heart (the saints);
تن ترا در حبس آب و گل کشد
the body leads you into the prison of water and earth.

هین غذای دل بده از همدلی
Oh, give your heart food from (conversation with) one who is in accord with it
رو بجو اقبال را از مقبلی
go, seek (spiritual) advancement from one who is advanced.

◈◉◈◉◈

تعظیم نعت مصطفی صلی الله علیه وسلم کی مذکور بود در آن چهیل
How honour was paid to the description of Mustafá (Mohammed), on whom be peace, which was mentioned in the Gospel.

بود در آن چهیل نام مصطفی
The name of Mustafá was in the Gospel

آن سر پیغامبران بحر صفا
the chief of the prophets, the sea of purity.

بود ذکر حلیه‌ها و شکل او
There was mention of his (external) characteristics and appearance;

بود ذکر غزو و صوم و اکل او
there was mention of his warring and fasting and eating.

طایفهٔ نصرانیان بهر ثواب
A party among the Christians, for the sake of the Divine reward,

چون رسیدندی بدان نام و خطاب
whenever (in reading the Gospel) they came to that name and discourse,

بوسه دادندی بر آن نام شریف
Would bestow kisses on that noble name

رو نهادندی بر آن وصف لطیف
and stoop their faces towards that beauteous description.

اندرین فتنه که گفتیم آن گروه
In this tribulation of which we have told,

ایمن از فتنه بدند و از شکوه
that party were secure from tribulation and dread,

ایمن از شر امیران و وزیر
Secure from the mischief of the amírs and the vizier,

در پناه نام احمد مستجیر
seeking refuge in the protection of the Name of Ahmad (Mohammed).

نسل ایشان نیز هم بسیار شد
Their offspring also multiplied:

نور احمد ناصر آمد یار شد
the Light of Ahmad aided and befriended them

وان گروه دیگر از نصرانیان
And the other party among the Christians

نام احمد داشتندی مستهان
(who) were holding the Name of Ahmad in contempt,

مستهان و خوار گشتند از فتن
They became contemptible and despised through dissensions
از وزیر شوم رای شوم فن
caused by the evil counselling and evil-plotting vizier;

هم مخبط دینشان و حکمشان
Moreover, their religion and their law became corrupted in
از پی طومارهای کژ بیان
consequence of the scrolls which set forth all perversely.

نام احمد این چنین یاری کند
The Name of Ahmad gives such help as this,
تا که نورش چون نگهداری کند
so that (one may judge) how his Light keeps guard (over his followers).

نام احمد چون حصاری شد حصین
Since the Name of Ahmad became (to the Christians) an impregnable fortress,
تا چه باشد ذات آن روح‌الامین
what then must be the Essence of that trusted Spirit?

بعد ازین خون‌ریز درمان ناپذیر
After this irremediable bloodshed which befell
کاندر افتاد از بلای آن وزیر
through the affliction (brought upon the Christians) by the vizier,

◈◉◈◉◈

حکایت پادشاه جهود دیگر کی در هلاک دین عیسی سعی نمود
The story of another Jewish king who endeavored to destroy the religion of Jesus.

یک شه دیگر ز نسل آن جهود
Another king, of the progeny of that Jew,
در هلاک قوم عیسی رو نمود
addressed himself to the destruction of the people of Jesus.

گر خبر خواهی ازین دیگر خروج
If you desire information about this second outbreak,
سوره بر خوان واسما ذات البروج
read the chapter of the Qur'án (beginning): By Heaven which hath the (zodiacal) signs

سنت بد کز شه اول بزاد
This second king set foot in the evil way
این شه دیگر قدم بر وی نهاد
that was originated by the former king.

هر که او بنهاد ناخوش سنتی
Whosoever establishes an evil way (practice),
سوی او نفرین رود هر ساعتی
towards him goes malediction every hour.

نیکوان رفتند و سنتها بماند
The righteous departed and their ways remained,
وز لئیمان ظلم و لعنتها بماند
and from the vile there remained (nothing but) injustice and execrations.

تا قیامت هر که جنس آن بدان
Until the Resurrection, the face of every congener of
در وجود آید بود رویش بدان
those wicked men who comes into existence is turned towards that one (who belongs to his own kind).

رگ رگست این آب شیرین و آب شور
Vein by vein is this sweet water and bitter water,
در خلایق می‌رود تا نفخ صور
flowing in(God's) creatures until the blast of the trumpet (at the Resurrection).

نیکوان را هست میراث از خوشاب
To the righteous is the inheritance of the sweet water. What is that inheritance?
آن چه میراثست اورثنا الکتاب
We have caused (those of Our servants whom We have chosen) to inherit the Book.

شد نیاز طالبان ار بنگری
If you will consider, the supplications of
شعله‌ها از گوهر پیغامبری
the seekers (of God) are rays (proceeding) from the substance of prophethood.

شعله‌ها با گوهران گردان بود
The rays are circling with the substances (whence they spring):
شعله آن جانب رود هم کان بود
the ray goes (ultimately) in the direction where that(substance) is.

نور روزن گرد خانه می‌دود
The window-gleam runs round the house,
زانک خور برجی به برجی می‌رود
because the sun goes from sign to sign of the zodiac.

هر که را با اختری پیوستگیست
Anyone who has affinity with a star (planet)
مر ورا با اختر خود هم‌تگیست
has a concurrence (of qualities) with his star.

طالعش گر زهره باشد در طرب
If his ascendant star be Venus,
میل کلی دارد و عشق و طلب
his whole inclination and love and desire is for joy;

ور بود مریخی خون‌ریزخو
And if he be one born under Mars, one whose nature is to shed blood,
جنگ و بهتان و خصومت جوید او
he seeks war and malignity and enmity.

اخترانند از ورای اختران
Beyond the (material) stars are stars
که احتراق و نحس نبود اندر آن
in which is no conflagration or sinister aspect,

سایران در آسمانهای دگر
(Stars) moving in other heavens,
غیر این هفت آسمان معتبر
not these seven heavens known to all,

راسخان در تاب انوار خدا
(Stars) immanent in the radiance of the light of God,
نه به هم پیوسته نه از هم جدا
neither joined to each other nor separate from each other.

هر که باشد طالع او زان نجوم
When any one's ascendant (fortune) is (from) those stars,
نفس او کفار سوزد در رجوم
his soul burns the infidels in driving (them) off.

خشم مریخی نباشد خشم او
His anger is not (like) the anger of the man born under Mars—perverse,
منقلب رو غالب و مغلوب خو
and of such nature that it is (now) dominant and (now) dominated.

نور غالب ایمن از نقص و غسق
The dominant light (of the saints) is secure from defect and dimness
درمیان اصبعین نور حق
between the two fingers of the Light of God

حق فشاند آن نور را بر جانها
God hath scattered that light over (all) spirits
مقبلان بر داشته دامانها
but only) the fortunate have held up their skirts (to receive it);

105

و آن نثار نور را وا یافته
And he (that is fortunate), having gained that strown largesse of ligh
روی از غیر خدا برتافته
has turned his face away from all except God

هر که را دامان عشقی نابده
Whosoever has lacked (such) a skirt of love
زان نثار نور بی بهره شده
is left without share in that strown largesse of light.

جزوها را روبها سوی کلست
The faces of particulars are set towards the universal:
بلبلان را عشق با روی گلست
nightingales are in love with the face of the rose.

گاو را رنگ از برون و مرد را
The ox has his colour outside,
از درون جو رنگ سرخ و زرد را
but in the case of a man seek the red and yellow hues within

رنگهای نیک از خم صفاست
The good colours are from the vat of purity
رنگ زشتان از سیاهابهٔ جفاست
the colour of the wicked is from the black water of iniquity.

صبغة الله نام آن رنگ لطیف
The baptism of God is the name of that subtle colour
لعنة الله بوی این رنگ کثیف
the curse of God is the smell of this gross colour.

آنچه از دریا به دریا می‌رود
That which is of the sea is going to the sea:
از همانجا کامد آنجا می‌رود
it is going to the same place whence it came

از سر که سیلهای تیزرو
From the mountain-top the swift-rushing torrents
وز تن ما جان عشق آمیز رو
and from our body the soul whose motion is mingled with love.

آتش کردن پادشاه جهود و بت نهادن پهلوی آتش که هر که این بت را سجود کند از آتش برست

How the Jewish king made a fire and placed an idol beside it, saying, "Whoever bows down to this idol shall escape the fire"

آن جهود سگ ببین چه رای کرد

Now see what a plan this currish Jew contrived!

پهلوی آتش بتی بر پای کرد

He set up an idol beside the fire,

کانک این بت را سجود آرد برست

Saying, "He that bows down to this idol is saved,

ور نیارد در دل آتش نشست

and if he bow not, he shall sit in the heart of the fire

چون سزای این بت نفس او نداد

Inasmuch as he did not give due punishment to this idol of self,

از بت نفسش بتی دیگر بزاد

from the idol of his self the other idol was born.

مادر بتها بت نفس شماست

The idol of your self is the mother of (all) idols,

زانک آن بت مار و این بت اژدهاست

because that (material) idol is (only) a snake, while this (spiritual) idol is a dragon.

آهن و سنگست نفس و بت شرار

The self is (as) iron and stone while the (material) idol is (as) the sparks:

آن شرار از آب می‌گیرد قرار

those sparks are quieted (quenched) by water.

سنگ و آهن زآب کی ساکن شود

(But) how should the stone and iron be allayed by water?

آدمی با این دو کی ایمن بود

How should a man, having these twain, be secure?

بت سیاهابه‌ست در کوزه نهان

The idol is the black water in a jug;

نفس مر آب سیه را چشمه دان

the self is a fountain for the black water.

آن بت منحوت چون سیل سیاه

That sculptured idol is like the black torrent;

نفس بتگر چشمه‌ای بر آب راه

the idol-making self is a fountain full of water for it.

107

صد سبو را بشکند یکپاره سنگ
A single piece of stone will break a hundred pitchers,
و آب چشمه می‌زهاند بی‌درنگ
but the fountain is jetting forth water incessantly.

بت‌شکستن سهل باشد نیک سهل
'Tis easy to break an idol, very easy;
سهل دیدن نفس را جهلست جهل
o regard the self as easy (to subdue) is folly, folly.

صورت نفس ار بجویی ای پسر
O son, if you seek (to know) the form of the self,
قصهٔ دوزخ بخوان با هفت در
read the story of Hell with its seven gates.

هر نفس مکری و در هر مکر زان
Every moment (there proceeds from the self) an act of deceit,
غرقه صد فرعون با فرعونیان
and in every one of those deceits a hundred Pharaohs are drowned together with their followers

در خدای موسی و موسی گریز
Flee to the God of Moses and to Moses,
آب ایمان را ز فرعونی مریز
do not from Pharaoh's quality (rebellious insolence) spill the water of the Faith.

دست را اندر احد و احمد بزن
Lay your hand on (cleave to) the One (God) and Ahmad
ای برادر وا ره از بوجهل تن
(Mohammed)! O brother, escape from the Bú Jahl of the body!

❦◉❦◉❦

به سخن آمدن طفل در میان آتش و تحریض کردن خلق را در افتادن آتش
How a child began to speak amidst the fire and urged the people to throw themselves into the fire

یک زنی با طفل آورد آن جهود
That Jew brought to that idol a woman with her child,
پیش آن بت و آتش اندر شعله بود
and the fire was blazing

طفل ازو بستد در آتش در فکند
He took the child from her and cast it into the fire:
زن بترسید و دل از ایمان بکند
the woman was affrighted and withdrew her heart from (abandoned) her

خواست تا او سجده آرد پیش بت
She was about to bow down before the idol
بانگ زد آن طفل انی لم امت
(when) the child cried, "Verily, I am not dead.

اندر آ ای مادر اینجا من خوشم
Come in, O mother: I am happy here,
گر چه در صورت میان آتشم
although in appearance I am amidst the fire.

چشم‌بندست آتش از بهر حجیب
The fire is a spell that binds the eye for the sake of screening (the truth);
رحمتست این سر برآورده ز جیب
this is (in reality) a Divine mercy which has raised its head from the collar

اندر آ مادر ببین برهان حق
Come in, mother, and see the evidence of God,
تا ببینی عشرت خاصان حق
that thou mayst behold the delight of God's elect.

اندر آ و آب بین آتش‌مثال
Come in, and see water that has the semblance of fire;
از جهانی کآتش است آبش مثال
from a world which is (really) fire and (only) has the semblance of water.

اندر آ اسرار ابراهیم بین
Come in, and see the mysteries of Abraham,
کو در آتش یافت سرو و یاسمین
who in the fire found cypress and jessamine.

مرگ می‌دیدم گه زادن ز تو
I was seeing death at the time of birth from thee:
سخت خوفم بود افتادن ز تو
sore was my dread of falling from thee;

چون بزادم رستم از زندان تنگ
when I was born, I escaped from the narrow prison
در جهان خوش‌هوای خوب رنگ
into a world of pleasant air and beautiful colour.

من جهان را چون رحم دیدم کنون
Now I deem the (earthly) world to be like the womb,
چون درین آتش بدیدم این سکون
since in this fire I have seen such rest:

اندرین آتش بدیدم عالمی
In this fire I have seen a world wherein
ذره ذره اندرو عیسی‌دمی
every atom possesses the (life-giving) breath of Jesus.

نک جهان نیست شکل هست ذات
Lo, (it is) a world apparently non-existent (but) essentially existent,
و آن جهان هست شکل بی‌ثبات
while that (other) world is apparently existent (but) has no permanence.

اندر آ مادر بحق مادری
Come in, mother, (I beseech thee) by the right of motherhood:
بین که این آذر ندارد آذری
see this fire, how it hath no fieriness.

اندر آ مادر که اقبال آمدست
Come in, mother, for felicity is come;
اندر آ مادر مده دولت ز دست
come in, mother, do not let fortune slip from thy hand.

قدرت آن سگ بدیدی اندر آ
Thou hast seen the power of that (Jewish) cur:
تا ببینی قدرت و لطف خدا
come in, that thou mayst see the power of God's grace

من ز رحمت می‌کشانم پای تو
Tis (only) out of pity that I am drawing thy feet (hither),
کز طرب خود نیستم پروای تو
for indeed such is my rapture that I have no care for thee.

اندر آ و دیگران را هم بخوان
Come in and call the others also,
کاندر آتش شاه بنهادست خوان
for the King has spread a (festal) table within the fire.

اندر آیید ای مسلمانان همه
O true believers, come in, all of you:
غیر عذب دین عذابست آن همه
except this sweetness('adhbí) all is torment ('adháb).

اندر آیید ای همه پروانه وار
Oh, come in, all of you, like moths;
اندرین بهره که دارد صد بهار
(come) into this fortune which hath a hundred springtimes."

بانگ می‌زد درمیان آن گروه
(Thus) he was crying amidst that multitude:
پر همی شد جان خلقان از شکوه
the souls of the people were filled with awe.

خلق خود را بعد از آن بی‌خویشتن
After that, the folk, men and women (alike),
می فکندند اندر آتش مرد و زن
cast themselves unwittingly into the fire—

بی موکل بی کشش از عشق دوست
Without custodian, without being dragged, for love of the Friend,
زانک شیرین کردن هر تلخ ازوست
because from Him is the sweetening of every bitterness

تا چنان شد کان عوانان خلق را
Until it came to pass that the (king's) myrmidons were
منع می‌کردند کآتش در میا
holding back the people, saying, "Do not enter the fire!"

آن یهودی شد سیه رو و خجل
The Jew became black-faced (covered with shame) and dismayed;
شد پشیمان زین سبب بیماردل
he became sorry and sick at heart,

کاندر ایمان خلق عاشق تر شدند
Because the people grew more loving (ardent) in their Faith
در فنای جسم صادق‌تر شدند
and more firm in mortification (faná) of the body.

مکر شیطان هم درو پیچید شکر
Thanks (be to God), the Devil's plot caught him in its toils;
دیو هم خود را سیه‌رو دید شکر
thanks (be to God), the Devil saw himself disgraced.

آنچه می‌مالید در روی کسان
That which he was rubbing (the shame he was inflicting)
جمع شد در چهرهٔ آن ناکس آن
on the faces of those persons (the Christians) was all accumulated on the visage of that vile wretch.

آنک می‌درید جامهٔ خلق چست
He who was busy rending the garment (honour and integrity) of the people
شد دریده آن او ایشان درست
his own (garment) was rent, (while) they were unhurt.

111

کج ماندن دهان آن مرد که نام محمد صلی الله علیه را به تسخر خواند
How the mouth remained awry of a man who pronounced the name of Mohammed, on whom be peace, derisively

آن دهان کژ کرد و از تسخر بخواند
He made his mouth wry and called the name of Ahmad

مر محمد را دهانش کژ بماند
(Mohammed) in derision: his mouth remained awry.

باز آمد کای محمد عفو کن
He came back, saying, "Pardon me, O Mohammed,

ای ترا الطاف و علم من لدن
O thou to whom belong the (Divine) gifts of esoteric knowledge

من ترا افسوس می‌کردم ز جهل
In my folly I was ridiculing thee,

من بدم افسوس را منسوب و اهل
(but) I myself was related to ridicule and deserving it."

چون خدا خواهد که پردهٔ کس درد
When God wishes to rend the veil of any one (expose him to shame),

میلش اندر طعنهٔ پاکان برد
He turns his inclination towards reviling holy men.

ور خدا خواهد که پوشد عیب کس
When God wishes to hide the blame of any one,

کم زند در عیب معیوبان نفس
he (that person) does not breathe a word of blame against the blameworthy.

چون خدا خواهد که مان یاری کند
When God wishes to help us,

میل ما را جانب زاری کند
He turns our inclination towards humble lament.

ای خنک چشمی که آن گریان اوست
Oh, happy the eye that is weeping for His sake!

وی همایون دل که آن بریان اوست
Oh, fortunate the heart that is seared for His sake!

آخر هر گریه آخر خنده‌ایست
The end of every weeping is laughter at last;

مرد آخربین مبارک بنده‌ایست
the man who foresees the end is a blessed servant (of God).

هر کجا آب روان سبزه بود
Wherever is flowing water, there is greenery:
هر کجا اشکی روان رحمت شود
wherever are running tears, (the Divine) mercy is shown.

باش چون دولاب نالان چشم تر
Be moaning and moist-eyed like the water-wheel,
تا ز صحن جانت بر روید خضر
that green herbs may spring up from the courtyard of your soul.

اشک خواهی رحم کن بر اشک‌بار
If you desire tears, have mercy on one who sheds tears;
رحم خواهی بر ضعیفان رحم آر
if you desire mercy, show mercy to the weak.

◈◈

عتاب کردن آتش را آن پادشاه جهود
How the fire reproached the Jewish king

رو به آتش کرد شه کای تندخو
The king turned his face to the fire, saying, "O fiercetempered one,
آن جهان سوز طبیعی خوت کو
where is thy world-consuming natural disposition?

چون نمی‌سوزی چه شد خاصیتت
How art thou not burning? What has become of thy specific property?
یا ز بخت ما دگر شد نیتت
Or has thy intention changed because of our fortune?

می‌نبخشایی تو بر آتش‌پرست
Thou hast no pity (even) on the fire-worshipper:
آنک نپرستد ترا او چون برست
how(then) has he been saved who does not worship thee?

هرگز ای آتش تو صابر نیستی
Never, O fire, art thou patient: how burnest thou not?
چون نسوزی چیست قادر نیستی
What is it? Hast thou not the power?

چشم‌بندست این عجب یا هوش‌بند
Is this a spell, I wonder, that binds the eye or the mind?
چون نسوزاند چنین شعلهٔ بلند
How does the lofty pyre not burn?

جادوی کردت کسی یا سیمیاست
Has some one bewitched thee? Or is it magic,
یا خلاف طبع تو از بخت ماست
or is thy unnatural behaviour from our fortune?"

گفت آتش من همانم ای شمن
The fire said: "I am the same, I am fire:
اندر آ تا تو ببینی تاب من
come in, that thou mayst feel my heat.

طبع من دیگر نگشت و عنصرم
My nature and element have not changed:
تیغ حقم هم بدستوری برم
I am the sword of God and by (His) leave I cut.

بر در خرگهٔ سگان ترکمان
The Turcoman dogs fawn
چاپلوسی کرده پیش میهمان
at the tent-door before the guest,

ور بخرگه بگذرد بیگانه رو
But if anyone having the face of a stranger pass by the tent
حمله بیند از سگان شیرانه او
he will see the dogs rushing at him like lions

من ز سگ کم نیستم در بندگی
I am not less than a dog in devotion
کم ز ترکی نیست حق در زندگی
nor is God less than a Turcoman in life (living power)."

آتش طبعت اگر غمگین کند
If the fire of your nature make you suffer pain,
سوزش از امر ملیک دین کند
it burns by command of the Lord of religion;

آتش طبعت اگر شادی دهد
If the fire of your nature give you joy,
اندرو شادی ملیک دین نهد
(that is because) the Lord of religion puts joy therein.

چونک غم بینی تو استغفار کن
When you feel pain, ask pardon of God:
غم بامر خالق آمد کار کن
(Only) by command of the Creator is pain operative.

114

چون بخواهد عین غم شادی شود
When He pleases, pain itself becomes joy
عین بند پای آزادی شود
bondage itself becomes freedom.

باد و خاک و آب و آتش بنده‌اند
Air and earth and water and fire are (His) slaves
با من و تو مرده با حق زنده‌اند
with you and me they are dead, but with God they are alive.

پیش حق آتش همیشه در قیام
Before God, fire is always standing (ready to do His behest)
همچو عاشق روز و شب پیچان مدام
writhing continually day and night, like a lover

سنگ بر آهن زنی بیرون جهد
If you strike stone on iron, it (the fire) leaps out:
هم به امر حق قدم بیرون نهد
'tis by God's command that it puts forth its foot.

آهن و سنگ هوا بر هم مزن
Do not strike together the iron and stone of injustice
کین دو می‌زایند همچون مرد و زن
for these two generate like man and woman.

سنگ و آهن خود سبب آمد ولیک
The stone and the iron are indeed causes,
تو به بالاتر نگر ای مرد نیک
but look higher, O good man!

کین سبب را آن سبب آورد پیش
For this (external) cause was produced by that (spiritual) cause
بی‌سبب کی شد سبب هرگز ز خویش
when did a cause ever proceed from itself without a cause?

و آن سببها کانبیا را رهبرند
And those causes which guide the prophets
آن سببها زین سببها برترند
on their way are higher than these (external) causes.

این سبب را آن سبب عامل کند
That (spiritual) cause makes this (external) cause operative;
باز گاهی بی بر و عاطل کند
sometimes, again, it makes it fruitless and ineffectual

این سبب را محرم آمد عقلها
Ordinary) minds are familiar with this (external) cause
و آن سببهاراست محرم انبیا
but the prophets are familiar with those (spiritual) causes

این سبب چه بود بتازی گو رسن
What is (the meaning of) this (word) "cause" (sabab) in Arabic? Say: "cord" (rasan).
اندرین چه این رسن آمد بفن
This cord came into this well (the world) by (Divine) artifice

گردش چرخه رسن را علت است
The revolution of the water-wheel causes the cord (to move)
چرخه گردان را ندیدن زلت است
(but) not to see the mover of the water-wheel is an error.

این رسنهای سببها در جهان
Beware, beware! Do not regard these cords of causation in the world
هان و هان زین چرخ سرگردان مدان
as (deriving their movement) from the giddy wheel (of heaven)

تا نمانی صفر و سرگردان چو چرخ
Lest you remain empty and giddy like the (celestial) wheel
تا نسوزی تو ز بی‌مغزی چو مرخ
lest through brainlessness you burn like markh wood.

باد آتش می‌شود از امر حق
By the command of God the wind devours (extinguishes) fire
هر دو سرمست آمدند از خمر حق
both are drunken with the wine of God.

آب حلم و آتش خشم ای پسر
from God too are the water of clemency and the fire of anger.
هم ز حق بینی چو بگشایی بصر
O son, when you open your eyes you will see that

گر نبودی واقف از حق جان باد
Had not the soul of the wind been informed by God,
فرق کی کردی میان قوم عاد
how would it have distinguished (the believers and unbelievers) amongst the people of 'Ád?

◈◉◈◉◈

قصه باد که در عهد هود علیه السلام قوم عاد را هلاک کرد
The story of the wind which destroyed the people of 'Ád in the time of (the prophet) Húd, on whom be peace

هود گرد مؤمنان خطی کشید
Húd drew a line round the believers:

نرم می‌شد باد کان جا می‌رسید
the wind would become soft (subside) when it reached that place,

هر که بیرون بود زان خط جمله را
(Although) it was dashing to pieces

پاره پاره می‌گسست اندر هوا
in the air all who were outside of the line.

همچنین شیبان شبان راعی می‌کشید
Likewise Shaybán the shepherd used to draw

گرد بر گرد رمه خطی پدید
a visible line round his flock

چون بجمعه می‌شد او وقت نماز
Whenever he went to the Friday service at prayer-time,

تا نیارد گرگ آنجا ترک تاز
in order that the wolf might not raid and ravage there:

هیچ گرگی در نرفتی اندر آن
No wolf would go into that (circle),

گوسفندی هم نگشتی زان نشان
nor would any sheep stray beyond that mark;

باد حرص گرگ و حرص گوسفند
The wind of the wolf's and sheeps' concupiscence

دایرهٔ مرد خدا را بود بند
was barred because of (by) the circle of the man of God.

همچنین باد اجل با عارفان
Even so, to those who know God ('árifán) the wind of Death

نرم و خوش همچون نسیم یوسفان
is soft and pleasant as the breeze (that wafts the scent) of (loved) ones like Joseph.

آتش ابراهیم را دندان نزد
The fire did not set its teeth in Abraham:

چون گزیدهٔ حق بود چونش گزد
how should it bite him, since he is the chosen of God?

ز آتش شهوت نسوزد اهل دین
The religious were not afflicted by the fire of lust
باقیان را برده تا قعر زمین
which bore all the rest down to the bottom of the earth.

موج دریا چون بامر حق بتاخت
The waves of the sea, when they charged on by God's command,
اهل موسی را ز قبطی وا شناخت
discriminated the people of Moses from the Egyptians.

خاک قارون را چو فرمان در رسید
The earth, when the (Divine) command came,
با زر و تختش به قعر خود کشید
drew Qárún(Korah) with his gold and throne into its lowest de pth.

آب و گل چون از دم عیسی چرید
The water and clay, when it fed on the breath of Jesus,
بال و پر بگشاد مرغی شد پرید
spread wings and pinions, became a bird, and flew.

هست تسبیحت بخار آب و گل
Your glorification (of God) is an exhalation from the water and clay (of your body):
مرغ جنت شد ز نفخ صدق دل
it became a bird of Paradise through the breathing (into it) of your heart's sincerity

کوه طور از نور موسی شد به رقص
Mount Mount Sinai, from (seeing) the radiance of Moses, began to dance,
صوفی کامل شد و رست او ز نقص
became a perfect Súfí, and was freed from blemish.

چه عجب گر کوه صوفی شد عزیز
What wonder if the mountain became a venerable Súfí?
جسم موسی از کلوخی بود نیز
The body of Moses also was (formed) from a piece of clay.

◈◈

طنز و انکار پادشاهان جهود و قبول نکردن نصیحت خاصان خویش
How the Jewish king scoffed and denied and would not accept the counsel of his intimates.

این عجایب دید آن شاه جهود
The king of the Jews beheld these marvellous things,
جز که طنز و جز که انکارش نبود
(but) he had naught (to say) except mockery and denial.

ناصحان گفتند از حد مگذران
His counsellors said, "Do not let (this injustice) go beyond bounds,
مرکب استیزه را چندین مران
do not drive the steed of obstinacy so far."

ناصحان را دست بست و بند کرد
He handcuffed the counsellors and confined them,
ظلم را در پیوند در پیوند کرد
he committed one injustice after another.

بانگ آمد کار چون اینجا رسید
When the matter reached this pass, a shout came
پای دار ای سگ که قهر ما رسید
"Hold thy foot (stop), O cur! For Our vengeance is come."

بعد از آن آتش چهل گز بر فروخت
After that, the fire blazed up forty ells high, became a ring
حلقه گشت و آن جهودان را بسوخت
became a ring, and consumed those Jews.

اصل ایشان بود آتش ز ابتدا
From fire was their origin in the beginning:
سوی اصل خویش رفتند انتها
they went (back) to their origin in the end.

هم ز آتش زاده بودند آن فریق
That company were born of fire:
جزوها را سوی کل باشد طریق
the way of particulars is towards the universal.

آتشی بودند مؤمن سوز و بس
They were only a fire to consume the true believers:
سوخت خود را آتش ایشان چو خس
their fire consumed itself like rubbish.

آنک بودست امه الهاویه
He whose mother is Háwiya (Hell-fire)
هاویه آمد مرورا زاویه
Háwiya shall become his cell (abode).

مادر فرزند جویان ویست
The mother of the child is (always) seeking it:
اصلها مر فرعها را در پیست
the fundamentals pursue the derivatives.

119

آبها در حوض اگر زندانیست
If water is imprisoned in a tank, the wind sucks it up,
باد نشفش می‌کند کار کانیست
for it (the wind) belongs to the original (source):

می‌رهاند می‌برد تا معدنش
It sets it free, it wafts it away to its source,
اندک اندک تا نبینی بردنش
little by little, so that you do not see its wafting;

وین نفس جانهای ما را همچنان
And our souls likewise this breath (of ours) steals away,
اندک اندک دزدد از حبس جهان
little by little, from the prison of the world.

تا الیه یصعد اطیاب الکلم
The perfumes of our (good) words ascend even unto Him,
صاعدا منا الی حیث علم
ascending from us whither God knoweth.

ترتقی انفاسنا بالمنتقی
Our breaths soar up with the choice (words),
متحفا منا الی دار البقا
as a gift from us, to the abode of everlastingness

ثم تاتینا مکافات المقال
Then comes to us the recompense of our speech,
ضعف ذاک رحمة من ذی الجلال
a double(recompense) thereof, as a mercy from (God) the Glorious;

ثم یلجینا الی امثالها
Then He causes us to repair to (makes us utter) good words like those (already uttered),
کی ینال العبد مما نالها
that His servant may obtain (something more) of what he has obtained.

هکذی تعرج و تنزل دائما
Thus do they (our good words) ascend while it (the Divine mercy) descends continually:
ذا فلا زلت علیه قائما
mayst thou never cease to keep up that (ascent and descent)!

پارسی گوییم یعنی این کشش
Let us speak Persian: the meaning is that this attraction
زان طرف آید که آمد آن چشش
omes from the same quarter whence came that savour

چشم هر قومی به سویی مانده‌ست
The eyes of every set of people remain (turned) in the direction
کان طرف یک روز ذوق رانده‌ست
where one day they satisfied a (longing for) delight.

ذوق جنس از جنس خود باشد یقین
The delight of (every) kind is certainly in its own kind(congener):
ذوق جزو از کل خود باشد ببین
the delight of the part, observe, is in its whole;

یا مگر آن قابل جنسی بود
Or else, that (part) is surely capable of (attachment to) a(different) kind and,
چون بدو پیوست جنس او شود
when it has attached itself thereto, becomes homogeneous with it,

همچو آب و نان که جنس ما نبود
As (for instance) water and bread, which were not our congeners,
گشت جنس ما و اندر ما فزود
became homogeneous with us and increased within us (added to our bulk and strength).

نقش جنسیت ندارد آب و نان
Water and bread have not the appearance of being our congeners,
ز اعتبار آخر آن را جنس دان
(but) from consideration of the end (final result) deem them to be homogeneous (with us).

ور ز غیر جنس باشد ذوق ما
And if our delight is (derived) from something not homogeneous,
آن مگر ماند باشد جنس را
that (thing) will surely resemble the congener.

آنک ماند ست باشد عاریت
That which (only) bears a resemblance is a loan:
عاریت باق نماند عاقبت
a loan is impermanent in the end.

مرغ را گر ذوق آید از صفیر
Although the bird is delighted by (the fowler's) whistle,
چونک جنس خود نیابد شد نفیر
it takes fright when it (sees him and) does not find its own congener.

تشنه را گر ذوق آید از سراب
Although the thirsty man is delighted by the mirage,
چون رسد در وی گریزد جوید آب
he runs away when he comes up to it, and seeks for water

مفلسان هم خوش شوند از زر قلب
Although the insolvent are pleased with base gold,
لیک آن رسوا شود در دار ضرب
yet that(gold) is put to shame in the mint.

تا زر اندودیت از ره نفکند
(Take heed) lest gildedness (imposture) cast you out of the(right) way,
تا خیال کژ ترا چه نفکند
lest false imagination cast you into the well.

از کلیله باز جو آن قصه را
Seek the story (illustrating this) from (the book of) Kalíla
واندر آن قصه طلب کن حصه را
and search out the moral (contained) in the story.

❊

بیان توکل و ترک جهد گفتن نخچیران بشیر
Setting forth how the beasts of chase told the lion to trust in God and cease from exerting himself.

طایفهٔ نخچیر در وادی خوش
A number of beasts of chase in a pleasant valley
بودشان از شیر دایم کش مکش
were continually harassed by a lion.

بس که آن شیر از کمین می در ربود
Inasmuch as the lion was (springing) from ambush and carrying them away,
آن چرا بر جمله ناخوش گشته بود
that pasturage had become unpleasant to them all.

حیله کردند آمدند ایشان بشیر
They made a plot: they came to the lion, saying,
کز وظیفه ما ترا داریم سیر
We will keep thee full-fed by means of a (fixed) allowance.

بعد ازین اندر پی صیدی میا
Do not go after any prey beyond thy allowance,
تا نگردد تلخ بر ما این گیا
in order that this grass may not become bitter to us."

❊

جواب گفتن شیر نخجیران را و فایده جهد گفتن
How the lion answered the beasts and explained the advantage of exertion

گفت آری گر وفا بینم نه مکر

"Yes," said he, "if I see (find) good faith (on your part),

مکرها بس دیده‌ام از زید و بکر

not fraud, for often have I seen (suffered) frauds from Zayd and Bakr.

من هلاک فعل و مکر مردمم

I am done to death by the cunning and fraud of men,

من گزیدهٔ زخم مار و کژدمم

I am bitten by the sting of (human) snake and scorpion;

مردم نفس از درونم در کمین

worse than all men in fraud and spite

از همه مردم بتر در مکر و کین

is the man of the flesh (nafs) lying in wait within me.

گوش من لایلدغ المؤمن شنید

My ear heard 'The believer is not bitten (twice),'

قول پیغامبر بجان و دل گزید

(and adopted this) saying of the Prophet with heart and soul."

ترجیح دادن نخجیران توکل را بر جحد و اکتساب
How the beasts asserted the superiority of trust in God to exertion and acquisition

جمله گفتند ای حکیم با خبر

They all said: "O knowing sage, let precaution alone:

الحذر دع لیس یغنی عن قدر

it is of no avail against the Divine decree.

در حذر شوریدن شور و شرست

In precaution is the embroilment of broil and woe:

رو توکل کن توکل بهترست

go, put thy trust in God: trust in God is better.

با قضا پنجه مزن ای تند و تیز

Do not grapple with Destiny, O fierce and furious one,

تا نگیرد هم قضا با تو ستیز

lest Destiny also pick a quarrel with thee.

مرده باید بود پیش حکم حق
One must be dead in presence of the decree of God,
تا نیاید زخم از رب الفلق
so that no blow may come from the Lord of the daybreak."

◆◉◆◉◆

ترجیح نهادن شیر جحد و اکتساب بر توکل و تسلیم
How the lion upheld the superiority of exertion and acquisition to trust in God and resignation.

گفت آری گر توکل رهبرست
"Yes," he said; "(but) if trust in God is the (true) guide,
این سبب هم سنت پیغمبرست
(yet use of) the means too is the Prophet's rule (Sunna)

گفت پیغامبر به آواز بلند
The Prophet said with a loud voice,
با توکل زانوی اشتر ببند
'While trusting in God bind the knee of thy camel.'

رمز الکاسب حبیب الله شنو
Hearken to the signification of 'The earner (worker) is beloved of God':
از توکل در سبب کاهل مشو
through trusting in God do not become neglectful as to the (ways and) means."

◆◉◆◉◆

ترجیح نهادن نخچیران توکل را بر اجتهاد
How the beasts preferred trust in God to exertion.

قوم گفتندش که کسب از ضعف خلق
The party answered him, saying, "Regard acquisition (work), arising from the infirmity of creatures,
لقمهٔ تزویر دان بر قدر حلق
as a mouthful of deceit proportionate to the size of the gullet.

نیست کسبی از توکل خوب تر
There is no work better than trust in God:
چیست از تسلیم خود محبوب تر
what, indeed, is dearer (to God) than resignation?

بس گریزند از بلا سوی بلا
Often do they flee from affliction (only) to (fall into) affliction;
بس جهند از مار سوی اژدها
often do they recoil from the snake (only) to (meet with) the dragon.

حیله کرد انسان و حیله‌ش دام بود
Man devised (something), and his device was a snare (wherein he was trapped):
آنک جان پنداشت خون‌آشام بود
that which he thought to be life was (actually) the drainer of his blood (his destroyer).

در ببست و دشمن اندر خانه بود
He locked the door while the foe was in the house:
حیلهٔ فرعون زین افسانه بود
the plot of Pharaoh was a story of this sort.

صد هزاران طفل کشت آن کینه‌کش
That vengeful man slew hundreds of thousands of babes,
وانک او می‌جست اندر خانه‌اش
while the one he was searching after was in his (Pharaoh's) house.

دیدهٔ ما چون بسی علت دروست
Since in our eyesight (foresight) there is much defect,
رو فنا کن دید خود در دید دوست
go, let your own sight pass away (faná) in the sight of the Friend (God).

دید ما را دید او نعم العوض
His sight for ours—what a goodly recompense!
یابی اندر دید او کل غرض
In His sight you will find the whole object of your desire.

طفل تا گیرا و تا پویا نبود
So long as the child could neither grasp (exert strength) nor run,
مرکبش جز گردن بابا نبود
he had nothing to ride on but his father's neck;

چون فضولی گشت و دست و پا نمود
When he became a busybody and plied hand and foot (exerted himself),
در عنا افتاد و در کور و کبود
he fell into trouble and wretchedness.

جانهای خلق پیش از دست و پا
The spirits of created beings, before (the creation of) hand and foot,
می‌پریدند از وفا اندر صفا
by reason of their faithfulness were flying in (the realm of) purity;

چون بامر اهبطوا بندی شدند
When they were constrained by the (Divine) command, Get ye down,
حبس خشم و حرص و خرسندی شدند
they became engaoled in anger and covetousness and contentment.

ما عیال حضرتیم و شیرخواه
We are the family of the Lord and craving after milk (like infants):
گفت الخلق عیال للاله
he (the Prophet) said, 'The people are God's family.'

آنک او از آسمان باران دهد
He who gives rain from heaven is also able,
هم تواند کو ز رحمت نان دهد
from His mercy, to give us bread."

❦◉❦◉❦

باز ترجیح نهادن شیر جهد را بر توکل
How the lion again pronounce d exertion to be superior to trust in God

گفت شیر آری ولی رب العباد
"Yes," said the lion; "but the Lord of
نردبانی پیش پای ما نهاد
His servants set a ladder before our feet.

پایه پایه رفت باید سوی بام
Step by step must we climb towards the roof
هست جبری بودن اینجا طمع خام
to be a necessitarian here is (to indulge in) foolish hopes.

پای داری چون کنی خود را تو لنگ
You have feet: why do you make yourself out to be lame?
دست داری چون کنی پنهان تو چنگ
you have hands: why do you conceal the fingers (whereby you grasp)?

خواجه چون بیلی به دست بنده داد
When the master put a spade in the slave's hand
بی زبان معلوم شد او را مراد
his object was made known to him (the slave) without (a word falling from his) tongue.

دست همچون بیل اشارتهای اوست
Hand and spade alike are His (God's) implicit signs;
آخراندیشی عبارتهای اوست
(our powers of) thinking upon the end are His explicit declarations.

126

چون اشارتهاش را بر جان نهی
When you take His signs to heart,
در وفای آن اشارت جان دهی
you will devote your life to fulfilling that indication (of His will).

پس اشارتهای اسرارت دهد
He will give you many hints (for the understanding) of mysteries,
بار بر دارد ز تو کارت دهد
He will remove the burden from you and give you (spiritual) authority.

حاملی محمول گرداند ترا
Do you bear (His burden)? He will cause you to be borne
قابلی مقبول گرداند ترا
Do you receive (His commands)? He will cause you to be received (into His favour).

قابل امر وی قایل شوی
If you accept His command, you will become the spokesman (thereof);
وصل جویی بعد از آن واصل شوی
if you seek union (with Him), thereafter you will become united

سعی شکر نعمتش قدرت بود
Freewill is the endeavour to thank (God) for His beneficence:
جبر تو انکار آن نعمت بود
your necessitarianism is the denial of that beneficence.

شکر قدرت قدرتت افزون کند
Thanksgiving for the power (of acting freely) increases your power;
جبر نعمت از کفت بیرون کند
necessitarianism takes the (Divine) gift (of freewill) out of your hand.

جبر تو خفتن بود در ره مخسپ
Your necessitarianism is (like) sleeping on the road: do not sleep!
تا نبینی آن در و درگه مخسپ
Sleep not, until you see the gate and the threshold!

هان مخسپ ای کاهل بی‌اعتبار
Beware! do not sleep, O inconsiderate necessitarian,
جز به زیر آن درخت میوه‌دار
save underneath that fruit-laden tree,

تا که شاخ افشان کند هر لحظه باد
So that every moment the wind may shake the boughs
بر سر خفته بریزد نقل و زاد
and shower upon the sleeper (spiritual) dessert and provision for the journey.

جبر و خفتن درمیان رهزنان
Necessitarianism is to sleep amidst highwaymen:
مرغ بی‌هنگام کی یابد امان
how should the untimely bird receive quarter?

ور اشارتهاش را بینی زنی
And if you turn up your nose at His signs, you deem(yourself) a man,
مرد پنداری و چون بینی زنی
but when you consider (more deeply), you are (only) a woman

این قدر عقلی که داری گم شود
This measure of understanding which you possess is lost:
سر که عقل از وی بپرد دم شود
a head from which the understanding is severed becomes a tail,

زانک بی‌شکری بود شوم و شنار
Because ingratitude is wickedness and disgrace
می‌برد بی‌شکر را در قعر نار
and brings the ingrate to the bottom of Hell-fire.

گر توکل می‌کنی در کار کن
If you are putting trust in God, put trust (in Him) as regards(your) work:
کشت کن پس تکیه بر جبار کن
sow (the seed), then rely upon the Almighty."

❖◉❖◉❖

باز ترجیح نهادن نخجیران توکل را بر جهد
How the beasts once more asserted the superiority of trust in God to exertion

جمله با وی بانگها بر داشتند
They all lifted up their voices (to dispute) with him,
کان حریصان که سببها کاشتند
saying, "Those covetous ones who sowed (the seed of) means

صد هزار اندر هزار از مرد و زن
Myriads on myriads of men and women
پس چرا محروم ماندند از زمن
why, then, did they remain deprived of fortune?

صد هزاران قرن ز آغاز جهان
From the beginning of the world myriads of generations
همچو اژدرها گشاده صد دهان
have opened a hundred mouths, like dragons:

مکرها کردند آن دانا گروه
Those clever people devised plots (of such power) that

که ز بن بر کنده شد زان مکر کوه
the mountain thereby was torn up from its foundation.

کرد وصف مکرهاشان ذوالجلال
The Glorious (God) described their plots (when He said):

لتزول منه اقلال الجبال
(though their guile be such) that the tops of the mountains might be moved thereby

جز که آن قسمت که رفت اندر ازل
(But) except the portion which came to pass (was predestined) in eternity,

روی ننمود از شکار و از عمل
nothing showed its face (accrued to them) from their scheming and doing.

جمله افتادند از تدبیر و کار
They all fell from (failed in) plan and act:

ماند کار و حکمهای کردگار
the acts and decrees of the Maker remained.

کسب جز نامی مدان ای نامدار
O illustrious one, do not regard work as aught but a name!

جهد جز وهمی مبندار ای عیار
O cunning one, think not that exertion is aught but a vain fancy!"

◆◉◆◉◆

نگریستن عزرائیل بر مردی
How 'Azrá'íl (Azrael) looked at a certain man,

و گریختن آن مرد در سرای سلیمان و تقریر ترجیح توکل بر جهد و قلت فایده جحد
and how that man fled to the palace of Solomon; and setting forth the superiority of trust in God to exertion and the uselessness of the latter

زاد مردی چاشتگاهی در رسید
One forenoon a freeborn (noble) man arrived

در سرا عدل سلیمان در دوید
and ran into Solomon's hall of justice,

رویش از غم زرد و هر دو لب کبود
His countenance pale with anguish and both lips blue.

پس سلیمان گفت ای خواجه چه بود
Then Solomon said, "Good sir, what is the matter?"

گفت عزرائیل در من این چنین
He replied, "Azrael cast on me such a look,
یک نظر انداخت پر از خشم و کین
so full of wrath and hate."

گفت هین اکنون چه می‌خواهی بخواه
"Come," said the king, "what (boon) do you desire now?
گفت فرما باد را ای جان پناه
Ask (it)!" "O protector of my life," said he, "command the wind,

تا مرا زینجا به هندستان برد
To bear me from here to India. Maybe,
بوک بنده کان طرف شد جان برد
when thy slave is come thither he will save his life."

نک ز درویشی گریزانند خلق
Lo, the people are fleeing from poverty:
لقمهٔ حرص و امل زانند خلق
hence are they a mouthful for (a prey to) covetousness and expectation.

ترس درویشی مثال آن هراس
The fear of poverty is like that (man's) terror:
حرص و کوشش را تو هندستان شناس
know thou that covetousness and striving are (like) India (in this tale).

باد را فرمود تا او را شتاب
He (Solomon) commanded the wind to bear him quickly over
برد سوی قعر هندستان بر آب
the water to the uttermost part of India.

روز دیگر وقت دیوان و لقا
Next day, at the time of conference and meeting,
پس سلیمان گفت عزرائیل را
Solomon said to Azrael:

کان مسلمان را بخشم از بهر آن
"Didst thou look with anger on that Moslem in order
بنگریدی تا شد آواره ز خان
that he might wander (as an exile) far from his home?"

گفت من از خشم کی کردم نظر
Azrael said, "When did I look (on him) angrily?
از تعجب دیدمش در رهگذر
I saw him as I passed by, (and looked at him) in astonishment,

که مرا فرمود حق کامروز هان
For God had commanded me, saying,
جان او را تو بهندستان ستان
'Hark, to-day do thou take his spirit in India.'

از عجب گفتم گر او را صد پرست
From wonder I said (to myself), '(Even) if he has a hundred wings,
او به هندستان شدن دور اندرست
'tis a far journey for him to be in India (to-day).'"

تو همه کار جهان را همچنین
In like manner judge of all the affairs of this world
کن قیاس و چشم بگشا و ببین
and open your eye and see!

از کی بگریزیم از خود ای محال
From whom shall we flee? From ourselves? Oh, absurdity!
از کی برباییم از حق ای وبال
From whom shall we take (ourselves) away? From God? Oh, crime!

◆◉◆◉◆

باز ترجیح نهادن شیر جهد را بر توکل و فواید جهد را بیان کردن
How the lion again declared exertion to be superior to trust in God and expounded the advantages of exertion.

شیر گفت آری ولیکن هم ببین
"Yes," said the lion; "but at the same time consider
جهدهای انبیا و مؤمنین
the exertions of the prophets and the true believers.

حق تعالی جهدشان را راست کرد
God, exalted is He, prospered their exertion
آنچه دیدند از جفا و گرم و سرد
and what they suffered of oppression and heat and cold.

حیله‌هاشان جمله حال آمد لطیف
Their plans were excellent in all circumstances:
کل شیء من ظریف هو ظریف
everything done by a goodly man is goodly.

دام‌هاشان مرغ گردونی گرفت
Their snares caught the Heavenly bird,
نقص‌هاشان جمله افزونی گرفت
all their deficiencies turned to increment."

جهد می‌کن تا توانی ای کیا
O master, exert thyself so long as thou canst
در طریق انبیاء و اولیا
in (following) the way of the prophets and saints!

با قضا پنجه زدن نبود جهاد
Endeavour is not a struggle with Destiny,
زانک این را هم قضا بر ما نهاد
because Destiny itself has laid this (endeavour) upon us.

کافرم من گر زیان کردست کس
I am an infidel if anyone has suffered loss a single moment
در ره ایمان و طاعت یک نفس
(while walking) in the way of faith and obedience.

سر شکسته نیست این سر را مبند
Your head is not broken: do not bandage this head. Exert yourself
یک دو روزک جهد کن باقی بخند
for a day or two (i.e. during this brief life), and laugh unto everlasting!

بد محالی جست کو دنیا بجست
An evil resort sought he that sought this world;
نیک حالی جست کو عقبی بجست
a good state sought he that sought the world to come.

مکرها در کسب دنیا باردست
Plots for gaining (the things of) this world are worthless,
مکرها در ترک دنیا واردست
(but) plots for renouncing this world are inspired (by God).

مکر آن باشد که زندان حفره کرد
The (right) plot is that he (the prisoner) digs a hole in his prison (in order to escape);
آنک حفره بست آن مکریست سرد
if he blocks up the hole, that is a foolish plot.

این جهان زندان و ما زندانیان
This world is the prison, and we are the prisoners:
حفره کن زندان و خود را وا رهان
prisoners: dig a hole in the prison and let yourself out!

چیست دنیا از خدا غافل بدن
What is this world? To be forgetful of God;
نه قماش و نقده و میزان و زن
it is not merchandise and silver and weighing-scales and women.

مال را کز بهر دین باشی حمول
As regards the wealth that you carry for religion's sake,
نعم مال صالح خواندش رسول
"How good is righteous wealth (for the righteous man)!" as the Prophet recited.

آب در کشتی هلاک کشتی است
Water in the boat is the ruin of the boat,
آب اندر زیر کشتی پشتی است
(but) water underneath the boat is a support.

چونک مال و ملک را از دل براند
Since he cast out from his heart (the desire for) wealth and possessions
زان سلیمان خویش جز مسکین نخواند
on that account Solomon did not call himself (by any name) but "poor."

کوزهٔ سربسته اندر آب زفت
The stoppered jar, (though) in rough water,
از دل پر باد فوق آب رفت
floated on the water because of its windfilled (empty) heart.

باد درویشی چو در باطن بود
When the wind of poverty is within (any one),
بر سر آب جهان ساکن بود
he rests at peace on the surface of the water of the world;

گر چه جملهٔ این جهان ملک ویست
Although the whole of this world is his kingdom,
ملک در چشم دل او لاشی‌ست
in the eye of his heart the kingdom is nothing.

پس دهان دل ببند و مهر کن
Therefore, stopper and seal the mouth of your heart,
پر کنش از باد کبر من لدن
and fill it from the inward ventilator.

جهد حقست و دوا حقست و درد
Exertion is a reality, and medicine and disease are realities:
منکر اندر نفی جهدش جهد کرد
the sceptic in his denial of exertion practised (and thereby affirmed) exertion.

مقرر شدن ترجیح جهد بر توکل
How the superiority of exertion to trust in God was established.

زین نمط بسیار برهان گفت شیر
The lion gave many proofs in this style,
کز جواب آن جبریان گشتند سیر
so that those necessitarians became tired of answering (him).

روبه و آهو و خرگوش و شغال
Fox and deer and hare and jackal abandoned
جبر را بگذاشتند و قیل و قال
necessity and (ceased from) disputation.

عهدها کردند با شیر ژیان
They made covenants with the furious lion,
کاندرین بیعت نیفتد در زیان
that he should incur no loss in this bargain,

قسم هر روزش بیاید بی‌جگر
(That) the daily ration should come to him without trouble,
حاجتش نبود تقاضایی دگر
and that he should not need to make a further demand.

قرعه بر هر که فتادی روز روز
Day by day the one on whom the lot fell
سوی آن شیر او دویدی همچو یوز
would run to the lion as (swiftly as) a cheetah

چون به خرگوش آمد این ساغر بدور
When this cup (of death) came round to the hare,
بانگ زد خرگوش کاخر چند جور
the hare cried out, "Why, how long (are we to endure this) injustice?"

◆◉◆◉◆

انکار کردن نخجیران بر خرگوش در تاخیر رفتن بر شیر
How the beasts of chase blamed the hare for his delay in going to the lion.

قوم گفتندش که چندین گاه ما
The company (of beasts) said to him:
جان فدا کردیم در عهد و وفا
All this time we have sacrificed our lives in troth and loyalty.

تو مجو بدنامی ما ای عنود
Do not thou seek to give us a bad name,
تا نرنجد شیر رو رو زود زود
O rebellious one! Lest the lion be aggrieved, go, go! Quick! Quick!"

❖

جواب گفتن خرگوش ایشان را
How the hare answered the beasts

گفت ای یاران مرا مهلت دهید
"O friends," said he, "grant me a respite,
تا بمکرم از بلا بیرون جهید
that by my cunning ye may escape from calamity

تا امان یابد بمکرم جانتان
That by my cunning your lives may be saved
ماند این میراث فرزندانتان
and this (safety) remain as a heritage to your children."

هر پیمبر امتان را در جهان
Every prophet amidst the peoples used to call them
همچنین تا مخلصی می‌خواندشان
after this manner to a place of deliverance,

کز فلک راه برون شو دیده بود
For he had seen from Heaven the way of escape,
در نظر چون مردمک پیچیده بود
(though) in (their) sight he was contracted (despicable) like the pupil of the eye.

مردمش چون مردمک دیدند خرد
Men regarded him as small like the pupil:
در بزرگی مردمک کس ره نبرد
none attained to (understanding of) the (real) greatness (worth) of the pupil

❖

اعتراض نخجیران بر سخن خرگوش
How the beasts objected to the proposal of the hare

قوم گفتندش که ای خرگوش دار
The company (of beasts) said to him:

خویش را اندازهٔ خرگوش دار
O donkey, listen(to us)! Keep thyself within the measure of a hare!

هین چه لافست این که از تو بهتران
Eh, what brag is this—(an idea) which thy betters

در نیاوردند اندر خاطر آن
never brought into their minds?

معجبی یا خود قضامان در پیست
Thou art self-conceited, or Destiny is pursuing us;

ور نه این دم لایق چون تو کیست
else, how is this speech suitable to one like thee?

❀◉❀◉❀

جواب خرگوش نخجیران را
How the hare again answered the beasts.

گفت ای یاران حقم الهام داد
He said: "O friends, God gave me inspiration:

مر ضعیفی را قوی رایی فتاد
to a weakling there came a strong judgement (wise counsel)."

آنچه حق آموخت مر زنبور را
That which God taught to the bees

آن نباشد شیر را و گور را
is not (belonging) to the lion and the wild ass.

خانه‌ها سازد پر از حلوای تر
It (the bee) makes houses of juicy halwá (sweetmeat):

حق برو آن علم را بگشاد در
God opened to it the door of that knowledge;

آنچه حق آموخت کرم پیله را
That which God taught to the silkworm

هیچ پیلی داند آن گون حیله را
does any elephant know such a device?

آدم خاکی ز حق آموخت علم
Adam, created of earth, learned knowledge from God:
تا به هفتم آسمان افروخت علم
knowledge shot beams up to the Seventh Heaven.

نام و ناموس ملک را در شکست
He (Adam) broke the name and fame (pride) of the angels,
کوری آنکس که در حق درشکست
to the confusion of that one who is in doubt concerning God.

زاهد ششصد هزاران ساله را
He (God) made the ascetic of so many thousand years
پوزبندی ساخت آن گوساله را
a muzzle for that young calf (Adam),

تا نتاند شیر علم دین کشید
That he (Adam) might not be able to drink the milk of knowledge of religion
تا نگردد گرد آن قصر مشید
and that he might not roam around that lofty castle.

علمهای اهل حس شد پوزبند
The sciences of the followers of (external) sense became a muzzle,
تا نگیرد شیر از آن علم بلند
so that he (the believer in sense-perception) might not receive milk from that sublime knowledge.

قطرهٔ دل را یکی گوهر فتاد
into the blood-drop (core) of the heart there fell a jewel
کان به دریاها و گردونها نداد
which He (God) gave not to the seas and skies.

چند صورت آخر ای صورت پرست
How long (this regard for) form? After all, O formworshipper,
جان بی‌معنیت از صورت نرست
has thy reality-lacking soul not (yet) escaped from form?

گر بصورت آدمی انسان بدی
If a human being were a man in virtue of form,
احمد و بوجهل خود یکسان بدی
Ahmad(Mohammed) and Bú Jahl would be just the same.

نقش بر دیوار مثل آدمست
The painting on the wall is like Adam:
بنگر از صورت چه چیز او کمست
see from the (pictured) form what thing in it is wanting.

جان کمست آن صورت با تاب را
The spirit is wanting in that resplendent form:
رو بجو آن گوهر کم یاب را
go, seek that jewel rarely found!

شد سر شیران عالم جمله پست
The heads of all the lions in the world were laid low
چون سگ اصحاب را دادند دست
They (God) gave a hand to (bestowed favour on) the dog of the Companions (of the Cave).

چه زیانستش از آن نقش نفور
What loss does it suffer from that abhorred shape,
چونک جانش غرق شد در بحر نور
inasmuch as its spirit was plunged in the ocean of light?

وصف و صورت نیست اندر خامه‌ها
Tis not in pens to describe (the outward) form:
عالم و عادل بود در نامه‌ها
(what is written) in letters is (qualities like) "learned" and "just";

عالم و عادل همه معنیست بس
(And qualities like) "learned" and "just" are only the spiritual essence
کش نیابی در مکان و پیش و پس
which thou wilt not find in (any) place or in front or behind.

می‌زند بر تن ز سوی لامکان
The sun of the spirit strikes (with its beams) on the body from the quarter where (the relation of) place does not exist:
می‌نگنجد در فلک خورشید جان
exist: it (that sun) is not contained in the sky.

◈◈

ذکر دانش خرگوش و بیان فضیلت و منافع دانستن
An account of the knowledge of the hare and an explanation of the excellence and advantages of knowledge

این سخن پایان ندارد هوش‌دار

This topic hath no end. Give heed!

هوش سوی قصهٔ خرگوش دار

Listen to the story of the hare.

گوش خر بفروش و دیگر گوش خر

Sell your asinine (corporeal) ear and buy another ear,

کین سخن را در نیابد گوش خر

for the asinine ear will not apprehend this discourse.

رو تو روبه‌بازی خرگوش بین

Go, behold the foxy tricks played by the hare;

مکر و شیراندازی خرگوش بین

behold how the hare made a plot to catch the lion.

خاتم ملک سلیمانست علم

Knowledge is the seal of the kingdom of Solomon:

جمله عالم صورت و جانست علم

the whole world is form, and knowledge is the spirit.

آدمی را زین هنر بیچاره گشت

are helpless before man.

خلق دریاها و خلق کوه و دشت

Because of this virtue, the creatures of the seas and those of mountain and plain

زو پلنگ و شیر ترسان همچو موش

Of him the pard and lion are afraid, like the mouse;

زو نهنگ و بحر در صفرا و جوش

from him the crocodile of the great river is in pallor and agitation.

زو پری و دیو ساحلها گرفت

From him peri and demon took to the shores (sought refuge):

هر یکی در جای پنهان جا گرفت

each took abode in some hiding-place.

آدمی را دشمن پنهان بسیست

Man hath many a secret enemy:

آدمی با حذر عاقل کسیست

the cautious man is a wise one.

خلق پنهان زشتشان و خوبشان
(There are) hidden creatures, evil and good:
می‌زند در دل بهر دم کوبشان
at every instant their blows are striking on the heart.

بهر غسل ار در روی در جویبار
If you go into the river to wash yourself,
بر تو آسیبی زند در آب خار
a thorn in the water inflicts a hurt upon you.

گر چه پنهان خار در آب‌ست پست
Although the thorn is hidden low in the water,
چونک در تو می‌خلد دانی که هست
you know it is there, since it is pricking you.

خارخار وحی‌ها و وسوسه
The pricks of (angelic) inspirations and (satanic) temptations are
از هزاران کس بود نه یک کسه
from thousands of beings, not (only) from one.

باش تا حس‌های تو مبدل شود
Wait (patiently) for your (bodily) senses to be transmuted,
تا ببینیشان و مشکل حل شود
so that you may see them (the hidden beings), and the difficulty may be solved,

تا سخن‌های کیان رد کرده‌ای
So that (you may see) whose words you have rejected
تا کیان را سرور خود کرده‌ای
and whom you have made your captain.

❖◉❖◉❖

باز طلبیدن نخجیران از خرگوش سر اندیشه او را
How the beasts requested the hare to tell the secret of his thought

بعد از آن گفتند کای خرگوش چست
Afterwards they said, "O nimble hare,
در میان آر آنچه در ادراک تست
communicate what is in thy apprehension.

ای که با شیری تو در پیچیده‌ای
O thou who hast grappled with a lion,
بازگو رایی که اندیشیده‌ای
declare the plan which thou hast thought of.

مشورت ادراک و هشیاری دهد
Counsel gives perception and understanding:
عقلها مر عقل را یاری دهد
the mind is helped by (other) minds.

گفت پیغامبر بکن ای رای‌زن
The Prophet said, 'O adviser, take counsel (with the trustworthy),
مشورت کالمستشار مؤتمن
for he whose counsel is sought is trusted.'"

◈◉◈◉◈

منع کردن خرگوش از راز ایشان را
How the hare withheld the secret from them

گفت هر رازی نشاید بازگفت
He said, "One ought not to say forth every secret:
جفت طاق آید گهی که طاق جفت
sometimes the even number turns out to be odd, and sometimes the odd number to be even"

از صفا گر دم زنی با آینه
If from guilelessness you breathe words to a mirror,
تیره گردد زود با ما آینه
the mirror at once becomes dim to us.

در بیان این سه کم جنبان لبت
Do not move your lip in explanation of these three things,
از ذهاب و از ذهب وز مذهبت
(namely) concerning your departure and your gold and your religion;

کین سه را خصمست بسیار و عدو
For to these three there is many an adversary and foe standing in
در کمینت ایستد چون داند او
wait for you when he knows (about any of them).

ور بگویی با یکی دو الوداع
And if you tell (only) one or two (a few people), farewell (to your secret):
کل سر جاوز الاثنین شاع
every secret that goes beyond the twain (who share it) is published abroad

گر دو سه پرنده را بندی بهم
If you tie two or three birds together,
بر زمین مانند محبوس از الم
they will remain on the ground, imprisoned by grief;

141

مشورت دارند سرپوشیده خوب
(But in truth) they hold a consultation well-disguised and mingled,
در کنایت با غلط‌افکن مشوب
in its (apparent) significance, with that which casts error (into the mind of any one who observes them).

مشورت کردی پیمبر بسته سر
(Similarly) the Prophet used to take counsel, (speaking) cryptically,
گفته ایشانش جواب و بی‌خبر
and they (his companions) would answer him and (would be) without knowledge (of his real meaning).

در مثالی بسته گفتی رای را
He would speak his opinion in a covert parable,
تا ندانند خصم از سر پای را
in order that the adversary might not know foot from head.

او جواب خویش بگرفتی ازو
He (the Prophet) would receive his answer from him (the adversary),
وز سؤالش می‌نبردی غیر بو
while the other would not catch the smell (drift) of his question.

قصه مکر خرگوش
The story of the hare's stratagem

ساعتی تاخیر کرد اندر شدن
He delayed awhile in going,

بعد از آن شد پیش شیر پنجه زن
then he went before the lion who rends (his prey) with claws.

زان سبب کاندر شدن او ماند دیر
Because he tarried late in going,

خاک را می‌کند و می‌غرید شیر
I said," cried the lion,

گفت من گفتم که عهد آن خسان
"that the promise of those vile ones would be vain—vain and frail and unfulfilled

خام باشد خام و سست و نارسان
Their palaver has duped me:

دمدمهٔ ایشان مرا از خر فکند
Their palaver has duped me:

چند بفریبد مرا این دهر چند
how long will this Time deceive me, how long?"

سخت در ماند امیر سست ریش
The prince that hath no strength in his beard

چون نه پس بیند نه پیش از احمقیش
is left sorely in the lurch when by reason of his folly he looks neither backwards nor forwards.

راه هموارست زیرش دامها
The road is smooth, and under it are pitfalls:

قحط معنی درمیان نامها
amidst the names there is a dearth of meaning.

لفظها و نامها چون دامهاست
Words and names are like pitfalls:

لفظ شیرین ریگ آب عمر ماست
the sweet (flattering) word is the sand for (the sand that sucks up) the water of our life.

آن یکی ریگی که جوشد آب ازو
The one sand whence water gushes

سخت کمیابست رو آن را بجو
is seldom to be found: go, seek it.

منبع حکمت شود حکمت‌طلب
He that searches after wisdom becomes a fountain of wisdom;
فارغ آید او ز تحصیل و سبب
he becomes independent of acquisition and (ways and) means.

لوح حافظ لوح محفوظی شود
The guarding tablet becomes a Guarded Tablet;
عقل او از روح محظوظی شود
his understanding becomes enriched by the Spirit.

چون معلم بود عقلش ز ابتدا
When a man's understanding has been his teacher,
بعد ازین شد عقل شاگردی ورا
after this the understanding becomes his pupil.

عقل چون جبریل گوید احمدا
The understanding says, like Gabriel, "O Ahmad
گر یکی گامی نهم سوزد مرا
if I take one (more) step, it will burn me;

تو مرا بگذار زین پس پیش ران
Do thou leave me, henceforth advance (alone):
حد من این بود ای سلطان جان
this is my limit, O sultan of the soul!"

هر که ماند از کاهلی بی‌شکر و صبر
Whoever, through heedlessness, remains without thanksgiving and patience (selfcontrol),
او همین داند که گیرد پای جبر
knows (no resource) but this, that he should follow in the heels of necessity (jabr).

هر که جبر آورد خود رنجور کرد
Anyone who pleads necessity (as an excuse) feigns himself to be ill,
تا همان رنجوریش در گور کرد
with the result that the (feigned) illness brings him to the grave.

گفت پیغمبر که رنجوری بلاغ
The Prophet said, "Illness (assumed) in jest brings (real) disease,
رنج آرد تا بمیرد چون چراغ
so that he (the jester) dies like a lamp."

جبر چه بود بستن اشکسته را
What is (the meaning of) jabr?
یا ببیوستن رگ بگسسته را
To bind up a broken (limb) or tie a severed vein.

چون درین ره پای خود نشکسته‌ای
Inasmuch as you have not broken your foot in this path,
بر کی می‌خندی چه پا را بسته ای
whom are you mocking? Why have you bandaged your foot?

وانک پایش در ره کوشش شکست
But as for him who broke his foot in the path of exertion,
در رسید او را براق و بر نشست
Buráq came up to him, and he mounted (and rode).

حامل دین بود او محمول شد
He was a bearer of the (true) religion, and he became one who is borne;
قابل فرمان بد او مقبول شد
he was an accepter of the (Divine) command, and he became accepted

تاکنون فرمان پذیرفتی ز شاه
Until now, he was receiving commands from the King;
بعد ازین فرمان رساند بر سپاه
henceforth he delivers the (King's) commands to the people.

تاکنون اختر اثر کردی درو
Until now, the stars were influencing him;
بعد ازین باشد امیر اختر او
henceforth he is the ruler of the stars.

گر ترا اشکال آید در نظر
If (on this account) perplexity arise in thy sight (mind),
پس تو شک داری در انشق القمر
then thou wilt have doubts concerning The moon was cloven asunder.

تازه کن ایمان نی از گفت زبان
Refresh thy faith, (but) not with talk of the tongue,
ای هوا را تازه کرده در نهان
O thou who hast secretly refreshed thy (evil) desire.

تا هوا تازه‌ست ایمان تازه نیست
So long as desire is fresh, faith is not fresh,
کین هوا جز قفل آن دروازه نیست
for 'tis this desire that locks (against thee) that gate

کرده‌ای تاویل حرف بکر را
Thou hast interpreted (and altered the meaning of) the virgin (uncorrupted) Word:
خویش را تاویل کن نه ذکر را
interpret (alter) thyself, not the (Divine) Book.

بر هوا تاویل قرآن می‌کنی
Thou interpretest the Qur'án according to thy desire:
پست و کژ شد از تو معنی سنی
by thee the sublime meaning is degraded and perverted.

{◉}{◉}

زیافت تاویل رکیک مگس
The baseness of the foul interpretation given by the fly

آن مگس بر برگ کاه و بول خر
The fly was lifting up his head,
همچو کشتیبان همی افراشت سر
like a pilot, on a blade of straw and (a pool of) ass's urine.

گفت من دریا و کشتی خوانده‌ام
"I have called (them) sea and ship," said he;
مدتی در فکر آن می‌مانده‌ام
"I have been pondering over that (interpretation) for a long while.

اینک این دریا و این کشتی و من
Look! here is this sea and this ship,
مرد کشتیبان و اهل و رای‌زن
and I am the pilot and skilled (in navigation) and judicious."

بر سر دریا همی راند او عمد
He was propelling the raft on the "sea":
می‌نمودش آن قدر بیرون ز حد
that (small) quantity appeared to him illimitable.

بود بی‌حد آن چمین نسبت بدو
That urine was boundless in relation to him:
آن نظر که بیند آن را راست کو
where was the vision that should see it truly?

عالمش چندان بود کش بینشست
His world extends (just) as far as his sight reaches;
چشم چندین بحر هم‌چندینشست
his eye is so big, his "sea" is big in the same proportion.

صاحب تاویل باطل چون مگس
So with the false interpreter (of the Qur'án): like the fly,
وهم او بول خر و تصویر خس
his imagination is (foul as) ass's urine and his conception (worthless as) a straw.

گر مگس تاویل بگذارد برای
If the fly leave off interpreting by (following his own) opinion,
آن مگس را بخت گرداند همای
Fortune will turn that fly into a humáy.

آن مگس نبود کش این عبرت بود
One who possesses this (Divine) indication (of the true meaning) is not a fly:
روح او نه در خور صورت بود
his spirit is not analogous to his (outward) form.

◈◉◈◉◈

تولیدن شیر از دیر آمدن خرگوش
How the lion roared wrathfully because the hare was late in coming.

همچو آن خرگوش کو بر شیر زد
As (for example) the hare who struck against the lion:
روح او کی بود اندر خورد قد
how was his spirit analogous to his stature?

شیر می‌گفت از سر تیزی و خشم
The lion from fury and rage was saying,
کز ره گوشم عدو بر بست چشم
"By means of my ear the enemy has bound up my eye.

مکرهای جبریانم بسته کرد
The tricks of the necessitarians have bound me (in captivity);
تیغ چوبینشان تنم را خسته کرد
their wooden sword has wounded my body.

زین سپس من نشنوم آن دمدمه
After this I will not hearken to their palaver:
بانگ دیوانست و غولان آن همه
all that is (only meant to deceive, like) the cry of demons and ghouls.

بر دران ای دل تو ایشان را مهایست
O my heart, tear them to pieces, do not lag;
پوستشان برکن کشان جز پوست نیست
rend their skins, for they have naught but skin

پوست چه بود گفته‌های رنگ رنگ
What is skin? Specious words,
چون زره بر آب کش نبود درنگ
like ripples on water which have no continuance.

این سخن چون پوست و معنی مغز دان
Know that these words are as the skin (rind), and the meaning is (as) the kernel;
چون نقش و معنی همچو جان
these words are as the form, and the meaning is like the spirit.

پوست باشد مغز بد را عیب‌پوش
The skin hides the defect of the bad kernel;
مغز نیکو را ز غیرت غیب‌پوش
it (also) hides jealously the secrets of the good kernel

چون قلم از باد بد دفتر ز آب
When the pen is of wind and the scroll of water,
هرچه بنویسی فنا گردد شتاب
whatever you write perishes speedily;

نقش آبست ار وفا جویی از آن
It is written on water: if you seek constancy from it,
بازگردی دستهای خود گزان
you will return biting your hands (in disappointment).

باد در مردم هوا و آرزوست
The wind in men is vanity and desire;
چون هوا بگذاشتی پیغام هوست
when you have abandoned vanity, (then) is (the time for) the message from Him (God).

خوش بود پیغام‌های کردگار
Sweet are the messages of the Maker,
کو ز سر تا پای باشد پایدار
for it (that message) from head to foot (from first to last) is enduring.

خطبهٔ شاهان بگردد و آن کیا
The khutbas for kings change (and pass), and their empire;
جز کیا و خطبه‌های انبیا
(all will pass) except the empire and khutbas (insignia) of the prophets,

زانک بوش پادشاهان از هواست
Because the pomp of kings is from (earthly) vanity,
بارنامهٔ انبیا از کبریاست
the glorious privilege of the prophets is from (Divine) Majesty.

از درمها نام شاهان برکنند
The names of kings are removed from the dirhems
نام احمد تا ابد بر می‌زنند
(but) the name of Ahmad (Mohammed) is stamped on them forever.

نام احمد نام جملهٔ انبیاست
The name of Ahmad is the name of all the prophets:
چونک صد آمد نود هم پیش ماست
when the hundred comes (is counted), ninety is with us as well.

◆◉◆◉◆

هم در بیان مکر خرگوش
Further setting forth the stratagem of the hare

در شدن خرگوش بس تاخیر کرد
The hare made much delay in going;
مکر را با خویشتن تقریر کرد
he rehearsed to himself the tricks (which he was about to play).

در ره آمد بعد تاخیر دراز
After long delay he came on (took) the road,
تا به گوش شیر گوید یک دو راز
that he might say one or two secrets into the ear of the lion.

تا چه عالمهاست در سودای عقل
Think, what worlds are in commerce with Reason!
تا چه با پهناست این دریای عقل
How wide is this ocean of Reason!

صورت ما اندرین بحر عذاب
In this sweet ocean our forms are moving fast,
می‌دود چون کاسه‌ها بر روی آب
like cups on the surface of water:

تا نشد پر بر سر دریا چو طشت
Until they become full, (they float) like bowls on the top of the sea,
چونک پر شد طشت در وی غرق گشت
(but) when the bowl is filled it sinks therein.

عقل پنهانست و ظاهر عالمی
Reason is hidden, and (only) a world (of phenomena) is visible:
صورت ما موج یا از وی نمی
our forms are the waves or a spray of it (of that hidden ocean).

هر چه صورت می وسیلت سازدش
Whatsoever (thing) the form makes (uses as) a means of approach to It (to Reason),
زان وسیلت بحر دور اندازدش
by that (same) means the ocean (of Reason) casts it (the form) far away.

تا نبیند دل دهندهٔ راز را
So long as the heart does not see the Giver of (its) conscience,
تا نبیند تیر دورانداز را
so long as the arrow does not see the far-shooting Archer,

اسپ خود را یاوه داند وز ستیز
He (who is thus blind) thinks his horse is lost,
می‌دواند اسپ خود در راه تیز
though (all the while) he is obstinately speeding his horse on the road.

اسپ خود را یاوه داند آن جواد
That fine fellow thinks his horse is lost,
و اسپ خود او را کشان کرده چو باد
while his horse is sweeping him onward like the wind.

در فغان و جست و جو آن خیره‌سر
In lamentation and inquiry that scatterbrain (runs) from door
هر طرف پرسان و جویان در بدر
to door in every direction, asking and searching:

کانک دزدید اسپ ما را کو و کیست
"Where and who is he that stole my horse?"
این که زیر ران تست ای خواجه چیست
What is this (animal) under thy thigh, O master?

آری این اسپست لیک این اسپ کو
"Yes, this is the horse, but where is the horse?"
با خود آی ای ای شهسوار اسپ‌جو
O dexterous rider in search of thy horse, come to thyself!

جان ز پیدایی و نزدیکیست گم
The Spirit is lost (to view) because of its being so manifest and near:
چون شکم پر آب و لب خشکی چو خم
how, having thy belly full of water, art thou dry-lipped like a jar?

کی ببینی سرخ و سبز و فور را
How wilt thou see red and green and russet,
تا نبینی پیش ازین سه نور را
unless before (seeing) these three (colours) thou see the light?

لیک چون در رنگ گم شد هوش تو
But since thy mind was lost (absorbed) in (perception of) the colour,
شد ز نور آن رنگها روپوش تو
those colours became to thee a veil from (debarred thee from contemplating) the light.

150

چونک شب آن رنگها مستور بود

Inasmuch as at night those colours were hidden,

پس بدیدی دید رنگ از نور بود

thou sawest that thy vision of the colour was (derived) from the light.

نیست دید رنگ بی‌نور برون

There is no vision of colour without the external light:

همچنین رنگ خیال اندرون

even so it is with the colour of inward phantasy.

این برون از آفتاب و از سها

This outward (light) is (derived) from the sun and from Suhá,

و اندرون از عکس انوار علا

while the inward (light) is from the reflexion of the beams of (Divine) Glory

نور نور چشم خود نور دلست

The light which gives light to the eye is in truth the light of the heart:

نور چشم از نور دلها حاصلست

the light of the eye is produced by the light of hearts.

باز نور نور دل نور خداست

Again, the light which gives light to the heart is the Light of God,

کو ز نور عقل و حس پاک و جداست

which is pure and separate from the light of intellect and sense.

شب نبد نور و ندیدی رنگها

At night there was no light: thou didst not see the colour;

پس به ضد نور پیدا شد ترا

then it (the light) was made manifest by the opposite of light (by darkness).

دیدن نورست آنگه دید رنگ

(First) comes the seeing of light, then the seeing of colour;

وین به ضد نور دانی بی‌درنگ

and this thou knowest immediately by the opposite of light (darkness).

رنج و غم را حق پی آن آفرید

God created pain and sorrow for the purpose that

تا بدین ضد خوشدلی آید پدید

happiness might be made manifest by means of this opposite.

پس نهانیها بضد پیدا شود

Hidden things, then, are manifested by means of their opposite;

چونک حق را نیست ضد پنهان بود

since God hath no opposite, He is hidden;

که نظر پر نور بود آنگه برنگ
For the sight fell (first) on the light, then on the colour:
ضد به ضد پیدا بود چون روم و زنگ
opposite is made manifest by opposite, like Greeks and Ethiopians.

پس به ضد نور دانستی تو نور
Therefore thou knewest light by its opposite:
ضد ضد را می‌نماید در صدور
opposite reveals opposite in (the process of) coming forth.

نور حق را نیست ضدی در وجود
The Light of God hath no opposite in (all) existence,
تا به ضد او را توان پیدا نمود
that by means of that opposite it should be possible to make Him manifest:

لاجرم ابصار ما لا تدرکه
Necessarily (therefore) our eyes do not perceive Him,
و هو یدرک بین تو از موسی و که
though He perceives (us): see this (fact) from (the case of) Moses and the mountain (Sinai)

صورت از معنی چو شیر از بیشه دان
Know that form springs from spirit (reality) as the lion from the jungle,
یا چو آواز و سخن ز اندیشه دان
or as voice and speech from thought.

این سخن و آواز از اندیشه خاست
This speech and voice arose from thought;
تو ندانی بحر اندیشه کجاست
thou knowest not where is the sea of thought,

لیک چون موج سخن دیدی لطیف
But since thou hast seen that the waves of speech are fair,
بحر آن دانی که باشد هم شریف
thou knowest that their sea also is noble.

چون ز دانش موج اندیشه بتاخت
When the waves of thought sped on from (the sea of) Wisdom,
از سخن و آواز او صورت بساخت
it (Wisdom) made (for them) the form of speech and voice.

از سخن صورت بزاد و باز مرد
The form was born of the Word and died again,
موج خود را باز اندر بحر برد
the wave drew itself back into the sea.

صورت از بی‌صورتی آمد برون
The form came forth from Formlessness and went back(thither),
باز شد که انا الیه راجعون
for Verily unto Him are we returning.

پس ترا هر لحظه مرگ و رجعتیست
Every instant, then, thou art dying and returning:
مصطفی فرمود دنیا ساعتیست
Mustafá declared that this world is (but) a moment

فکر ما تیریست از هو در هوا
Our thought is an arrow (shot) from Him (Hú) into the air(hawá):
در هوا کی پاید آید تا خدا
how should it stay in the air? It comes (back) to God.

هر نفس نو می‌شود دنیا و ما
Every moment the world is renewed, and we are unaware of
بی‌خبر از نو شدن اندر بقا
its being renewed whilst it remains (the same in appearance).

عمر همچون جوی نو نو می‌رسد
Life is ever arriving anew, like the stream,
مستمری می‌نماید در جسد
though in the body it has the semblance of continuity.

آن ز تیزی مستمر شکل آمدست
From its swiftness it appears continuous,
چون شرر کش تیز جنبانی بدست
like the spark which thou whirlest rapidly with thy hand.

شاخ آتش را بجنبانی بساز
If thou whirl a firebrand with dexterity,
در نظر آتش نماید بس دراز
it appears to the sight as a very long (line of) fire.

این درازی مدت از تیزی صنع
The swift motion produced by the action of God presents this length of duration
می‌نماید سرعت‌انگیزی صنع
as (a phenomenon arising) from the rapidity of Divine action

طالب این سر اگر علامه ایست
Even if the seeker of this mystery is an exceedingly learned man, (say to him), "Lo,
نک حسام‌الدین که سامی نامه ایست
Husámu'ddín, who is a sublime book (where you will find the mystery revealed)."

رسیدن خرگوش به شیر
The hare's coming to the lion and the lion's anger with him

شیر اندر آتش و در خشم و شور
The lion, incensed and wrathful and frantic,

دید کان خرگوش می‌آید ز دور
saw the hare coming from afar,

می‌دود بی‌دهشت و گستاخ او
Running undismayed and confidently,

خشمگین و تند و تیز و ترش‌رو
looking angry and fierce and fell and sour,

کز شکسته آمدن تهمت بود
For by coming humbly (he thought) suspicion would be (excited),

وز دلیری دفع هر ریبت بود
while by boldness every cause of doubt would be removed.

چون رسید او پیشتر نزدیک صف
When he came further on, near to the "shoe-row,"

بانگ بر زد شیرها ای ناخلف
the lion shouted— "Ha, villain!

من که پیلان را ز هم بدریده‌ام
I who have torn oxen limb from limb,

من که گوش شیر نر مالیده‌ام
I who have rubbed the ear of the ferocious elephant

نیم خرگوشی که باشد که چنین
Who (what) is a half-witted (feeble) hare,

امر ما را افکند او بر زمین
that he should thus throw on the ground (disregard) my behest?"

ترک خواب غفلت خرگوش کن
Abandon the hare's slumber and heedlessness!

غرهٔ این شیر ای خرگوش کن
Give ear, O donkey, to the roaring of this lion!

◆◉◆◉◆

عذر گفتن خرگوش
The hare's apology

گفت خرگوش الامان عذریم هست
Mercy!" cried the hare, "I have an excuse,
گر دهد عفو خداوندیت دست
if thy Lordship's pardon come to my aid."

گفت چه عذر ای قصور ابلهان
"What excuse?" said he. "Oh, the shortsightedness of fools!
این زمان آیند در پیش شهان
Is this the time for them to come into the presence of kings?

مرغ بی‌وقتی سرت باید برید
Thou art an untimely bird: thy head must be cut off.
عذر احمق را نمی‌شاید شنید
off. One ought not to hear the excuse of a fool.

عذر احمق بتر از جرمش بود
The fool's excuse is worse than his crime;
عذر نادان زهر هر دانش بود
the excuse of the ignorant is the poison that kills wisdom.

عذرت ای خرگوش از دانش تهی
Thy excuse, O hare, is devoid of wisdom:
من نه خرگوشم که در گوشم نهی
what hare am I that? thou shouldst put it in my ear?"

گفت ای شه ناکسی را کس شمار
"O king," he replied, "account a worthless one to be worthy:
عذر استم دیده‌ای را گوش دار
hearken to the excuse of one who has suffered oppression.

خاص از بهر زکات جاه خود
In particular, as an alms (thank-offering) for thy high estate,
گمرهی را تو مران از راه خود
do not drive out of thy way one whose way is lost.

بحر کو آبی به هر جو می‌دهد
The ocean, which gives some water to every stream,
هر خسی را بر سر و رو می‌نهد
lays on its head and face (surface) every piece of rubbish.

کم نخواهد گشت دریا زین کرم
By this bounty the sea will not become less:
از کرم دریا نگردد بیش و کم
the sea is neither increased nor diminished by its bounty."

گفت دارم من کرم بر جای او
The lion said, "I will bestow bounty in its (proper) place,
جامهٔ هر کس برم بالای او
I will cut every one's clothes according to his stature."

گفت بشنو گر نباشم جای لطف
"Listen," cried the hare, "if I am not a fit object for (thy) grace,
سر نهادم پیش اژدرهای عنف
I lay my head before the dragon of (thy) violence.

من بوقت چاشت در راه آمدم
At breakfast-time I set out on the way,
با رفیق خود سوی شاه آمدم
I came towards the king with my comrade.

با من از بهر تو خرگوشی دگر
That party (of beasts) had appointed, for thy sake,
جفت و همره کرده بودند آن نفر
another hare to go along with me as consort and companion

شیری اندر راه قصد بنده کرد
On the road a lion attacked thy humble slave,
قصد هر دو همره آینده کرد
attacked both the companions in travel who were coming (to thee).

گفتمش ما بنده شاهنشهیم
I said to him, 'We are the slaves of the King of kings,
خواجه تاشان که آن درگهیم
the lowly fellow-servants of that (exalted) court.'

گفت شاهنشه کی باشد شرم دار
He said, 'The King of kings! Who is he? Be ashamed!
پیش من تو یاد هر ناکس میار
Do not make mention of every base loon in my presence.

هم ترا و هم شهت را بر درم
Both thee and thy king I will tear to pieces,
گر تو با یارت بگردید از درم
if thou and thy friend turn back from my door.'

گفتمش بگذار تا بار دگر
I said to him, 'Let me behold once more
روی شه بینم برم از تو خبر
the face of the king and bear the news of thee (to him).'
گفت همره را گرو نه پیش من
He said, 'Place thy comrade with me (in my keeping) as a pledge; otherwise,
ور نه قربانی تو اندر کیش من
thou art a sacrifice (thy life is forfeit) according to my law.'
لابه کردیمش بسی سودی نکرد
We entreated him much: it was no use.
یار من بستد مرا بگذاشت فرد
He seized my friend and left me to go alone.
یارم از زفتی دو چندان بد که من
My friend, from his plumpness,
هم بلطف و هم بخوبی هم بتن
made three of me both in comeliness and beauty and (size of) body.
بعد ازین زان شیر این ره بسته شد
Henceforth this road is barred by that lion:
حال ما این بود و با تو گفته شد
the thread of our covenants is broken.
از وظیفه بعد ازین اومید بر
Cut off (abandon) hope of the allowance henceforth;
حق همی گویم ترا والحق مر
I am telling thee the truth, and truth is bitter.
گر وظیفه بایدت ره پاک کن
If thou want the allowance, clear the way! hey,
هین بیا و دفع آن بی‌باک کن
come on and repel that irreverent one!"

جواب گفتن شیر خرگوش را و روان شدن با او
How the lion answered the hare and set off with him.

گفت بسم الله بیا تا او کجاست
"Come on in God's name," said he, "let me see where he is!

پیش در شو گر همی گویی تو راست
Go thou in front, if thou art speaking truth,

تا سزای او و صد چون او دهم
That I may give him and a hundred like him the punishment they deserve,

ور دروغست این سزای تو دهم
or if this is a lie, that I may give thy deserts to thee."

اندر آمد چون قلاووزی به پیش
The hare set out on the way, (going) in front like a guide,

تا برد او را به سوی دام خویش
that he might lead him towards his snare,

سوی چاهی کو نشانش کرده بود
Towards the well which he had designated:

چاه مغ را دام جانش کرده بود
he had made the deep well a snare for his (the lion's) life.

می‌شدند این هر دو تا نزدیک چاه
(Thus) were these twain going till (they arrived) near the well. Look,

اینت خرگوشی چو آبی زیر کاه
you, (this was) a hare (deceitful) as a (pool of) water (hidden) under straw.

آب کاهی را به هامون می‌برد
The water bears a blade of straw (down) to the plain:

آب کوهی را عجب چون می‌برد
how, I wonder, will the straw bear away a mountain?

دام مکر او کمند شیر بود
The snare of his (the hare's) guile was a noose for the lion:

طرفه خرگوشی که شیری می‌ربود
a marvellous hare (he), who was carrying off a lion (as his prey)!

موسیی فرعون را با رود نیل
A Moses draws Pharaoh,

می‌کشد با لشکر و جمع ثقیل
with his army and mighty host, into the river Nile;

پشه‌ای نمرود را با نیم پر
A single gnat with half a wing
می‌شکافد بی‌محابا درز سر
intrepidly the suture of Nimrod's skull.

حال آن کو قول دشمن را شنود
Behold the state of him who hearkened to the words of his enemy,
بین جزای آنک شد یار حسود
and the retribution of him who became the friend of the envious one

حال فرعونی که هامان را شنود
The state of a Pharaoh who hearkened to Haman,
حال نمرودی که شیطان را شنود
Haman, and the state of a Nimrod who hearkened to Satan.

دشمن ار چه دوستانه گویدت
Albeit the enemy speak to thee in friendly wise,
دام دان گر چه ز دانه گویدت
know (his words to be) the snare, though he speak to thee of the grain (bait).

گر ترا قندی دهد آن زهر دان
If he give thee some candy, regard it as poison;
گر بتن لطفی کند آن قهر دان
if he do a kindness to thy body, regard it as cruelty.

چون قضا آید نبینی غیر پوست
When the (Divine) destiny comes to pass, you see naught but the skin (outward appearance):
دشمنان را باز نشناسی ز دوست
you do not distinguish enemies from friends.

چون چنین شد ابتهال آغاز کن
Since the case is thus, begin humble supplication;
ناله و تسبیح و روزه ساز کن
set about lamenting and glorifying (God) and fasting.

ناله می‌کن کای تو علام الغیوب
Lament continually, crying, "O Thou who well knowest the hidden things,
زیر سنگ مکر بد ما را مکوب
do not crush us beneath the stone of evil contrivance.

گر سگی کردیم ای شیرآفرین
O Creator of the lion, if we have wrought currishness,
شیر را مگمار بر ما زین کمین
do not set the lion (to spring) on us from this covert.

آب خوش را صورت آتش مده
Do not give to sweet water the form of fire,
اندر آتش صورت آبی منه
do not put upon fire the form of water.

از شراب قهر چون مستی دهی
When Thou makest (us) drunken with the wine of Thy wrath,
نیستها را صورت هستی دهی
Thou givest to things non-existent the form of existence."

چیست مستی بند چشم از دید چشم
What is (this) drunkenness? That which binds(prevents) the eye from (true) eyesight,
تا نماند سنگ گوهر پشم یشم
so that a (common) stone appears a jewel, and wool (pashm) a jasper (yashm).

چیست مستی حسها مبدل شدن
What is (this) drunkenness? The perversion of the senses,
چوب گز اندر نظر صندل شدن
change of tamarisk-wood into sandal-wood in the (perverted) sight.

قصه هد هد و سلیمان در بیان اینکه چون قضا آید چشم های روشن بسته شود
Story of the hoopoe and Solomon, showing that when the Divine destiny comes to pass, clear eyes are sealed.

چون سلیمان را سراپرده زدند
When the tent-pavilion was pitched for Solomon,

جمله مرغانش به خدمت آمدند
the birds came before him to pay obeisance.

هم‌زبان و محرم خود یافتند
They found (him) speaking the same tongue (as themselves) and familiar with them:

پیش او یک یک بجان بشتافتند
one by one they sped with (eager) soul into his presence.

جمله مرغان ترک کرده چیک چیک
All the birds, having ceased from twittering,

با سلیمان گشته افصح من اخیک
with Solomon became more distinct (spoke more articulately) than your own brother.

همزبانی خویشی و پیوندی است
To speak the same tongue is a kinship and affinity:

مرد با نامحرمان چون بندی است
a man, (when he is) with those in whom he cannot confide, is like a prisoner in chains.

ای بسا هندو و ترک همزبان
Oh, many are the Indians and Turks that speak the same tongue;

ای بسا دو ترک چون بیگانگان
oh, many the pair of Turks that are as strangers (to each other).

پس زبان محرمی خود دیگرست
Therefore the tongue of mutual understanding is different indeed:

همدلی از همزبانی بهترست
to be one in heart is better than to be one in tongue.

غیرنطق و غیر ایما و سجل
Without speech and without sign or scroll,

صد هزاران ترجمان خیزد ز دل
hundreds of thousands of interpreters arise from the heart.

جمله مرغان هر یکی اسرار خود
The birds, all and each, their secrets

از هنر وز دانش و از کار خود
of skill and knowledge and practice

با سلیمان یک بیک وا می‌نمود
Were revealing, one by one, to Solomon,
از برای عرضه خود را می‌ستود
and were praising themselves by way of submitting a request

از تکبر نه و از هستی خویش
Not from pride and self-conceit,
بهر آن تا ره دهد او را به پیش
(but) in order that he might give them access to him.

چون بباید برده را از خواجه‌ای
When a captive wants a lord (to buy him as a slave),
عرضه دارد از هنر دیباجه‌ای
slave), he offers a preface (summary account) of his talent;

چونک دارد از خریداریش ننگ
(But) when he is ashamed (disgusted) at his buying him,
خود کند بیمار و کر و شل و لنگ
he makes himself out to be sick and palsied and deaf and lame

نوبت هدهد رسید و پیشه‌اش
The turn came for the hoopoe and his craft
و آن بیان صنعت و اندیشه‌اش
and the explanation of his skill and thoughtfulness

گفت ای شه یک هنر کان کهترست
"O king," said he, "I will declare (only) one talent,
بازگویم گفت کوته بهترست
which is an inferior one; 'tis better to speak briefly."

گفت بر گو تا کدامست آن هنر
"Tell on," said Solomon; "let me hear what talent that is
گفت من آنگه که باشم اوج بر
The hoopoe said, "At the time when I am at the zenith,

بنگرم از اوج با چشم یقین
I gaze from the zenith with the eye of certainty
من ببینم آب در قعر زمین
and I see the water at the bottom of the earth,

تا کجایست و چه عمقستش چه رنگ
So that (I know) where it is and what is its depth;
از چه می‌جوشد ز خاکی یا ز سنگ
what its colour is, whence it gushes forth—from clay or from rock.

ای سلیمان بهر لشگرگاه را

O Solomon, for the sake of thine army's camping-place keep

در سفر می‌دار این آگاه را

this wise one (beside thee) on thy expeditions."

پس سلیمان گفت ای نیکو رفیق

Then said Solomon, "O good companion

در بیابانهای بی آب عمیق

in waterless far-stretching wastes!"

❖◉❖◉❖

طعنه زاغ در دعوی هدهد

How the crow impugned the claim of the hoopoe

زاغ چون بشنود آمد از حسد

When the crow heard (this), from envy he came and said to Solomon,

با سلیمان گفت کو کژ گفت و بد

He has spoken false and ill.

از ادب نبود به پیش شه مقال

It is not respectful to speak in the king's presence,

خاصه خودلاف دروغین و محال

in particular (to utter) lying and absurd self-praise.

گر مر او را این نظر بودی مدام

If he had always had this (keen) sight,

چون ندیدی زیر مشتی خاک دام

how would not he have seen the snare beneath a handful of earth?

چون گرفتار آمدی در دام او

How would he have been caught in the snare?

چون قفس اندر شدی ناکام او

How would he have gone into the cage willy-nilly?"

پس سلیمان گفت ای هدهد رواست

Then Solomon said: "O hoopoe, is it right

کز تو در اول قدح این درد خاست

that these dregs have risen from thee at the first cup?

چون نمایی مستی ای خورده تو دوغ

O thou who hast drunk buttermilk,

پیش من لافی زنی آنگه دروغ

how dost thou pretend intoxication and brag in my presence and tell lies besides?"

163

جواب گفتن هد هد طعنه زاغ
The hoopoe's answer to the attack of the crow.

گفت ای شه بر من عور گدای
words against me, bare beggar as I am.

قول دشمن مشنو از بهر خدای
He said, "O king, for God's sake do not listen to the enemy's

گر به بطلانست دعوی کردنم
If this which I claim is not (true),

من نهادم سر بیر این گردنم
I lay my head (before thee): sever this neck of mine.

زاغ کو حکم قضا را منکرست
The crow, who disbelieves in the (absolute) authority of the Divine destiny,

گر هزاران عقل دارد کافرست
is an infidel, though he have thousands of wits.

در تو تا کافی بود از کافران
Whilst there is in you a single k (derived) from the káfirán (infidels),

جای گند و شهوتی چون کاف ران
you are the seat of stench and lust, velut rima femoris.

من ببینم دام را اندر هوا
I see the snare (when I am) in the air,

گر نپوشد چشم عقلم را قضا
if the Divine destiny do not muffle the eye of my intelligence.

چون قضا آید شود دانش بخواب
When the Divine destiny comes, wisdom goes to sleep,

مه سیه گردد بگیرد آفتاب
the moon becomes black, the sun is stopped (from shining).

از قضا این تعبیه کی نادرست
How is this disposal (of things) by the Divine destiny (to be called) singular?

از قضا دان کو قضا را منکرست
Know that it is by the Divine destiny that he (the infidel) disbelieves in the Divine destiny.

قصه ادم علیه السلام
The story of Adam, on whom be peace,

و بستن قضا نظر او را ازمراعات صریح نهی و ترک تاویل
and how the Divine destiny sealed up his sight so that he failed to observe the plain meaning of the prohibition and to refrain from interpreting it.

بوالبشر کو علم الاسما بگست
The father of mankind, who is the lord of He (God) taught(Adam) the Names,

صد هزاران علمش اندر هر رگست
hath hundreds of thousands of sciences in every vein.

اسم هر چیزی چنان کان چیز هست
To his soul accrued (knowledge of) the name of everything,

تا به پایان جان او را داد دست
even as that thing exists (in its real nature) unto the end (of the world).

هر لقب کو داد آن مبدل نشد
No title that he gave became changed:

آنک چستش خواند او کاهل نشد
that one whom he called 'brisk' did not become 'lazy.'

هر که اول مؤمنست اول بدید
Whoso is (to be) a believer at the last, he saw at the first;

هر که آخر کافر او را شد پدید
whoso is (to be) an infidel at the last, to him it became manifest.

اسم هر چیزی تو از دانا شنو
Do thou hear the name of everything from the knower:

سر رمز علم الاسما شنو
hear the inmost meaning of the mystery of He taught the Names.

اسم هر چیزی بر ما ظاهرش
With us, the name of everything is its outward (appearance);

اسم هر چیزی بر خالق سرش
with the Creator, the name of everything is its inward(reality).

نزد موسی نام چوبش بد عصا
In the eyes of Moses the name of his rod was 'staff';

نزد خالق بود نامش اژدها
in the eyes of the Creator its name was 'dragon.'

بد عمر را نام اینجا بت‌پرست
Here the name of 'Umar was 'idolater,'

لیک مؤمن بود نامش در الست
but in Alast. his name was 'believer.'

آنک بد نزدیک ما نامش منی
That of which the name, with us, was 'seed' was,
پیش حق این نقش بد که با منی
in the sight of God, thou who art at this moment beside me.

صورتی بود این منی اندر عدم
This 'seed' was a form (idea) in non-existence (potentiality), existent with God,
پیش حق موجود نه بیش و نه کم
neither more nor less (than the form in which it appeared externally).

حاصل آن آمد حقیقت نام ما
In brief, that which is our end
پیش حضرت کان بود آن چهام ما
is really our name with God.

مرد را بر عاقبت نامی نهد
He bestows on a man a name according to his final state,
نی بر آن کو عاریت نامی نهد
not according to that (state) to which He gives the name of 'a loan.'

چشم آدم چون به نور پاک دید
Inasmuch as the eye of Adam saw by means of the Pure Light,
جان و سر نامها گشتش پدید
the soul and inmost sense of the names became evident to him.

چون ملک انوار حق در وی بیافت
Since the angels perceived in him the rays of God,
در سجود افتاد و در خدمت شتافت
they fell in worship and hastened to do homage.

مدح این آدم که نامش می‌برم
The Adam like this whose name I am celebrating,
قاصرم گر تا قیامت بشمرم
if I praise(him) till the Resurrection, I fall short (of what is due).

این همه دانست و چون آمد قضا
All this he knew; (yet) when the Divine destiny came,
دانش یک نهی شد بر وی خطا
he was at fault in the knowledge of a single prohibition,

کای عجب نهی از پی تحریم بود
Wondering whether the prohibition was for the purpose of making unlawful (the thing prohibited),
یا به تاویلی بد و توهیم بود
or whether it admitted of an interpretation and was a cause of perplexity.

در دلش تاویل چون ترجیح یافت
When (the view that it admitted of) interpretation prevailed in his mind,
طبع در حیرت سوی گندم شتافت
his nature hastened in bewilderment towards the wheat.

باغبان را خار چون در پای رفت
When the thorn went into the foot of the gardener (Adam),
دزد فرصت یافت کالا برد تفت
the thief (Satan) found an opportunity and quickly carried off the goods.

چون ز حیرت رست باز آمد به راه
As soon as he escaped from bewilderment, he returned into the (right) road;
دید برده دزد رخت از کارگاه
(then) he saw that the thief had carried off the wares from the shop.

ربنا انا ظلمنا گفت و آه
He cried, 'O Lord, we have done wrong,' and 'Alas,'
یعنی آمد ظلمت و گم گشت راه
that is to say, 'darkness came and the way was lost.'

پس قضا ابری بود خورشیدپوش
This Divine destiny is a cloud that covers the sun:
شیر و اژدرها شود زو همچو موش
thereby lions and dragons become as mice.

من اگر دامی نبینم گاه حکم
If I (the hoopoe) do not see a snare in the hour of Divine ordainment,
من نه تنها جاهلم در راه حکم
tis not I alone who am ignorant in the course of Divine ordainment."

ای خنک آن کو نکوکاری گرفت
Oh, happy he that clave to righteousness,
زور را بگذاشت او زاری گرفت
he (that) let (his own) strength go and took to supplication!

گر قضا پوشد سیه همچون شبت
If the Divine destiny shrouds thee in black like night,
هم قضا دستت بگیرد عاقبت
yet the Divine destiny will take thy hand (and guide thee) at the last.

گر قضا صد بار قصد جان کند
If the Divine destiny a hundred times attempts thy life,
هم قضا جانت دهد درمان کند
yet the Divine destiny gives thee life and heals thee.

این قضا صد بار اگر راهت زند
This Divine destiny, if a hundred times it waylays thee,
بر فراز چرخ خرگاهت زند
(nevertheless) pitches thy tent on the top of Heaven.

از کرم دان این که می‌ترساندت
Know that this is from the loving kindness (of God),
تا به ملک ایمنی بنشاندت
that He terrifies thee in order that He may establish thee in the kingdom of security.

این سخن پایان ندارد گشت دیر
This subject hath no end. 'Tis late.
گوش کن تو قصهٔ خرگوش و شیر
Hearken (now) to the story of the hare and the lion.

❧◉❧◉❧

پا واپس کشیدن خرگوش از شیر چون نزدیک چاه رسید
How the hare drew back from the lion when he approached the well.

چونک نزد چاه آمد شیر دید
When the lion came near the well,
کز ره آن خرگوش ماند و پا کشید
he saw that the hare lagged on the way and stepped back.

گفت پا واپس کشیدی تو چرا
He said, "Why have you stepped back?
پای را واپس مکش پیش اندر آ
Do not step back come on!"

گفت کو پایم که دست و پای رفت
The hare said, "Where is my (power to move a) foot? for (both) hand and foot are gone.
جان من لرزید و دل از جای رفت
My soul trembles and my heart (courage) has fled.

رنگ رویم را نمی‌بینی چو زر
Seest thou not the colour of my face (pale) as gold?
ز اندرون خود می‌دهد رنگم خبر
My colour indeed is giving knowledge of my inward state.

حق چو سیما را معرف خوانده‌ست
Since God has called the (external) sign (aspect) informative,
چشم عارف سوی سیما مانده‌ست
the eye of the gnostic has remained turned towards the sign.

رنگ و بو غماز آمد چون جرس
Colour and scent are significant like a bell:
از فرس آگه کند بانگ فرس
the neigh of a horse makes (one) acquainted with the horse.

بانگ هر چیزی رساند زو خبر
The sound made by anything conveys knowledge of it,
تا بدانی بانگ خر از بانگ در
that you may distinguish the bray of an ass from the creak of a door.

گفت پیغامبر به تمییز کسان
Touching the discrimination of persons (one from another), the Prophet said,
مرء مخفی لدی طی اللسان
'A man is hidden when his tongue is folded up.'

رنگ رو از حال دل دارد نشان
The colour of the face indicates the state of the heart:
رحمتم کن مهر من در دل نشان
have pity on me, implant love of me in thy heart.

رنگ روی سرخ دارد بانگ شکر
A red complexion has the sound of (declares and expresses) thankfulness (satisfaction);
بانگ روی زرد دارد صبر و نکر
the sound (signification) of a pale complexion is patience and unthankfulness.

در من آمد آنک دست و پا برد
There has come upon me that which took away hand and foot,
رنگ رو و قوت و سیما برد
took away colour of face and strength and (every outward) mark;

آنک در هر چه در آید بشکند
That which shatters everything it comes upon,
هر درخت از بیخ و بن او بر کند
tears up every tree from root and bottom;

در من آمد آنک ازوی گشت مات
There has come upon me that by which man and animal,
آدمی و جانور جامد نبات
mineral and plant have been checkmated.

این خود اجزا اند کلیات ازو
These indeed are (only) parts, (but) wholes (too) are by him
زرد کرده رنگ و فاسد کرده بو
(Doom) made yellow in hue and corrupt in odour,

تا جهان گه صابرست و گه شکور
So that the world is now patient, now thankful;
بوستان گه حله پوشد گاه عور
the garden now puts on a robe (of verdure) and again is bare.

آفتابی کو بر آید نارگون
The sun, which rises fire-coloured,
ساعتی دیگر شود او سرنگون
at another hour sinks headlong.

اختران تافته بر چار طاق
Stars shining in the four quarters (of the sky) are,
لحظه لحظه مبتلای احتراق
from time to time, afflicted with (consumed by) burning.

ماه کو افزود ز اختر در جمال
The moon, which excels the stars in beauty,
شد ز رنج دق او همچون خیال
becomes like a phantom from the malady of a hectic fever.

این زمین با سکون با ادب
This earth, quiet and controlled,
اندر آرد زلزله‌ش در لرز تب
is thrown by earthquakes into feverish tremors.

ای بسا که زین بلای مر دریگ
Oh, from this inherited woe many a mountain
گشته است اندر جهان او خرد و ریگ
in the world has become tiny fragments and (grains of) sand.

این هوا با روح آمد مقترن
This air is conjoined with the (vital) spirit,
چون قضا آید وبا گشت و عفن
(but) when the Divine destiny comes, it turns foul and stinking

آب خوش کو روح را همشیره شد
The sweet water that was a sister (congenial) to the spirit,
در غدیری زرد و تلخ و تیره شد
(after standing) in a pool, became yellow and bitter and turbid.

آتشی کو باد دارد در بروت
The fire that has wind in its moustache
هم یکی بادی برو خواند یموت
a single puff of wind calls death upon it.

حال دریا ز اضطراب و جوش او
The state of the sea (is such that) from its agitation
فهم کن تبدیلهای هوش او
commotion (you may) perceive the changes of its mind.

چرخ سرگردان که اندر جست و جوست
The whirling heaven, which is (ever engaged) in seeking and searching
حال او چون حال فرزندان اوست
its state is like the state of its children;

گه حضیض و گه میانه گاه اوج
Now nadir, now middle, now zenith:
اندرو از سعد و نحسی فوج فوج
therein are host on host of stars fortunate and unlucky.

از خود ای جزوی ز کلها مختلط
From thyself, O part made up of wholes,
فهم می‌کن حالت هر منبسط
apprehend the state of every simple (uncompounded) thing.

چونک کلیات را رنجست و درد
Inasmuch as wholes suffer grief and pain,
جزو ایشان چون نباشد روی زرد
how should their part not be pale-faced (sick and subject to decay)?

خاصه جزوی کو ز اضدادست جمع
Especially a part which is composed of contraries
ز آب و خاک و آتش و بادست جمع
of water and earth and fire and air.

این عجب نبود که میش از گرگ جست
It is no wonder that the sheep recoiled from the wolf;
این عجب کین میش دل در گرگ بست
wonder is that this sheep set its heart on (became friendly with) the wolf.

زندگانی آشتی ضدهاست
Life is the peace (harmony) of contraries;
مرگ آنک اندر میانش جنگ خاست
death is the fact that war arose between them.

لطف حق این شیر را و گور را
The grace of God has given amity to this lion and wild-ass
الف دادست این دو ضد دور را
these two far distant contraries.

چون جهان رنجور و زندانی بود
Since the world is sick and a prisoner,
چه عجب رنجور اگر فانی بود
what wonder if the sick one is passing away?"

خواند بر شیر او ازین رو پندها
From this point of view he (the hare) recited counsels to the lion.
گفت من پس مانده‌ام زین بندها
"I have lagged behind," said he, "because of these bonds."

پرسیدن شیر از سبب پای واپس کشیدن خرگوش
How the lion asked the reason of the hare's drawing back

شیر گفتش تو ز اسباب مرض
The lion said to him, "Amongst (all) the causes of your malady tell

این سبب گو خاص کاینستم غرض
the special cause, for this is my object."

گفت آن شیر اندرین چه ساکنست
"That lion," he said, "lives in this well:

اندرین قلعه ز آفات آمنست
within this fortress he is safe from harms."

قعر چه بگزید هر که عاقلست
Everyone who is wise chose the bottom of the well

زانک در خلوت صفاهای دلست
because spiritual joys are (to be attained only) in solitude.

ظلمت چه به که ظلمتهای خلق
The darkness of the well is better than the dark shades of the world:

سر نبرد آنکس که گیرد پای خلق
he that followed at the heels of the world never saved his head.

گفت پیش آ زخمم او را قاهرست
Come on," said the lion; "my blow subdues him:

تو ببین کان شیر در چه حاضرست
him: see thou whether that lion is in the well at present."

گفت من سوزیده‌ام زان آتشی
The hare answered, "I am consumed with (dread of) that fieriness (wrath):

تو مگر اندر بر خویشم کشی
perhaps thou wilt take me beside thee,

تا به پشت تو من ای کان کرم
That with thy support, O mine of generosity,

چشم بگشایم بچه در بنگرم
I may open my eyes and look into the well."

◈◉◈◉◈

و آن خرگوش را نظر کردن شیر در چاه و دیدن عکس خود را
How the lion looked into the well and saw the reflexion of himself and the hare in the water

چونک شیر اندر بر خویشش کشید
When the lion took him to his side,

در پناه شیر تا چه می‌دوید
under the lion's protection he began to run towards the well.

چونک در چه بنگریدند اندر آب
As soon as they looked at the water in the well,

اندر آب از شیر و او در تافت تاب
there shone forth in the water the light (reflected) from the lion and him (the hare).

شیر عکس خویش دید از آب تفت
The lion saw his own reflexion: from the water

شکل شیری در برش خرگوش زفت
shone the image of a lion with a plump hare at his side.

چونک خصم خویش را در آب دید
When he beheld his adversary in the water,

مر ورا بگذاشت و اندر چه جهید
he left him (the hare) and sprang into the well.

در فتاد اندر چهی کو کنده بود
He fell into the well which he had dug,

زانک ظلمش در سرش آینده بود
because his iniquity was coming (back) on his own head.

چاه مظلم گشت ظلم ظالمان
The iniquity of evil-doers became (for them) a dark well:

این چنین گفتند جملهٔ عالمان
well: so have said all the wise.

هر که ظالم‌تر چهش با هول‌تر
The more iniquitous one is, the more frightful is his well:

عدل فرموده‌ست بتر را بتر
(Divine) Justice has ordained worse (punishment) for worse (sin).

ای که تو از جاه ظلمی می‌کنی
O you who from iniquity are digging a well (for others),

دانک بهر خویش چاهی می‌کنی
others), you are making a snare for yourself.

گرد خود چون کرم پیله بر متن
Do not weave (a cocoon) round yourself, like the silkworm.
بهر خود چه می‌کنی اندازه کن
You are digging a well for yourself (to fall in): dig with moderation (not too deep).

مر ضعیفان را تو بی‌خصمی مدان
Deem not the weak to be without a champion:
از نبی ذا جاء نصر الله خوان
recite from the Qur'án (the words), When the help of God shall come.

گر تو پیلی خصم تو از تو رمید
If you are an elephant and your foe fled from you,
نک جزا طیرا ابابیلت رسید
lo, the retribution came upon you, birds in flocks.

گر ضعیفی در زمین خواهد امان
If any poor man on the earth beg for mercy,
غلغل افتد در سپاه آسمان
a loud tumult falls on (arises among) the Host of Heaven.

گر بدندانش گزی پر خون کنی
If you bite him with your teeth and make him bleed,
درد دندانت بگیرد چون کنی
toothache will attack you—how will you do (then)?

شیر خود را دید در چه وز غلو
The lion saw himself in the well,
خویش را نشناخت آن دم از عدو
and in his fury he did not know himself at that moment from the enemy.

عکس خود را او عدو خویش دید
He regarded his own reflexion as his enemy:
لاجرم بر خویش شمشیری کشید
necessarily he drew a sword against himself.

ای بسا ظلمی که بینی در کسان
Oh, many an iniquity that you see in others
خوی تو باشد دریشان ای فلان
is your own nature (reflected) in them, O reader!

اندریشان تافته هستی تو
In them shone forth all that you are
از نفاق و ظلم و بد مستی تو
in your hypocrisy and iniquity and insolence.

آن توی و آن زخم بر خود می‌زنی
You are that (evil-doer), and you are striking those blows at yourself:
بر خود آن دم تار لعنت می‌تنی
'tis yourself you are cursing at that moment.

در خود آن بد را نمی‌بینی عیان
You do not see clearly the evil in yourself,
ورنه دشمن بودی خود را بجان
else you would hate yourself with (all) your soul.

حمله بر خود می‌کنی ای ساده مرد
You are assaulting yourself, O simpleton,
همچو آن شیری که بر خود حمله کرد
like the lion who made a rush at himself.

چون به قعر خوی خود اندر رسی
When you reach the bottom of your own nature,
پس بدانی کز تو بود آن ناکسی
then you will know that that vileness was from yourself.

شیر را در قعر پیدا شد که بود
At the bottom (of the well) it became manifest to the lion
نقش او آنکش دگر کس می‌نمود
that he who seemed to him to be another was (really) his own image.

هر که دندان ضعیفی می‌کند
Whoever tears out the teeth of a poor wretch
کار آن شیر غلط‌بین می‌کند
is doing what the falsely-seeing lion did.

می‌ببیند خال بد بر روی عم
O you who see the bad reflexion on the face of your uncle,
عکس خال تست آن از عم مرم
it is not your uncle that is bad, it is you: do not run away from yourself!

مؤمنان آیینهٔ همدیگرند
The Faithful are mirrors to one another:
این خبر می از پیمبر آورند
this saying is related from the Prophet.

پیش چشمت داشتی شیشهٔ کبود
You held a blue glass before your eye:
زان سبب عالم کبودت می‌نمود
for that reason the world seemed to you to be blue.

گر نه کوری این کبودی دان ز خویش
Unless you are blind, know that this blueness comes from yourself:
خویش را بد گو مگو کس را تو بیش
speak ill of yourself, speak no more ill of any one (else).

مؤمن ار ینظر بنور الله نبود
If the true believer was not seeing by the Light of God,
غیب مؤمن را برهنه چون نمود
how did things unseen appear naked (plainly revealed) to the true believer?

چون که تو ینظر بنار الله بدی
Inasmuch as you were seeing by the Fire of God,
در بدی از نیکوی غافل شدی
you did not discern the difference between good and evil.

اندک اندک آب بر آتش بزن
Little by little throw water on the fire,
تا شود نار تو نور ای بوالحزن
that your fire may become light, O man of sorrow!

تو بزن یا ربنا آب طهور
Throw Thou, O Lord, the purifying water,
تا شود این نار عالم جمله نور
that this world-fire may become wholly light.

آب دریا جمله در فرمان تست
All the water of the sea is under Thy command;
آب و آتش ای خداوند آن تست
command; water and fire, O Lord, are Thine.

گر تو خواهی آتش آب خوش شود
If Thou willest, fire becomes sweet water;
ور نخواهی آب هم آتش شود
and if Thou willest not, even water becomes fire.

این طلب در ما هم از ایجاد تست
This search (aspiration) in us is also brought into existence by Thee;
رستن از بیداد یا رب داد تست
deliverance from iniquity is Thy gift, O Lord.

بی‌طلب تو این طلب‌مان داده‌ای
Without (our) seeking Thou hast given us this search,
گنج احسان بر همه بگشاده‌ای
Thou hast given (us) gifts without number and (without) end.

مژده بردن خرگوش سوی نخچیران که شیر در چاه افتاد
How the hare brought to the beasts of chase the news that the lion had fallen into the well

چونک خرگوش از رهایی شاد گشت
When the hare was gladdened by deliverance (from the lion),
سوی نخچیران دوان شد تا به دشت
he began to run towards the beasts until (he came to) the desert.

شیر را چون دید در چه کشته زار
Having seen the lion miserably slain in the well,
چرخ می‌زد شادمان تا مرغزار
he was skipping joyously all the way to the meadow,

دست می‌زد چون رهید از دست مرگ
Clapping his hands because he had escaped from the hand of Death;
سبز و رقصان در هوا چون شاخ و برگ
fresh and dancing in the air, like bough and leaf.

شاخ و برگ از حبس خاک آزاد شد
Bough and leaf were set free from the prison of earth,
سر برآورد و حریف باد شد
lifted their heads, and became comrades of the wind;

برگها چون شاخ را بکشافتند
The leaves, when they had burst (forth from) the bough,
تا به بالای درخت اشتافتند
made haste to reach the top of the tree;

با زبان شطاه شکر خدا
With the tongue of (seed that put forth) its sprouts
می‌سراید هر بر و برگی جدا
each fruit and tree severally is singing thanks to God,

که بپرورد اصل ما را ذوالعطا
Saying, "The Bounteous Giver nourished our root
تا درخت استغلظ آمد و استوی
until the tree grew big and stood upright."

جانهای بسته اندر آب و گل
(Even so) the spirits bound in clay,
چون رهند از آب و گلها شاددل
when they escape glad at heart from their (prisons of) clay,

در هوای عشق حق رقصان شوند
Begin to dance in the air of Divine Love
همچو قرص بدر بی‌نقصان شوند
and become flawless like the full moon's orb,

چشمان در رقص و جانها خود مپرس
Their bodies dancing, and their souls—nay, do not ask (how their souls fare);
وانک گرد جان از آنها خود مپرس
and those things from which comes the soul's delight—nay, do not ask (of those things)!

شیر را خرگوش در زندان نشاند
The hare lodged the lion in prison.
ننگ شیری کو ز خرگوشی بماند
Shame on a lion who was discomfited by a hare!

درچنان ننگی و آنگه این عجب
He is in such a disgrace, and still—this is a wonder
فخر دین خواهد که گویندش لقب
he would fain be addressed by the title of Fakhr-i Dín.

ای تو شیری در تک این چاه فرد
O thou lion that liest at the bottom of this lonely well,
نقش چون خرگوش خونت ریخت و خورد
thy hare-like soul (nafs) has shed and drunk thy blood;

نفس خرگوشت به صحرا در چرا
Thy hare-soul is feeding in the desert,
تو بقعر این چه چون و چرا
(whilst) thou art (lying) at the bottom of this well of "How?" and "Why?"

سوی نخچیران دوید آن شیرگیر
That lion-catcher (the hare) ran towards the beasts,
کابشروا یا قوم اذ جاء البشیر
crying, "Rejoice, O people, since the announcer of joy is come.

مژده مژده ای گروه عیش ساز
Glad news! Glad news, O company of merry-makers!
کان سگ دوزخ به دوزخ رفت باز
That hell-hound has gone back to Hell.

مژده مژده کان عدو جانها
Glad news! Glad news! The enemy of your lives
کند قهر خالقش دندانها
his teeth have been torn out by the vengeance of his Creator.

آنک از پنجه بسی سرها بکوفت
He who smote many heads with his claws
همچو خس جاروب مرگش هم بروفت
him too the broom of Death has swept away like rubbish."

❦◉❦◉❦

جمع شدن نخجیران گرد خرگوش و ثنا گفتن او را
How the beasts gathered round the hare and spoke in praise of him.

جمع گشتند آن زمان جمله وحوش
Then all the wild beasts assembled,
شاد و خندان از طرب در ذوق و جوش
joyous and laughing gleefully in rapture and excitement.

حلقه کردند او چو شمعی در میان
They formed a ring, he (the hare) in the midst like a candle:
سجده آوردند و گفتندش که هان
all the animals of the desert bowed (in homage) to him.

تو فرشتهٔ آسمانی یا پری
"Art thou a heavenly angel or a peri?
نی تو عزرائیل شیران نری
No, thou art the Azrael of fierce lions.

هرچه هستی جان ما قربان تست
Whatever thou art, our souls are offered in sacrifice to thee.
دست بردی دست و بازویت درست
Thou hast prevailed. Health to thy hand and arm!

راند حق این آب را در جوی تو
God turned this water into thy stream.
آفرین بر دست و بر بازوی تو
Blessing on thy hand and arm!

بازگو تا چون سگالیدی به مکر
Explain how thou didst meditate with guile,
آن عوان را چون بمالیدی به مکر
and how thou didst guilefully wipe out that ruffian.

بازگو تا قصه درمانها شود
Explain, in order that the tale may be the means of curing (our malady);
بازگو تا مرهم جانها شود
explain, that it may be a salve for our souls.

بازگو کز ظلم آن استم نما
Explain! for in consequence of the iniquity of that tyrant

صد هزاران زخم دارد جان ما
our souls have myriads of wounds."

گفت تایید خدا بد ای مهان
O Sirs," said he, "it was (by) God's aid;

ورنه خرگوشی کی باشد در جهان
else, who in the world is a hare (who am I, that I should have been able to do this)?

قوتم بخشید و دل را نور داد
He (God) bestowed power on me and gave light to my heart:

نور دل مر دست و پا را زور داد
the light in my heart gave strength to hand and foot."

از بر حق می‌رسد تفضیلها
From God come preferments (to high position),

باز هم از حق رسد تبدیلها
from God also come changes (which bring one to low estate).

حق بدور نوبت این تایید را
God in (due) course and turn is ever

می‌نماید اهل ظن و دید را
displaying this (Divine) aid to doubters and seers (alike).

◈◈◈

پند دادن خرگوش نخجیران را که بدین شاد مشوید
Advise of Nabbit Nakhjiran: Do Not Be Happy with this

هین بملک نوبتی شادی مکن
Take heed! Do not exult in a kingdom bestowed in turns (passing from one to another),

ای تو بستهٔ نوبت آزادی مکن
O thou who art the bondsman of Vicissitude, do not act as though thou wert free!

آنک ملکش برتر از نوبت تنند
(But) those for whom is prepared a kingdom beyond Vicissitude,

برتر از هفت آن چهمش نوبت زنند
for them the drums (of sovereignty) are beaten beyond the Seven Planets.

برتر از نوبت ملوک باقیند
Beyond Vicissitude are the kings everlasting

دور دایم روحها با ساقیند
their spirits are circling with the Cupbearer perpetually.

ترک این شرب ار بگویی یک دو روز

If thou wilt renounce this drinking (of worldly pleasures) for a day or two (for thy brief lifetime),

در کنی اندر شراب خلد پوز

thou wilt dip thy mouth in the drink of Paradise

❀❀❀

تفسیر رجعنا من الجهادالاصغر الی الجهاد الاکبر

Commentary on (the Tradition) "We have returned from the lesser Jihád to the greater Jihád."

ای شهان کشتیم ما خصم برون

O kings, we have slain the outward enemy,

ماند خصمی زو بتر در اندرون

(but) there remains within (us) a worse enemy than he.

کشتن این کار عقل و هوش نیست

To slay this (enemy) is not the work of reason and intelligence:

شیر باطن سخرهٔ خرگوش نیست

the inward lion is not subdued by the hare.

دوزخست این نفس و دوزخ اژدهاست

This carnal self (nafs) is Hell, and Hell is a dragon

کو به دریاها نگردد کم و کاست

which is not diminished by oceans (of water).

هفت دریا را در آشامد هنوز

It would drink up the Seven Seas,

کم نگردد سوزش آن خلق‌سوز

and still the blazing of that consumer of all creatures would not become less.

سنگها و کافران سنگ‌دل

Stones and stony-hearted infidels enter it

اندر آیند اندرو زار و خجل

miserable and shamefaced,

هم نگردد ساکن از چندین غذا

(But) still it is not appeased by all this food,

تا ز حق آید مرورا این ندا

ntil there comes to it from God this call

سیر گشتی سیر گوید نه هنوز

"Art thou filled, art thou filled?" It says, "Not yet;

اینت آتش اینت تابش اینت سوز

lo, here is the fire, here is the glow, here is the burning!"

عالمی را لقمه کرد و در کشید
It made a mouthful of and swallowed a whole world,
معده‌اش نعره زنان هل من مزید
its belly crying aloud, "Is there any more?"

حق قدم بر وی نهد از لامکان
God, from (the realm) where place is not,
آنگه او ساکن شود از کن فکان
sets His foot on it: then it subsides at (the command) Be, and it was.

چونک جزو دوزخست این نفس ما
Inasmuch as this self of ours is a part of Hell,
طبع کل دارد همیشه جزوها
and the parts always have the nature of the whole,

این قدم حق را بود کو را کشد
To God (alone) belongs this foot (power) to kill it:
غیر حق خود کی کمان او کشد
who, indeed, but God should draw its bow (vanquish it)?

در کمان ننهند الا تیر راست
Only the straight arrow is put on the bow,
این کمان را بازگون کژ تیرهاست
(but) this bow (of the self) has (its) arrows bent back and crooked.

راست شو چون تیر و واره از کمان
Be straight, like an arrow, and escape from the bow,
کز کمان هر راست بجهد بی‌گمان
for without doubt every straight (arrow) will fly from the bow (to its mark).

چونک واگشتم ز پیگار برون
When I turned back from the outer warfare,
روی آوردم به پیگار درون
I set my face towards the inner warfare.

قد رجعنا من جهاد الاصغریم
We have returned from the lesser Jihád,
با نبی اندر جهاد اکبریم
we are engaged along with the Prophet in the greater Jihád.

قوت از حق خواهم و توفیق و لاف
I pray God to grant me strength and aid and (the right of) boasting,
تا به سوزن بر کنم این کوه قاف
that I may root up with a needle this mountain of Qáf.

سهل شیری دان که صفها بشکند
Deem of small account the lion (champion) who breaks the ranks (of the enemy):
شیر آنست آن که خود را بشکند
the (true) lion is he that breaks (conquers) himself.

◆◉◆◉

آمدن رسول روم تا نزد عمر و دیدن کرامات او
How the ambassador of Rúm came to the Commander of the Faithful, 'Umar, and witnessed the gifts of grace with which 'Umar, was endowed

تا عمر آمد ز قیصر یک رسول
To 'Umar in Medina there came through
در مدینه از بیابان نغول
the wide desert an ambassador from the Emperor of Rúm.

گفت کو قصر خلیفه ای حشم
He said, "O ye attendants, where is the palace of the Caliph,
تا من اسپ و رخت را آنجا کشم
that I may take thither my horse and baggage?"

قوم گفتندش که او را قصر نیست
The folk said to him, "He has no palace:
مر عمر را قصر جان روشنی است
'Umar's (only) palace is an illumined spirit.

گرچه از میری ورا آوازه‌ایست
Though he has a (great) renown from being Commander (of the Faithful),
همچو درویشان مر او را کازه‌ایست
he has (no dwelling except) a hut, like the poor.

ای برادر چون ببینی قصر او
O brother, how wilt thou behold his palace,
چونک در چشم دلت رستست مو
when hair has grown in the eye of thy heart?

چشم دل از مو و علت پاک آر
Purge thy heart's eye of hair and defect,
وانگه آن دیدار قصرش چشم دار
and then hope to behold his palace.

هر که را هست از هوسها جان پاک
Whoever hath a spirit purged of (sensual) desires will at once behold
زود بیند حضرت و ایوان پاک
the Presence and the Holy Porch

چون محمد پاک شد زین نار و دود
When Mohammed was purged of this fire and smoke (of human passions),
هر کجا رو کرد وجه الله بود
wheresoever he turned his face, was the Face of Allah.

چون رفیقِ وسوسهٔ بدخواه را
Inasmuch as thou art a friend to the evil suggestions of the malign one (Satan)
کی بدانی ثم وجه الله را
how wilt thou know (the true meaning of) There is the Face of Allah?

هر که را باشد ز سینه فتح باب
Everyone in whose breast the gate is opened will behold
او ز هر شهری ببیند آفتاب
from every city the sun (shining).

حق پدیدست از میان دیگران
God is manifest amongst others
همچو ماه اندر میان اختران
as the moon amidst the stars

دو سر انگشت بر دو چشم نه
Lay two finger-ends on thy two eyes,
هیچ بینی از جهان انصاف ده
and wilt thou see aught of the world? Deal justly

گر نبینی این جهان معدوم نیست
If thou dost not see this world, (yet) it is not non-existent:
عیب جز ز انگشت نفس شوم نیست
the fault lies not save in the finger of thy evil self

تو ز چشم انگشت را بردار هین
Come, lift the finger from thine eye
وانگهانی هرچه می‌خواهی ببین
and then behold whatsoever thou wishest.

نوح را گفتند امت کو ثواب
To Noah his people said, 'Where is the Divine recompense?
گفت او زان سوی و استغشوا ثیاب
He said, 'On the other side of they cover themselves with their garments.

رو و سر در جامه‌ها پیچیده‌اید
Ye have wrapped your faces and heads in your clothes
لاجرم با دیده و نادیده‌اید
of necessity ye have eyes and see not.'

آدمی دیدست و باقی پوستست
Man is eye, and (all) the rest is (worthless) skin:
دید آنست آن که دید دوستست
the sight of that (eye) is (consists in) seeing the Beloved.

چونک دید دوست نبود کور به
When there is not sight of the Beloved, it (the eye) is better blind;
دوست کو باقی نباشد دور به
the beloved who is not everlasting is better afar

چون رسول روم این الفاظ تر
When the ambassador of Rúm admitted these fresh (spiritual) words into his hearing (gave ear to them),
در سماع آورد شد مشتاق‌تر
he became more full of longing.

دیده را بر جستن عمر گماشت
He fixed his eye on seeking 'Umar,
رخت را و اسپ را ضایع گذاشت
he let his baggage and horse be lost.

هر طرف اندر پی آن مرد کار
He was going in every direction after that man of (great) accomplishment
می‌شدی پرسان او دیوانه‌وار
inquiring madly for him,

کین چنین مردی بود اندر جهان
Saying, "Can there be in the world such a man,
وز جهان مانند جان باشد نهان
and he be hid, like the spirit, from the world?"

جست او را تاش چون بنده بود
He sought him, that he might be as a slave to him:
لاجرم جوینده یابنده بود
inevitably the seeker is a finder.

دید اعرابی زنی او را دخیل
An Arab woman of the desert saw that he was a stranger guest. "Look,"
گفت عمر نک به زیر آن نخیل
said she, "there is 'Umar under that palm.

زیر خرمابن ز خلقان او جدا
There he is under the palm-tree, apart from the people:
زیر سایه خفته بین سایهٔ خدا
behold the Shadow of God asleep in the shade!"

یافتن رسول روم عمر را خفته در زیر درخت

How the ambassador of Rúm found the Commander of the Faithful, 'Umar, may God be well-pleased with him, sleeping under the palm-tree.

آمد او آنجا و از دور ایستاد

He came thither and stood afar off;

مر عمر را دید و در لرز اوفتاد

he saw 'Umar and fell a-trembling.

هیبتی زان خفته آمد بر رسول

An awe came upon the ambassador from that slumbering man,

حالتی خوش کرد بر جانش نزول

a sweet ecstasy lodged in his soul.

مهر و هیبت هست ضد همدگر

Love and awe are contrary to each other:

این دو ضد را دید جمع اندر جگر

he saw these two contraries united in his heart.

گفت با خود من شهان را دیده‌ام

He said to himself: "I have seen (many) kings,

پیش سلطانان مه و بگزیده‌ام

I have been great (in esteem) and chosen (for honour) in the presence of sultans:

از شهانم هیبت و ترسی نبود

I had no awe or dread of kings,

هیبت این مرد هوشم را ربود

(but) awe of this man has robbed me of my wits.

رفته‌ام در بیشهٔ شیر و پلنگ

I have gone into a jungle of lions and leopards,

روی من زیشان نگردانید رنگ

and my face did not change colour because of them;

بس شدستم در مصاف و کارزار

Often where the ranks are arrayed on the field of battle have I become (fierce

همچو شیر آن دم که باشد کارزار

as a lion at the time when the affair is grievous (desperate);

بس که خوردم بس زدم زخم گران

Many a heavy blow have I suffered and inflicted,

دل قوی‌تر بوده‌ام از دیگران

I have been stouter in heart than (all) the others.

بی‌سلاح این مرد خفته بر زمین
This man is asleep on the earth, unarmed,
من به هفت اندام لرزان چیست این
(and yet) I am trembling in my seven limbs (my whole body): what is this?

هیبت حقست این از خلق نیست
This is awe of God, it is not from created beings,
هیبت این مرد صاحب دلق نیست
it is not awe of this man who wears the frock of a dervish.

هر که ترسید از حق او تقوی گزید
Whoever is afraid of God and has chosen fear of God (as his religion),
ترسد از وی جن و انس و هر که دید
the Jinn and mankind and everyone who sees (him) are afraid of him."

ندرین فکرت به حرمت دست بست
Thus meditating, he folded his hands reverently.
بعد یک ساعت عمر از خواب جست
After a while 'Umar sprang up from sleep.

◈◈

سلام کردن رسول روم بر عمر

How the ambassador of Rúm saluted the Commander of the Faithful, may God be well pleased with him.

کرد خدمت مر عمر را و سلام
He did homage to 'Umar and salaamed:
گفت پیغامبر سلام آنگه کلام
the Prophet said, "(First) the salaam, then the talk."

پس علیکش گفت و او را پیش خواند
Then he ('Umar) said, "To thee (greeting)," called him (to come) forward,
ایمنش کرد و به پیش خود نشاند
reassured him, and bade him sit down by his side.

لاتخافوا هست نزل خایفان
Fear ye not is the hospitality offered to those who fear:
هست در خور از برای خایف آن
fear: that is proper (entertainment) for one who is afraid.

هر که ترسد مر ورا ایمن کنند
When any one is afraid, they make him (feel) secure;
مر دل ترسنده را ساکن کنند
they soothe (his) fearful heart.

آنک خوفش نیست چون گویی مترس
How should you say "Fear not" to one who has no fear?
درس چه دهی نیست او محتاج درس
Why give lessons (to him)? He needs no lessons.

آن دل از جا رفته را دلشاد کرد
He ('Umar) made that disturbed mind (be) of good cheer
خاطر ویرانش را آباد کرد
And made his desolate heart (be) flourishing (happy).

بعد از آن گفتش سخنهای دقیق
Afterwards he addressed to him subtle discourses
وز صفات پاک حق نعم الرفیق
f the holy attributes of God how good a Friend is He!

وز نوازشهای حق ابدال را
And of the loving kindnesses of God to the Abdál (saints),
تا بداند او مقام و حال را
in order that he might know maqám and hál (passing state).

حال چون جلوه‌ست زان زیبا عروس
The hál is like the unveiling of that beauteous bride,
وین مقام آن خلوت آمد با عروس
while the maqám is the (king's) being alone with the bride.

جلوه بیند شاه و غیر شاه نیز
The unveiling is witnessed by the king and by others as well,
وقت خلوت نیست جز شاه عزیز
(but) at the time of being alone (with the bride) there is no one except the mighty king.

جلوه کرده خاص و عامان را عروس
The bride unveils before commons and nobles (alike);
خلوت اندر شاه باشد با عروس
in the bridal chamber the king is (alone) with the bride

هست بسیار اهل حال از صوفیان
There is many a one of the Súfís who enjoys hál,
نادرست اهل مقام اندر میان
(but) he that has attained to maqám is rare amongst them

از منازلهای جانش یاد داد
He ('Umar) reminded him of the stages traversed by the soul,
وز سفرهای روانش یاد داد
and he reminded him of the journeys of the spirit,

189

وز زمانی کز زمان خالی بدست
And of the Time which has (ever) been void of time,
وز مقام قدس که اجلالی بدست
and of the Station of Holiness which has (ever) been majestical,

وز هوایی کاندرو سیمرغ روح
And of the atmosphere wherein the Símurgh of the spirit,
پیش ازین دیدست پرواز و فتوح
before this (material life), has flown and experienced (the bounty of Divine) grace,

هر یکی پروازش از آفاق بیش
Every single flight thereof (being) greater than the horizons
وز امید و نهمت مشتاق بیش
(of this world) and greater than the hope and greed of the longing lover.

چون عمر اغیار رو را یار یافت
When 'Umar found the stranger in appearance a friend (in reality),
جان او را طالب اسرار یافت
he found (that) his soul (was) seeking (to learn) the (Divine) mysteries.

شیخ کامل بود و طالب مشتهی
The Shaykh ('Umar) was adept and the disciple (the ambassador) eager:
مرد چابک بود و مرکب درگهی
the man (rider) was quick (dexterous) and the beast belonged to the royal court (was nobly bred and docile).

دید آن مرشد که او ارشاد داشت
That spiritual guide ('Umar) perceived that he (the ambassador) possessed (the capacity for receiving) guidance
تخم پاک اندر زمین پاک کاشت
he sowed the good seed in the good soil.

سوال کردن رسول روم از عمر
How the ambassador of Rúm questioned the Commander of the Faithful, may God be well-pleased with him.

مرد گفتش کای امیرالمؤمنین
The man said to him, "O Commander of the Faithful,

جان ز بالا چون در آمد در زمین
how did the spirit come to the earth from above?

مرغ بی‌اندازه چون شد در قفس
How did the infinite bird go into the cage?"

گفت حق بر جان فسون خواند و قصص
He replied, "God recited spells and incantations over the spirit.

بر عدم‌ها کان ندارد چشم و گوش
When He recites spells over the non-existences which have no eye or ear,

چون فسون خواند همی آید به جوش
they begin to stir.

از فسون او عدم‌ها زود زود
Because of His spells the non-existences at that very moment

خوش معلق می‌زند سوی وجود
are dancing joyously into existence.

باز بر موجود افسونی چو خواند
When, again, He recited a spell over the existent,

زو دو اسپه در عدم موجود راند
at His word the existent marched (back) post-haste into nonexistence.

گفت در گوش گل و خندانش کرد
He spake into the ear of the rose and made it laughing(blooming);

گفت با سنگ و عقیق کانش کرد
He spake to the stone and made it a cornelian of the mine.

گفت با جسم آیتی تا جان شد او
He spake to the body a sign (message), so that it became spirit;

گفت با خورشید تا رخشان شد او
He spake to the sun, so that it became radiant.

باز در گوشش دمد نکتهٔ مخوف
Again He puts into its ear a fearful saying,

در رخ خورشید افتد صد کسوف
and upon the face of the sun fall a hundred eclipses.

تا به گوش ابر آن گویا چه خواند
Consider what that Speaker chanted into the ear of the cloud,
کو چو مشک از دیدهٔ خود اشک راند
so that it poured tears from its eye, like a waterskin.

تا به گوش خاک حق چه خوانده است
Consider what God has chanted into the ear of the earth,
کو مراقب گشت و خامش مانده است
so that it became regardful and has (ever since) remained silent."

در تردد هر که او آشفته است
Whosoever in perplexity is sorely troubled,
حق به گوش او معما گفته است
God has spoken the riddle into his ear,

تا کند محبوسش اندر دو گمان
That He may imprison him in two (doubtful) thoughts, (namely),
آن کنم آن گفت یا خود ضد آن
"Shall I do what He told (me) or the contrary thereof?"

هم ز حق ترجیح یابد یک طرف
From (the decree of) God also, one side obtains the preponderance,
زان دو یک را برگزیند زان کنف
and from that (Divine) quarter he chooses one of the two (alternatives).

گر نخواهی در تردد هوش جان
If thou wouldst not have the mind of thy spirit in (a state of) perplexity,
کم فشار این پنبه اندر گوش جان
do not stuff this cotton-wool into thy spiritual ear,

تا کنی فهم آن معماهاش را
So that thou mayst understand those riddles of His,
تا کنی ادراک رمز و فاش را
so that thou mayst apprehend (both) the secret sign and the open.

پس محل وحی گردد گوش جان
Then the spiritual ear becomes the place where wahy(inspiration) descends
وحی چه بود گفتنی از حس نهان
What is wahy? A speech hidden from sense-perception.

گوش جان و چشم جان جز این حس است
The spiritual ear and eye are other than this sense-perception,
گوش عقل و گوش ظن زین مفلس است
the ear of (discursive) reason and the ear of opinion are destitute of this (inspiration).

لفظ جبرم عشق را بی‌صبر کرد
The word "compulsion" (jabr) made me impatient(uncontrollable) for love's sake,
وانک عاشق نیست حبس جبر کرد
while it confined in (the prison of) compulsion him who is not a lover.

این معیت با حقست و جبر نیست
This is union with God, and it is not compulsion:
این تجلی مه است این ابر نیست
this is the shining forth of the moon, this is not a cloud

ور بود این جبر جبر عامه نیست
And if this be compulsion, it is not the compulsion of (suffered by) the vulgar:
جبر آن اماره خودکامه نیست
it is not the compulsion of (exerted by) the evil-commanding self-willed (soul).

جبر را ایشان شناسند ای پسر
O son, (only) they know (the real meaning of) compulsion
که خدا بگشادشان در دل بصر
in whose hearts God has opened the sight (of the spiritual eye).

غیب و آینده بریشان گشت فاش
To them the unseen things of the future became manifest;
ذکر ماضی پیش ایشان گشت لاش
to them recollection of the past became naught.

اختیار و جبر ایشان دیگرست
Their freewill and compulsion is different (from that of ordinary men):
قطره‌ها اندر صدفها گوهرست
in oyster-shells drops (of rain) are pearls.

هست بیرون قطرهٔ خرد و بزرگ
Outside (of the shell) it is a drop of water, small or great,
در صدف آن در خردست و سترگ
(but) within the shell it is a small or big pearl.

طبع ناف آهوست آن قوم را
Those persons have the nature of the muskdeer's gland:
از برون خون و درونشان مشکها
externally they are (as) blood, while within them is the fragrance of musk

تو مگو کین مایه بیرون خون بود
Do not say, "This substance externally is blood:
چون رود در ناف مشکی چون شود
how should it become a musky perfume when it goes into the gland?"

تو مگو کین مس برون بد محتقر
Do not say, "This copper externally was despicable:
در دل اکسیر چون گیرد گهر
should it assume nobility in the heart (midst) of the elixir?"

اختیار و جبر در تو بد خیال
In thee (the matter of) freewill and compulsion was a (mere) fancy,
چون درِ ایشان رفت شد نور جلال
(but) when it went into them it became the light of (Divine) Majesty.

نان چو در سفره‌ست باشد آن جماد
When bread is (wrapped) in the tablecloth it is the inanimate thing (so-called),
در تن مردم شود او روح شاد
(but) in the human body it becomes the glad spirit (of life).

در دل سفره نگردد مستحیل
It does not become transmuted in the heart of (within) the table-cloth:
مستحیلش جان کند از سلسبیل
the (animal) soul transmutes it with (the water of) Salsabíl.

قوت جانست این ای راست خوان
O thou who readest aright, such is the power of the soul:
تا چه باشد قوت آن جان جان
what, then, must be the power of that Soul of soul?

گوشت پارهٔ آدمی با عقل و جان
The piece of flesh which is Man, endowed with intelligence and soul,
می‌شکافد کوه را با بحر و کان
cleaves the mountain by means of water-channel and mine.

زور جان کوه کن شق حجر
The strength of the mountain-riving soul is (shown in) the splitting of rocks
زور جان جان در انشق القمر
the strength of the Soul of soul in the moon was split asunder.

گر گشاید دل سر انبان راز
If the heart should open the lid of the wallet of (this) mystery
جان به سوی عرش سازد ترک تاز
the soul would rush (in rapture) towards the highest heaven.

اضافت کردن آدم علیه‌السلام آن زلت را به خویشتن
How Adam imputed that fault (which he had committed) to himself,

کی ربنا ظلمنا و اضافت کردن ابلیس گناه خود را به خدای تعالی کی بما اغویتنی
saying, "O Lord, we have done wrong," and how Iblís imputed his own sin to God, saying, "Because Thou hast seduced me"

کرد حق و کرد ما هر دو ببین
Consider both our action and the action of God.

کرد ما را هست دان پیداست این
Regard our action as existent. This is manifest.

گر نباشد فعل خلق اندر میان
If the action of created beings be not in the midst (obviously existent),

پس مگو کس را چرا کردی چنان
then say not to anyone, "Why have you acted thus?

خلق حق افعال ما را موجدست
The creative act of God brings our actions into existence:

فعل ما آثار خلق ایزدست
our actions are the effects of the creative act of God.

ناطقی یا حرف بیند یا غرض
A rational being perceives either the letter (the outer sign) or the (inner) purpose (the spirit):

کی شود یک دم محیط دو عرض
how should he comprehend two accidents at once?

گر به معنی رفت شد غافل ز حرف
If he goes (turns his mind) to the spirit, he becomes unheedful of the letter:

پیش و پس یک دم نبیند هیچ طرف
no eye sees forward and backward at the same moment.

آن زمان که پیش‌بینی آن زمان
At the time when you look in front,

تو پس خود کی ببینی این بدان
how at the same time can you look behind you? Recognise this.

چون محیط حرف و معنی نیست جان
Inasmuch as the soul does not comprehend (both) the letter and the spirit,

چون بود جان خالق این هر دوان
how should the soul be the creator of them both?

حق محیط جمله آمد ای پسر
O son, (only) God comprehends both:

وا ندارد کارش از کار دگر
the (one) action does not hinder Him from the other action.

گفت شیطان که بما اغویتنی
Satan said Because Thou hast seduced me:
کرد فعل خود نهان دیو دنی
the vile Devil concealed his own act.

گفت آدم که ظلمنا نفسنا
dam said We have done wrong unto ourselves:
او ز فعل حق نبد غافل چو ما
he was not, like us, unheedful of the action of God.

در گنه او از ادب پنهانش کرد
From respect he concealed it (the action of God) in(regard to) the sin:
زان گنه بر خود زدن او بر بخورد
by casting the sin upon himself he ate fruit (was blessed).

بعد توبه گفتش ای آدم نه من
After his repentance, He (God) said to him, "O Adam,
آفریدم در تو آن جرم و محن
did not I create in thee that sin and (those) tribulations?

نه که تقدیر و قضای من بد آن
Was it not My foreordainment and destiny?
چون به وقت عذر کردی آن نهان
How didst thou conceal that at the time of excusing thyself?"

گفت ترسیدم ادب نگذاشتم
He (Adam) said, "I was afraid, (so) I did not let respect go (did not fail to observe due respect)."

گفت هم من پاس آنت داشتم
He (God) said, "I too have observed it towards thee."

هر که آرد حرمت او حرمت برد
Whoever brings reverence gets reverence (in return):
هر که آرد قند لوزینه خورد
whoever brings sugar eats almond-cake.

طیبات از بهر کی للطیبین
For whom are the good women? For the good men.
یار را خوش کن برنجان و ببین
Treat thy friend with honour; offend (him) and see (what will happen).

یک مثال ای دل بی فرق بیار
O heart, bring (forward) a parable for the sake of (illustrating) a difference,
تا بدانی جبر را از اختیار
that thou mayst know (what distinguishes) compulsion from freewill.

دست کان لرزان بود از ارتعاش
a hand that is shaking from (morbid or involuntary) tremor and (the case of)
وانک دستی تو بلرزانی ز جاش
a person whose hand you cause to shake (by knocking it away) from its place.

هر دو جنبش آفریدهٔ حق شناس
Know that both (these) movements are created by God,
لیک نتوان کرد این با آن قیاس
but it is impossible to compare the latter with the former.

زان پشیمانی که لرزانیدیش
You are sorry for having caused it (his hand) to shake:
مرتعش را کی پشیمان دیدیش
how is the man afflicted with (a morbid) tremor not sorry?

بحث عقلست این چه عقل آن حیله گر
This is the intellectual quest.
تا ضعیفی ره برد آنجا مگر
perchance (by its means) a man of weak understanding may find his way to that place

بحث عقلی گر در و مرجان بود
(Yet) the intellectual quest, though it be (fine as) pearls and coral,
آن دگر باشد که بحث جان بود
is other than the spiritual quest.

بحث جان اندر مقامی دیگرست
The spiritual quest is on another plane:
بادهٔ جان را قوامی دیگرست
the spiritual wine has another consistency.

آن زمان که بحث عقلی ساز بود
At the time when the intellectual quest was in keeping (with the circumstances),
این عمر با بوالحکم همراز بود
this 'Umar was intimate with Bu 'l-Hakam,

چون عمر از عقل آمد سوی جان
(But) when 'Umar went away from intellect towards spirit
بوالحکم بوجهل شد در حکم آن
Bu 'l-Hakam became Bú Jahl (the father of ignorance) in the case of that (spiritual quest).

سوی حس و سوی عقل او کاملست
He is perfect on the side of sense-perception and understanding,
گرچه خود نسبت به جان او جاهلست
though indeed he is ignorant in regard to the spirit.

بحث عقل و حس اثر دان یا سبب
Know that the quest of the intellect and the senses is (concerned with) effects or secondary causes.

بحث جانی یا عجب یا بوالعجب
The spiritual quest is either wonder or the father of wonder (either wonderful or beyond wonder)

ضوء جان آمد نماند ای مستضی
The illumination of the spirit comes: (then) there remains not, O thou who seekest illumination,

لازم و ملزوم و نافی مقتضی
conclusion and premise or that which contradicts (a statement) (or) that which renders (its acceptance) necessary,

زانک بینایی که نورش بازغست
Because the seer on whom His (God's) Light is dawning is

از دلیل چون عصا بس فارغست
quite independent of the (logical) proof which resembles a (blind man's) staff

❖◉❖◉❖

تفسیر و هو معکم این ما کنتم
Commentary on "And He is with you wheresoever ye be."

بار دیگر ما به قصه آمدیم
Once more we come back to the tale:

ما از آن قصه برون خود کی شدیم
when, indeed, did we go forth from the tale?

گر به جهل آییم آن زندان اوست
If we come to ignorance, that is His prison,

ور به علم آییم آن ایوان اوست
and if we come to knowledge, that is His palace;

ور به خواب آییم مستان وییم
And if we come to sleep, we are His intoxicated ones;

ور به بیداری به دستان وییم
and if to wakefulness, we are in His hands;

ور بگرییم ابر پر زرق وییم
And if we weep, we are a cloud laden with the bounty dispensed by Him;

ور بخندیم آن زمان برق وییم
at that time we are His lightning;

ور بخشم و جنگ عکس قهر اوست
And if (we come) to wrath and war, 'tis the reflexion of His Might;
ور بصلح و عذر عکس مهر اوست
and if to peace and forgiveness, 'tis the reflexion of His Love.

ما کییم اندر جهان پیچ پیچ
Who are we? In this tangled world what indeed hath
چون الف او خود چه دارد هیچ هیچ
He (who is single) like alif? Nothing, nothing.

❖◉❖◉❖

سؤال کردن رسول روم از عمر رضی‌الله عنه از سبب ابتلای ارواح با این آب و گل جسم

How the ambassador asked 'Umar, may God be well-pleased with him, concerning the cause of the tribulation suffered by spirits in these bodies of clay.

گفت یا عمر چه حکمت بود و سر
He said, "O 'Umar, what was the wisdom and mystery
حبس آن صافی درین جای کدر
of imprisoning that pure one (the spirit) in this dirty place?

آب صافی در گلی پنهان شده
The pure water has become hidden in mud:
جان صافی بستهٔ ابدان شده
the pure spirit has become bound in bodies."

گفت تو بحثی شگرفی می‌کنی
He ('Umar) said, "Thou art making a profound inquiry,
معنیی را بند حرفی می‌کنی
thou art confining a meaning in a word.

حبس کردی معنی آزاد را
Thou hast imprisoned the free (unconditioned) meaning,
بند حرفی کرده‌ای تو یاد را
thou hast bound the wind in a word.

از برای فایده این کرده‌ای
This thou hast done for a benefit (good purpose),
تو که خود از فایده در پرده‌ای
O thou who thyself art blind to the benefit (good purpose) of God

آنک از وی فایده زاییده شد
He from whom (every) benefit was born,
چون نبیند آنچه ما را دیده شد
how should He not see that which was seen by us?

صد هزاران فایده‌ست و هر یکی
There are myriads of benefits
صد هزاران پیش آن یک اندکی
and every myriad is (but) a few beside that one.

آن دم نطقت که جزو جزوهاست
The breath of thy speech, which is a part of the parts (bodily members), became beneficial:
فایده شد کل کل خالی چراست
why (then) is the whole of the whole (the universal connexion of spirit and body) devoid

تو که جزوی کار تو با فایده‌ست
Thou who art a part—thy act (of speaking) is beneficial:
پس چرا در طعن کل آری تو دست
why(then) dost thou lift thy hand to assail the whole?

گفت را گر فایده نبود مگو
If there is no benefit in speech, do not speak; and if there is,
ور بود هل اعتراض و شکر جو
leave off making objections, and endeavour to give thanks."

شکر یزدان طوق هر گردن بود
Thanksgiving to God is a collar on every neck (every one's duty);
نی جدال و رو ترش کردن بود
it is not (thanksgiving) to dispute and make one's face look sour.

گر ترش‌رو بودن آمد شکر و بس
If thanksgiving is only to look sour,
پس چو سرکه شکرگویی نیست کس
then there is no thanksgiver like vinegar.

سرکه را گر راه باید در جگر
If vinegar wants (to find) the way to the liver,
گو بشو سرکنگبین او از شکر
let it become oxymel by (being mixed with) sugar.

معنی اندر شعر جز با خبط نیست
The meaning in poetry has no sureness of direction:
چون قلاسنگست و اندر ضبط نیست
direction: it is like the sling, it is not under control.

❁◉❁◉❁

200

در معنی آنک من اراد ان یجلس مع الله فلیجلس مع اهل التصوف
On the inner sense of "Let him who desires to sit with God sit with the Súfis."

آن رسول از خود بشد زین یک دو جام

The ambassador became beside himself from these one or two cups (of spiritual discourse):

نی رسالت یاد ماندش نی پیام

neither embassage nor message remained in his memory.

واله اندر قدرت الله شد

He became distraught at the power of God.

آن رسول اینجا رسید و شاه شد

The ambassador arrived at this place (state) and became a king.

سیل چون آمد به دریا بحر گشت

When the torrent reached the sea, it became the sea;

دانه چون آمد به مزرع گشت کشت

when the seed reached the cornland, it became the crop of corn.

چون تعلق یافت نان با بوالبشر

When the bread attained to connexion with the animal (man),

نان مرده زنده گشت و با خبر

the dead bread became living and endowed with knowledge.

موم و هیزم چون فدای نار شد

When the wax and firewood were devoted to the fire,

ذات ظلمانی او انوار شد

their dark essence became (filled with) light.

سنگ سرمه چونک شد در دیدگان

When the (powdered) stone of antimony went into the eyes,

گشت بینایی شد آنجا دیدبان

it turned to sight and there became a scout (one who observes the enemy from some point of vantage).

ای خنک آن مرد کز خود رسته شد

Oh, happy is the man who was freed from himself

در وجود زنده‌ای پیوسته شد

and united with the existence of a living one!

وای آن زنده که با مرده نشست

Alas for the living one who consorted with the dead!

مرده گشت و زندگی از وی بجست

He became dead, and life sped away from him.

چون تو در قرآن حق بگریختی
When you have fled (for refuge) to the Qur'án of God,
با روان انبیا آمیختی
you have mingled with the spirit of the prophets.

هست قرآن حالهای انبیا
The Qur'án is (a description of) the states of the prophets,
ماهیان بحر پاک کبریا
(who are) the fishes of the holy sea of (Divine) Majesty.

ور بخوانی و نه‌ای قرآن‌پذیر
And if you read and do not accept (take to heart) the Qur'án,
انبیا و اولیا را دیده گیر
suppose you have seen the prophets and saints (what will that avail you?);

ور پذیرایی چو بر خوانی قصص
But if you are accepting (the Qur'án), when you read the stories (of the prophets),
مرغ جانت تنگ آید در قفس
the bird, your soul, will be distressed in its cage.

مرغ کو اندر قفس زندانیست
The bird that is a prisoner in a cage,
می‌نجوید رستن از نادانیست
(if it) is not seeking to escape, 'tis from ignorance.

روحهایی کز قفسها رسته‌اند
The spirits which have escaped from their cages
انبیاء رهبر شایسته‌اند
are the prophets, (those) worthy guides.

از برون آوازشان آید ز دین
From without comes their voice, (telling) of religion,
که ره رستن ترا اینست این
(and crying), "This, this is the way of escape for thee.

ما بذین رستیم زین تنگین قفس
By this we escaped from this narrow cage:
جز که این ره نیست چارهٔ این قفس
there is no means of escape from this cage but this way,

خویش را رنجور سازی زار زار
(That) thou shouldst make thyself ill, exceedingly wretched,
تا ترا بیرون کنند از اشتهار
in order that thou mayst be let out from (the cage of) reputation."

که اشتهار خلق بند محکمست
Worldly reputation is a strong chain:
در ره این از بند آهن کی کمست
chain: in the Way how is this less than a chain of iron?

◆◉◆◉

قصهٔ بازرگان کی طوطی محبوس او را پیغام داد به طوطیان هندوستان هنگام رفتن به تجارت
The story of the merchant to whom the parrot gave a message for the parrots of India on the occasion of his going (thither) to trade.

بود بازرگان و او را طوطیی
There was a merchant, and he had a parrot
در قفس محبوس زیبا طوطیی
imprisoned in a cage, a pretty parrot.

چونک بازرگان سفر را ساز کرد
When the merchant made ready for travel
سوی هندستان شدن آغاز کرد
and was about to depart to India,

هر غلام و هر کنیزک را ز جود
Because of his generosity he said to each male slave and each handmaid,
گفت بهر تو چه آرم گوی زود
"What shall I bring (home) for you? Tell (me) quickly."

هر یکی از وی مرادی خواست کرد
Each one asked him for some object of desire:
جمله را وعده بداد آن نیک مرد
that good man gave his promise to them all.

گفت طوطی را چه خواهی ارمغان
He said to the parrot, "What present would you like me
کارمت از خطهٔ هندوستان
to bring for you from the land of India?"

گفتش آن طوطی که آنجا طوطیان
The parrot said, "When thou seest the parrots there,
چون ببینی کن ز حال من بیان
explain my plight (and say),

کان فلان طوطی که مشتاق شماست
Such and such a parrot, who is longing for you,
از قضای آسمان در حبس ماست
is in my prison by the destiny of Heaven.

بر شما کرد او سلام و داد خواست
She salutes you and asks for justice and desires (to learn)
وز شما چاره و ره ارشاد خواست
from you the means and way of being rightly guided.

گفت می شاید که من در اشتیاق
She says, "Is it meet that I in yearning (after you)
جان دهم اینجا بمیرم در فراق
should give up the ghost and die here in separation?

این روا باشد که من در بند سخت
Is this right—(that) I (should be) in grievous bondage,
گه شما بر سبزه گاهی بر درخت
while ye are now on green plants, now on trees?

این چنین باشد وفای دوستان
The faith kept by friends, is it like this?
من درین حبس و شما در گلستان
I in this prison and ye in the rose-garden.

یاد آرید ای مهان زین مرغ زار
O ye noble ones, call to mind this piteous bird,
یک صبوحی درمیان مرغزار
a morning-draught amongst the meadows!

یاد یاران یار را میمون بود
Happy it is for a friend to be remembered by friends,
خاصه کان لیلی و این مجنون بود
in particular, when that (beloved) is Laylá and this (lover) Majnún.

ای حریفان بت موزون خود
O ye who consort with your charming and adored one,
من قدحها می‌خورم پر خون خود
am I to be drinking cups filled with my own blood?

یک قدح می‌نوش کن بر یاد من
(O thou who art my beloved), quaff one cup of wine in memory of me,
گر نمی‌خواهی که بدهی داد من
if thou desirest to do me justice,

یا بیاد این فتادهٔ خاک‌بیز
Or (at least), when thou hast drunk,
چونک خوردی جرعه‌ای بر خاک ریز
spill one draught on the earth in memory of this fallen one who sifts dust.

ای عجب آن عهد و آن سوگند کو
Oh, where, I wonder, is that covenant and oath?
وعده‌های آن لب چون قند کو
Where are the promises of that lip like candy?

گر فراق بنده از بد بندگیست
If thy having forsaken thy slave is because of (his) ill service (to thee)—when thou doest ill to the ill-doer,
چون تو با بد بد کنی پس فرق چیست
then what is the difference (between master and slave)?

ای بدی که تو کنی در خشم و جنگ
Oh, the ill thou doest in wrath and quarrel
با طرب تر از سماع و بانگ چنگ
is more delightful than music and the sound of the harp.

ای جفای تو ز دولت خوبتر
Oh, thy cruelty is better than felicity,
و انتقام تو ز جان محبوبتر
and thy vengeance dearer than life.

نار تو اینست نورت چون بود
This is thy fire: how (what) must be thy light!
ماتم این تا خود که سورت چون بود
This is (thy) mourning, so how (what) indeed must be thy festival!

از حلاوتها که دارد جور تو
In respect of the sweetnesses which thy cruelty hath,
وز لطافت کس نیابد غور تو
and in respect of thy beauty, no one gets to the bottom of thee.

نالم و ترسم که او باور کند
I complain, and (yet) I fear lest he believe me
وز کرم آن جور را کمتر کند
and from kindness make that cruelty less.

عاشقم بر قهر و بر لطفش بجد
I am exceedingly enamoured of his violence and his gentleness:
بوالعجب من عاشق این هر دو ضد
'tis marvelous (that) I (am) in love with both these contraries.

والله ار زین خار در بستان شوم
By God, if (I escape) from this thorn (of sorrow) and enter the garden (of joy),
همچو بلبل زین سبب نالان شوم
because of this I shall begin to moan like the nightingale.

این عجب بلبل که بگشاید دهان
This is a wondrous nightingale that opens his mouth
تا خورد او خار را با گلستان
to eat thorns and roses together.

این چه بلبل این نهنگ آتشیست
What nightingale is this? (Nay), 'tis a fiery monster:
جمله ناخوشها ز عشق او را خوشیست
because of (his) love all unsweet things are sweetness to him.

عاشق کلست و خود کلست او
He is a lover of the Universal, and he himself is the Universal:
عاشق خویشست و عشق خویش‌جو
he is in love with himself and seeking his own love.

❖◉❖◉❖

صفت اجنحهٔ طیور عقول الهی
Description of the wings of the birds that are Divine Intelligences.

قصهٔ طوطی جان زین سان بود
Such-like is the tale of the parrot which is the soul:
کو کسی کو محرم مرغان بود
where is that one who is the confidant of (the spiritual) birds?

کو یکی مرغی ضعیفی بی‌گناه
Where is a bird, weak and innocent,
و اندرون او سلیمان با سپاه
and within him Solomon with (all) his host?

چون بنالد زار بی‌شکر و گله
When he moans bitterly, without thanksgiving or complaint,
افتد اندر هفت گردون غلغله
complaint, a noise of tumult falls on (arises in) the Seven Spheres (of Heaven).

هر دمش صد نامه صد پیک از خدا
At every moment (there come) to him from God a hundred missives, a hundred couriers:
یا ربی زو شصت لبیک از خدا
from him one (cry of) "O my Lord!" and from God a hundred (cries of) "Labbayka

زلت او به ز طاعت نزد حق
In the sight of God his backsliding is better than obedience;
پیش کفرش جمله ایمانها خلق
beside his infidelity all faiths are tattered (worthless).

هر دمی او را یکی معراج خاص
Every moment he hath an ascension (to God) peculiar to himself:
بر سر تاجش نهد صد تاج خاص
He (God) lays upon his crown a hundred peculiar crowns.

صورتش بر خاک و جان بر لامکان
His form is on earth and his spirit in "no-place,"
لامکانی فوق وهم سالکان
a "no-place" beyond the imagination of travellers (on the mystic Way):

لامکانی نه که در فهم آیدت
Not such a "no-place" that it should come into thy understanding
هر دمی در وی خیالی زایدت
a fancy about it should be born in thee every moment;

بل مکان و لامکان در حکم او
Nay, place and "no-place" are in his control,
همچو در حکم بهشتی چار جو
just as the four (Paradisal) rivers are in the control of one who dwells in Paradise.

شرح این کوته کن و رخ زین بتاب
Cut short the explanation of this and avert thy face from it:
دم مزن والله اعلم بالصواب
do not breathe a word (more)—and God knows best what is right.

باز می‌گردیم ما ای دوستان
We return from this (matter), O friends,
سوی مرغ و تاجر و هندوستان
to the bird and the merchant and India.

مرد بازرگان پذیرفت این پیام
The merchant accepted this message
کو رساند سوی جنس از وی سلام
that he would convey the greeting from her (the parrot) to her congeners.

دیدن خواجه طوطیان هندوستان را در دشت و پیغام رسانیدن از آن طوطی
How the merchant saw the parrots of India in the plain and delivered the parrot's message.

چونک تا اقصای هندستان رسید
When he reached the farthest bounds of India,
در بیابان طوطیی چندی بدید
he saw a number of parrots in the plain.

مرکب استانید پس آواز داد
He halted his beast; then he gave voice,
آن سلام و آن امانت باز داد
delivered the greeting and (discharged) the trust.

طوطیی زان طوطیان لرزید بس
One of those parrots trembled exceedingly,
اوفتاد و مرد و بگسستش نفس
fell, and died, and its breath stopped.

شد پشیمان خواجه از گفت خبر
The merchant repented of having told the news,
گفت رفتم در هلاک جانور
and said, "I have gone about to destroy the creature.

این مگر خویشست با آن طوطیک
This one, surely, is kin to that little parrot (of mine):
این مگر دو جسم بود و روح یک
they must have been two bodies and one spirit.

این چرا کردم چرا دادم پیام
Why did I do this? Why did I give the message?
سوختم بیچاره را زین گفت خام
I have consumed the poor creature by this raw (foolish) speech."

این زبان چون سنگ و هم آهن وشست
This tongue is like stone and is also fire-like,
وآنچه بجهد از زبان چون آتشست
and that which springs from the tongue is like fire.

سنگ و آهن را مزن بر هم گزاف
Do not vainly strike stone and iron against each other,
گه ز روی نقل و گه از روی لاف
now for the sake of relating (a story), now for the sake of boasting,

زانک تاریکست و هر سو پنبه زار
Because it is dark, and on every side are fields of cotton:
درمیان پنبه چون باشد شرار
how should sparks be amongst cotton?

ظالم آن قومی که چشمان دوختند
Iniquitous are those persons who shut their eyes
زان سخنها عالمی را سوختند
by such (vain) words set a whole world ablaze.

عالمی را یک سخن ویران کند
A single word lays waste a (whole) world,
روبهان مرده را شیران کند
turns dead foxes into lions.

جانها در اصل خود عیسی‌دمند
Spirits in their original nature have the (life-giving) breath of Jesus,
یک زمان زخمند و گاهی مرهمند
(but while they remain embodied) one breath of it (the spirit) is a wound, and the other a plaster

گر حجاب از جانها بر خاستی
If the (bodily) screen were removed from the spirits,
گفت هر جانی مسیح آساستی
the speech of every spirit would be like (the breath of) the Messiah.

گر سخن خواهی که گویی چون شکر
If you wish to utter words like sugar,
صبر کن از حرص و این حلوا مخور
refrain from concupiscence and do not eat this sweetmeat (the desires of the flesh).

صبر باشد مشتهای زیرکان
Self-control is the thing desired by the intelligent;
هست حلوا آرزوی کودکان
sweetmeat is what children long for.

هرکه صبر آورد گردون بر رود
Whoever practises self-control ascends to Heaven,
هر که حلوا خورد واپس‌تر رود
whoever eats sweetmeat falls farther behind.

تفسیر قول فریدالدین عطار قدس الله روحه
Commentary on the saying of Farídu'ddín 'Attár, -may God sanctify his spirit-

تو صاحب نفسی ای غافل میان خاک خون می‌خوری که صاحب‌دل اگر زهری خورد آن انگبین باشد
"Thou art a sensualist: O heedless one, drink blood (mortify thyself) amidst the dust (of thy bodily existence), For if the spiritualist drink a poison, it will be (to him as) an antidote

صاحب دل را ندارد آن زیان
It does not harm the spiritualist (saint)

گر خورد او زهر قاتل را عیان
he drink deadly poison for all to see,

زانک صحت یافت و از پرهیز رست
Because he has attained to (spiritual) health and has been set free from (the need for) abstinence,

طالب مسکین میان تب درست
(while) the poor seeker (of God) is (still) in the (state of) fever.

گفت پیغامبر که ای مرد جری
The Prophet said, "O bold seeker, beware!

هان مکن با هیچ مطلوبی مری
Do not contend with anyone who is sought."

در تو نمرودیست آتش در مرو
In thee is a Nimrod: do not go into the fire.

رفت خواهی اول ابراهیم شو
If thou wish to go in, first become Abraham!

چون نه‌ای سباح و نه دریایی
When thou art neither a swimmer nor a seaman,

در میفکن خویش از خودرایی
do not cast thyself (into the sea) from a (feeling of) self-conceit.

او ز آتش ورد احمر آورد
He (the saint) fetches pearls from the bottom of the sea,

از زیانها سود بر سر آورد
from losses he brings gain to the surface.

کاملی گر خاک گیرد زر شود
If a perfect man (saint) take earth, it becomes gold;

ناقص ار زر برد خاکستر شود
if an imperfect one has carried away gold, it becomes ashes.

چون قبول حق بود آن مرد راست
Since that righteous man is accepted of God,

دست او در کارها دست خداست
his hand in (all) things is the hand of God.

دست ناقص دست شیطانست و دیو
The hand of the imperfect man is the hand of Devil and demon
زانک اندر دام تکلیفست و ریو
because he is in the trap of imposition and guile.

جهل آید پیش او دانش شود
If ignorance come to him (the perfect man), it becomes knowledge,
جهل شد علمی که در منکر رود
(but) the knowledge that goes into the imperfect man becomes ignorance.

هرچه گیرد علتی علت شود
Whatever an ill man takes becomes illness,
کفر گیرد کاملی ملت شود
(but) if a perfect man takes infidelity, it becomes religion.

ای مری کرده پیاده با سوار
thou who, being on foot, hast contended with a horseman,
سر نخواهی برد اکنون پای دار
thou wilt not save thy head. Now hold thy foot (desist)!

◆◉◆◉◆

تعظیم ساحران مر موسی را علیه‌السلام کی چه می‌فرمایی اول تو اندازی عصا
How the magicians paid respect to Moses, on whom be peace, saying, "What dost thou command? Wilt thou cast down thy rod first, or shall we?"

ساحران در عهد فرعون لعین
The magicians in the time of the accursed Pharaoh,
چون مری کردند با موسی بکین
when they contended with Moses in enmity,

لیک موسی را مقدم داشتند
Yet gave Moses the precedence
ساحران او را مکرم داشتند
the magicians held him in honour

زانک گفتندش که فرمان آن تست
Because they said to him, "'Tis for thee to command:
گر همی خواهی عصا تو فکن نخست
(if) thou wishest to be the first, do thou cast down thy rod first (of all)."

گفت نی اول شما ای ساحران
"Nay," said he, "first do ye, O magicians,
افکنید آن مکرها را درمیان
cast down those tricks (objects of enchantment) into the middle (where all can see them)."

این قدر تعظیم دینشان را خرید
This amount of respect purchased their (belief in) (the true) religion,
کز مری آن دست و پاهاشان برید
so that it (the true belief) cut off the hands and feet of their contention

ساحران چون حق او بشناختند
When the magicians acknowledged his (Moses') right,
دست و پا در جرم آن در باختند
they sacrificed their hands and feet (as a penance) for the sin of that (contention).

لقمه و نکته‌ست کامل را حلال
To the perfect man (every) mouthful (of food) and (every) saying is lawful.
تو نه‌ای کامل مخور می‌باش لال
Thou art not perfect: do not eat, be mute,

چون تو گوشی او زبان نی جنس تو
Inasmuch as thou art an ear and he a tongue,
گوشها را حق بفرمود انصتوا
not thy congener: God said to the ears, "Be silent."

کودک اول چون بزاید شیرنوش
When the sucking babe is born,
مدتی خامش بود او جمله گوش
at first it keeps silence for a while, it is all ear.

مدتی می‌بایدش لب دوختن
For a while it must close its lips
از سخن تا او سخن آموختن
from speech, until it learns to speak;

ور نباشد گوش و تی‌تی می‌کند
And if it is not (silent like) an ear but makes babbling sounds,
خویشتن را گنگ گیتی می‌کند
it makes itself the dumbest creature in the world.

کر اصلی کش نبد ز آغاز گوش
He that is deaf by nature, he that had no ear at the beginning,
لال باشد کی کند در نطق جوش
is dumb: how should he burst into speech?

زانک اول سمع باید نطق را
Since, in order to speak, one must first hear,
سوی منطق از ره سمع اندر آ
do thou come to speech by the way of hearing.

وادخلوا الابیات من ابوابها
Enter ye the houses by their doors,
واطلبوا الاغراض فی اسبابها
and seek ye the ends in their causes.

نطق کان موقوف راه سمع نیست
There is no speech independent of the way
جز که نطق خالق بی‌طمع نیست
of hearing except the speech of the Creator who is without want.

مبدعست او تابع استاد نی
He is the Originator, He follows no master;
مسند جمله ورا اسناد نی
He is the support of all things, He hath no support,

باقیان هم در حرف هم در مقال
(While) the rest, (engaged) in handicrafts and talk,
تابع استاد و محتاج مثال
follow a master and have need of a pattern.

زین سخن گر نیستی بیگانه ای
If thou art not alien to (unfit to hear) this discourse,
دلق و اشکی گیر در ویرانه‌ای
assume the frock of a dervish and (take to shedding) tears in some deserted place,

زانک آدم زان عتاب از اشک رست
Because Adam by means of tears escaped from that reproof:
اشک تر باشد دم توبه پرست
moist tears are the breath (speech) of the penitent.

بهر گریه آمد آدم بر زمین
For weeping's sake Adam came (down) to the earth,
تا بود گریان و نالان و حزین
that he might be weeping and moaning and sorrowful.

آدم از فردوس و از بالای هفت
Adam, (cast out) from Paradise and from above the Seven (Heavens),
پای ماچان از برای عذر رفت
went to the "she-row" for the purpose of excusing himself.

گر ز پشت آدمی وز صلب او
If thou art from the back of Adam and from his loins,
در طلب می‌باش هم در طلب او
be constant in seeking (forgiveness) amongst his company.

ز آتش دل و آب دیده نقل ساز
Prepare a dessert of heart-fire (burning grief) and eye-water
بوستان از ابر و خورشیدست باز
the garden is made open (blooming) by cloud and sun.

تو چه دانی ذوق آب دیدگان
What dost thou know of the taste of the water of the eyes?
عاشق نانی تو چون نادیدگان
Thou art a lover of bread, like the blind (beggars).

گر تو این انبان ز نان خالی کنی
If thou make this wallet empty of bread,
پر ز گوهرهای اجلالی کنی
thou wilt make it full of glorious jewels.

طفل جان از شیر شیطان باز کن
Wean the babe, thy soul, from the Devil's milk,
بعد از آنش با ملک انباز کن
and after that make it consort with the Angel.

تا تو تاریک و ملول و تیره‌ای
Whilst thou art dark and vexed and gloomy,
دان که با دیو لعین همشیره‌ای
know that thou art sucking from the same breast as the accursed Devil.

لقمه‌ای کو نور افزود و کمال
The mouthful that gave increase of light and perfection
آن بود آورده از کسب حلال
is obtained from lawful earnings.

روغنی کاید چراغ ما کشد
The oil that comes and quenches our lamp
آب خوانش چون چراغی را کشد
when it quenches a lamp, call it water.

علم و حکمت زاید از لقمهٔ حلال
From the lawful morsel are born knowledge and wisdom;
عشق و رقت آید از لقمهٔ حلال
from the lawful morsel come love and tenderness.

چون ز لقمه تو حسد بینی و دام
When from a morsel thou seest (arise) envy and guile,
جهل و غفلت زاید آن را دان حرام
ignorance and heedlessness are born (of it), know that it is unlawful.

هیچ گندم کاری و جو بر دهد
Wilt thou sow wheat and will it produce barley?
دیده‌ای اسپی که کرهٔ خر دهد
Hast thou seen a mare bring forth an ass's colt?

لقمه تخمست و برش اندیشه‌ها
The morsel is seed, and thoughts are its fruit;
لقمه بحر و گوهرش اندیشه‌ها
the morsel is the sea, and thoughts are its pearls

زاید از لقمهٔ حلال اندر دهان
From the lawful morsel in the mouth is born
میل خدمت عزم رفتن آن جهان
the inclination to serve (God) and the resolve to go to yonder world.

❖❖❖

باز گفتن بازرگان با طوطی آنچه دید از طوطیان هندوستان
How the merchant related to the parrot what he had witnessed on the part of the parrots of India.

کرد بازرگان تجارت را تمام
The merchant finished his trading
باز آمد سوی منزل دوستکام
and returned home glad at heart.

هر غلامی را بیاورد ارمغان
He brought a present for every male slave,
هر کنیزک را ببخشید او نشان
he gave a token to every slave-girl.

گفت طوطی ارمغان بنده کو
"Where is my present?" asked the parrot.
آنچه دیدی و آنچه گفتی بازگو
"Relate what thou hast said and seen."

گفت نه من خود پشیمانم از آن
Nay," said he, "indeed I am repenting of that (which I said),
دست خود خایان و انگشتان گزان
gnawing my hand and biting my fingers (in remorse).

من چرا پیغام خامی از گزاف
Why, from ignorance and folly,
بردم از بی‌دانشی و از نشاف
did I idly bear (such) an inconsiderate message?"

گفت ای خواجه پشیمانی ز چیست
"O master," said the parrot, "what is thy repentance for?
چیست آن کین خشم و غم را مقتضیست
What is it that causes this anger and grief?"

گفت گفتم آن شکایتهای تو
I told thy complaints," said he,
با گروهی طوطیان همتای تو
to a company of parrots resembling thee.

آن یکی طوطی ز دردت بوی برد
One parrot got scent of (understood) thy pain:
زهره‌اش بدرید و لرزید و بمرد
her heart broke, and she trembled and died.

من پشیمان گشتم این گفتن چه بود
I became sorry, (thinking) 'why did I say this?'
لیک چون گفتم پشیمانی چه سود
but what was the use of repenting after I had said it?"

نکته‌ای کان جست ناگه از زبان
Know that a word which suddenly shot from the tongue
همچو تیری دان که آن جست از کمان
tongue is like an arrow shot from the bow.

وا نگردد از ره آن تیر ای پسر
O son, that arrow does not turn back on its way:
بند باید کرد سیلی را ز سر
you must dam a torrent at the source.

چون گذشت از سر جهانی را گرفت
When it left the source behind, it swept over a world
گر جهان ویران کند نبود شگفت
if it lays waste the world, 'tis no wonder.

فعل را در غیب اثرها زادنیست
There is an unseen bringing forth of effects to (our) action,
و آن موالیدش بحکم خلق نیست
and the results born of it are not in the control of (human) creatures:

بی‌شریکی جمله مخلوق خداست
Those results are all created by God without any partner,
آن موالید ار چه نسبتشان به ماست
though they are imputed to us.

زید پرانید تیری سوی عمرو
Zayd let fly an arrow in the direction of 'Amr:
عمرو را بگرفت تیرش همچو نمر
his arrow gripped 'Amr like a leopard.

مدت سالی همی زایید درد
During a long time, a (whole) year, it was producing pain:
دردها را آفریند حق نه مرد
pains are created by God, not by man.

زید رامی آن دم ار مرد از وجل
If Zayd who shot (the arrow) died of fright at the moment
دردها می‌زاید آنجا تا اجل
pains are continually being produced there (in 'Amr's body) until ('Amr's) death.

زان موالید وجع چون مرد او
Inasmuch as he ('Amr) died from the results of the hurt (inflicted on him),
زید را از اول سبب قتال گو
for this cause call Zayd, who shot (the arrow), the murderer.

آن وجعها را بدو منسوب دار
Impute those pains to him,
گرچه هست آن جمله صنع کردگار
though all of them are the work of the Creator.

همچنین کشت و دم و دام و جماع
So with sowing and breathing (speaking) and (laying) snares and sexual intercourse
آن موالیدست حق را مستطاع
the results of those (actions) are amenable to (determined by the will of) God.

اولیا را هست قدرت از اله
The saints possess power (derived) from God:
تیر جسته باز آرندش ز راه
they turn back from its course the arrow that has sped.

بسته درهای موالید از سبب
When the saint repents, he closes the doors of the results
چون پشیمان شد ولی زان دست رب
from the cause by that hand (power) of the Lord.

گفته ناگفته کند از فتح باب
Through the opening of the door (of Divine grace), he makes unsaid what has been said,
تا از آن نه سیخ سوزد نه کباب
so that neither spit nor roast-meat is burnt thereby.

از همه دلها که آن نکته شنید
He wipes out the saying from all the minds that heard it,
آن سخن را کرد محو و ناپدید
and makes it imperceptible

گرت برهان باید و حجت مها
O sire, if thou must needs have demonstration and proof (of this),
بازخوان من آیة او ننسها
"(Whatever) verse (We cancel) or cause to be forgotten

آیت انسوکم ذکری بخوان
Read the verse "They made you forget My warning":
قدرت نسیان نهادنشان بدان
acknowledge their (the saints') power to put forgetfulness (in men's hearts).

چون به تذکیر و به نسیان قادرند
Since they are able to make (you) remember and forget,
بر همه دلهای خلقان قاهرند
they are mighty over all the hearts of (God's) creatures.

چون بنسیان بست او راه نظر
When he (the saint) has blocked the road of (your) mental perception by means of forgetfulness
کار نتوان کرد ور باشد هنر
it is impossible (for you) to act, even if there be virtue (in you).

خلتم سخریة اهل السمو
Think ye those exalted ones are a laughing-stock?
از نبی خوانید تا انسوکم
Recite from the Qur'án as far as (the words) "They made you forget."

صاحب ده پادشاه جسمهاست
He that owns a village is king over bodies;
صاحب دل شاه دلهای شماست
he that owns a heart is king over your hearts.

فرع دید آمد عمل بی هیچ شک
Without any doubt, action (practice) is a branch of (subordinate to) seeing (theory):
پس نباشد مردم الا مردمک
therefore, Man is nothing but "the little man" (the pupil of the eye).

من تمام این نیارم گفت از آن
I dare not expound the whole of this (subject):
منع می آید ز صاحب مرکزان
hindrance thereto is coming from those who are at the centre.

چون فراموشی خلق و یادشان با ویست و او رسد فریادشان
Inasmuch as the forgetfulness and recollection of (God's) creatures are with him (depend on the perfect saint), and he comes at their call for help,

صد هزاران نیک و بد را آن بهی
hundreds of thousands of good and evil (thoughts),

می‌کند هر شب ز دلهاشان تهی
Every night that glorious one is emptying from their hearts

روز دلها را از آن پر می‌کند
in the daytime he is filling their hearts

آن صدفها را پر از در می‌کند
he is filling those oystershells with pearls.

آن همه اندیشهٔ پیشانها
By (Divine) guidance (after sleep is past) all those thoughts of

می‌شناسند از هدایت خانها
former things recognize the spirits (to which they were attached).

پیشه و فرهنگ تو آید به تو
Your handicraft and skill come (back) to you,

تا در اسباب بگشاید به تو
that they may open to you the door of (ways and) means.

پیشهٔ زرگر بهنگر نشد
The goldsmith's craft did not go to the ironsmith;

خوی این خوش‌خو با آن منکر نشد
the disposition of the good-natured man did not go to the disagreeable one.

پیشه‌ها و خلقها همچون جهاز
On the day of Resurrection, the handicrafts and dispositions will come,

سوی خصم آیند روز رستخیز
like articles of property, to the claimant (owner).

پیشه‌ها و خلقها از بعد خواب
After sleep also, the handicrafts and dispositions

واپس آید هم به خصم خود شتاب
come back in haste to him that claims them as his.

پیشه‌ها و اندیشه‌ها در وقت صبح
At the hour of dawn the handicrafts and thoughts went to the

هم بدآنجا شد که بود آن حسن و قبح
same place where that good and evil (formerly) were.

چون کبوترهای پیک از شهرها
Like carrier pigeons,
سوی شهر خویش آرد بهرها
they bring things useful (to know) from (other) cities to their own city.

شنیدن آن طوطی حرکت آن طوطیان و مردن آن طوطی در قفص و نوحهٔ خواجه بر وی
How the parrot heard what those parrots had done, and died in the cage, and how the merchant made lament for her.

چون شنید آن مرغ کان طوطی چه کرد
When the bird heard what that (other) parrot had done,
پس بلرزید اوفتاد و گشت سرد
she trembled exceedingly, fell, and became cold.

خواجه چون دیدش فتاده همچنین
The merchant, seeing her thus fallen,
بر جهید و زد کله را بر زمین
sprang up and dashed his cap on the ground.

چون بدین رنگ و بدین حالش بدید
When he saw her in this guise and in this state,
خواجه بر جست و گریبان را درید
the merchant sprang forward and tore the breast of his garment.

گفت ای طوطی خوب خوش حنین
He said, "O beautiful parrot with thy sweet cry,
این چه بودت این چرا گشتی چنین
what is this that has happened to thee? Why hast thou become like this?

ای دریغا مرغ خوش‌آواز من
Oh, alas for my sweet-voiced bird!
ای دریغا همدم و همراز من
Oh, alas for my bosom-friend and confidant!

ای دریغا مرغ خوش‌الحان من
Oh, alas for my melodious bird,
راح روح و روضه و ریحان من
the wine of my spirit and my garden and my sweet basil!

گر سلیمان را چنین مرغی بدی
Had Solomon possessed a bird like this,
کی خود او مشغول آن مرغان شدی
how indeed should he have become occupied with those (other) birds?

ای دریغا مرغ کارزان یافتم
Oh, alas for the bird which I gained cheaply,
زود روی از روی او بر تافتم
and (so) soon turned my face away from her countenance!

ای زبان تو بس زیانی بر وری
O tongue, thou art a great damage to me,
چون توی گویا چه گویم من ترا
(but) since thou art speaking, what should I say to thee?

ای زبان هم آتش و هم خرمنی
O tongue, thou art both the fire and the stack:
چند این آتش درین خرمن زنی
how long wilt thou dart this fire upon this stack?

در نهان جان از تو افغان می‌کند
Secretly my soul is groaning because of thee,
گرچه هر چه گوییش آن می‌کند
although it is doing whatsoever thou biddest it.

ای زبان هم گنج بی‌پایان توی
O tongue, thou art a treasure without end. O tongue,
ای زبان هم رنج بی‌درمان توی
thou art also a disease without remedy.

هم صفیر و خدعهٔ مرغان توی
Thou art at once a whistle and decoy for birds,
هم انیس وحشت هجران توی
and a comforter in the desolation of absence (from the Beloved).

چند امانم می‌دهی ای بی امان
How long wilt thou grant me mercy, O merciless one,
ای تو زه کرده به کین من کمان
O thou who hast drawn the bow to take vengeance on me?

نک بپرانیده‌ای مرغ مرا
Lo, thou hast made my bird fly away.
در چراگاه ستم کم کن چرا
Do not browse (any more) in the pasture of injustice!

یا جواب من بگو یا داد ده
Either answer me or give redress or mention to me
یا مرا ز اسباب شادی یاد ده
(what will be) the means of (producing) joy.

ای دریغا نور ظلمت سوز من
Oh, alas for my darkness-consuming dawn!
ای دریغا صبح روز افروز من
Oh, alas for my day-enkindling light!

ای دریغا مرغ خوش پرواز من
Oh, alas for my bird of goodly flight,
ز انتها پریده تا آغاز من
that has flown from my end (my last state) to my beginning (my first state).

عاشق رنجست نادان تا ابد
The ignorant man is in love with pain unto everlasting.
خیز لا اقسم بخوان تا فی کبد
Arise and read (in the Qur'án) I swear as far as (the words) in trouble.

از کبد فارغ بدم با روی تو
With thy face I was free from trouble,
وز زبد صافی بدم در جوی تو
and in thy river I was unsoiled by froth.

این دریغاها خیال دیدنست
These cries of 'Alas' are (caused by) the phantasy (idea) of seeing (the Beloved)
وز وجود نقد خود ببریدنست
and (by) separation from my present existence.

غیرت حق بود و با حق چاره نیست
'Twas the jealousy of God, and there is no device against God:
کو دلی کز عشق حق صد پاره نیست
where is a heart that is not (shattered) in a hundred pieces by God's love?

غیرت آن باشد که او غیر همه ست
The jealousy (of God) is this, that He is other than all things,
آنک افزون از بیان و دمدمه ست
that He is beyond explanation and the noise of words.

ای دریغا اشک من دریا بدی
Oh, alas! Would that my tears were an ocean,
تا نثار دلبر زیبا بدی
that they might be strewn as an offering to the fair charmer!

طوطی من مرغ زیرکسار من
My parrot, my clever-headed bird,
ترجمان فکرت و اسرار من
the interpreter of my thought and inmost consciousness,

هرچه روزی داد و ناداد آیدم
She has told me from the first, that I might remember it,
او ز اول گفته تا یاد آیدم
whatsoever should come to me as my allotted portion of right and wrong."

طوطیی کآید ز وحی آواز او
The parrot whose voice comes from (Divine) inspiration
پیش از آغاز وجود آغاز او
and whose beginning was before the beginning of existence

اندرون تست آن طوطی نهان
That parrot is hidden within thee:
عکس او را دیده تو بر این و آن
thou hast seen the reflexion of her upon this and that

می برد شادیت را تو شاد ازو
She takes away thy joy, and because of her thou art rejoicing:
می‌پذیری ظلم را چون داد ازو
thou receivest injury from her as though it were justice.

ای که جان را بهر تن می‌سوختی
O thou who wert burning the soul for the body's sake,
سوختی جان را و تن افروختی
thou hast burned (destroyed) the soul and illumined (delighted) the body.

سوختم من سوخته خواهد کسی
I am burning (with love of God): does anyone want tinder,
تا زمن آتش زند اندر خسی
let him set his rubbish ablaze with fire from me.

سوخته چون قابل آتش بود
Inasmuch as tinder is combustible,
سوخته بستان که آتش‌کش بود
take tinder that catches fire (readily).

ای دریغا ای دریغا ای دریغ
O alas, O alas, O alas
کانچنان ماهی نهان شد زیر میغ
that such a moon became hidden under the clouds!

چون زنم دم کآتش دل تیز شد
How should I utter a word? —for the fire in my heart is grown fierce,
شیر هجر آشفته و خونریز شد
the lion of separation (from the Beloved) has become raging and blood-shedding

223

آنک او هشیار خود تندست و مست
One that even when sober is violent and furious,
چون بود چون او قدح گیرد به دست
how will it be when he takes the wine-cup in his hand?

شیر مستی کز صفت بیرون بود
The furious Lion who is beyond description is
از بسیط مرغزار افزون بود
too great for (cannot be contained in) the wide expanse of the meadow

قافیه اندیشم و دلدار من
I am thinking of rhymes, and my Sweetheart says to me,
گویدم مندیش جز دیدار من
Do not think of aught except vision of Me.

خوش نشین ای قافیه‌اندیش من
Sit at thy ease, My rhyme-meditating (friend):
قافیهٔ دولت توی در پیش من
in My presence thou art rhymed with (attached to) felicity.

حرف چه بود تا تو اندیشی از آن
What are words that thou shouldst think of them?
حرف چه بود خار دیوار رزان
What are words? Thorns in the hedge of the vineyard.

حرف و صوت و گفت را بر هم زنم
I will throw word and sound and speech into confusion,
تا که بی این هر سه با تو دم زنم
that without these three I may converse with thee.

آن دمی کز آدمش کردم نهان
That word which I kept hidden from Adam I will speak to thee,
با تو گویم ای تو اسرار جهان
O (thou who art the) consciousness of the world.

آن دمی را که نگفتم با خلیل
(I will tell to thee) that word which I did not communicate to Abraham,
و آن غمی را که نداند جبرئیل
and that pain (love) which Gabriel does not know."

آن دمی کز وی مسیحا دم نزد
That word of which the Messiah (Jesus) breathed not a word God,
حق ز غیرت نیز بی ما هم نزد
from jealousy, did not utter even without má.

ما چه باشد در لغت اثبات و نفی
What is má in language? Positive and negative.
من نه اثباتم منم بی‌ذات و نفی
I am not positive, I am selfless and negated

من کسی در ناکسی در یافتم
I found (true) individuality in non-individuality:
پس کسی در ناکسی در بافتم
therefore, I wove (my) individuality into non-individuality.

جمله شاهان بندهٔ بندهٔ خودند
All kings are enslaved to their slaves,
جمله خلقان مردهٔ مردهٔ خودند
all people are dead (ready to die) for one who dies for them.

جمله شاهان پست پست خویش را
All kings are prostrate before one who is prostrate before them,
جمله خلقان مست مست خویش را
all people are intoxicated with (love for) one who is intoxicated with them.

می‌شود صیاد مرغان را شکار
The fowler becomes a prey to the birds
تا کند ناگه ایشان را شکار
in order that of a sudden he may make them his prey.

بی‌دلان را دلبران جسته بجان
The hearts of heart-ravishers are captivated by those who have lost their hearts (to them):
جمله معشوقان شکار عاشقان
all loved ones are the prey of (their) lovers.

هر که عاشق دیدیش معشوق دان
Whomsoever thou didst deem to be a lover,
کو به نسبت هست هم این و هم آن
regard (him) as the loved one, for relatively he is both this and that.

تشنگان گر آب جویند از جهان
If they that are thirsty seek water from the world,
آب جوید هم به عالم تشنگان
(yet) water too seeks in the world them that are thirsty.

چونک عاشق اوست تو خاموش باش
Inasmuch as He is (thy) lover, do thou be silent:
او چو گوشت می‌کشد تو گوش باش
as He is pulling thine ear, be thou (all) ear.

بند کن چون سیل سیلانی کند
Dam the torrent (of ecstasy) when it runs in flood;
ور نه رسوایی و ویرانی کند
else it will work shame and ruin.

من چه غم دارم که ویرانی بود
What care I though ruin be (wrought)?
زیر ویران گنج سلطانی بود
Under the ruin there is a royal treasure.

غرق حق خواهد که باشد غرق‌تر
He that is drowned in God wishes to be more drowned,
همچو موج بحر جان زیر و زبر
(while) his spirit (is tossed) up and down like the waves of the sea,

زیر دریا خوشتر آید یا زبر
(Asking), "Is the bottom of the sea more delightful, or the top?
تیر او دلکش‌تر آید یا سپر
Is His (the Beloved's) arrow more fascinating, or the shield?"

پاره کردهٔ وسوسه باشی دلا
O heart, thou art torn asunder by evil suggestion
گر طرب را باز دانی از بلا
if thou recognise any difference between joy and woe.

گر مرادت را مذاق شکرست
Although the object of thy desire has the taste of sugar,
بی‌مرادی نه مراد دلبرست
is not absence of any object of desire (in thee) the object of the Beloved's desire?

هر ستاره‌اش خونبهای صد هلال
Every star of His is the blood-price of a hundred new moons:
خون عالم ریختن او را حلال
it is lawful for Him to shed the blood of the (whole) world.

ما بها و خونبها را یافتیم
We gained the price and the blood-price:
جانب جان باختن بشتافتیم
we hastened to gamble our soul away.

ای حیات عاشقان در مردگی
Oh, the life of lovers consists in death:
دل نیابی جز که در دل‌بردگی
thou wilt not win the (Beloved's) heart except in losing thine own.

من دلش جسته به صد ناز و دلال
I sought (to win) His heart with a hundred airs and graces,
او بهانه کرده با من از ملال
(but) He made excuses to me (put me off) in disdain.

گفتم آخر غرق تست این عقل و جان
I said, "After all, this mind and soul (of mine) are drowned in Thee." "Begone," said He,
گفت رو رو بر من این افسون مخوان
begone! Do not chant these spells over Me (do not seek thus to beguile Me).

من ندانم آنچه اندیشیده‌ای
Do not I know what thought thou hast conceived?
ای دو دیده دوست را چون دیده‌ای
O thou who hast seen double, how hast thou regarded the Beloved?

ای گران جهان خوار دیدستی ورا
O gross-spirited one, thou hast held Me in light esteem,
زانک بس ارزان خریدستی ورا
because thou hast bought Me very cheaply.

هرکه او ارزان خرد ارزان دهد
He that buys cheaply gives cheaply:
گوهری طفلی به قرصی نان دهد
a child will give a pearl for a loaf of bread."

غرق عشقی‌ام که غرقست اندرین
I am drowned in a love (so deep) that therein are drowned
عشقهای اولین و آخرین
the first loves and the last.

مجملش گفتم نکردم زان بیان
I have told it summarily, I have not explained it (at length),
ورنه هم افهام سوزد هم زبان
otherwise both (thy) perceptions and (my) tongue would be consumed.

من چو لب گویم لب دریا بود
When I speak of "lip," 'tis the lip (shore) of the Sea;
من چو لا گویم مراد الا بود
when I say "not," the intended meaning is "except."

من ز شیرینی نشستم رو ترش
By reason of (inward) sweetness I sit with sour face:
من ز بسیاری گفتارم خمش
from fullness of speech I am silent,

تا که شیرینی ما از دو جهان
my sweetness may be kept hidden from the two worlds.

در حجاب رو ترش باشد نهان
That in the mask of sour-facedness

تا که در هر گوش ناید این سخن
In order that this subject may not come to every ear,

یک همی گویم ز صد سر لدن
I am telling (only) one out of a hundred esoteric mysteries.

◈◈

تفسیر قول حکیم
Commentary on the saying of the Hakím (Saná'í):

بهرچ از راه و امانی چه کفر آن حرف و چه ایمان بهرچ از دوست دورافتی چه زشت آن نقش و چه زیبا در معنی قوله علیه‌السلام ان سعدا لغیور و انا اغیر من سعد و الله اغیر منی و من غیرته حرم الفواحش ما ظهر منها و ما بطن

"Anything that causes thee to be left behind on the Way, what matter whether it be infidelity or faith? Any form that causes thee to fall far from the Beloved, what matter whether it be ugly or beautiful?"—and (a discourse) on the meaning of the words of the Prophet, on whom be peace: "Verily, Sa'd is jealous, and I am more jealous than Sa'd, and Allah is more jealous than I; and because of His jealousy He hath forbidden foul actions both outward and inward.

جمله عالم زان غیور آمد که حق
The whole world became jealous because God is superior

برد در غیرت برین عالم سبق
to all the world in jealousy.

او چو جانست و جهان چون کالبد
He is like the spirit, and the world is like the body:

کالبد از جان پذیرد نیک و بد
the body receives from the spirit (both) good and evil.

هر که محراب نمازش گشت عین
Anyone whose prayer-niche is turned to the (mystical) revelation,

سوی ایمان رفتنش می‌دان تو شین
do thou regard his going (back) to (the traditional) faith as shameful

هر که شد مر شاه را او جامه دار
Anyone who has become Master of the robes to the King,

هست خسران بهر شاهش اتجار
it is loss for him to traffic on the King's behalf.

هر که با سلطان شود او همنشین
Anyone who becomes the intimate friend of the Sultan,
بر درش شستن بود حیف و غبین
it is an injury and swindle (for him) to wait at his door.

دستبوسش چون رسید از پادشاه
When (the privilege of) kissing the (King's) hand has been bestowed on him by the King,
گر گزیند بوس پا باشد گناه
it is a sin if he prefers to kiss the (King's) foot.

گرچه سر بر پا نهادن خدمتست
Although to lay the head on the (King's) foot is an act of obeisance,
پیش آن خدمت خطا و زلتست
(yet) compared with the former act of obeisance it is a fault and backsliding.

شاه را غیرت بود بر هر که او
The King is jealous of any one who,
بو گزیند بعد از آن که دید رو
after having seen the face, prefers the (mere) scent.

غیرت حق بر مثل گندم بود
To speak in parables, God's jealousy is the wheat,
کاه خرمن غیرت مردم بود
(while) men's jealousy is the straw in the stack.

اصل غیرتها بدانید از اله
Know that the root of (all) jealousies is in God:
آن خلقان فرع حق بی‌اشتباه
those of mankind are an offshoot from God, without resemblance

شرح این بگذارم و گیرم گله
I will leave the explanation of this and will begin to complain
از جفای آن نگار ده دله
will begin to complain of the cruelty of that fickle Beauty.

نالم ایرا ناله‌ها خوش آیدش
I wail because wailings are pleasant to Him:
از دو عالم ناله و غم بایدش
He wants from the two worlds wailing and grief.

چون ننالم تلخ از دستان او
How should I not wail bitterly on account of His deceit,
چون نیم در حلقهٔ مستان او
since I am not in the circle of those intoxicated with Him?

چون نباشم همچو شب بی روز او
How should I not mourn, like night, without His day
بی وصال روی روز افروز او
and without the favour of His day-illuming countenance?

ناخوش او خوش بود در جان من
His unsweetness is sweet in my soul:
جان فدای یار دل رنجان من
may my soul be sacrificed to the Beloved who grieves my heart!

عاشقم بر رنج خویش و درد خویش
I am in love with my grief and pain
بهر خشنودی شاه فرد خویش
for the sake of pleasing my peerless King.

خاک غم را سرمه سازم بهر چشم
I make the dust of sorrow a salve for mine eye,
تا ز گوهر پر شود دو بحر چشم
that the two seas of mine eyes may be filled with pearls.

اشک کان از بهر او بارند خلق
The tears which people shed for His sake
گوهرست و اشک پندارند خلق
are pearls and people think they are tears.

من ز جان جان شکایت می‌کنم
I am complaining of the Soul of the soul,
من نیم شاکی روایت می‌کنم
(but in truth) I am not complaining: I am (only) relating

دل همی‌گوید کزو رنجیده‌ام
My heart is saying, "I am tormented by Him,"
وز نفاق سست می‌خندیده‌ام
and I have (long) been laughing at its poor pretence.

راستی کن ای تو فخر راستان
Do (me) right, O glory of the righteous,
ای تو صدر و من درت را آستان
O Thou who art the dais, and I the threshold of Thy door!

آستانه و صدر در معنی کجاست
Where are threshold and dais in reality?
ما و من کو آن طرف کان یار ماست
In the quarter where our Beloved is, where are "we" and "I"?

ای رهیده جان تو از ما و من
O Thou whose soul is free from "we" and "I,"
ای لطیفهٔ روح اندر مرد و زن
O Thou who art the subtle essence of the spirit in man and woman,

مرد و زن چون یک شود آن یک توی
When man and woman become one, Thou art that One;
چونک یکها محو شد انک توی
when the units are wiped out, lo, Thou art that (Unity).

این من و ما بهر آن بر ساختی
Thou didst contrive this "I" and "we" in order
تا تو با خود نرد خدمت باختی
that Thou mightst play the game of worship with Thyself,

تا من و توها همه یک جان شوند
That all "I's" and "thou's" should become one soul
عاقبت مستغرق جانان شوند
and at last should be submerged in the Beloved.

این همه هست و بیا ای امر کن
All this is (true), and do Thou come, O (Lord of the) Creative Word,
ای منزه از بیا و از سخن
O Thou who transcendest "Come" and (all) speech!

جسم جسمانه تواند دیدنت
The body can see Thee (only) in bodily fashion:
در خیال آرد غم و خندیدنت
It fancies (pictures to itself) Thy sadness or laughter.

دل که او بستهٔ غم و خندیدنست
(such bodily attributes as) sadness and laughter is worthy of seeing Thee
تو مگو کو لایق آن دیدنست
Do not say that the heart that is bound by

آنک او بستهٔ غم و خنده بود
He who is bound by sadness and laughter
او بدین دو عاریت زنده بود
is living by means of these two borrowed (transient and unreal) things.

باغ سبز عشق کو بی منتهاست
In the verdant garden of Love, which is without end,
جز غم و شادی درو بس میوه‌هاست
there are many fruits besides sorrow and joy.

عاشقی زین هر دو حالت برترست
Love is higher than these two states of feeling:
بی بهار و بی خزان سبز و ترست
without spring and without autumn it is (ever) green and fresh.

ده زکات روی خوب ای خوب رو
Pay the tithe on Thy fair face, O Beauteous One:
شرح جان شرحه شرحه بازگو
relate the story of the soul that is rent in pieces,

کز کرشم غمزه‌ای غمازه‌ای
For by the coquetry of a glance One who is given
بر دلم بنهاد داغی تازه‌ای
to glancing amorously has branded my heart anew.

من حلالش کردم ار خونم بریخت
I absolved Him if He shed my blood:
من همی‌گفتم حلال او می گریخت
I was saying, "It is lawful (I absolve Thee)," and He was fleeing (from me).

چون گریزانی ز نالهٔ خاکیان
Since Thou art fleeing from the lament of those who are (as) dust,
غم چه ریزی بر دل غمناکیان
why pourest Thou sorrow on the hearts of the sorrowful?

ای که هر صبحی که از مشرق بتافت
O Thou, whom every dawn that shone from the East found
همچو چشمهٔ مشرقت در جوش یافت
overflowing (with abundant grace) like the bright fountain (of the sun),

چون بهانه دادی این شیدات را
How didst Thou give (nothing but) evasion to Thy frenzied lover,
ای بها نه شکر لبهات را
O Thou the sugar of whose lips hath no price?

ای جهان کهنه را تو جان نو
O Thou who art a new soul to the old world,
از تن بی جان و دل افغان شنو
hear the cry (that comes) from my body (which is) without soul and heart.

شرح گل بگذار از بهر خدا
Leave the tale of the Rose! For God's sake
شرح بلبل گو که شد از گل جدا
set forth the tale of the Nightingale that is parted from the Rose!

از غم و شادی نباشد جوش ما
Our emotion is not caused by grief and joy,
با خیال و وهم نبود هوش ما
our consciousness is not related to fancy and imagination.

حالتی دیگر بود کان نادرست
There is another state (of consciousness), which is rare:
تو مشو منکر که حق بس قادرست
do not thou disbelieve, for God is very mighty.

تو قیاس از حالت انسان مکن
Do not judge from the (normal) state of man,
منزل اندر جور و در احسان مکن
do not abide in wrong-doing and in well-doing.

جور و احسان رنج و شادی حادثست
Wrong-doing and well-doing, grief and joy, are things that come into existence;
حادثان میرند و حقشان وارثست
those who come into existence die; God is their heir.

صبح شد ای صبح را صبح و پناه
'Tis dawn. O Thou who art the support and refuge of the dawn,
عذر مخدومی حسام‌الدین بخواه
ask pardon (for me) of my Lord Husámu'ddín!

عذرخواه عقل کل و جان توی
Thou art He who asketh pardon of the Universal Mind and Soul,
جان جان و تابش مرجان توی
Thou art the Soul of the soul and the Splendour of the coral.

تافت نور صبح و ما از نور تو
The light of dawn has shone forth, and from Thy light we are
در صبوحی با می منصور تو
engaged in drinking the morning-drink with the wine of Thy Mansúr

دادهٔ تو چون چنین دارد مرا
Inasmuch as Thy gift keeps me thus (enravished),
باده کی بود کو طرب آرد مرا
who(what) is (other) wine that it should bring me rapture?

باده در جوشش گدای جوش ماست
Wine in ferment is a beggar suing for our ferment;
چرخ در گردش گدای هوش ماست
Heaven in revolution is a beggar suing for our consciousness.

باده از ما مست شد نه ما ازو
Wine became intoxicated with us, not we with it;
قالب از ما هست شد نه ما ازو
the body came into being from us, not we from it.

ما چو زنبوریم و قالبها چو موم
We are as bees, and bodies are as wax (honeycomb):
خانه خانه کرده قالب را چو موم
we have made the body, cell by cell, like wax.

❀◉❀◉❀

رجوع به حکایت خواجهٔ تاجر
Reverting to the tale of the merchant who went to trade (in India).

بس دراز است این حدیث خواجه گو
This (discourse) is very long. Tell the story of the merchant,
تا چه شد احوال آن مرد نکو
that we may see what happened to that good man.

خواجه اندر آتش و درد و حنین
The merchant in fire (burning grief) and anguish and yearning
صد پراکنده همی‌گفت این چنین
was uttering a hundred distracted phrases like this,

گه تناقض گاه ناز و گه نیاز
Now self-contradiction, now disdain, now supplication,
گاه سودای حقیقت گه مجاز
now passion for reality, now metaphor (unreality).

مرد غرقه گشته جانی می‌کند
The drowning man suffers an agony of soul
دست را در هر گیاهی می‌زند
and clutches at every straw.

تا کدامش دست گیرد در خطر
For fear of (losing) his head (life),
دست و پایی می‌زند از بیم سر
he flings about (both) hand and foot to see whether any one will take his hand (help him) in peril

دوست دارد یار این آشفتگی
The Friend loves this agitation:
کوشش بیهوده به از خفتگی
it is better to struggle vainly than to lie still.

آنک او شاهست او بی‌کار نیست
He who is the King (of all) is not idle,
ناله از وی طرفه کو بیمار نیست
complaint from Him would be a marvel, for He is not ill.

بهر این فرمود رحمان ای پسر
For this reason said the Merciful (God), O son,
کل یوم هو فی شان ای پسر
"Every day He is (busy) in an affair," O son.

اندرین ره می‌تراش و می‌خراش
In this Way be thou ever scraping and scratching (exerting thyself to the utmost):
تا دم آخر دمی فارغ مباش
until thy last breath do not be unoccupied for a moment,

تا دم آخر دمی آخر بود
So that thy last breath may be a last breath
که عنایت با تو صاحب سر بود
in which the (Divine) favour is thy bosomfriend.

هر چه می‌کوشند اگر مرد و زنست
Whatsoever the soul which is in man and woman strives to do,
گوش و چشم شاه جان بر روزنست
the ear and eye of the soul's King are at the window.

◆◉◆◉◆

برون انداختن مرد تاجر طوطی را از قفس و پریدن طوطی مرده
How the merchant cast the parrot out of the cage and how the dead parrot flew away.

بعد از آنش از قفس بیرون فکند
After that, he cast her out of the cage.
طوطیک پرید تا شاخ بلند
The little parrot flew to a lofty bough.

طوطی مرده چنان پرواز کرد
The dead parrot made such a (swift) flight
کآفتاب شرق ترکی تاز کرد
as when the orient sun rushed onward.

خواجه حیران گشت اندر کار مرغ
The merchant was amazed at the action of the bird:
بی‌خبر ناگه بدید اسرار مرغ
without understanding he suddenly beheld the mysteries of the bird.

روی بالا کرد و گفت ای عندلیب
He lifted up his face and said, "O nightingale,
از بیان حال خودمان ده نصیب
give us profit(instruction) by explaining thy case.

او چه کرد آنجا که تو آموختی
What did she (the parrot) do there (in India),
ساختی مکری و ما را سوختی
hat thou didst learn, devise a trick, and burn us (with grief)"?

گفت طوطی کو به فعلم پند داد
The parrot said, "She by her act counselled me
که رها کن لطف آواز و وداد
Abandon thy charm of voice and thy affection (for thy master),

زانک آوازت ترا در بند کرد
Because thy voice has brought thee into bondage':
خویشتن مرده پی این پند کرد
she feigned herself dead for the sake of (giving me) this counsel,

یعنی ای مطرب شده با عام و خاص
Meaning (to say), 'O thou who hast become a singer to high and low,
مرده شو چون من که تا یابی خلاص
become dead like me, that thou mayst gain release.'"

دانه باشی مرغکانت بر چنند
If you are a grain, the little birds will peck you up;
غنچه باشی کودکانت بر کنند
up; if you are a bud, the children will pluck you off.

دانه پنهان کن بکلی دام شو
Hide the grain (bait), become wholly a snare;
غنچه پنهان کن گیاه بام شو
hide the bud, become the grass on the roof.

هر که داد او حسن خود را در مزاد
Anyone who offers his beauty to auction,
صد قضای بد سوی او رو نهاد
a hundred evil fates set out towards him (and overtake him).

چشمها و خشمها و رشکها
Plots and angers and envies pour upon his head,
بر سرش ریزد چو آب از مشکها
like water from waterskins.

دشمنان او را ز غیرت می‌درند
Foes tear him to pieces from jealousy;
دوستان هم روزگارش می‌برند
even friends take his lifetime away.

آنک غافل بود از کشت و بهار
He that was heedless of the sowing and the springtide,
او چه داند قیمت این روزگار
how should he know the value of this lifetime?

در پناه لطف حق باید گریخت
You must flee to the shelter of God's grace,
کو هزاران لطف بر ارواح ریخت
who shed thousand-fold grace upon (our) spirits

تا پناهی یابی آنگه چون پناه
That you may find a shelter. Then how (will you lack) shelter?
آب و آتش مر ترا گردد سپاه
Water and fire will become your army.

نوح و موسی را نه دریا یار شد
Did not the sea become a friend to Noah and Moses?
نه بر اعداشان بکین قهار شد
Did it not become overbearing in vengeance against their enemies?

آتش ابراهیم را نه قلعه بود
Was not the fire a fortress for Abraham,
تا برآورد از دل نمرود دود
so that it raised smoke (sighs of despair) from the heart of Nimrod?

کوه یحیی را نه سوی خویش خواند
Did not the mountain call Yahyá (John the Baptist) to itself
قاصدانش را به زخم سنگ راند
and drive off his pursuers with blows of stone?

گفت ای یحیی بیا در من گریز
"O Yahyá," it said, "come, take refuge in me,
تا پناهت باشم از شمشیر تیز
that I may be thy shelter from the sharp sword."

◆◉◆◉◆

وداع کردن طوطی خواجه را و پریدن
How the parrot bade farewell to the merchant and flew away.

یک دو پندش داد طوطی بی‌نفاق
The parrot gave him one or two counsels full of(spiritual) savour

بعد از آن گفتش سلام الفراق
The merchant said to her, "Go, God protect thee!

خواجه گفتش فی امان الله برو
Just now thou hast shown to me a new Way."

مر مرا اکنون نمودی راه نو
Said the merchant to himself, "This is the counsel for me;

خواجه با خود گفت کین پند منست
I will take her Way, for this Way is shining with light.

راه او گیرم که این ره روشنست
I will take her Way, for this Way is shining with light.

جان من کمتر ز طوطی کی بود
How should my soul be meaner than the parrot?

جان چنین باید که نیکوپی بود
The soul ought to follow a good track like this."

مضرت تعظیم خلق و انگشت‌نمای شدن
The harmfulness of being honoured by the people and of becoming conspicuous.

تن قفس شکلست تن شد خار جان
The body is cage-like: the body, amidst the cajoleries of those

در فریب داخلان و خارجان
who come in and go out, became a thorn to the soul.

اینش گوید من شوم همراز تو
This one says to him, "I will be thy confidant,"

وآنش گوید نی منم انباز تو
and that one says, "Nay, I am thy partner."

اینش گوید نیست چون تو در وجود
This one says to him, "There is none in existence like

در جمال و فضل و در احسان و جود
thee for beauty and eminence and for kindness and liberality."

آنش گوید هر دو عالم آن تست
That one says to him, "Both the worlds are thine,
جمله جانهامان طفیل جان تست
all our souls are thy soul's parasites."

او چو بیند خلق را سرمست خویش
When he sees the people intoxicated with (desire for) him,
از تکبر می‌رود از دست خویش
because of arrogance he loses self-control.

او نداند که هزاران را چو او
He does not know that the Devil has cast thousands
دیو افکندست اندر آب جو
like him into the water of the river (of destruction).

لطف و سالوس جهان خوش لقمه‌ایست
The world's flattery and hypocrisy is a sweet morsel:
کمترش خور کان پر آتش لقمه‌ایست
eat less of it (eat it not), for it is a morsel full of fire.

آتشش پنهان و ذوقش آشکار
Its fire is hidden and its taste is manifest:
دود او ظاهر شود پایان کار
its smoke becomes visible in the end.

تو مگو آن مدح را من کی خورم
Do not say, "How should I swallow that praise? He is speaking from desire (for reward):
از طمع می‌گوید او پی می‌برم
I am on his track (and see quite well what he is after)."

مادحت گر هجو گوید بر ملا
If your belauder should satirise you in public,
روزها سوزد دلت زان سوزها
your heart would burn for (many) days on account of those scorches

گر چه دانی کو ز حرمان گفت آن
Although you know that he (only) said it in disappointment
کان طمع که داشت از تو شد زیان
because the hopes he had of you brought him no gain,

آن اثر می‌ماندت در اندرون
(Yet) the effect thereof is remaining within you.
در مدیح این حالتت هست آزمون
The same experience happens to you in the case of praise.

آن اثر هم روزها باقی بود
The effect of that too lasts for many days
مایهٔ کبر و خداع جان شود
and becomes a source of arrogance and deception of the soul,

لیک ننماید چو شیرینست مدح
But it does not show itself, because praise is sweet;
بد نماید زانک تلخ افتاد قدح
the evil shows itself, because blame is bitter.

همچو مطبوخست و حب کان را خوری
It (blame) is like (bitter) decoctions and pills which you swallow
تا بدیری شورش و رنج اندری
and for a long time you are in disturbance and pain,

ور خوری حلوا بود ذوقش دمی
Whereas, if you eat halwá (sweetmeat), its taste is momentary:
این اثر چون آن نمی‌پاید همی
this effect, like the other, is not enduring forever.

چون نمی‌پاید همی‌پاید نهان
Since it does not endure (perceptibly), it endures imperceptibly:
هر ضدی را تو به ضد او بدان
recognise every opposite by means of its opposite.

چون شکر پاید نهان تاثیر او
When the effect of sugar endures (remains latent),
بعد حینی دمل آرد نیش‌جو
after a while it produces boils that call for the lancet.

نفس از بس مدحها فرعون شد
The fleshly soul was made a Pharaoh by (receiving) many praises:
کن ذلیل النفس هونا لا تسد
be lowly of spirit through meekness, do not domineer.

تا توانی بنده شو سلطان مباش
So far as you can, become a slave, do not be a monarch
زخم کش چون گوی شو چوگان مباش
Suffer blows: become like the ball, do not be the bat.

ورنه چون لطفت نماند وین جمال
Otherwise, when this elegance and beauty remains with you no more,
از تو آید آن حریفان را ملال
you will be loathed by those companions.

آن جماعت کت همی‌دادند ریو
The set of people who used to flatter you deceitfully
چون ببینندت بگویندت که دیو
when they behold you will call you a devil.

جمله گویندت چو بینندت بدر
When they see you at their doors, they all will cry,
مرده‌ای از گور خود بر کرد سر
Truly a dead man has risen from the grave."

همچو امرد که خدا نامش کنند
(You will be) like the beardless youth whom they address as "Lord"
تا بدین سالوس در دامش کنند
that by this hypocrisy they may make entrap him.

چونک در بدنامی آمد ریش او
As soon as he has grown a beard in infamy,
دیو را ننگ آید از تفتیش او
the Devil is ashamed to search after him

دیو سوی آدمی شد بهر شر
The Devil approaches Man for the sake of wickedness:
سوی تو ناید که از دیوی بتر
he does not approach you because you are worse than the Devil.

تا تو بودی آدمی دیو از پیت
So long as you were a man the Devil
می‌دوید و می‌چشانید او میت
was running at your heels and bidding you taste (his) wine.

چون شدی در خوی دیوی استوار
Since you have become confirmed in devilry,
می‌گریزد از تو دیو نابکار
the good-for-nothing Devil is fleeing from you!

آنک اندر دامنت آویخت او
He who (formerly) clung to your skirt fled
چون چنین گشتی ز تو بگریخت او
from you when you became like this.

❖◉❖◉❖

تفسیر ما شاء الله کان
Explanation of (the Tradition) "Whatsoever God wills cometh to pass."

این همه گفتیم لیک اندر بسیچ
We have spoken all these words, but in preparing ourselves (for the journey before us) we are naught

بی‌عنایات خدا هیچیم هیچ
naught without the favours of God.

بی عنایات حق و خاصان حق
Without the favours of God and God's elect ones

گر ملک باشد سیاهستش ورق
angel though he be, his page is black

ای خدا ای فضل تو حاجت روا
O God, O Thou whose bounty fulfils (every) need,

با تو یاد هیچ کس نبود روا
it is not allowable to mention any one beside Thee.

این قدر ارشاد تو بخشیده‌ای
This amount of guidance Thou hast bestowed (upon us);

تا بدین بس عیب ما پوشیده‌ای
till this (present time) Thou hast covered up many a fault of ours

قطرهٔ دانش که بخشیدی ز پیش
Cause the drop of knowledge which Thou gavest

متصل گردان به دریاهای خویش
(us) heretofore to become united with Thy seas.

قطرهٔ علمست اندر جان من
In my soul there is a drop of knowledge:

وارهانش از هوا وز خاک تن
deliver it from sensuality and from the body's clay,

پیش از آن کین خاکها خسفش کنند
Before these clays drink it up,

پیش از آن کین بادها نشفش کنند
before these winds absorb it,

گر چه چون نشفش کند تو قادری
Although, when they absorb it

کش ازیشان وا ستانی وا خری
Thou art able to take it back from them and redeem it.

قطره‌ای کو در هوا شد یا که ریخت
The drop that vanished in the air or was spilled (on the earth)
از خزینهٔ قدرت تو کی گریخت
when did it flee (escape) from the storehouse of Thy omnipotence?

گر در آید در عدم یا صد عدم
If it enter into non-existence or a hundred non-existences,
چون بخوانیش او کند از سر قدم
it will make a foot of its head (will return in headlong haste) when Thou callest it.

صد هزاران ضد ضد را می‌کشد
Hundreds of thousands of opposites are killing their opposites:
بازشان حکم تو بیرون می‌کشد
Thy decree is drawing them forth again (from non-existence).

از عدمها سوی هستی هر زمان
There is caravan on caravan, O Lord,
هست یا رب کاروان در کاروان
O Lord, (speeding) continually from non-existence towards existence.

خاصه هر شب جمله افکار و عقول
In particular, every night all thoughts and understandings
نیست گردد غرق در بحر نغول
become naught, plunged in the deep Sea;

باز وقت صبح آن اللهیان
Again at the time of dawn those Divine ones
بر زنند از بحر سر چون ماهیان
lift up their heads from the Sea, like fishes

در خزان آن صد هزاران شاخ و برگ
In autumn the myriads of boughs and leaves
از هزیمت رفته در دریای مرگ
go in rout into the sea of Death,

زاغ پوشیده سیه چون نوحه گر
(While) in the garden the crow clothed in black like a mourner
در گلستان نوحه کرده بر خضر
makes lament over the (withered) greenery.

باز فرمان آید از سالار ده
Again from the Lord of the land comes the edict (saying) to Non-existence,
مر عدم را کآنچه خوردی باز ده
"Give back what thou hast devoured!

آنچه خوردی وا ده ای مرگ سیاه
Give up, O black Death,
از نبات و دارو و برگ و گیاه
what thou hast devoured of plants and healing herbs and leaves and grass!"

ای برادر عقل یکدم با خود آر
O brother, collect thy wits for an instant (and think):
دم بدم در تو خزانست و بهار
from moment to moment (incessantly) there is autumn and spring within thee

باغ دل را سبز و تر و تازه بین
Behold the garden of the heart, green and moist and fresh,
پر ز غنچه و ورد و سرو و یاسمین
full of buds and roses and cypresses;

ز انبهی برگ پنهان گشته شاخ
Boughs hidden by the multitude of leaves,
ز انبهی گل نهان صحرا و کاخ
vast plain and high palace hidden by the multitude of flowers.

این سخنهایی که از عقل کلست
These words, which are from Universal Reason
بوی آن گلزار و سرو و سنبلست
are the scent of those flowers and cypresses and hyacinths

بوی گل دیدی که آنجا گل نبود
Didst thou (ever) smell the scent of a rose where no rose was?
جوش مل دیدی که آنجا مل نبود
Didst thou (ever) see the foaming of wine where no wine was?

بو قلاووزست و رهبر مر ترا
The scent is thy guide and conducts thee on thy way:
می‌برد تا خلد و کوثر مر ترا
it will bring thee to Eden and Kawthar.

بو دوای چشم باشد نورساز
The scent is a remedy for the (sightless) eye; (it is) light-making:
شد ز بویی دیدهٔ یعقوب باز
the eye of Jacob was opened by a scent.

بوی بد مر دیده را تاری کند
The foul scent darkens the eye
بوی یوسف دیده را یاری کند
the scent of Joseph succours the eye.

تو که یوسف نیستی یعقوب باش
Thou who art not a Joseph, be a Jacob: be (familiar), like him,
همچو او با گریه و آشوب باش
with weeping and sore distress.

بشنو این پند از حکیم غزنوی
Hearken to this counsel from the Sage of Ghazna,
تا بیابی در تن کهنه نوی
that thou mayst feel freshness in thy old body:

ناز را رویی بباید همچو ورد
"Disdain needs a face like the rose;
چون نداری گرد بدخویی مگرد
when thou hast not (such a face), do not indulge in ill-temper.

زشت باشد روی نازیبا و ناز
Ugly is disdain in an uncomely face
سخت باشد چشم نابینا و درد
grievous is eye-ache in an unseeing eye."

پیش یوسف نازش و خوبی مکن
In the presence of Joseph do not give thyself airs and behave like a beauty:
جز نیاز و آه یعقوبی مکن
offer nothing but the supplication and sighs of Jacob.

معنی مردن ز طوطی بد نیاز
The meaning of dying (as conveyed) by the parrot was supplication (self-abasement):
در نیاز و فقر خود را مرده ساز
make thyself dead in supplication and poverty (of spirit),

تا دم عیسی ترا زنده کند
That the breath of Jesus may revive
همچو خویشت خوب و فرخنده کند
thee and make thee fair and blessed as itself.

از بهاران کی شود سرسبز سنگ
How should a rock be covered with verdure by the Spring?
خاک شو تا گل نمایی رنگ رنگ
Become earth, that thou mayst display flowers of many a hue.

سالها تو سنگ بودی دل خراش
Years hast thou been a heart-jagging rock:
آزمون را یک زمانی خاک باش
once, for the sake of experiment, be earth!

داستان پیر چنگی
The story of the old harper

کی در عهد عمر رضی الله عنه از بهر خدا روز بی‌نوایی چنگ زد میان گورستان

who in the time of 'Umar, may God be well-pleased with him, on a day when he was starving played the harp for God's sake in the graveyard.

آن شنیدستی که در عهد عمر

Hast thou heard that in the time of 'Umar

بود چنگی مطربی با کر و فر

there was a harper, a fine and glorious minstrel?

بلبل از آواز او بی‌خود شدی

The nightingale would be made beside herself by his voice:

یک طرب ز آواز خوبش صد شدی

by his beautiful voice one rapture would be turned into a hundred.

مجلس و مجمع دمش آراستی

His breath was an ornament to assembly and congregation,

وز نوای او قیامت خاستی

and at his song the dead would arise.

همچو اسرافیل کآوازش بفن

(He was) like Isráfil (Seraphiel), whose voice will cunningly

مردگان را جان در آرد در بدن

bring the souls of the dead into their bodies,

یار سایل بود اسرافیل را

Or he was (like) an accompanist to Isráfil,

کز سماعش پر برستی فیل را

for his music would make the elephant grow wings.

سازد اسرافیل روزی ناله را

One day Isráfil will make a shrill sound and

جان دهد پوسیدهٔ صدساله را

will give life to him that has been rotten for a hundred years.

انبیا را در درون هم نغمه‌هاست

The prophets also have (spiritual) notes within,

طالبان را زان حیات بی‌بهاست

whence there comes life beyond price to them that seek (God).

نشنود آن نغمه‌ها را گوش حس

The sensual ear does not hear those notes,

کز ستم‌ها گوش حس باشد نجس

for the sensual ear is defiled by iniquities.

نشنود نغمهٔ پری را آدمی
The note of the peri is not heard by man,
کو بود ز اسرار پریان اعجمی
for he is unable to apprehend the mysteries of the peris,
گرچه هم نغمهٔ پری زین عالمست
Although the note of the peri too belongs to this world.
نغمهٔ دل برتر از هر دو دمست
The note of the heart is higher than both breaths (notes),
که پری و آدمی زندانیند
For peri and man (alike) are prisoners:
هر دو در زندان این نادانیند
both are (captive) in the prison of this ignorance.
معشر الجن سورهٔ رحمان بخوان
Recite O community of Jinn (and men) in the Súratu l'-Rahmán;
تستطیعوا تنفذوا را باز دان
recognise (the meaning of) if ye be able to pass forth.
نغمه‌های اندرون اولیا
The inward notes of the saints say,
اولا گوید که ای اجزای لا
at first, "O ye particles of lá (not=not-being),
هین ز لای نفی سرها بر زنید
Take heed, lift up your heads from the lá of negation,
این خیال و وهم یکسو افکنید
put forth your heads from this fancy and vain imagining.
ای همه پوسیده در کون و فساد
O ye who all are rotten in (the world of) generation and corruption,
جان باقیتان نروید و نزاد
your everlasting soul neither grew nor came to birth."
گر بگویم شمه‌ای زان نغمه‌ها
If I tell (even) a tittle of those (saintly) notes,
جانها سر بر زنند از دخمه‌ها
the souls will lift up their heads from the tombs.
گوش را نزدیک کن کان دور نیست
Put thine ear close, for that (melody) is not far off,
لیک نقل آن به تو دستور نیست
but 'tis not permitted to convey it to thee.

هین که اسرافیل وقتند اولیا
Hark! for the saints are the Isráfils of the (present) time:
مرده را زیشان حیاتست و نما
from them to the dead comes life and freshness.

جان هر یک مرده‌ای از گور تن
At their voice the dead souls in the body's grave
بر جهد ز آوازشان اندر کفن
start up in their winding-sheets

گوید این آواز ز آواها جداست
He (that is thus awakened) says, "This voice is separate from (all other) voices:
زنده کردن کار آواز خداست
to quicken (the dead) is the work of the voice of God.

ما بمردیم و بکلی کاستیم
We (had) died and were entirely decayed:
بانگ حق آمد همه بر خاستیم
the call of God came: we all arose."

بانگ حق اندر حجاب و بی حجاب
The call of God, (whether it be) veiled or unveiled,
آن دهد کو داد مریم را ز جیب
bestows that which He bestowed on Mary from His bosom.

ای فناتان نیست کرده زیر پوست
O ye who are rotten with death (in your hearts) underneath the skin,
باز گردید از عدم ز آواز دوست
return from non-existence at the voice of the Friend!

مطلق آن آواز خود از شه بود
Absolutely, indeed, that voice is from the King (God),
گرچه از حلقوم عبدالله بود
though it be from the larynx of God's servant.

گفته او را من زبان و چشم تو
He (God) has said to him (the saint), "I am thy tongue and eye;
من حواس و من رضا و خشم تو
I am thy senses and I am thy good pleasure and thy wrath.

رو که بی یسمع و بی یبصر توی
Go, for thou art (he of whom God saith), 'By Me he hears and by Me he sees':
سر توی چه جای صاحب سر توی
thou art the consciousness what is the occasion of 'Thou art the possessor of the consciousness'?

چون شدی من کان لله از وله
Since thou hast become, through bewilderment, 'He that belongs to God,'
من ترا باشم که کان الله له
I am thine, for 'God shall belong to him.'

گه توی گویم ترا گاهی منم
Sometimes I say to thee, ''Tis thou,' sometimes,
هر چه گویم آفتاب روشنم
''Tis I': whatever I say, I am the Sun illuminating (all).

هر کجا تابم ز مشکات دمی
Wheresoever I shine forth from the lamp-niche of a breath (Divine word),
حل شد آنجا مشکلات عالمی
there the difficulties of a (whole) world are resolved.

ظلمتی را کآفتابش بر نداشت
The darkness which the (earthly) sun did not remove,
از دم ما گردد آن ظلمت چو چاشت
through My breath that darkness becomes like bright morning."

آدمی را او بخویش اسما نمود
To an Adam He in His own person showed the (Divine) Names;
دیگران را ز آدم اسما می‌گشود
to the rest He was revealing the Names by means of Adam.

خواه ز آدم گیر نورش خواه ازو
Do thou receive His light either from Adam or from Himself
خواه از خم گیر می خواه از کدو
take the wine either from the jar or from the gourd (cup),

کین کدو با خنب پیوستست سخت
For this gourd is very closely connected with the jar:
نی چو تو شاد آن کدوی نیکبخت
the blessed gourd is not rejoiced (by the same causes) as thou art.

گفت طوبی من رآنی مصطفی
Mustafá (Mohammed) said, "Happy he that has seen me
والذی یبصر لمن وجهی رای
and he that looks at him that saw my face.

چون چراغی نور شمعی را کشید
When a lamp has derived (its) light from a candle,
هر که دید آن را یقین آن شمع دید
every one that sees it (the lamp) certainly sees the candle

همچنین تا صد چراغ ار نقل شد
If transmission (of the light) occurs in this way till a hundred lamps (are lighted)
دیدن آخر لقای اصل شد
the seeing of the last (lamp) becomes a meeting with the original (light)

خواه از نور پسین بستان تو آن
Either take it from the hindmost light
هیچ فرق نیست خواه از شمع جان
there is no difference—or from the candle of the Spirit.

خواه بین نور از چراغ آخرین
Either behold the light (of God) from the lamp of the last (saints),
خواه بین نورش ز شمع غابرین
or behold His light from the candle of those who have gone before.

◆◉◆◉◆

در بیان این حدیث کی ان لربکم فی ایام دهرکم نفحات الا فتعر ضوا لها

Explanation of the Tradition, "Verily, your Lord hath, during the days of your time, certain breathings: oh, address yourselves to (receive) them."

گفت پیغامبر که نفحتهای حق
The Prophet said,
اندرین ایام می‌آرد سبق
"In these days the breathings of God prevail:

گوش و هش دارید این اوقات را
Keep ear and mind (attentive) to these (spiritual) influences,
در ربایید این چنین نفحات را
catch up such-like breathings."

نفحه آمد مر شما را دید و رفت
The (Divine) breathing came, beheld you, and departed:
هر که را می‌خواست جان بخشید و رفت
it gave life to whom it would, and departed.

نفحهٔ دیگر رسید آگاه باش
Another breathing has arrived. Be thou heedful,
تا ازین هم وانمانی خواجه تاش
that thou mayst not miss this one too, O comrade.

جان ناری یافت از وی انطفا
The soul of fire gained therefrom extinction;
مرده پوشید از بقای او قبا
from its everlastingness the dead (soul) put on the mantle (of eternal life)

تازگی و جنبش طوبیست این
This is the freshness and movement of the Túbá-tree
همچو جنبشهای حیوان نیست این
this is not like the movements of animals.

گر در افتد در زمین و آسمان
If it fall on earth and heaven,
زهره‌هاشان آب گردد در زمان
their galls will turn to water at once

خود ز بیم این دم بی منتها
Truly, from fear of this infinite breath
باز خوان فابین ان یحملنها
recite (the words of the Qur'án) but they refused to bear it

ورنه خود اشفقن منها چون بدی
Else, how should (the words) they shrank from it have been
گرنه از بیمش دل که خون شدی
unless from fear of it the heart of the mountain had become blood?

دوش دیگر لون این می‌داد دست
Yesternight this (breath) presented itself (to me) in a different guise
لقمهٔ چندی درآمد ره ببست
some morsels (of food) came in and barred the way.

بهر لقمه گشته لقمانی گرو
For a morsel's sake a Luqmán has become (held in custody as) a pledge
وقت لقمانست ای لقمه برو
'tis thetime for Luqmán: begone, O morsel

از هوای لقمهٔ این خارخار
These pricks (of the flesh) for desire of a morsel!
از کف لقمان همی جوید خار
Seek ye always (to draw forth) the thorn from the sole of Luqmán

در کف او خار و سایه ش نیز نیست
In his sole there is (really) no thorn or even the shadow of it
لیکتان از حرص آن تمییز نیست
but because of concupiscence ye have not that discernment.

خار دان آن را که خرما دیده‌ای
Know that the thorn is that which thou,
زانک بس نان کور و بس نادیده‌ای
because thou art very greedy and very blind, hast deemed to be a date.

251

جان لقمان که گلستان خداست

Inasmuch as Luqmán's spirit is the rose-garden of God

پای جانش خستهٔ خاری چراست

why is the foot of his spirit wounded by a thorn?

اشتر آمد این وجود خارخوار

This thorn-eating existence is (like) a camel

مصطفی زادی برین اشتر سوار

and upon this camel one born of Mustafá (Mohammed) is mounted.

اشترا تنگ گلی بر پشت تست

O camel, on thy back is a bale of roses,

کز نسیمش در تو صد گلزار رست

from the perfume of which a hundred rosaries grew within thee

میل تو سوی مغیلانست و ریگ

Thy inclination is towards thorn-bushes and sand:

تا چه گل چینی ز خار مردریگ

I wonder what roses thou wilt gather from worthless thorns.

ای بگشته زین طلب از کو بکو

O thou who in this search hast roamed from one quarter to another,

چند گویی کین گلستان کو و کو

how long wilt thou say, "Where, where is this rose-garden?

پیش از آن کین خار پا بیرون کنی

Until thou extract this thorn in thy foot,

چشم تاریکست جولان چون کنی

thine eye is dark (blind): how wilt thou go about?

آدمی کو می‌نگنجد در جهان

Man, who is not contained in the world

در سر خاری همی گردد نهان

becomes hidden in the point of a thorn!

مصطفی آمد که سازد همدمی

Mustafá (Mohammed) came (into the world) to make harmony:

کلمینی یا حمیرا کلمی

(he would say) "Speak to me, O Humayrá, speak!"

ای حمیرا اندر آتش نه تو نعل

O Humayrá, put the horse-shoe in the fire,

تا ز نعل تو شود این کوه لعل

that by means of thy horse-shoe this mountain may become (glowing with love, like) rubies.

این حمیرا لفظ تانیثست و جان
This "Humayrá" is a feminine word,

نام تانیثش نهند این تازیان
and the Arabs call the (word for) "spirit" feminine;

لیک از تانیث جان را باک نیست
But there is no fear (harm) to the Spirit from being feminine:

روح را با مرد و زن اشراک نیست
the Spirit has no association (nothing in common) with man and woman.

از مؤنث وز مذکر برترست
It is higher than feminine and masculine:

این نی آن جانست کز خشک و ترست
this is not that spirit which is composed of dryness and moisture.

این نه آن جانست کافزاید ز نان
This is not that spirit which is increased by (eating) bread,

یا گهی باشد چنین گاهی چنان
or which is sometimes like this and sometimes like that.

خوش کنندهست و خوش و عین خوشی
It is a doer of (what is) sweet, and (it is) sweet, and the essence of sweetness.

بی خوشی نبود خوشی ای مرتشی
Without (inward) sweetness there is no sweetness, O taker of bribes!

چون تو شیرین از شکر باشی بود
When thou art (made) sweet by sugar

کان شکر گاهی ز تو غایب شود
it may be that at some time that sugar will vanish from thee;

چون شکر گردی ز تاثیر وفا
(But) when thou becomest sugar from the effect produced by faithfulness

پس شکر کی از شکر باشد جدا
then how should sugar be parted from sugar?

عاشق از خود چون غذا یابد رحیق
When the lover (of God) is fed from (within) himself with pure wine

عقل آنجا گم شود گم ای رفیق
there reason becomes lost, lost, O comrade

عقل جزوی عشق را منکر بود
Partial (discursive) reason is a denier of Love,

گرچه بنماید که صاحب سر بود
hough it may give out that it is a confidant.

زیرک و داناست اما نیست نیست
It is clever and knowing, but it is not naught (devoid of self-existence):
تا فرشته لا نشد آهرمنیست
until the angel has become naught, he is an Ahriman (Devil).

او بقول و فعل یار ما بود
It (partial reason) is our friend in word and deed
چون بحکم حال آیی لا بود
(but) when you come to the case of inward feeling (ecstasy), it is naught (of no account).

لا بود چون او نشد از هست نیست
It is naught because it did not (pass away) from existence and become nonexistent:
چونک طوعا لا نشد کرها بسیست
since it did not become naught willingly there is many a one unwillingly.

جان کمالست و ندای او کمال
The Spirit is perfection and its call is perfection
مصطفی گویان ارحنا یا بلال
Mustafá (Mohammed) used to say, "Refresh us, O Bilál!

ای بلال افراز بانگ سلسلت
O Bilál, lift up thy mellifluous voice (drawn)
زان دمی کاندر دمیدم در دلت
from that breath which I breathed into thy heart

زان دمی کادم از آن مدهوش گشت
From that breath by which Adam was dumbfounded
هوش اهل آسمان بیهوش گشت
and the wits of the people of Heaven were made witless

مصطفی بیخویش شد زان خوب صوت
Mustafá became beside himself at that beautiful voice
شد نمازش از شب تعریس فوت
his prayer escaped him (was left unperformed) on the night of the ta'rís.

سر از آن خواب مبارک بر نداشت
He did not raise his head from that blessed sleep
تا نماز صبحدم آمد بچاشت
the (time of the) dawn prayer had advanced to (the time of) forenoon.

در شب تعریس پیش آن عروس
On the night of the ta'rís his holy spirit gained
یافت جان پاک ایشان دستبوس
kissing hands in the presence of the Bride.

عشق و جان هر دو نهاند و ستیر
Love and the Spirit are, both of them, hidden and veiled:
گر عروسش خوانده‌ام عیبی مگیر
if I have called Him (God) the Bride, do not find fault.

از ملولی یار خامش کردمی
I would have been silent from (fear of) the Beloved's displeasure,
گر همو مهلت بدادی یکدمی
if He had granted me a respite for one moment,

لیک می‌گوید بگو هین عیب نیست
But He keeps saying, "Say on! Come, 'tis no fault,
جز تقاضای قضای غیب نیست
'tis but the requirement of the (Divine) destiny in the World Unseen.

عیب باشد کو نبیند جز که عیب
The fault is (in him) who sees nothing but fault
عیب کی بیند روان پاک غیب
how should the Pure Spirit of the Invisible see fault?

عیب شد نسبت به مخلوق جهول
Fault arises (only) in relation to the ignorant creature,
نی به نسبت با خداوند قبول
not in relation to the Lord of favour

کفر هم نسبت به خالق حکمتست
Infidelity, too, is wisdom in relation to the Creator
چون به ما نسبت کنی کفر آفتست
(but) when you impute it to us, infidelity is a noxious thing.

ور یکی عیبی بود با صد حیات
And if there be one fault together with a hundred advantages (excellences),
بر مثال چوب باشد در نبات
it resembles the wood (woody stalk) in the sugarcane.

در ترازو هر دو را یکسان کشند
Both (sugar and stalk) alike are put into the scales,
زانک آن هر دو چو جسم و جان خوشند
because they both are sweet like body and soul.

پس بزرگان این نگفتند از گزاف
Not idly, therefore, the great (mystics) said this:
جسم پاکان عین جان افتاد صاف
The body of the holy ones (the saints) is essentially pure as (their) spirit."

گفتشان و نفسشان و نقششان
Their speech and soul and form
جمله جان مطلق آمد بی نشان
all (this) is absolute spirit without (external) trace.

جان دشمن دارشان جسمست صرف
The spirit that regards them with enmity is a mere body
چون زیاد از نرد او اسمست صرف
like the plus in (the game called) nard, it is a mere name.

آن به خاک اندر شد و کل خاک شد
That one (the body of the enemy of the saints) went into the earth (grave) and became earth entirely;
وین نمک اندر شد و کل پاک شد
this (holy body) went into the salt and became entirely pure

آن نمک کز وی محمد املحست
The (spiritual) salt through which Mohammed is more refined (than all others):
زان حدیث با نمک او افصحست
he is more eloquent than that salt-seasoned (elegantly expressed) Hadíth.

این نمک باقیست از میراث او
This salt is surviving in his heritage:
با توند آن وارثان او بجو
those heirs of his are with thee. Seek them!

پیش تو شسته ترا خود پیش کو
He (the spiritual heir of Mohammed) is seated in front of thee, (but) where indeed is thy "front"?
پیش هستت جان پیش‌اندیش کو
He is before thee, (but) where is the soul that thinks "before"?

گر تو خود را پیش و پس داری گمان
If thou fancy thou hast a "before" and "behind,"
بستهٔ جسمی و محرومی ز جان
thou art tied to body and deprived of spirit.

زیر و بالا پیش و پس وصف تنست
"Below" and "above," "before" and "behind" are attributes of the body
بی‌جهتها ذات جان روشنست
the essence of the bright spirit is without relations (not limited by relations of place)

برگشا از نور پاک شه نظر
Open thy (inward) vision with the pure light of the King
تا نپنداری تو چون کوته‌نظر
Beware of fancying, like one who is short-sighted,

256

که همینی در غم و شادی و بس
That thou art only this very (body living) in grief and joy.

ای عدم کو مر عدم را پیش و پس
O (thou who art really) non-existence, where (are) "before" and "behind" (appertaining) to non-existence?

روز بارانست می‌رو تا به شب
"Tis a day of rain: journey on till night

نه ازین باران از آن باران رب
not (sped) by this (earthly) rain but by the rain of the Lord.

❦◉❦◉❦

قصهٔ سوال کردن عایشه رضی الله عنها از مصطفی صلی‌الله علیه و سلم
The story of 'Á'isha, may God be well-pleased with her, how she asked Mustafá (Mohammed), on whom be peace, saying,

کی امروز باران بارید چون تو سوی گورستان رفتی جامه‌های تو چون تر نیست
"It rained to-day: since thou wentest to the graveyard, how is it that thy clothes are not wet?"

مصطفی روزی به گورستان برفت
One day Mustafá went to the graveyard:

با جنازهٔ مردی از یاران برفت
he went with the bier of a man (who was one) of his friends.

خاک را در گور او آگنده کرد
He made the earth so that it filled his grave:

زیر خاک آن دانه‌اش را زنده کرد
he quickened his seed under the earth.

این درختانند همچون خاکیان
These trees are like the interred ones:

دستها بر کرده‌اند از خاکدان
they have lifted up their hands from the earth.

سوی خلقان صد اشارت می‌کنند
They are making a hundred signs to the people

وانک گوشستش عبارت می‌کنند
and speaking plainly to him that hath ears (to hear).

با زبان سبز و با دست دراز
With green tongue and with long hand

از ضمیر خاک می‌گویند راز
they are telling secrets from the earth's conscience (inmost heart).

257

همچو بطان سر فرو برده به آب
(Sunk in earth) like ducks that have plunged their heads in water,
گشته طاووسان و بوده چون غراب
they have peacocks, though (in winter) they were as crows.

در زمستانشان اگر محبوس کرد
If during the winter He imprisoned them (in ice and snow),
آن غرابان را خدا طاووس کرد
God made those "crows" "peacocks" (in spring).

در زمستانشان اگر چه داد مرگ
Although He put them to death in winter,
زنده‌شان کرد از بهار و داد برگ
He revived them by means of spring and gave (them) leaves

منکران گویند خود هست این قدیم
The sceptics say, "This (creation), surely, is eternal:
این چرا بندیم بر رب کریم
why should we fix it on a beneficent Lord?"

کوری ایشان درون دوستان
God, in despite of them, caused (spiritual) gardens and plots
حق برویانید باغ و بوستان
of sweet flowers to grow in the hearts of His friends.

هر گلی کاندر درون بویا بود
Every rose that is sweet-scented within,
آن گل از اسرار کل گویا بود
that rose is telling of the secrets of the Universal.

بوی ایشان رغم آنف منکران
Their scent, to the confusion of the sceptics,
گرد عالم می‌رود پرده دران
is going round the world, rending the veil (of doubt and disbelief).

منکران همچون جعل زان بوی گل
The sceptics, (shrinking) from the scent of the rose like a beetle,
یا چو نازک مغز در بانگ دهل
or like a delicate (sensitive) brain at the noise of the drum,

خویشتن مشغول می‌سازند و غرق
Feign themselves to be occupied and absorbed,
چشم می‌دزدند ازین لمعان برق
and withdraw their eyes from the flash and the lightning.

چشم می‌دزدند و آنجا چشم نی
They withdraw their eyes, but no eye is there:
چشم آن باشد که بیند مأمنی
the eye is that which sees a place of safety.

چون ز گورستان پیمبر بازگشت
When the Prophet returned from the graveyard,
سوی صدیقه شد و همراز گشت
he went to the Siddíqa and confided (in her).

چشم صدیقه چو بر رویش فتاد
As soon as the eye of the Siddíqa fell upon his countenance,
پیش آمد دست بر وی می‌نهاد
she advanced and began to lay her hand on him,

بر عمامه و روی او و موی او
On his turban and his face and his hair,
بر گریبان و بر و بازوی او
on his collar and chest and arm.

گفت پیغامبر چه می‌جویی شتاب
Said the Prophet, "What art thou seeking so hastily?"
گفت باران آمد امروز از سحاب
She replied, "To-day rain fell from the clouds:

جامه‌هاات می‌بجویم در طلب
I am searching thy garments in quest (of moisture),
تر نمی‌یابم ز باران ای عجب
I do not feel them wet with the rain. Oh, how wonderful!"

گفت چه بر سر فکندی از ازار
The Prophet said, "What wrap hast thou thrown over thy head?"
گفت کردم آن ردای تو خمار
Said she, "I made that ridá (plaid) of thine (serve as) a head-covering."

گفت بهر آن نمود ای پاک‌جیب
He said, "O pure-bosomed one,
چشم پاکت را خدا باران غیب
that is why God revealed to thy pure eye the rain of the Unseen

نیست آن باران ازین ابر شما
That rain is not from your clouds:
هست ابری دیگر و دیگر سما
there are other clouds and another sky."

تفسیر بیت حکم رضی‌الله عنه
Commentary on the verse of Hakím (Saná'í):

«آسمانهاست در ولایت جان کارفرمای آسمان جهان» «در ره روح پست و بالاهاست کوههای بلند و دریاهاست»
"In the realm of the soul are skies lording over the sky of this world. In the Way of the spirit there are lowlands and highlands, there are lofty mountains and seas."

غیب را ابری و آبی دیگرست
The Unseen World has other clouds and water

آسمان و آفتابی دیگرست
it has another sky and sun.

ناید آن الا که بر خاصان پدید
That is not discerned save by the elect;

باقیان فی لبس من خلق جدید
the rest are in doubt as to a new creation.

هست باران از پی پروردگی
There is rain for the sake of nurture;

هست باران از پی پژمردگی
there is (also) rain for the sake of decay.

نفع باران بهاران بوالعجب
Marvellous is the benefit of the rain of springtime,

باغ را باران پاییزی چو تب
(but) to the garden the autumnal rain is like a (consuming) fever.

آن بهاری نازپروردش کند
That vernal (rain) makes it tenderly nurtured (flourishing),

وین خزانی ناخوش و زردش کند
while this autumnal (rain) makes it sickly and wan.

همچنین سرما و باد و آفتاب
Similarly know that cold and wind and sun

بر تفاوت دان و سررشته بیاب
are at variance (produce various effects); and find the clue.

همچنین در غیب انواعست این
Even so in the Unseen World there are these different sorts,

در زیان و سود و در ربح و غبین
(consisting) in loss and gain and in profit and defraudment(damage).

این دم ابدال باشد زان بهار
This breath of the Abdál (saints) is from that (spiritual) springtide:

در دل و جان روید از وی سبزه‌زار
from it there grows a green garden in heart and soul.

260

فعل باران بهاری با درخت
the (same) effect (as that) of the spring rain on the tree.
آید از انفاسشان در نیکبخت
From their breaths there comes (is produced) in him who is fortunate

گر درخت خشک باشد در مکان
If there be in the place a dry tree,
عیب آن از باد جان افزا مدان
do not deem its defect to be due to the life quickening wind

باد کار خویش کرد و بر وزید
The wind did its own work and blew on:
آنک جانی داشت بر جانش گزید
he that had a soul chose it in preference to his soul.

❀◉❀◉❀

در معنی این حدیث کی اغتنموا برد الربیع الی آخره
On the meaning of the Tradition, "Take advantage of the coolness of the spring season, etc."

گفت پیغامبر ز سرمای بهار
The Prophet said, "Give heed, my friends!
تن مپوشانید یاران زینهار
Do not cover your bodies from the cold of spring,

زانک با جان شما آن می‌کند
For it does to your
کان بهاران با درختان می‌کند
spirits the same thing that spring does to the trees;

لیک بگریزید از سرد خزان
But flee from the cold of autumn,
کان کند کو کرد با باغ و رزان
for it does what autumn did to the garden and the vines."

راویان این را به ظاهر برده‌اند
The traditionists have referred this (saying) to the outward (sense),
هم بر آن صورت قناعت کرده‌اند
and have been content with that same (outward) form.

بی‌خبر بودند از جان آن گروه
That class (of people) were ignorant of the spirit:
کوه را دیده ندیده کان بکوه
they saw the mountain, they did not see the mine in the mountain.

آن خزان نزد خدا نفس و هواست
In the sight of God that "autumn" is the flesh (nafs) and (its) desires:
عقل و جان عین بهارست و بقاست
the reason and the spirit are the essence of spring and are everlasting life.

مر ترا عقلیست جزوی در نهان
Thou hast a partial reason hidden (within thee):
کامل العقلی بجو اندر جهان
(now) in this world seek one whose reason is perfect.

جزو تو از کل او کلی شود
Through his whole thy part is made whole (and perfect):
عقل کل بر نفس چون غلی شود
Universal Reason is like a shackle on the neck of the flesh.

پس بتاویل این بود کانفاس پاک
Therefore, according to the (right) interpretation, it (the meaning) is this,
چون بهارست و حیات برگ و تاک
that the holy breaths are like spring and the life of leaf and vine.

از حدیث اولیا نرم و درشت
The sayings of the saints, whether soft or rough, do not thou cover thy body (against them),
تن مپوشان زانک دینت راست پشت
for they are the support of thy religion.

گرم گوید سرد گوید خوش بگیر
Whether he (the saint) speak hot or cold, receive (his words) with joy:
تا ز گرم و سرد بجهی وز سعیر
thereby thou wilt escape from the hot and cold (of Nature) and from Hell-fire.

گرم و سردش نوبهار زندگیست
His "hot" and "cold" is life's new season of spring,
مایهٔ صدق و یقین و بندگیست
the source of sincerity and faith and service.

زان کزو بستان جانها زنده است
Inasmuch as the garden of the spirits is living through him,
زین جواهر بحر دل آگنده است
and the sea of (his) heart is filled with these pearls,

بر دل عاقل هزاران غم بود
Thousands of griefs lie (heavy) on a wise man's heart,
گر ز باغ دل خلالی کم شود
if from the garden of his heart (even) a toothpick fail (be missing).

پرسیدن صدیقه رضی‌الله عنها از مصطفی صلی‌الله علیه و سلم کی سر باران امروزینه چه بود
How the Siddíqa ('Á'isha), may God be well-pleased with her, asked Mustafá, God bless him and give him peace, saying, "What was the inner meaning of to-day's rain?"

گفت صدیقه که ای زبدهٔ وجود
The Siddíqa said, "O (thou who art the) cream of existence,

حکمت باران امروزین چه بود
what was the (true) reason of to-day's rain?

این ز بارانهای رحمت بود یا
Was it (one) of the rains of mercy,

بهر تهدیدست و عدل کبریا
or (was it) for the sake of menace and the justice of (Divine) Majesty?

این از آن لطف بهاریات بود
Was it from the favour of the vernal attributes,

یا ز پاییزی پر آفات بود
or from a baneful autumnal attribute?"

گفت این از بهر تسکین غمست
He said, "This (rain) was for the purpose of allaying the grief

کز مصیبت بر نژاد آدمست
that is upon the race of Adam in calamity.

گر بر آن آتش بماندی آدمی
If man were to remain in that fire (of grief),

بس خرابی در فتادی و کمی
much ruin and loss would befall.

این جهان ویران شدی اندر زمان
This world would at once become desolate:

حرصها بیرون شدی از مردمان
(all) selfish desires would go forth from men."

استن این عالم ای جان غفلتست
Forgetfulness (of God), O beloved, is the pillar (prop) of this world:

هوشیاری این جهان را آفتست
(spiritual) intelligence is a bane to this world.

هوشیاری زان جهانست و چو آن
Intelligence belongs to that (other) world,

غالب آید پست گردد این جهان
and when it prevails, this world is overthrown.

هوشیاری آفتاب و حرص یخ
Intelligence is the sun and cupidity the ice;
هوشیاری آب و این عالم وسخ
intelligence is the water and this world the dirt.

زان جهان اندک ترشح می‌رسد
A little trickle (of intelligence) is coming from yonder world,
تا نغرد در جهان حرص و حسد
that cupidity and envy may not roar (too loudly) in this world.

گر ترشح بیشتر گردد ز غیب
If the trickle from the Unseen should become greater,
نه هنر ماند درین عالم نه عیب
in this world neither virtue nor vice will be left.

این ندارد حد سوی آغاز رو
This (topic) has no bound. Go to the starting-point,
سوی قصهٔ مرد مطرب باز رو
go back to the tale of the minstrel.

◈◈◈

بقیهٔ قصهٔ پیر چنگی و بیان مخلص آن
The remainder of the story of the old harper and the explanation of its issue (moral)

مطربی کز وی جهان شد پر طرب
That minstrel by whom the world was filled with rapture,
رسته ز آوازش خیالات عجب
from whose voice wondrous phantasies grew (arose in the minds of those who heard him),

از نوایش مرغ دل پران شدی
At whose song the bird of the soul would take wing,
وز صدایش هوش جان حیران شدی
and at whose note the mind of the spirit would be distraught

چون برآمد روزگار و پیر شد
When time passed and he grew old,
باز جانش از عجز پشه‌گیر شد
from weakness the falcon, his soul, became a catcher of gnats.

پشت او خم گشت همچون پشت خم
His back became bent like the back of a wine-jar,
ابروان بر چشم همچون پالدم
jar, the brows over his eyes like a crupper-strap.

گشت آواز لطیف جان‌فزاش
His charming soul-refreshing voice became

زشت و نزد کس نیرزیدی بلاش
ugly and worth nothing to anyone.

آن نوای رشک زهره آمده
The tone that had (once) been the envy of Zuhra (Venus)

همچو آواز خر پیری شده
Venus) was now like the bray of an old donkey.

خود کدامین خوش که او ناخوش نشد
Truly, what fair thing is there that did not become foul,

یا کدامین سقف کان مفرش نشد
or what roof that did not become a carpet?

غیر آواز عزیزان در صدور
Except the voices of holy men in their breasts,

که بود از عکس دمشان نفخ صور
from the repercussion of whose breath is the blast of the trumpet (of Resurrection).

اندرونی کاندرونها مست ازوست
(Theirs is) the heart by which (all) hearts are made drunken,

نیستی کین هستهامان هست ازوست
(theirs is) the nonexistence whereby these existences of ours are made existent.

کهربای فکر و هر آواز او
He (the saint) is the amber (magnet) of (all) thought and of every voice;

لذت الهام و وحی و راز او
he is the (inward) delight of revelation and inspiration and (Divine) mystery.

چونک مطرب پیرتر گشت و ضعیف
When the minstrel grew older and feeble,

شد ز بی کسبی رهین یک رغیف
through not earning(anything) he became indebted for a single loaf of bread.

گفت عمر و مهلتم دادی بسی
He said, "Thou hast given me long life and respite:

لطفها کردی خدایا با خسی
O God, Thou hast bestowed (many) favours on a vile wretch.

معصیت ورزیده‌ام هفتاد سال
For seventy years I have been committing sin,

باز نگرفتی ز من روزی نوال
(yet) not for one day hast Thou withheld Thy bounty from me.

نیست کسب امروز مهمان توام
I (can) earn nothing: to-day I am Thy guest,
چنگ بهر تو زنم کان توام
I will play the harp for Thee, I am Thine."

چنگ را برداشت و شد الله‌جو
He took up his harp and went in search of God
سوی گورستان یثرب آه‌گو
to the graveyard of Medina, crying "Alas!"

گفت خواهم از حق ابریشم بها
He said, "I crave of God the price of silk (for harpstrings),
کو به نیکویی پذیرد قلبها
for He in His kindness accepts adulterated coin."

چونک زد بسیار و گریان سر نهاد
He played the harp a long while and (then), weeping, laid his head down:
چنگ بالین کرد و بر گوری فتاد
he made the harp his pillow and dropped on a tomb.

خواب بردش مرغ جانش از حبس رست
Sleep overtook him: the bird, his soul,
چنگ و چنگی را رها کرد و بجست
escaped from captivity, it let harp and harper go and darted away.

گشت آزاد از تن و رنج جهان
It became freed from the body and the pain of this world
در جهان ساده و صحرای جان
in the simple (purely spiritual) world and the vast region of the soul.

جان او آنجا سرایان ماجرا
There his soul was singing what had befallen (it), saying,
کاندرین جا گر بماندندی مرا
"If they would but let me stay here,

خوش بدی جانم درین باغ و بهار
Happy would be my soul in this garden and springtide,
مست این صحرا و غیبی لاله‌زار
drunken with this (far stretching) plain and mystic anemonefield.

بی پر و بی پا سفر می‌کردمی
Without head or foot I would be journeying,
بی لب و دندان شکر می‌خوردمی
without lip or tooth I would be eating sugar.

ذکر و فکری فارغ از رنج دماغ
With a memory and thought free from brain-sickness,
کردمی با ساکنان چرخ لاغ
I would frolic with the dwellers in Heaven.

چشم بسته عالمی می‌دیدمی
With eye shut I would be seeing a (whole) world,
ورد و ریحان بی کفی می‌چیدمی
without a hand I would be gathering roses and basil."

مرغ آبی غرق دریای عسل
The water-bird (his soul) was plunged in a sea of honey
عین ایوبی شراب و مغتسل
the fountain of Job, to drink and wash in,

که بدو ایوب از پا تا به فرق
Whereby Job, from his feet to the crown of his head,
پاک شد از رنجها چون نور شرق
head, was purged of afflictions (and made pure) like the light of the sunrise.

مثنوی در حجم گر بودی چو چرخ
If the Mathnawí were as the sky in magnitude, not half the portion of this (mystery) would find room in it,
در نگنجیدی درو زین نیم برخ
not half the portion of this (mystery) would find room in it,

کان زمین و آسمان بس فراخ
For the exceeding broad earth and sky (of the material world caused my heart,
کرد از تنگی دلم را شاخ شاخ
from (their) narrowness (in comparison with the spiritual universe), to be rent in pieces;

وین جهانی کاندرین خوابم نمود
And this world that was revealed to me in this dream (of the minstrel)
از گشایش پر و بالم را گشود
has spread wide my wings and pinions because of (its vast) expansion.

این جهان و راهش ار پیدا بدی
If this world and the way to it were manifest,
کم کسی یک لحظه‌ای آنجا بدی
no one would remain there (in the material world) for a single moment.

امر می‌آمد که نه طامع مشو
The (Divine) command was coming (to the minstrel)— "Nay,
چون ز پایت خار بیرون شد برو
be not covetous: inasmuch as the thorn is out of thy foot, depart"

مول مولی می‌زد آنجا جان او
(Whilst) his soul was lingering there in
در فضای رحمت و احسان او
the spacious demesne of His (God's) mercy and beneficence.

◆◉◆◉◆

خواب گفتن هاتف مر عمر را رضی الله عنه
How the heavenly voice spoke to 'Umar, may God be well-pleased with him, while he was asleep, saying,

کی چندین زر از بیت المال بن مرد ده کی در گورستان خفته است
"Give a certain sum of gold from the public treasury to the man who is sleeping in the graveyard."

آن زمان حق بر عمر خوابی گماشت
Then God sent such a drowsiness upon 'Umar

تا که خویش از خواب نتوانست داشت
that he was unable to keep himself from slumber.

در عجب افتاد کین معهود نیست
He fell into amazement saying, "This is (a thing) unknown.

این ز غیب افتاد بی مقصود نیست
This has fallen from the Unseen, 'tis not without purpose."

سر نهاد و خواب بردش خواب دید
He laid his head down, and slumber overtook him.

کامدش از حق ندا جانش شنید
He dreamed that a voice came to him from God: his spirit heard

آن ندایی کاصل هر بانگ و نواست
That voice which is the origin of every cry and sound:

خود ندا آنست و این باقی صداست
that indeed is the (only) voice, and the rest are echoes.

ترک و کرد و پارسی‌گو و عرب
Turcoman and Kurd and Persian-speaking man and Arab

فهم کرده آن ندا بی گوش و لب
have understood that voice without (help of) ear or lip.

خود چه جای ترک و تاجیکست و زنگ
Ay, (but) what of Turcomans, Persians, and Ethiopians?

فهم کردست آن ندا را چوب و سنگ
(Even) wood and stone have understood that voice.

هر دمی از وی همی‌آید الست
Every moment there is coming from Him (the call), "Am not I (your Lord)?
جوهر و اعراض می‌گردند هست
" and substance and accidents are becoming existent.

گر نمی‌آید بلی زیشان ولی
If (the answer) "Yea" is not coming from them
آمدنشان از عدم باشد بلی
yet their coming from non-existence (into existence) is (equivalent to) "Yea."

زآنچه گفتم من ز فهم سنگ و چوب
concerning the friendliness (awareness) of stone and wood.
در بیانش قصه‌ای هشدار خوب
Listen to a goodly tale in explanation of what I have said

❧◉❧◉❧

نالیدن ستون حنانه چون برای پیغامبر صلی الله علیه و سلم منبر ساختند
How the moaning pillar complained when they made a pulpit for the Prophet, on whom be peace

کی جماعت انبوه شد گفتند ما روی مبارک ترا بهنگام وعظ نمی‌بینیم و شنیدن رسول و صحابه آن ناله را و سال و جواب مصطفی صلی الله علیه و سلم با ستون صریح

for the multitude had become great, and said, "We do not see thy blessed face when thou art exhorting us"—and how the Prophet and his Companions heard that complaint, and how Mustafá conversed with the pillar in clear language. the moaning pillar complained when they made a

استن حنانه از هجر رسول
The moaning pillar was complaining of (its) separation from the Prophet,
ناله می‌زد همچو ارباب عقول
just as rational beings (might do).

گفت پیغامبر چه خواهی ای ستون
The Prophet said, "O pillar, what dost thou want?"
گفت جانم از فراقت گشت خون
It said, "My soul is turned to blood because of parting from thee.

مسندت من بودم از من تاختی
I was thy support: (now) thou hast run away from me:
بر سر منبر تو مسند ساختی
thou hast devised a place to lean against upon the pulpit."

گفت خواهی که ترا نخلی کنند
"Dost thou desire," said he, "to be made a date-palm,
شرق و غربی ز تو میوه چنند
(so that) the people of the East and the West shall gather fruit from thee?

یا در آن عالم حقت سروی کند
Or that He (God) should make thee a cypress in yonder world,
تا تر و تازه بمانی تا ابد
so that thou wilt remain everlastingly fresh and flourishing?"

گفت آن خواهم که دایم شد بقاش
It replied, "I desire that whereof the life is enduring forever."
بشنو ای غافل کم از چوبی مباش
Hearken, O heedless one! Be not thou less than a piece of wood!

آن ستون را دفن کرد اندر زمین
He (the Prophet) buried that pillar in the earth,
تا چو مردم حشر گردد یوم دین
that it may be raised from the dead, like mankind, on the day of Resurrection,

تا بدانی هر که را که یزدان بخواند
That (hence) thou mayst know that everyone whom God has called
از همه کار جهان بی کار ماند
(to Himself) remains disengaged from all the work of this world

هر که را باشد ز یزدان کار و بار
Whosoever hath his work and business from God,
یافت بار آنجا و بیرون شد ز کار
gains admission there and goes forth from (abandons worldly) work.

آنک او را نبود از اسرار داد
He that hath no gift (portion) of spiritual mysteries,
کی کند تصدیق او نالهٔ جماد
how should he believe in the complaining of inanimate things?

گوید آری نه ز دل بهر وفاق
He says "Yes," not from his heart (but) for agreement's sake,
تا نگویندش که هست اهل نفاق
lest people should say that he is a hypocrite (in his religion).

گر نبندی واقفان امر کن
Unless there were knowers of the (Divine) command "Be!",
در جهان رد گشته بودی این سخن
this doctrine (that inanimate things are capable of speech) would have been rejected in the world

صد هزاران ز اهل تقلید و نشان
Myriads of conformists and legalists are cast
افکندشان نیم وهمی در گمان
into the abyss (of destruction) by a single taint (of doubt),
که بظن تقلید و استدلالشان
For their conformity and their drawing evidence from logical proofs
قایمست و جمله پر و بالشان
and all their wings and wing-feathers depend on opinion.

شبهه‌ای انگیزد آن شیطان دون
The vile Devil raises a doubt (in their minds):
در فتند این جمله کوران سرنگون
all these blind ones fall in headlong.

پای استدلالیان چوبین بود
The leg of the syllogisers is of wood:
پای چوبین سخت بی تمکین بود
a wooden leg is very infirm,

غیر آن قطب زمان دیده‌ور
Unlike the Qutb (supreme saint) of the age, the possessor of (spiritual) vision,
کز ثباتش کوه گردد خیره سر
by whose steadfastness the mountain is made giddy-headed (amazed).

پای نابینا عصا باشد عصا
The blind man's leg is a staff, a staff,
تا نیفتد سرنگون او بر حصا
so that he may not fall headlong on the pebbles.

آن سواری کو سپه را شد ظفر
The cavalier that became (the cause of) victory for the army,
اهل دین را کیست سلطان بصر
who is he for (the army of) the religious? One possessed of (spiritual) sight.

با عصا کوران اگر ره دیده‌اند
If, with (the aid of) a staff, the blind have seen their way,
در پناه خلق روشن‌دیده‌اند
(yet only) under the protection of (other) people are they clearsighted.

گر نه بینایان بدندی و شهان
Were there no men of vision and (spiritual) kings,
جمله کوران مرده‌اندی در جهان
all the blind in the world would be dead.

نه ز کوران کشت آید نه درود
From the blind comes neither sowing nor reaping
نه عمارت نه تجارتها و سود
nor cultivation nor tradings and profit.

گر نکردی رحمت و افضالتان
If He (God) did not bestow mercy and grace upon you,
در شکستی چوب استدلالتان
the wood of your logical deduction would break.

این عصا چه بود قیاسات و دلیل
What is this staff? Inferences and (logical) demonstration.
آن عصا که دادشان بینا جلیل
Who gave them (the blind) that staff? The all-seeing and almighty One.

چون عصا شد آلت جنگ و نفیر
Since the staff has become a weapon of quarrel and attack,
آن عصا را خرد بشکن ای ضریر
break that staff to pieces, O blind man!

او عصاتان داد تا پیش آمدیت
He gave you the staff that ye might approach (Him):
آن عصا از خشم هم بر وی زدیت
ith that staff ye struck even at Him in your anger.

حلقهٔ کوران به چه کار اندرید
O company of the blind, what are ye doing?
دیدبان را در میانه آورید
Bring the seer between (you and God)!

دامن او گیر کو دادت عصا
Lay hold of His skirt who gave thee the staff:
در نگر کادم چه‌ها دید از عصا
consider what (dreadful) things Adam suffered from disobedience.

معجزهٔ موسی و احمد را نگر
Consider the miracles of Moses and Ahmad (Mohammed),
چون عصا شد مار و استن با خبر
how the staff became a serpent and the pillar was endowed with knowledge.

از عصا ماری و از استن حنین
From the staff (came) a serpent and from the pillar a moaning:
پنج نوبت می‌زنند از بهر دین
they (the staff and the pillar) are beating five times daily for the sake of the Religion.

گرنه نامعقول بودی این مزه
Unless this savour (perception of spiritual truths) were nonintellectual,
کی بدی حاجت به چندین معجزه
how should all these miracles have been necessary?

هرچه معقولست عقلش می‌خورد
Whatever is intelligible, the intellect is swallowing
بی بیان معجزه بی جر و مد
it without the evidence of miracles and without contention.

این طریق بکر نامعقول بین
This virgin (untrodden) Way deem unintelligible,
در دل هر مقبلی مقبول بین
deem (it) accepted in the heart of every fortunate (elect) one.

همچنان کز بیم آدم دیو و دد
As in fear of Adam devil and wild
در جزایر در رمیدند از حسد
beast fled to the islands, from envy,

هم ز بیم معجزات انبیا
So in fear of the miracles of the prophets
سر کشیده منکران زیر گیا
have the sceptics slunk away under the grass,

تا به ناموس مسلمانی زیند
That they may live in hypocrisy with the reputation of being Moslems,
در تسلس تا ندانی که کیند
and that you may not know who they are.

همچو قلابان بر آن نقد تباه
Like counterfeiters, they smear the base
نقره می‌مالند و نام پادشاه
coin with silver and (inscribe on it) the name of the King.

ظاهر الفاظشان توحید و شرع
The outward form of their words is profession of the Divine Unity and the religion (of Islam):
باطن آن همچو در نان تخم صرع
the inward meaning thereof is like darnel (?) seed in bread.

فلسفی را زهره نه تا دم زند
The philosopher has not the stomach (courage) to breathe a word:
دم زند دین حقش بر هم زند
if he utter a word, the true Religion will confound him.

دست و پای او جماد و جان او
His hand and foot are inanimate,

هر چه گوید آن دو در فرمان او
and whatever his spirit says(commands), those two are under its control.

با زبان گر چه تهمت می‌نهند
Albeit they (the sceptics) propound (reasons for) suspicion with their tongues,

دست و پاهاشان گواهی می‌دهند
their hands and feet give testimony (against them).

❖❖❖

اظهار معجزهٔ پیغمبر صلی الله علیه و سلم
How the Prophet, on whom be peace, manifested a miracle

به سخن آمدن سنگریزه در دست ابوجهل علیه اللعنه و گواهی دادن سنگ‌ریزه بر حقیت محمد صلی الله علیه و سلم به رسالت او
by the speaking of the gravel in the hand of Abú Jahl— God's curse on him! —and by the gravel's bearing witness to the truth of Mohammed, on whom be God's blessing and peace.

سنگها اندر کف بوجهل بود
There were some pebbles in the hand of Bú Jahl:

گفت ای احمد بگو این چیست زود
"O Ahmad," said he, "tell quickly what this is.

گر رسولی چیست در مشتم نهان
If thou art the Messenger (of God), what is hidden in my fist? (Speak),

چون خبر داری ز راز آسمان
since thou hast knowledge of the mysteries of Heaven."

گفت چون خواهی بگویم آن چه‌هاست
He said, "How dost thou wish (me to do)? Shall I say what those (hidden) things are,

یا بگویند آن که ما حقیم و راست
or shall they declare that I am truthful and right?"

گفت بوجهل این دوم نادرترست
Bú Jahl said, "This second (thing) is more extraordinary."

گفت آری حق از آن قادرترست
"Yes," said the Prophet, "(but) God hath greater power than that."

از میان مشت او هر پاره سنگ
Without delay, from the middle of his (closed) fist every pebble

در شهادت گفتن آمد بی درنگ
began to pronounce the (Moslem's) profession of faith.

لا اله گفت و الا الله گفت
Each said, "There is no god" and (each) said, "except Allah";
گوهر احمد رسول الله سفت
(each) threaded the pearl of "Ahmad is the Messenger of Allah."

چون شنید از سنگها بوجهل این
When Bú Jahl heard this from the pebbles,
زد ز خشم آن سنگها را بر زمین
in his anger he dashed those pebbles on the ground.

❁◉❁◉❁

بقیهٔ قصهٔ مطرب
The rest of the story of the minstrel,

و پیغام رسانیدن امیرالمؤمنین عمر رضی الله عنه باو آنچه هاتف آواز داد
and how the Commander of the Faithful, 'Umar, may God be wellpleased with him, conveyed to him the message spoken by the heavenly voice.

باز گرد و حال مطرب گوش دار
Turn back and hear the plight of the minstrel,
زانک عاجز گشت مطرب ز انتظار
for the minstrel had (now) become desperate from waiting (so long).

بانگ آمد مر عمر را کای عمر
The voice (of God) came to 'Umar, saying,
بندهٔ ما را ز حاجت باز خر
"O 'Umar, redeem Our servant from want.

بنده‌ای داریم خاص و محترم
We have a servant, a favourite and highly esteemed one:
سوی گورستان تو رنجه کن قدم
take the trouble to go on foot to the graveyard.

ای عمر بر جه ز بیت المال عام
O 'Umar, spring up and put in thy hand full
هفتصد دینار در کف نه تمام
thy hand full seven hundred dínárs from the public treasury.

پیش او بر کای تو ما را اختیار
Carry them to him (and say), 'O thou who art Our choice,
این قدر بستان کنون معذور دار
accept this sum now and excuse (Us for offering such a small gift).

275

این قدر از بهر ابریشم بها
Spend this amount on the price (purchase) of silk:
خرج کن چون خرج شد اینجا بیا
silk: when it is spent, come here (again).'"

پس عمر زان هیبت آواز جست
Then 'Umar in awe of that voice
تا میان را بهر این خدمت ببست
sprang up that he might gird his loins for this service

سوی گورستان عمر بنهاد رو
Umar set his face towards the graveyard with the purse under his arm,
در بغل همیان دوان در جست و جو
running in search (of God's favourite).

گرد گورستان دوانه شد بسی
Long did he run round about the graveyard:
غیر آن پیر او ندید آنجا کسی
no one was there but that poor old man.

گفت این نبود دگر باره دوید
He said, "This is not he," and ran once more.
مانده گشت و غیر آن پیر او ندید
He became tired out and saw none but the old man.

گفت حق فرمود ما را بنده‌ایست
He said, "God said, 'We have a servan
صافی و شایسته و فرخنده‌ایست
he is a pure and worthy and blessed one.'

پیر چنگی کی بود خاص خدا
How should an old harper be the chosen of God?
حبذا ای سر پنهان حبذا
O Hidden Mystery, how excellent, how excellent art Thou!"

بار دیگر گرد گورستان بگشت
Once again he wandered about the graveyard,
همچو آن شیر شکاری گرد دشت
like the hunting lion about the desert.

چون یقین گشتش که غیر پیر نیست
When it became certain to him that none was there except the old man, he said,
گفت در ظلمت دل روشن بسی ست
"Many an illumined heart is (to be found) in darkness."

276

آمد او با صد ادب آنجا نشست
He came and sat down there (beside him) with a hundred marks of respect.
بر عمر عطسه فتاد و پیر جست
'Umar happened to sneeze, and the old man sprang to his feet.

مر عمر را دید ماند اندر شگفت
He saw 'Umar and stood fixed in amazement:
عزم رفتن کرد و لرزیدن گرفت
he resolved to go and began to tremble (with fear).

گفت در باطن خدایا از تو داد
He said within himself, "O God, help, I beseech thee!
محتسب بر پیری چنگی فتاد
The Inspector has fallen upon a poor old harper."

چون نظر اندر رخ آن پیر کرد
When 'Umar looked on the old man's countenance,
دید او را شرمسار و روی زرد
he saw him ashamed and pale

پس عمر گفتش مترس از من مرم
Then 'Umar said to him, "Fear not, do not flee from me,
کت بشارتها ز حق آورده‌ام
for I have brought thee glad tidings from God.

چند یزدان مدحت خوی تو کرد
How often has God praised thy disposition,
تا عمر را عاشق روی تو کرد
so that He has made 'Umar in love with thy face!

پیش من بنشین و مهجوری مساز
Sit down beside me and do not make separation (between us),
تا بگوشت گویم از اقبال راز
that I may say into thine ear the secret (message) from (the Divine) favour.

حق سلامت می‌کند می‌پرسدت
God sends thee greeting and asks
چونی از رنج و غمان بی‌حدت
thee how thou farest in thy distress and boundless sorrows.

نک قراضهٔ چند ابریشم بها
Lo, here are some pieces of gold to pay for silk.
خرج کن این را و باز اینجا بیا
Spend them and come back to this place."

پیر لرزان گشت چون این را شنید
The old man heard this, trembling all over

دست می‌خایید و بر خود می‌طپید
and biting his hand and tearing his garment,

بانگ می زد کای خدای بی‌نظیر
Crying, "O God who hast no like!"

بس که از شرم آب شد بیچاره پیر
inasmuch as the poor old man was melted with shame.

چون بسی بگریست و از حد رفت درد
After he had wept long and his grief had gone beyond (all) bounds,

چنگ را زد بر زمین و خرد کرد
he dashed his harp on the earth and broke it to bits.

گفت ای بوده حجابم از اله.
He said, "O thou (harp) that hast been to me a curtain (debarring me) from God,

ای مرا تو راهزن از شاه‌راه
O thou (that hast been) to me a brigand (cutting me off) from the King's highway,

ای بخورده خون من هفتاد سال
O thou that hast drunk my blood for seventy years,

ای ز تو رویم سیه پیش کمال
O thou because of whom my face is black (disgraced) before (the Divine) perfection!

ای خدای با عطای با وفا
Have mercy, O bounteous God who keepest faith,

رحم کن بر عمر رفته در جفا
faith, on a life passed in iniquity!

داد حق عمری که هر روزی از آن
God gave (me) a life, the value of every single day

کس نداند قیمت آن در جهان
whereof none knoweth except Him.

خرج کردم عمر خود را دم بدم
I have spent my life, breath by breath:

در دمیدم جمله را در زیر و بم
I have breathed it all away in treble and bass.

آه کز یاد ره و پردهٔ عراق
Ah me, that in minding the (musical) mode and rhythm of 'Iráq

رفت از یادم دم تلخ فراق
the bitter moment of parting (from this world) went out of my mind (was forgotten).

وای کز تری زیر افکند خرد
Alas that from the liquid freshness of the minor zírafgand

خشک شد کشت دل من دل بمرد
the seed sown in my heart dried up, and my heart died.

وای کز آواز این بیست و چهار
Alas that from (my preoccupation with) the sound of these four-and-twenty

کاروان بگذشت و بیگه شد نهار
the caravan passed and the day grew late."

ای خدا فریاد زین فریادخواه
O God, help (me) against this (self of mine) that is seeking help (from Thee):

داد خواهم نه ز کس زین دادخواه
I seek justice (redress) from no one (else, but only) from this justice-seeking (self).

داد خود از کس نیابم جز مگر
I shall not get justice for myself from anyone except,

زانک او از من بمن نزدیکتر
surely, from Him who is nearer to me than I;

کین منی از وی رسد دم دم مرا
For this "I-hood" comes to me from Him moment by moment:

پس ورا بینم چو این شد کم مرا
therefore, when this has failed me, I see (only) Him,

همچو آن کو با تو باشد زرشمر
As (when you are with) one who is counting out gold to you,

سوی او داری نه سوی خود نظر
you keep your gaze (directed) towards him, not towards yourself.

گردانیدن عمر رضی الله عنه نظر او را از مقام گریه

How 'Umar, may God be well-pleased with him, bade him (the harper) turn his gaze from the stage of weeping,

که نیستی هست کی هستی است بمقام استغراق

which is (self-) existence, to the stage of absorption (in God), which is non-existence (of self).

پس عمر گفتش که این زاری تو

Then 'Umar said to him, "This wailing

هست هم آثار هشیاری تو

of thine is also (one of) the marks of thy sobriety (self-consciousness).

راه فانی گشته راهی دیگرست

The way of him that has passed away (from selfconsciousness) is another way,

زانک هشیاری گناهی دیگرست

because sobriety is another sin.

هست هشیاری ز یاد ما مضی

Sobriety exists (arises) from recollection of what is past:

ماضی و مستقبلت پردهٔ خدا

past and future are to thee a curtain (separating thee) from God.

آتش اندر زن بهر دو تا بکی

Cast fire on them both: how long, because of these twain,

پر گره با شی ازین هر دو چو نی

wilt thou be full of knots (joints) like a reed?

تا گره با نی بود همراز نیست

Whilst the reed is knotted, it is not a sharer of secrets:

همنشین آن لب و آواز نیست

it is not the companion of the (flute-player's) lip and voice.

چون بطوفی خود بطوفی مرتدی

When thou art (engaged) in going about (seeking God) thou art indeed wrapped in (thy) going about:

چون به خانه آمدی هم با خودی

when thou hast come home, thou art still with thyself (self-conscious).

ای خبرهات از خبر دهٔ بی خبر

O thou whose knowledge is without knowledge of the Giver of knowledge,

توبهٔ تو از گناه تو بتر

thy repentance is worse than thy sin.

ای تو از حال گذشته توبه جو
O thou that seekest to repent of a state that is past,
کی کنی توبه ازین توبه بگو
say, when wilt thou repent of this repentance?

گاه بانگ زیر را قبله کنی
At one time thou turnest to the (low) sound of the treble,
گاه گریهٔ زار را قبله زنی
at another thou dost kiss (art in love with) weeping and wailing.

چونک فاروق آینهٔ اسرار شد
When Fárúq ('Umar) became a reflector of mysteries,
جان پیر از اندرون بیدار شد
the old man's heart was awakened from within.

همچو جان بی‌گریه و بی‌خنده شد
He became without weeping or laughter
جانش رفت و جان دیگر زنده شد
like the soul: his (animal) soul departed and the other soul came to life.

حیرتی آمد درونش آن زمان
In that hour such a bewilderment arose within him
که برون شد از زمین و آسمان
that he went forth from earth and heaven

جست و جویی از ورای جست و جو
A seeking and searching beyond (all) seeking and search:
من نمی‌دانم تو می‌دانی بگو
I know not (how to describe it); (if) you know, tell!

حال و قالی از ورای حال و قال
Words and feelings beyond (all) feelings and words
غرقه گشته در جمال ذوالجلال
he had become drowned in the beauty of the Lord of majesty,

غرقه‌ای نه که خلاصی باشدش
Drowned, not in such wise that there should be for him any deliverance,
یا به جز دریا کسی بشناسدش
or that any one should know him except the (Divine) Ocean.

عقل جزو از کل گویا نیستی
Partial reason would not be telling of (the mysteries of) the Universal (Reason),
گر تقاضا بر تقاضا نیستی
if there were not demand after demand

چون تقاضا بر تقاضا می‌رسد
Since demand after demand is arriving,

موج آن دریا بدینجا می‌رسد
the waves of that Sea (Universal Reason) reach this place (the world of partial reason).

چونک قصهٔ حال پیر اینجا رسید
Now that the story of the old man's (spiritual) experiences has come to this point,

پیر و حالش روی در پرده کشید
the old man and his experiences have withdrawn behind the veil.

پیر دامن را ز گفت و گو فشاند
The old man has shaken his skirt free from talk and speech:

نیم گفته در دهان ما بماند
half of the tale has remained in our mouth (has not been told).

از پی این عیش و عشرت ساختن
It behoves (us), for the sake of procuring (such) delight and enjoyment,

صد هزاران جان بشاید باختن
to gamble away (sacrifice) hundreds of thousands of souls (lives).

در شکار بیشهٔ جان باز باش
In chase of the spiritual forest be (as) a falcon,

همچو خورشید جهان جان‌باز باش
be one who gambles his soul (life) away, like the sun of this world.

جان‌فشان افتاد خورشید بلند
The lofty sun is life-diffusing:

هر دمی تی می‌شود پر می‌کنند
every moment it becomes empty and is filled.

جان فشان ای آفتاب معنوی
O Sun of Reality, diffuse spiritual life,

مر جهان کهنه را بنما نوی
show forth newness to this old world!

در وجود آدمی جان و روان
Soul and spirit are coming from

می‌رسد از غیب چون آب روان
the Unseen into human existence, like running water.

❁◉❁◉❁

تفسیر دعای آن دو فرشته
Commentary on the prayer of the two angels

که هر روز بر سر هر بازاری منادی می‌کنند کی اللهم اعط کل منفق خلفا اللهم اعط کل ممسک تلفا و بیان کردن کی آن منفق مجاهد راه حقست نی مسرف راه هوا

who daily make proclamation in every market, saying, "O God, bestow on every prodigal some boon in exchange! O God, bestow on every niggard some bane (in return)"; and an explanation that the prodigal is he that strives earnestly in the Way of God, not he that squanders his wealth in the way of sensuality.

گفت پیغامبر که دایم بهر پند
The Prophet said, "For admonishment's sake

دو فرشته خوش منادی می‌کنند
two angels are always making goodly proclamation,

کای خدایا منفقان را سیر دار
Saying, 'O God, keep the prodigals fully satisfied,

هر درمشان را عوض ده صد هزار
give hundred-thousandfold recompense for every dirhem that they spend.

ای خدایا ممسکان را در جهان
O God, do not give the niggards

تو مده الا زیان اندر زیان
in this world anything but loss upon loss!'"

ای بسا امساک کز انفاق به
Oh, (there is) many an act of niggardliness that is better than prodigality:

مال حق را جز به امر حق مده
do not bestow what belongs to God except by the command of God,

تا عوض یابی تو گنج بی‌کران
That thou mayst gain infinite treasure in return,

تا نباشی از عداد کافران
and that thou mayst not be numbered among the infidels

کاشتران قربان همی‌کردند تا
Who were offering camels in sacrifice

چیره گردد تیغشان بر مصطفی
in order that their swords might prevail against Mustafá.

امر حق را باز جو از واصلی
Endeavour to find out the command of God from one who is united (with God):

امر حق را در نیابد هر دلی
not every heart understands the command of God,

چون غلام یاغیی کو عدل کرد
As (for example) the slave, the enemy (of God),
مال شه بر یاغیان او بذل کرد
who did justice bestowed what belonged to the King upon those who rebelled against Him

در نبی انذار اهل غفلتست
In the Qur'án there is warning to
کان همه انفاقهاشان حسرتست
the heedless that all their spendings are a (cause of) bitter grief to them

عدل این یاغی و داداش نزد شاه
What increase does the equity and justice of this enemy produce in the sight of the King?
چه فزاید دوری و روی سیاه
Banishment and a black countenance (disgrace).

سروران مکه در حرب رسول
The chiefs of Mecca (when) at war with the Prophet
بدشان قربان به اومید قبول
offered sacrifice in hope of (Divine) favour.

بهر این مؤمن همی گوید ز بیم
On this account the true believer is saying in his prayer,
در نماز اهد الصراط المستقیم
from fear, "Lead (us) in the right path!"

آن درم دادن سخی را لایقست
It beseems the generous man thus to give money,
جان سپردن خود سخای عاشقست
verily the generosity of the lover is the surrender of his soul(life).

نان دهی از بهر حق نانت دهند
If you give bread for God's sake, you will be given bread (in return);
جان دهی از بهر حق جانت دهند
if you give your life for God's sake, you will be given life (in return).

گر بریزد برگهای این چنار
If the leaves of this plane-tree drop off,
برگ بی‌برگیش بخشد کردگار
the Creator will bestow on it the provision of leaflessness (spiritual poverty).

گر نماند از جود در دست تو مال
If because of your liberality no wealth remains in your hand,
کی کند فضل الهت پای‌مال
how should the bounty of God let you be down-trodden?

هر که کارد گردد انبارش تهی
When any one sows, his barn becomes empty (of seed),
لیکش اندر مزرعه باشد بهی
but there is goodliness in his cornfield;

وانک در انبار ماند و صرفه کرد
And, if he leaves it (the seed) in the barn and saves it up
اشپش و موش حوادث پاک خورد
weevils and mice and calamities (of time and decay) devour it.

این جهان نفیست در اثبات جو
This world is negation (of reality): seek (reality) in affirmation (of God).
صورتت صفرست در معنیت جو
Your form (body) is void (of reality): seek in your essence.

جان شور تلخ پیش تیغ بر
Bring the briny bitter (animal) soul to the sword:
جان چون دریای شیرین را بخر
buy the (heavenly) soul that is like a great sweet river.

ور نمی‌دانی شدن زین آستان
And if you cannot become (one of the frequenters) of this threshold (sublime court),
باری از من گوش کن این داستان
at least hear from me the following tale.

285

قصهٔ خلیفه
The story of the Caliph

کی در کرم در زمان خود از حاتم طائی گذشته بود و نظیر خود نداشت
who in his time surpassed Hátim of Tayyi' in generosity and had no rival.

یک خلیفه بود در ایام پیش
In former days there was a Caliph

کرده حاتم را غلام جود خویش
who made Hátim the slave of his liberality.

رایت اکرام و داد افراشته
He had raised high the banner of munificence and largesse,

فقر و حاجت از جهان بر داشته
he had removed poverty and want from the world.

بحر و در از بخششش صاف آمده
He was a sea of pearls, pure bounty:

داد او از قاف تا قاف آمده
his largesse reached from Qáf to Qáf.

در جهان خاک ابر و آب بود
In this world of dust he was the cloud and the rain:

مظهر بخشایش وهاب بود
he was the centre wherein the bounty of the Giver of all displayed itself.

از عطااش بحر و کان در زلزله
His gifts caused sea and mine to quake (tremble with shame):

سوی جودش قافله بر قافله
caravan on caravan (were hastening) towards his liberality.

قبلهٔ حاجت در و دروازهاش
His gate and portal was the point to which Need turned:

رفته در عالم بجود آوازهاش
the fame of his munificence had gone (far and wide) into the world.

هم عجم هم روم هم ترک و عرب
Persians and Greeks, Turcomans and Arabs,

مانده از جود و سخااش در عجب
were lost in amazement at his liberality and generosity.

آب حیوان بود و دریای کرم
He was the Water of Life and the Ocean of Bounty:

زنده گشته هم عرب زو هم عجم
by him both Arabs and foreigners were revived.

قصهٔ اعرابی درویش و ماجرای زن با او به سبب قلت و درویشی
Story of the poor Arab of the desert and his wife's altercation with him because of (their) penury and poverty.

یک شب اعرابی زنی مر شوی را
One night a Bedouin woman said to her husband

گفت و از حد برد گفت و گوی را
and she carried (her) talk beyond bounds

کین همه فقر و جفا ما می‌کشیم
"We are suffering all this poverty and hardship:

جمله عالم در خوشی ما ناخوشیم
all the world are (living) in happiness, we (alone) are unhappy.

نان مان نه نان خورش‌مان درد و رشک
We have no bread, our (only) condiment is anguish and envy:

کوزه‌مان نه آب‌مان از دیده اشک
we have no jug, our (only) water is the tears (that flow) from our eyes.

جامهٔ ما روز تاب آفتاب
Our garment by day is the burning sunshine;

شب نهالین و لحاف از ماهتاب
at night our bed and coverlet is (made) of the moonbeams.

قرص مه را قرص نان پنداشته
We fancy the disk of the moon is a disk (round cake) of bread

دست سوی آسمان برداشته
and lift up our hands towards the sky.

ننگ درویشان ز درویشی ما
The (poorest of the) poor feel shame at our poverty:

روز شب از روزی اندیشی ما
day is turned to night (darkened) by our anxiety about our daily portion (of food).

خویش و بیگانه شده از ما رمان
Kinsfolk and strangers have come to flee

بر مثال سامری از مردمان
from us in like fashion as Sámirí from men.

گر بخواهم از کسی یک مشت نسک
If I beg a handful of lentils from someone,

مر مرا گوید خمش کن مرگ و جسک
he says to me, 'Be silent, O death and plague!'

مر عرب را فخر غزوست و عطا
The Arabs take pride in fighting and giving:
در عرب تو همچو اندر خط خطا
thou amongst the Arabs art like a fault in writing."

چه غزا ما بی‌غزا خود کشته‌ایم
What fighting (can we do)? We are killed without fighting,
ما به تیغ فقر بی سرگشته‌ایم
we are made giddy (utterly distracted) by the sword of want.

چه عطا ما بر گدایی می‌تنیم
What gifts (can we make)? We are continually in beggary,
مر مگس را در هوا رگ می‌زنیم
we are slitting the vein of (slaughtering) the gnat in the air.

گر کسی مهمان رسد گر من منم
If any guest arrive, if I am I
شب بخسپد دلقش از تن بر کنم
I will go for his tattered cloak when he falls asleep at night.

◈◉◈◉◈

مغرور شدن مریدان محتاج به مدعیان مزور
How disciples (novices in Súfism) are beguiled in their need by false impostors

و ایشان را شیخ و محتشم و واصل پنداشتن و نقل را از نقد فرق نادانستن و بر بسته را از بر رسته
and imagine them to be Shaykhs and venerable personages and (saints) united (with God), and do not know the difference between fact (naqd) and fiction (naql) and between what is tied on (artificially) and what has grown up (naturally).

بهر این گفتند دانایان بفن
For this reason the wise have said with knowledge,
میهمان محسنان باید شدن
'One must become the guest of those who confer benefits.'

تو مرید و میهمان آن کسی
Thou art the disciple and guest of one who,
کو ستاند حاصلت را از خسی
from his vileness, robs thee of all thou hast.

نیست چیره چون ترا چیره کند
He is not strong: how should he make thee strong?
نور ندهد مر ترا تیره کند
He does not give light, (nay) he makes thee dark.

چون ورا نوری نبود اندر قِران
Since he had no light (in himself),
نور کی یابند از وی دیگران
how in association (with him) should others obtain light from him?

همچو اعمش کو کند داروی چشم
(He is) like the half-blind healer of eyes:
چه کشد در چشمها الّا که یشم
what should he put in (people's) eyes except wool?

حال ما اینست در فقر و عنا
Such is our state in poverty and affliction:
هیچ مهمانی مبا مغرور ما
may no guest be beguiled by us!

قحط ده سال ار ندیدی در صور
If thou hast never seen a ten years' famine in (visible) forms,
چشمها بگشا و اندر ما نگر
open thine eyes and look at us.

ظاهر ما چون درون مدعی
Our outward appearance is like the inward reality of the impostor:
در دلش ظلمت زبانش شعشعی
darkness in his heart, his tongue flashy (plausible).

از خدا بویی نه او را نه اثر
He has no scent or trace of God,
دعویش افزون ز شیث و بوالبشر
(but) his pretension is greater than (that of) Seth and the Father of mankind (Adam).

دیو ننموده ورا هم نقش خویش
The Devil (is so ashamed of him that he) has not shown to him even his portrait,
او همی‌گوید ز ابدالیم بیش
(yet) he (the impostor) is saying, 'We are of the Abdál and are more (we are superior even to them).'

حرف درویشان بدزدیده بسی
He has stolen many an expression used by dervishes,
تا گمان آید که هست او خود کسی
in order that he himself may be thought to be a (holy) personage.

خرده گیرد در سخن بر بایزید
In his talk he cavils at Báyazíd,
ننگ دارد از درون او یزید
(although) Yazíd would be ashamed of his existence.

بی‌نوا از نان و خوان آسمان

(He is) without (any) portion of the bread and viands of Heaven:

پیش او ننداخت حق یک استخوان

God did not throw a single bone to him.

او ندا کرده که خوان بنهاده‌ام

He has proclaimed, 'I have laid out the dishes,

نایب حقم خلیفه زاده‌ام

I am the Vicar of God, I am the son of the (spiritual) Khalífa:

الصلا ساده‌دلان پیچ پیچ

Welcome (to the feast), O simple-hearted ones,

تا خورید از خوان جودم سیر هیچ

Tormented that from my bounteous table ye may eat your fill of nothing.

سالها بر وعدهٔ فردا کسان

Some persons, (relying) on the promise of 'To-morrow,'

گرد آن در گشته فردا نارسان

have wandered for years around that door, (but) 'To-morrow' never comes.

دیر باید تا که سر آدمی

It needs a long time for the inmost conscience of a man to become evident,

آشکارا گردد از بیش و کمی

more and less (both in great and small matters),

زیر دیوار بدن گنجست یا

(So that we may know whether) beneath the wall of his body there is treasure,

خانهٔ مارست و مور و اژدها

or whether there is the house of snake and ant and dragon.

چونک پیدا گشت کو چیزی نبود

When it became clear that he was naught (worthless),

عمر طالب رفت آگاهی چه سود

(by that time) the life of the seeker (disciple) had passed: what use (was) the knowledge (to him)?

در بیان آنک نادر افتد کی مریدی در مدعی مزور اعتقاد بصدق ببندد

Explaining how it may happen, (though) rarely, that a disciple sincerely puts his faith in a false impostor

کی او کسی است و بدین اعتقاد به مقامی برسد کی شیخش در خواب ندیده باشد و آب و آتش او را گزند نکند و شیخش را گزند کند ولیکن بنادر نادر

(and believes) that he is a (holy) personage, and by means of this faith attains unto a (spiritual) degree which his Shaykh has never (even) dreamed of, and (then) fire and water do him no hurt, though they hurt his Shaykh; but this occurs very seldom.

لیک نادر طالب آید کز فروغ

But exceptionally comes (the case of) a disciple to whom,

در حق او نافع آید آن دروغ

because of his (spiritual) illumination, that falsehood (of the impostor) is beneficial.

او به قصد نیک خود جایی رسد

He, by his goodly purpose, attains unto a (high) degree,

گرچه جان پنداشت و آن آمد جسد

although he fancied (the impostor to be) soul, and that (soul) proved to be (only) body.

چون تحری در دل شب قبله را

(It is) like trying to find the qibla in the heart (depth) of night:

قبله نی و آن نماز او روا

the qibla is not (found), but his (the seeker's) prayer is valid.

مدعی را قحط جان اندر سرست

The impostor has a dearth of soul within,

لیک ما را قحط نان بر ظاهرست

but we have a dearth of bread without.

ما چرا چون مدعی پنهان کنیم

Why should we conceal (our poverty) like the impostor

بهر ناموس مزور جان کنیم

and suffer agony for the sake of false reputation?"

صبر فرمودن اعرابی زن خود را و فضیلت صبر و فقر بیان کردن با زن
How the Bedouin bade his wife be patient and declared to her the excellence of patience and poverty.

شوی گفتش چند جویی دخل و کشت
Her husband said to her, "How long wilt thou seek income and seed-produce?
خود چه ماند از عمر افزون‌تر گذشت
What indeed is left of (our) life? Most (of it) is past.

عاقل اندر بیش و نقصان ننگرد
The sensible man does not look at increase or deficiency,
زانک هر دو همچو سیلی بگذرد
because both (these) will pass by like a torrent.

خواه صاف و خواه سیل تیره‌رو
Whether it (life) be pure (clear and untroubled) or whether it be a turbid flood,
چون نمی‌پاید دمی از وی مگو
do not speak of it, since it is not enduring for a moment.

اندرین عالم هزاران جانور
In this world thousands of animals are living happily,
می‌زید خوش‌عیش بی زیر و زبر
happily, without up and down (anxiety).

شکر می‌گوید خدا را فاخته
The dove on the tree is uttering thanks to God,
بر درخت و برگ شب نا ساخته
though her food for the night is not (yet) ready.

حمد می‌گوید خدا را عندلیب
The nightingale is singing glory to God (and saying),
کاعتماد رزق بر تست ای مجیب
I rely on Thee for my daily bread, O Thou who answerest (prayer).'

باز دست شاه را کرده نوید
The falcon has made the king's hand his joy (the place in which he takes delight),
از همه مردار ببریده امید
and has given up hope of (has become indifferent to) all carrion.

همچنین از پشه‌گیری تا به پیل
Similarly, you may take (every animal) from the gnat to the elephant:
شد عیال الله و حق نعم المعیل
they all have become God's family (dependent on Him for their nourishment),
and what an excellent nourisher is God!

این همه غمها که اندر سینه‌هاست
All these griefs that are within our breasts
از بخار و گرد باد و بود ماست
arise from the vapour and dust of our existence and wind (vain desire).

این غمان بیخ کن چون داس ماست
These uprooting griefs are as a scythe to us:
این چنین شد و آنچنان وسواس ماست
this is such and such or that that is such and such is a temptation (of the Devil) to us.

دان که هر رنجی ز مردن پاره‌ایست
Know that every pain is a piece of Death:
جزو مرگ از خود بران گر چاره‌ایست
expel (that) part of Death from thee, if there be a means (of doing so).

چون ز جزو مرگ نتوانی گریخت
When thou canst not flee from the part of Death,
دان که کلش بر سرت خواهند ریخت
know that the whole of it will be poured upon thy head.

جزو مرگ ار گشت شیرین مر ترا
If the part of Death has become sweet to thee,
دان که شیرین می‌کند کل را خدا
know that God will make the whole sweet.

دردها از مرگ می‌آید رسول
Pains are coming from Death as (his) messengers:
از رسولش رو مگردان ای فضول
do not avert thy face from his messenger, O foolish one!

هر که شیرین می‌زید او تلخ مرد
Whoever lives sweetly (pleasantly) dies bitterly (painfully):
هر که او تن را پرستد جان نبرد
whoever serves his body does not save his soul.

گوسفندان را ز صحرا می‌کشند
Sheep are driven from the plains (to the town):
آنک فربه‌تر مر آن را می‌کشند
the fatter they are, the quicker they are killed.

شب گذشت و صبح آمد ای تمر
The night is past and dawn is come.
چند گیری این فسانهٔ زر ز سر
O my soul, how long wilt thou take up (again) the tale of gold from the beginning?

تو جوان بودی و قانع‌تر بدی
Thou wert young (once), and (then) thou wert more contented:
زر طلب گشتی خود اول زر بدی
(now) thou hast become a seeker of gold, (but) at first thou wert gold indeed (precious and perfect)

رز بدی پر میوه چون کاسد شدی
Thou wert a fruitful vine: how hast thou become unsaleable(worthless)?
وقت میوه پختنت فاسد شدی
How hast thou become rotten when thy fruit is ripening?

میوه‌ات باید که شیرین‌تر شود
Thy fruit ought to become sweeter
چون رسن تابان نه واپس‌تر رود
and not move farther backwards like rope-makers.

جفت مانی جفت باید هم‌صفت
Thou art my wife: the wife must be of the same quality
تا برآید کارها با مصلحت
(as the husband) in order that things may go rightly.

جفت باید بر مثال همدگر
The married pair must match one another:
در دو جفت کفش و موزه در نگر
look at a pair of shoes or boots.

گر یکی کفش از دو تنگ آید به پا
If one of the shoes is too tight for the foot,
هر دو جفتش کار ناید مر ترا
the pair of them is of no use to thee.

جفت در یک خرد وان دیگر بزرگ
Hast thou ever seen one leaf of a (folding) door small and the other large,
جفت شیر بیشه دیدی هیچ گرگ
or a wolf mated with the lion of the jungle?

راست ناید بر شتر جفت جوال
A pair of sacks on a camel do not balance
آن یکی خالی و این پر مال مال
properly when one is small and the other of full size.

من روم سوی قناعت دل‌قوی
I march with stout heart towards contentment:
تو چرا سوی شناعت می‌روی
why art thou betaking thyself to revilement?"

مرد قانع از سر اخلاص و سوز
In this fashion the contented man, moved by sincerity and ardour,
زین نسق می‌گفت با زن تا بروز
was talking to his wife till daybreak.

نصحیت کردن زن مر شوی را
How the wife counselled her husband, saying,

کی سخن افزون از قدم و از مقام خود مگو تقولون ما لا تفعلون کی این سخنها اگرچه راستست این مقام توکل ترا نیست و این سخن گفتن فوق مقام و معاملهٔ خود زیان دارد و کبر مقتا عند الله باشد

"Don't talk any more about thy merit and (spiritual) rank 'why say ye that which ye do not?' for although these words are true, yet thou hast not attained to the degree of trust in God, and to speak thus above thy station and devotional practice is harmful and 'exceedingly hateful in the sight of God.'"

زن بر و زد بانگ کای ناموس کیش
The wife cried out at him, saying, "O thou who makest reputation thy religion,

من فسون تو نخواهم خورد بیش
I will not swallow thy spells (deceiving speeches) any more.

ترهات از دعوی و دعوت مگو
Don't talk nonsense in thy presumption and pretension:

رو سخن از کبر و از نخوت مگو
begone, don't speak from pride and arrogance.

چند حرف طمطراق و کار بار
How long (wilt thou utter) pompous and artificial phrases?

کار و حال خود ببین و شرم دار
Look at thine own acts and feelings and be ashamed!

کبر زشت و از گدایان زشت تر
Pride is ugly, and in beggars (all the) more ugly:

روز سرد و برف وانگه جامه تر
(it is like) wet clothes after a cold snowy day.

چند دعوی و دم و باد و بروت
How long (this) pretension and palaver and bluster,

ای ترا خانه چو بیت العنکبوت
O thou whose house is (frail) as the house of the spider?

از قناعت کی تو جان افروختی
When hast thou illumined thy soul by contentment?

از قناعتها تو نام آموختی
Of contentment thou hast learned (only) the name.

گفت پیغامبر قناعت چیست گنج
The Prophet said, 'What is contentment?

گنج را تو وا نمی‌دانی ز رنج
A treasure.' Thou canst not distinguish the gain from the pain.

این قناعت نیست جز گنج روان
This contentment is the soul's treasure: do not thou boast (of possessing it),
تو مزن لاف ای غم و رنج روان
O (thou who art) grief and pain to my soul.

تو مخوانم جفت کمتر زن بغل
Don't call me thy mate, don't flap so much.
جفت انصافم نیم جفت دغل
I am the mate of justice, I am not the mate of fraud.

چون قدم با میر و با بگ می‌زنی
How art thou walking (consorting) with amír and bey,
چون ملخ را در هوا رگ می‌زنی
when thou art slitting the veins of (killing for food) the locust in the air?

با سگان زین استخوان در چالشی
Thou art contending with dogs for the sake of a bone,
چون نی اشکم تهی در نالشی
thou art wailing like an empty-bellied reed-pipe.

سوی من منگر بخواری سست سست
Don't look at me dully (coldly) with contempt,
تا نگویم آنچه در رگهای تست
lest I tell (others) what is in thy veins (disclose thy hidden faults).

عقل خود را از من افزون دیده‌ای
Thou hast deemed thy understanding superior to mine, (but)
مر من کم‌عقل را چون دیده‌ای
how hast thou (truly) seen me, who am deficient in understanding?

همچو گرگ غافل اندر ما مجه
Don't spring upon me like a reckless wolf!
ای ز ننگ عقل تو بی‌عقل به
Oh, better be without understanding (mad) than (suffer) the disgrace of (having) thy understanding

چونک عقل تو عقیلهٔ مردمست
Since thy understanding is a shackle for mankind,
آن نه عقلست آن که مار و کزدمست
it is not understanding: it is a snake and scorpion.

خصم ظلم و مکر تو الله باد
May God be the enemy of thy iniquity and deceit!
فضل و عقل تو ز ما کوتاه باد
May the deceitfulness of thy understanding fall short of (fail to injure) us!

هم تو ماری هم فسون‌گر این عجب
Thou art both the snake and the charmer—oh,
مارگیر و ماری ای ننگ عرب
wonderful! Thou art (both) the snakecatcher and the snake, O thou disgrace to the Arabs!

زاغ اگر زشتی خود بشناختی
If the crow knew its ugliness,
همچو برف از درد و غم بگداختی
from grief and sorrow it would melt like snow.

مرد افسونگر بخواند چون عدو
The charmer chants (a spell) as an enemy (does);
او فسون بر مار و مار افسون برو
he is(casting) a spell upon the snake and the snake is (casting) a spell upon him.

گر نبودی دام او افسون مار
If his trap were not (devised by him as) a spell for the snake (a means of catching it),
کی فسون مار را گشتی شکار
how would he become a prey to the snake's spell?

مرد افسون‌گر ز حرص کسب و کار
The charmer, from greed and (desire of) getting and making (money),
در نیابد آن زمان افسون مار
is not conscious of the snake's spell at the time.

مار گوید ای فسون‌گر هین و هین
The snake says, 'O charmer, beware, beware!
آن خود دیدی فسون من ببین
Thou hast beheld thine own spell (and its effect upon me): now behold mine!

تو به نام حق فریبی مر مرا
Thou beguilest me with the Name of God
تا کنی رسوای شور و شر مرا
in order that thou mayst expose me to shame and confusion

نام حقم بست نی آن رای تو
The Name of God enthralled me, not thy contrivance:
نام حق را دام کردی وای تو
madest the Name of God a trap: woe to thee!

نام حق بستاند از تو داد من
The Name of God will take vengeance from thee on my behalf:
من به نام حق سپردم جان و تن
I commit my soul and body to the Name of God.

یا به زخم من رگ جانت برد
Either it will sever the vein of thy life by my stroke,
یا که همچون من به زندانت برد
or it will bring thee into a prison as (it has brought) me."

زن ازین گونه خشن گفتارها
Rough speeches of this sort, (whole) volumes,
خواند بر شوی جوان طومارها
the woman recited to her youthful husband

❖◉❖◉❖

نصیحت کردن مرد مر زن را
How the man counselled his wife, saying,

کی در فقیران به خواری منگر و در کار حق به گمان کمال نگر و طعنه مزن در فقر و فقیران به خیال و گمان بی‌نوایی خویشتن
"Do not look with contempt on the poor, but regard the work of God as perfect, and do not let thy vain thought and opinion of thine own penury cause thee to sneer at poverty and revile the poor."

گفت ای زن تو زنی یا بوالحزن
O woman," said he, "art thou a woman or the father of sorrow?
فقر فخر آمد مرا بر سر مزن
Poverty is (my) pride, and do not thou beat me on the head (lash me with thy reproaches).

مال و زر سر را بود همچون کلاه
Wealth and gold are as a cap to the head:
کل بود او کز کله سازد پناه
'tis the bald man that makes a shelter of his cap,

آنک زلف جعد و رعنا باشدش
(But) he that has curly and beautiful
چون کلاهش رفت خوشتر آیدش
locks is happier when his cap is gone.

مرد حق باشد بماند بصر
The man of God (the saint) resembles the eye:
پس برهنه به که پوشیده نظر
therefore (his) sight is better bare (unveiled) than covered.

وقت عرضه کردن آن برده فروش
When a slave-dealer offers (slaves) for sale,
بر کند از بنده جامهٔ عیب پوش
he removes from the (sound) slave the garment that hides defects.

ور بود عیبی برهنه ش کی کند
But if there be any defect, how should he strip (the slave)?
بل بجامه خدعه‌ای با وی کند
Nay, he tricks him (the purchaser) by means of the garment.

گوید ای شرمنده است از نیک و بد
'This one,' says he, 'is ashamed of good and evil:
از برهنه کردن او از تو رمد
stripping him would cause him to run away from thee.'

خواجه در عیبست غرقه تا به گوش
The (rich) merchant is plunged in vice up to the ears,
خواجه را مالست و مالش عیب‌پوش
(but) the merchant has money, and his money covers his vice,

کز طمع عیبش نبیند طامعی
For because of cupidity none that is covetous sees his vice:
گشت دلها را طمعها جامعی
feelings of cupidity are a bond uniting (men's) hearts;

ور گدا گوید سخن چون زر کان
And if a beggar speak a word like the (pure) gold of the mine,
ره نیابد کالهٔ او در دکان
his wares will not find the way to the shop.

کار درویشی ورای فهم تست
The affair of (spiritual) poverty is beyond thy apprehension:
سوی درویشی بمنگر سست سست
do not look on poverty with contempt,

زانک درویشان ورای ملک و مال
Because dervishes are beyond property and wealth:
روزیی دارند ژرف از ذوالجلال
they possess an abundant portion from the Almighty.

حق تعالی عادلست و عادلان
The High God is just, and how should the just behave
کی کنند استمگری بر بی‌دلان
tyrannously to the dispirited (poor and weak)?

آن یکی را نعمت و کالا دهند
(How should they) give fortune and goods to that one,
وین دگر را بر سر آتش نهند
while they put this one on the fire?

آتشش سوزا که دارد این گمان
The fire burns him because he hath this thought about
بر خدا و خالق هر دو جهان
the Lord who created both worlds.

فقر فخری از گزافست و مجاز
Is (the saying) 'Poverty is my pride' vain and false?
نه هزاران عز پنهانست و ناز
false? No; 'tis thousands of hidden glories and disdains.

از غضب بر من لقبها راندی
Thou in anger hast poured nicknames on me:
یارگیر و مارگیرم خواندی
thou hast called me a catcher (deceiver) of friends and a catcher of snakes.

گر بگیرم برکنم دندان مار
If I catch the snake, I extract its fangs
تاش از سرکوفتن نبود ضرار
in order that I may save it from having its head crushed.

زانک آن دندان عدو جان اوست
Because those fangs are an enemy to its life,
من عدو را می‌کنم زین علم دوست
I am making the enemy a friend by means of this skill.

از طمع هرگز نخوانم من فسون
Never do I chant my spell from (motives of) cupidity:
این طمع را کرده‌ام من سرنگون
I have turned this cupidity upside down (I have entirely vanquished it).

حاش لله طمع من از خلق نیست
God forbid! I desire nothing from created beings:
از قناعت در دل من عالمیست
through contentment there is a (whole) world within my heart.

بر سر امرودبن بینی چنان
Thou, (sitting) on the top of the pear-tree, seest (things) like that:
زان فرود آ تا نماند آن گمان
come down from it, that the (evil) thought may not continue.

چون که بر گردی تو سرگشته شوی
When thou turnest round and round and becomest giddy, thou seest the house turning round,
خانه را گردنده بینی و آن توی
and 'tis thou (thyself) art that (revolving object).

در بیان آنک جنبیدن هر کسی از آنجا

Explaining how every one's movement (action) proceeds from the place

آفتاب را کبود نماید و سرخ سرخ نماید چون تابه‌ها از رنگها ( ) کی ویست هر کس را از چنبرهٔ وجود خود بیند تابهٔ کبود بیرون آید سپید شود از همه تابه‌های دیگر او راست‌گوتر باشد و امام باشد

where he is, (so that) he sees every one (else) from the circle of his own self-existence: a blue glass shows the sun as blue, a red glass as red, (but) when the glass escapes from (the sphere of) colour, it becomes white, (and then) it is more truthful than all other glasses and is the Imám exemplar to them all).

دید احمد را ابوجهل و بگفت
Abú Jahl saw Ahmad (Mohammed) and said,

زشت نقشی کز بنی‌هاشم شکفت
'Tis an ugly figure that has sprung from the sons of Háshim!'

گفت احمد مر ورا که راستی
Ahmad said to him, 'Thou art right,

راست گفتی گرچه کار افزاستی
thou hast spoken truth, although thou art impertinent.'

دید صدیقش بگفت ای آفتاب
The Siddíq (Abú Bakr) saw him and said,

نی ز شرق نی ز غربی خوش بتاب
O Sun, thou art neither of East nor of West: shine beauteously!'

گفت احمد راست گفتی ای عزیز
Ahmad said, 'Thou hast spoken the truth, O dear friend,

ای رهیده تو ز دنیای نه چیز
O thou that hast escaped from this world of nothingness.'

حاضران گفتند ای صدر الوری
They that were present said, 'O king,

راست‌گو گفتی دو ضدگو را چرا
why didst thou call both of them truth-tellers when they contradicted each other?'

گفت من آیینه‌ام مصقول دست
He replied, 'I am a mirror polished by the (Divine) hand:

ترک و هندو در من آن بیند که هست
Turcoman and Indian behold in me that which exists (in themselves).'

ای زن ار طماع می‌بینی مرا
O wife, if thou deemest me very covetous,

زین تحری زنانه برتر آ
rise above this womanish care (for worldly things).

آن طمع را ماند و رحمت بود

This (state of mine) resembles cupidity and (in reality) it is a (Divine) mercy:

کو طمع آنجا که آن نعمت بود

where that (spiritual) blessing is, where is cupidity?

امتحان کن فقر را روزی دو تو

Make trial of poverty for a day or two,

تا به فقر اندر غنا بینی دوتو

that thou mayst see (find) in poverty double riches.

صبر کن با فقر و بگذار این ملال

Have patience with poverty and abandon this disgust,

زانک در فقرست عز ذوالجلال

because in poverty there is the light of the Lord of glory.

سرکه مفروش و هزاران جان ببین

Do not look sour, and (thou wilt) see thousands of souls plunged,

از قناعت غرق بحر انگبین

through contentment, in an ocean of honey.

صد هزاران جان تلخی‌کش نگر

Behold hundreds of thousands of bitterly suffering souls

همچو گل آغشته اندر گلشکر

steeped in rose-syrup, like the rose.

ای دریغا مر ترا گنجا بدی

Oh, alas, would that thou hadst comprehension,

تا ز جانم شرح دل پیدا شدی

so that the unfolded tale of my heart might be shown forth to thee from my soul.

این سخن شیرست در پستان جان

This discourse is milk in the teat of the soul

بی کشنده خوش نمی‌گردد روان

it will not flow well without someone to suck (the teat).

مستمع چون تشنه و جوینده شد

When the hearer has become thirsty and craving

واعظ ار مرده بود گوینده شد

the preacher, (even) if he be (as good as) dead, becomes eloquent.

مستمع چون تازه آمد بی‌ملال

When the hearer is fresh and without fatigue (not bored),

صدزبان گردد به گفتن گنگ و لال

the dumb and mute will find a hundred tongues to speak withal.

چونک نامحرم در آید از درم
When a stranger comes in at my door,
پرده در پنهان شوند اهل حرم
the women of the harem hide themselves in the veil,

ور در آید محرمی دور از گزند
But if a harmless relative should come in,
برگشایند آن ستیران روی‌بند
those covered ones will lift up their faceveils.

هرچه را خوب و خوش و زیبا کنند
Everything that is made beautiful and fair and lovely is made
از برای دیدهٔ بینا کنند
(so) for the eye of him that sees.

کی بود آواز چنگ و زیر و بم
How should the sound of melody and treble and bass
از برای گوش بی‌حس اصم
be(made) for the insentient ear of one who is deaf?

مشک را بیهوده حق خوش‌دم نکرد
Not in vain did God make musk fragrant:
بهر حس کرد و پی اخشم نکرد
He made it(so) for the sense (of smell), He did not make it for one whose nostrils are stopped

حق زمین و آسمان بر ساخته ست
God hath fashioned the earth and the sky,
در میان بس نار و نور افراخته ست
He hath raised in the midst much fire and light.

این زمین را از برای خاکیان
(He made) this earth for those (created) of clay,
آسمان را مسکن افلاکیان
(He made) heaven to be the abode of the celestials.

مرد سفلی دشمن بالا بود
The low (base) man is the enemy of what is high:
مشتری هر مکان پیدا بود
the purchaser (seeker) of each place (Heaven or Hell) is manifest (made known by his actions).

ای ستیره هیچ تو بر خاستی
O chaste woman, hast thou ever risen up
خویشتن را بهر کور آراستی
and decked thyself for the sake of him that is blind?

303

گر جهان را پر در مکنون کنم
If I should fill the world with hidden pearls (of wisdom),
روزی تو چون نباشد چون کنم
how should I fare since they are not thy portion

ترک جنگ و رهزنی ای زن بگو
O wife, take leave of quarrelling and waylaying,
ور نمی‌گویی به ترک من بگو
and if thou wilt not, (then) take leave of me!

مر مرا چه جای جنگ نیک و بد
What room have I for quarrelling with the good or the bad?
کین دلم از صلحها هم می‌رمد
for this heart of mine is recoiling (even) from acts of peace.

گر خمش گردی وگر نه آن کنم
If thou keep silence, ('tis well), and if not,
که همین دم ترک خان و مان کنم
I will so do that at this very moment I will leave my house and home."

❖◉❖◉❖

مراعات کردن زن شوهر را و استغفار کردن از گفتهٔ خویش
How the wife paid regard to her husband and begged God to forgive her for what she had said.

زن چو دید او را که تند و توسنست
When the wife saw that he was fierce and unmanageable,
گشت گریان گریه خود دام زنست
she began to weep: tears in sooth are a woman's lure.

گفت از تو کی چنین پنداشتم
She said, "When did I imagine such (words) from thee?
از تو من امید دیگر داشتم
I hoped of thee something different."

زن در آمد از طریق نیستی
The wife approached by the way of self-naughting (selfabasement).
گفت من خاک شمام نی ستی
"I am thy dust," said she, "not (worthy to be) thy lady-wife.

جسم و جان و هرچه هستم آن تست
Body and soul and all I am is thine:
حکم و فرمان جملگی فرمان تست
he entire authority and command belongs to thee.

304

گر ز درویشی دلم از صبر جست
If because of poverty my heart has lost patience,
بهر خویشم نیست آن بهر تو است
it is not for my own sake, but for thine.

تو مرا در دردها بودی دوا
Thou hast been my remedy in afflictions:
من نمی‌خواهم که باشی بی‌نوا
I am unwilling that thou shouldst be penniless.

جان تو کز بهر خویشم نیست این
On my soul and conscience, this is not for my own sake:
از برای تستم این ناله و حنین
this wailing and moaning is on account of thee.

خویش من والله که بهر خویش تو
(I swear) by God that at every moment my self
هر نفس خواهد که میرد پیش تو
would fain die for thy self before thee.

کاش جانت کش روان من فدا
Would that thy soul, to which my soul is devoted,
از ضمیر جان من واقف بدی
were aware of my soul's inmost thoughts!

چون تو با من این چنین بودی بظن
Inasmuch as thou hast such (an ill) opinion of me,
هم ز جان بیزار گشتم هم ز تن
I am grown weary both of soul and of body.

خاک را بر سیم و زر کردیم چون
I cast earth on (renounce) silver and gold,
تو چنینی با من ای جان را سکون
since thou behavest thus to me, O comfort of my soul.

تو که در جان و دلم جا می‌کنی
Thou who dwellest in my soul and heart,
زین قدر از من تبرا می‌کنی
wilt thou declare thyself to be quit of me for this (small) amount

تو تبرا کن که هستت دستگاه
Be quit (then)! for thou hast the power,
ای تبرای ترا جان عذرخواه
(but) oh, my soul pleads against thy making this declaration.

یاد می‌کن آن زمانی را که من
Remember the time when I

چون صنم بودم تو بودی چون شمن
was (beautiful) as the idol, and thou (adoring) as the idolater

بنده بر وفق تو دل افروختست
Thy slave has kindled her heart (in eagerness) to comply with thee:

هرچه گویی پخت گوید سوختست
whatever thou callest 'cooked,' she says it is 'burnt.'

من سپاناخ تو با هرچم پزی
Whatever thou mayst cook me with, I am thy spinach:

یا ترش‌با یا که شیرین می‌سزی
whether (thou art) sour broth (to me) or sweet, thou art worthy (of my affection).

کفر گفتم نک بایمان آمدم
I uttered infidelity (blasphemy): lo, I have returned to

پیش حکمت از سر جان آمدم
the true faith, I am come (to submit) with all my soul to thy command.

خوی شاهانهٔ ترا نشناختم
I did not know thy kingly nature,

پیش تو گستاخ خر در تاختم
I rudely urged my beast(intruded) before thee.

چون ز عفو تو چراغی ساختم
Since I have made (for myself) a lamp of thy forgiveness,

توبه کردم اعتراض انداختم
forgiveness, I repent, I cast away (abandon) opposition.

می‌نهم پیش تو شمشیر و کفن
I am laying before thee sword and winding-sheet:

می‌کشم پیش تو گردن را بزن
I am bending my neck towards thee: smite!

از فراق تلخ می‌گویی سخن
Thou art talking of bitter separation (from me):

هر چه خواهی کن ولیکن این مکن
do whatever thou wilt, but do not this.

در تو از من عذرخواهی هست سر
Thy conscience within thee is a pleader on my behalf,

با تو بی من او شفیعی مستمر
it is a perpetual intercessor with thee in my absence.

عذر خواهم در درونت خلق تست
What pleads within thee for me is thy (noble) nature:
ز اعتماد او دل من جرم جست
from reliance on it my heart sought (to) sin (against thee).

رحم کن پنهان ز خود ای خشمگین
Have mercy, unbeknown to thyself (without any self-conceit), O angry one,
ای که خلقت به ز صد من انگبین
O thou whose nature is better than a hundred maunds of honey."

زین نسق می‌گفت با لطف و گشاد
In this fashion was she speaking graciously and winningly:
در میانه گریه‌ای بر وی فتاد
meanwhile a (fit of) weeping came upon her.

گریه چون از حد گذشت و های های
When the tears and sobs passed beyond bounds
زو که بی گریه بد او خود دلربای
from her who was fascinating even without tears

شد از آن باران یکی برق پدید
There appeared from that rain a lightning-flash (that)
زد شراری در دل مرد وحید
shot a spark of fire into the heart of the lonely man.

آنک بندۀ روی خوبش بود مرد
She by whose beauteous face man was enslaved,
چون بود چون بندگی آغاز کرد
how will it be when she begins to play the (humble) slave?

آنک از کبرش دلت لرزان بود
She at whose haughtiness thy heart is trembling,
چون شوی چون پیش تو گریان شود
how wilt thou fare when she falls aweeping before thee?

آنک از نازش دل و جان خون بود
She from whose disdain thy heart and soul are bleeding,
چونک آید در نیاز او چون بود
how will it be when she turns to entreaty?

آنک در جور و جفااش دام ماست
She in whose tyranny and cruelty we are snared,
عذر ما چه بود چو او در عذر خاست
what plea shall we have when she rises to plead?

زین للناس حق آراستست
(The love of desired things, women, etc.) is decked out for men (made attractive to them):
زآنچه حق آراست چون دانند جست
God has arranged it: how can they escape from what God has arranged?

چون پی یسکن الیهاش آفرید
Inasmuch as He created her (the woman) that he (Adam) might take comfort in her,
کی تواند آدم از حوا برید
how can Adam be parted from Eve?

رستم زال ار بود وز حمزه بیش
Though he (the husband) be Rustam son of Zál and greater than Hamza (in valour),
هست در فرمان اسیر زال خویش
as regards authority he is his old woman's (his wife's) captive.

آنک عالم مست گفتش آمدی
He (the Prophet), to whose words the (whole) world was enslaved (obedient),
کلمینی یا حمیرا می‌زدی
used to cry, "Speak to me, O Humayrá!"

آب غالب شد بر آتش از لهیب
The water prevailed over (extinguished) the fire by its dread onset,
زآتش او جوشد چو باشد در حجیب
(but) the fire makes it seethe when it (the water) is screened (hidden in the cauldron).

چونک دیگی حایل آمد هر دو را
When a cauldron comes between (them), O king,
نیست کرد آن آب را کردش هوا
it (the fire) annihilates the water and converts it into air.

ظاهرا بر زن چو آب ار غالبی
If outwardly thou art dominating thy wife, like the (firequenching) water,
باطنا مغلوب و زن را طالبی
(yet) inwardly thou art dominated and art seeking (the love of) thy wife.

این چنین خاصیتی در آدمیست
This is characteristic of Man (alone):
مهر حیوان را کمست آن از کمیست
to the (other) animals love is wanting, and that arises from inferiority

در بیان این خبر کی انهن یغلبن العاقل و یغلبهن الجاهل
Explanation of the Tradition, "Verily, they (women) prevail over the wise man, and the ignorant man prevails over them."

گفت پیغامبر که زن بر عاقلان
The Prophet said that woman prevails

غالب آید سخت و بر صاحب دلان
exceedingly over the wise and intelligent,

باز بر زن جاهلان چیره شوند
(While), on the other hand, ignorant men prevail over woman,

زانک ایشان تند و بس خیره روند
for in them the fierceness of the animal is imprisoned.

کم بودشان رقت و لطف و وداد
They lack tenderness, kindness, and affection,

زانک حیوانیست غالب بر نهاد
because animality predominates over their (human) nature.

مهر و رقت وصف انسانی بود
Love and tenderness are human qualities,

خشم و شهوت وصف حیوانی بود
anger and lust are animal qualities.

پرتو حقست آن معشوق نیست
She (woman) is a ray of God, she is not that (earthly) beloved:

خالقست آن گویی مخلوق نیست
she is creative, you might say she is not created.

◈◈◈

تسلیم کردن مرد خود را بآنچه التماس زن بود
How the man yielded to his wife's request

از طلب معیشت و آن اعتراض زن را اشارت حق دانستن
that he should seek the means of livelihood, and regarded her opposition (to him) as a Divine indication man it is a fact.

به نزد عقل هر داننده ای هست
To the mind of every knowing man it is a fact

کی با گردنده گرداننده ای هست
that with the revolving object there is one that causes it to revolve

مرد زان گفتن پیشمان شد چنان
The man became as sorry for that speech

کز عوانی ساعت مردن عوان
(of his) as at the hour of death a tyrannical officer (is sorry) for his tyranny.

گفت خصم جان جان چون آمدم
He said, "How did I become the adversary of (her who is) the life of my soul?

بر سر جان من لگدها چون زدم
How did I bestow kicks on the head of my soul?"

چون قضا آید فرو پوشد بصر
When the (Divine) destiny comes, it muffles the sight,

تا نداند عقل ما پا را ز سر
so that our intellect cannot distinguish foot from head.

چون قضا بگذشت خود را می خورد
As soon as the destiny is past, it (the intellect) devours itself

پرده بدریده گریبان می درد
rending the veil (without regard for appearances), it tears its bosom.

مرد گفت ای زن پیشمان می شوم
The man said, "O wife, I am repenting:

گر بدم کافر مسلمان می شوم
if I have been an infidel, I will (now) become a Moslem.

من گنه کار توم رحمی بکن
I am a sinner against thee: have mercy,

بر مکن یکبارگیم از بیخ و بن
do not dig me up all at once from root and foundation

کافر پیر ار پشیمان می شود
If the old infidel is repenting,

چونک عذر آرد مسلمان می شود
he becomes a Moslem when he pleads for pardon.

حضرت پر رحمتست و پر کرم
He (God) is the merciful and bountiful Lord:

عاشق او هم وجود و هم عدم
both existence and non-existence are in love with Him.

کفر و ایمان عاشق آن کبریا
(Both) infidelity and faith are lovers of that Majesty,

مس و نقره بنده آن کیمیا
both copper and silver are slaves to that Elixir.

در بیان آنک موسی و فرعون هر دو مسخر مشیت‌اند
Explaining that both Moses and Pharaoh are subject to the Divine Will,

چنانک زهر و پازهر و ظلمات و نور و مناجات کردن فرعون بخلوت تا ناموس نشکند
like antidote and poison and darkness and light, and how Pharaoh conversed in solitude with God, praying that He would not destroy his (good) reputation.

موسی و فرعون معنی را رهی
Moses and Pharaoh were servants (worshippers) of Reality,

ظاهر آن ره دارد و این بی‌رهی
(though) outwardly the former keeps the way (is rightly guided), while the latter has lost the way

روز موسی پیش حق نالان شده
In the daytime Moses was making lament (supplication) to God:

نیمشب فرعون هم گریان بده
at midnight Pharaoh would begin to weep,

کین چه غلست ای خدا بر گردنم
Saying, "O God, what shackle is this on my neck?

ورنه غل باشد کی گوید من منم
Were it not for the shackle, who would say 'I am I'?

زانک موسی را منور کرده‌ای
By that (will) whereby Thou hast made Moses to be illumined,

مر مرا زان هم مکدر کرده‌ای
by that (same will) Thou hast made me to be darkened;

زانک موسی را تو مه رو کرده‌ای
By that whereby Thou hast made Moses' face like the moon

ماه جانم را سیه رو کرده‌ای
Thou hast made the moon of my soul to be black-faced (eclipsed).

بهتر از ماهی نبود استاره‌ام
My star was not better than a moon (so that it should be exempt from eclipse):

چون خسوف آمد چه باشد چاره‌ام
since it has suffered eclipse, what help have I?

نوبتم گر رب و سلطان می‌زنند
If they beat drums in my honour (proclaiming me) as Lord and Sultan,

مه گرفت و خلق پنگان می‌زنند
('tis like as when) the moon is eclipsed and the people beat bowls (of metal).

می‌زنند آن طاس و غوغا می‌کنند
They beat those bowls and raise a clamour:

ماه را زان زخمه رسوا می‌کنند
they put the moon to shame by their blows.

من که فرعونم ز خلق ای وای من
I, who am Pharaoh, oh, woe is me because of (what is being done by) the people:
زخم طاس آن ربی الاعلای من
my (title of) 'My supreme Lord' is (like) the blows on the bowl (since it proclaims my eclipse)

خواجه تاشانیم اما تیشه ات
We (Moses and I) are fellow-servants (to Thee),
می‌شکافد شاخ را در بیشه ات
but Thy axe is cleaving the sappy boughs in Thy forest;

باز شاخی را موصل می‌کند
Then it makes one bough to be firmly planted,
شاخ دیگر را معطل می‌کند
another bough to be left uncared for.

شاخ را بر تیشه دستی هست نی
The bough has no power against the axe:
هیچ شاخ از دست تیشه جست نی
no bough escaped from the power of the axe.

حق آن قدرت که آن تیشه تراست
(I entreat Thee) by the truth of the might which belongs to Thy axe,
از کرم کن این کژیها را تو راست
do Thou graciously make these crooked (perverse) actions (of ours) straight (righteous)."

باز با خود گفته فرعون ای عجب
Once more Pharaoh said to himself,
من نه دریا ربناام جمله شب
"Oh, wonderful! Am not I (occupied) the whole night in (crying) 'O our Lord'?

در نهان خاکی و موزون می‌شوم
In secret I am growing humble and harmonious:
چون به موسی می‌رسم چون می‌شوم
when I reach Moses, how am I becoming (so different)?

رنگ زر قلب ده‌تو می‌شود
The colour (gilt) of base gold is (laid on) in ten coats:
پیش آتش چون سیه رو می‌شود
how is it becoming black-faced in the presence of the fire?

نه که قلب و قالبم در حکم اوست
Is it not (true) that my heart (spirit) and body are under His control,
لحظه‌ای مغزم کند یک لحظه پوست
(so that) at one moment He makes me a kernel, at another moment a rind?

312

سبز گردم چونک گوید کشت باش
When He bids me be a cornfield, I become green;
زرد گردم چونک گوید زشت باش
when He bids me be ugly, I become yellow.

لحظه‌ای ماهم کند یک دم سیاه
At one moment He makes me a moon, at another black."
خود چه باشد غیر این کار اله
How, indeed, is the action of God other than this?

پیش چوگانهای حکم کن فکان
Before the (blows of the) bat of His decree, "Be, and it was,"
می‌دویم اندر مکان و لامکان
we are running (like balls) in Space and beyond.

چونک بی‌رنگی اسیر رنگ شد
Since colourlessness (pure Unity) became the captive of colour (manifestation in the phenomenal world),
موسی با موسی در جنگ شد
a Moses came into conflict with a Moses.

چون به بی‌رنگی رسی کان داشتی
When you attain unto the colourlessness which you (originally) possessed,
موسی و فرعون دارند آشتی
Moses and Pharaoh are at peace (with each other).

گر ترا آید برین نکته سئوال
If it occurs to you to ask questions about this mystery,
رنگ کی خالی بود از قیل و قال
(I reply), how should (the world of) colour be devoid of contradiction?

این عجب کین رنگ از بی درنگ خاست
The marvel is that this colour arose from that which is colourless:
رنگ با بی‌رنگ چون در جنگ خاست
how did colour arise to war with the colourless?

چونک روغن را ز آب اسرشته اند
The original source of oil (the oil producing tree) is made to grow by means of water
آب با روغن چرا ضد گشته اند
how (then) does it (oil) finally become opposed to water?

چون گل از خارست و خار از گل چرا
Since the rose springs from the thorn, and the thorn from the rose
هر دو در جنگند و اندر ماجرا
why are both of them at war and (engaged) in recrimination?

یا نه جنگست این برای حکمتست
Or is this not (really) war? Is it for (the Divine) purpose, (and is it) an artifice

همچو جنگ خر فروشان صنعتست
like the bickering of those who sell asses?

یا نه اینست و نه آن حیرانیست
Or is it neither this nor that? Is it bewilderment?

گنج باید جست این ویرانیست
The treasure must be sought and this (bewilderment) is the ruin (where it is hidden).

آنچه تو گنجش توهم می کنی
That which you imagine to be the treasure

زان توهم گنج را گم می کنی
through that vain imagination you are losing the treasure.

چون عمارت دان تو وهم و رایها
Know that fancies and opinions are like the state of cultivation:

گنج نبود در عمارت جایها
treasure is not (to be found) in cultivated spots.

در عمارت هستی و جنگی بود
In the state of cultivation there is existence and strife(contrariety):

نیست را از هستها ننگی بود
the non-existent is ashamed of (all) existent things.

نه که هست از نیستی فریاد کرد
It is not the case that the existent implored help against (sought to escape from) nonexistence;

بلک نیست آن هست را واداد کرد
nay, ('twas) the nonexistent(that) repelled the existent.

تو مگو که من گریزانم ز نیست
Do not say, "I am fleeing from the non-existent";

بلک او از تو گریزانست بیست
nay, it is fleeing from you. Stop! (Do not fancy yourself to be fleeing.)

ظاهرا می خواندت او سوی خود
Outwardly it is calling you towards itself,

وز درون می راندت با چوب رد
but inwardly it is driving you away with the cudgel of rejection.

نعلهای بازگونه ست ای سلیم
O man of sound heart (mind), 'tis (a case of) reversed shoes:

نفرت فرعون می دان از کلیم
know that the rebelliousness of Pharaoh was (really) from (caused by) Moses.

سبب حرمان اشقیا از دو جهان
The reason why the unblest are disappointed of both worlds,

کی خسر الدنیا و اخرة
(according to the text) "he has lost this life and the life to come."

چون حکیمک اعتقادی کرده است
The wretched philosopher being firmly convinced that

کآسمان بیضه زمین چون زرده است
the sky is an egg and the earth like its yolk,

گفت سایل چون بماند این خاکدان
Someone asked him how this earth remains,

در میان این محیط آسمان
in the midst of this surrounding expanse of sky,

همچو قندیلی معلق در هوا
Suspended in the air like a lamp,

نه باسفل می‌رود نه بر علا
moving neither to the bottom nor to the top.

آن حکیمش گفت کز جذب سما
The philosopher said to him, "It remains in the air

از جهات شش بماند اندر هوا
because of the attraction exerted by the sky from (all) six directions.

چون ز مغناطیس قبهٔ ریخته
(The sky is) like a vault moulded (made) of lodestone:

درمیان ماند آهنی آویخته
(the earth like) a suspended piece of iron remains in the middle."

آن دگر گفت آسمان با صفا
Said the other, "How should the pure sky

کی کشد در خود زمین تیره را
draw the dark earth to itself?

بلک دفعش می‌کند از شش جهات
Nay, it is repelling it (the earth) from (all) six directions:

زان بماند اندر میان عاصفات
hence it (the earth) remains (suspended) amidst the violent winds (currents)."

پس ز دفع خاطر اهل کمال
(Similarly), then, because of the repulsion exerted by the hearts of the perfect (saints),

جان فرعونان بماند اندر ضلال
the spirits of Pharaohs remain in perdition.

پس ز دفع این جهان و آن جهان
Therefore, through being rejected by this world and by that world,
مانده‌اند این بی‌رهان بی این و آن
these lost ones have been left without either this or that.

سرکشی از بندگان ذوالجلال
If you turn away your head from the (holy) servants of the Almighty
دان که دارند از وجود تو ملال
know that they are disgusted by your existence.

کهربا دارند چون پیدا کنند
They possess the amber when they display it
کاه هستی ترا شیدا کنند
they make the straw of your existence frenzied (with desire for it).

کهربای خویش چون پنهان کنند
When they conceal their amber,
زود تسلیم ترا طغیان کنند
they quickly make your submission (to God) rebellion (against Him).

آنچنان که مرتبهٔ حیوانیست
That (position which you hold in relation to them) is like the stage of animality,
کو اسیر و سغبهٔ انسانیست
which is captive and subject to (the stage of) humanity.

مرتبهٔ انسان به دست اولیا
Know that the stage of humanity is subject to the power
سغبه چون حیوان شناسش ای کیا
of the saints as the animal (is subject to man), O master.

بندهٔ خود خواند احمد در رشاد
Ahmad (Mohammed) in righteousness called (the people of
جمله عالم را بخوان قل یا عباد
the whole world his servants: read (the text), "Say, O My servants."

عقل تو همچون شتربان تو شتر
Your intellect is like the camel-driver, and you are the camel:
می‌کشاند هر طرف در حکم مر
it drives you in every direction under its bitter control.

عقل عقلند اولیا و عقل‌ها
The saints are the intellect of intellect, and (all) intellects
بر مثال اشتران تا انتها
(from the beginning) to the end are (under their control) like camels.

اندریشان بنگر آخر ز اعتبار
Come now, look upon them with (profound) consideration: there is (but) one guide,
یک قلاووزست جان صد هزار
and a hundred thousand souls (following him).

چه قلاووز و چه اشتربان بیاب
What is the guide and what the camel-driver?
دیده‌ای کان دیده بیند آفتاب
Get thee an eye that may behold the Sun!

یک جهان در شب بمانده میخ دوز
o, the world has been left nailed fast in night,
منتظر موقوف خورشیدست و روز
(while) day is waiting expectantly, depending on the sun.

اینت خورشیدی نهان در ذره‌ای
Here is a sun hidden in a mote,
شیر نر در پوستین بره‌ای
a fierce lion in the fleece of a lamb.

اینت دریایی نهان در زیر کاه
Here is an ocean hidden beneath straw:
پا برین که هین منه با اشتباه
beware, do not step on this straw with hesitancy.

اشتباهی و گمانی را درون
(But) a feeling of hesitancy and doubt in the heart
رحمت حقست بهر رهنمون
is a Divine mercy in regard to the (spiritual) guide.

هر پیمبر فرد آمد در جهان
Every prophet came alone into this world:
فرد بود آن رهنمایش در نهان
he was alone, and (yet) he had a hundred unseen worlds within him.

عالک کبری بقدرت سحر کرد
By his power he enchanted the macrocosm (universe),
کرد خود را در کهین نقشی نورد
he enfolded himself in a very small frame.

ابلهانش فرد دیدند و ضعیف
The foolish deemed him to be lonely and weak:
کی ضعیفست آن که با شه شد حریف
how is he weak who has become the King's companion?

317

ابلهان گفتند مردی بیش نیست
The foolish said, "He is a man, nothing more":
وای آنکو عاقبت‌اندیش نیست
woe to him that recks not of the end!

◆◉◆◉◆

حقیر و بی‌خصم دیدن دیده‌های حس صالح و ناقهٔ صالح علیه‌السلام را
How the eyes of (external) sense regarded Sálih and his she-camel as despicable and without a champion;

چون خواهد کی حق لشکری را هلاک کند در نظر ایشان حقیر نماید خصمان را و اندک اگرچه غالب باشد آن خصم و یقللکم فی اعینهم لیقضی الله امراً کان مفعولا
(for) when God is about to destroy an army He makes their adversaries appear despicable and few in their sight, even though the adversary be superior in strength: and He was making you few in their eyes, that God might bring to pass a thing that was to be done."

ناقهٔ صالح بصورت بد شتر
The she-camel of Sálih was in (outward) form a camel:
پی بریدندش ز جهل آن قوم مر
that bitter (graceless) tribe hamstrung (and slaughtered) her in their folly.

از برای آب چون خصمش شدند
When they became her foes on account of the water (which she shared with them),
نان کور و آب کور ایشان بدند
they were blind to bread and blind to water (ungrateful for the blessings of God).

ناقة الله آب خورد از جوی و میغ
God's she-camel drank water from brook and cloud:
آب حق را داشتند از حق دریغ
they (really) withheld God's water from God.

ناقهٔ صالح چو جسم صالحان
The she-camel of Sálih became, like the bodies of righteous men,
شد کمینی در هلاک طالحان
an ambush for the destruction of the wicked,

تا بر آن امت ز حکم مرگ و درد
That (you may see) what (the Divine command), Let God's she-camel have her portion of water
ناقةالله و سقیاها چه کرد
wrought against that people, through the ordainment of death and woe.

318

شحنهٔ قهر خدا زیشان بجست
The vengeance, which is God's minister,
خونبهای اشتری شهری درست
demanded from them an entire town as the blood-price of a single camel.

روح همچون صالح و تن ناقه است
His (the prophet's or saint's) spirit is like Sálih, and his body is the she-camel:
روح اندر وصل و تن در فاقه است
the spirit is in union (with God), the body in want (distress).

روح صالح قابل آفات نیست
The Sálih-spirit is not susceptible to afflictions:
زخم بر ناقه بود بر ذات نیست
the blows fall on the camel (body), not on the essence (spirit).

کس نیابد بر دل ایشان ظفر
No one gains victory over their (the saints') hearts
بر صدف آمد ضرر نی بر گهر
harm comes (only) to the oyster-shell, not to the pearl.

روح صالح قابل آزار نیست
The Sálih-spirit is not capable of being hurt:
نور یزدان سغبهٔ کفار نیست
the light of God is not subject to infidels.

حق از آن پیوست با جسمی نهان
God became secretly united with a body
تاش آزارند و بینند امتحان
that they (the infidels) might hurt (it) and suffer tribulation,

بی‌خبر کزار این آزار اوست
Not knowing that to hurt this (body) is to hurt (offend) Him:
آب این خم متصل با آب جوست
the water in this jar is joined with the water in the river

زان تعلق کرد با جسمی اله
God became connected with a body
تا که گردد جمله عالم را پناه
in order that he (the prophet or saint) might become a refuge for the whole world.

ناقهٔ جسم ولی را بنده باش
Be a slave to the camel, which is the saint's body,
تا شوی با روح صالح خواجه تاش
that you may become the fellow servant of the Sálih-spirit

گفت صالح چونک کردید این حسد
Sálih said (to the people of Thamúd), "Inasmuch as ye have shown this envy,
بعد سه روز از خدا نقمت رسد
after three days the punishment will arrive from God.

بعد سه روز دگر از جانستان
After three more days there will come from the Taker of life
آفتی آید که دارد سه نشان
a calamity that hath three signs.

رنگ روی جمله تان گردد دگر
The colour of all your faces will be changed
رنگ رنگ مختلف اندر نظر
(they will be of) colours different to look at.

روز اول رویتان چون زعفران
On the first day your faces will be like saffron,
در دوم رو سرخ همچون ارغوان
on the second your faces will be red like arghawán (flowers of the Judas-tree).

در سوم گردد همه روها سیاه
On the third, all your faces will become black:
بعد از آن اندر رسد قهر اله
after that, the vengeance of God will arrive.

گر نشان خواهید از من زین وعید
If ye desire from me the sign of this threatened chastisement
کرهٔ ناقه به سوی که دوید
the she-camel's foal has run towards the mountains:

گر توانیدش گرفتن چاره هست
If ye can catch him, there is help (for you);
ورنه خود مرغ امید از دام جست
else the bird of hope hath surely escaped from the snare.

کس نتانست اندر آن کره رسید
None was able to overtake the foal:
رفت در کهسارها شد ناپدید
he went into the mountains and vanished

گفت دیدیت آن قضا معلن شدست
Sálih said, "Ye see, the (Divine) destiny has been divulged
صورت اومید را گردن زدست
and has beheaded the phantom of your hope."

کرهٔ ناقه چه باشد خاطرش
What is the she-camel's foal? His (the saint's) heart

که بجا آرید ز احسان و برش
which ye may bring back to its place (win again) by means of well-doing and piety.

گر بجا آید دلش رستید از آن
If his heart comes back (is reconciled), ye are saved from that (Divine punishment)

ورنه نومیدیت و ساعد را گزان
otherwise ye are despairing and biting your fore-arms (in remorse).

چون شنیدند این وعید منکدر
When they heard this dark threat,

چشم بنهادند و آن را منتظر
they cast down their eyes and waited for it (to be fulfilled).

روز اول روی خود دیدند زرد
On the first day they saw their faces yellow:

می‌زدند از ناامیدی آه سرد
from despair they were sighing heavily.

سرخ شد روی همه روز دوم
On the second day the faces of all became red:

نوبت اومید و توبه گشت گم
the time for hope and repentance was (irretrievably) lost

شد سیه روز سیم روی همه
On the third day all their faces became black

حکم صالح راست شد بی ملحمه
the prediction of Sálih came true without (possibility of) dispute.

چون همه در ناامیدی سر زدند
When they all gave themselves up to despair

همچو مرغان در دو زانو آمدند
they fell on their knees, like (crouching) birds.

در نبی آورد جبریل امین
Gabriel, the trusted (angel), brought in the Qur'án

شرح این زانو زدن را جاثمین
the description of this kneeling, (which is described by the word) játhimín.

زانو آن دم زن که تعلیمت کنند
Do thou kneel at the time when they (the saints) are teaching

وز چنین زانو زدن بیمت کنند
thee and bidding thee dread such a kneeling as this.

منتظر گشتند زخم قهر را
They (the people of Thamúd) were waiting for the stroke of vengeance
قهر آمد نیست کرد آن شهر را
the vengeance came and annihilated that town.

صالح از خلوت بسوی شهر رفت
Sálih went from his solitude to the town
شهر دید اندر میان دود و نفت
he beheld the town amidst (wrapt in) smoke and naphtha

ناله از اجزای ایشان می‌شنید
He heard (the sound of) wailing from their limbs:
نوحه پیدا نوحه گویان ناپدید
the lamentation was plain (to hear), those who uttered it (were) invisible.

ز استخوانهاشان شنید او ناله‌ها
He heard wailings from their bones:
اشک ریزان جانشان چون ژاله‌ها
tears of blood (poured) from their spirits shedding tears, like hailstones.

صالح آن بشنید و گریه ساز کرد
Sálih heard that and set to weeping:
نوحه بر نوحه گران آغاز کرد
he began to lament for them that made lamentation.

گفت ای قومی به باطل زیسته
He said, "O people that lived in vanity,
وز شما من پیش حق بگریسته
and on account of you I wept before God!

حق بگفته صبر کن بر جورشان
God said (to me), 'Have patience with their iniquity
پندشان ده بس نماند از دورشان
give them counsel, not much remains of their (allotted) period.'

من بگفته پند شد بند از جفا
I said, 'Counsel is barred by ill-treatment:
شیر پند از مهر جوشد وز صفا
the milk of counsel gushes forth from love and joy.

بس که کردید از جفا بر جای من
Much ill-treatment have ye bestowed on me,
شیر پند افسرد در رگهای من
(so that) the milk of counsel is curdled in my veins.'

حق مرا گفته ترا لطفی دهم
God said to me, 'I will give thee a boon,
بر سر آن زخمها مرهم نهم
I will lay a plaster on those wounds (of thine).'

صاف کرده حق دلم را چون سما
God made my heart clear as the sky,
روفته از خاطرم جور شما
He swept your oppression out of my mind.

در نصیحت من شده بار دگر
I went (back) once more to admonition,
گفته امثال و سخنها چون شکر
I spake parables and words (sweet) as sugar,

شیر تازه از شکر انگیخته
I produced fresh milk from the sugar,
شیر و شهدی با سخن آمیخته
I mingled milk and honey with my words.

در شما چون زهر گشته آن سخن
In you those words became like poison
زانک زهرستان بدیت از بیخ و بن
because ye were filled with poison from the root and foundation.

چون شوم غمگین که غم شد سرنگون
How should I be grieved that grief is overthrown?
غم شما بودیت ای قوم حرون
Ye were grief (to me), O obstinate people.

هیچ کس بر مرگ غم نوحه کند
Does anyone lament the death of grief?
ریش سر چون شد کسی مو بر کند
Does anyone tear out his hair when the sore on his head is removed?"

رو بخود کرد و بگفت ای نوحه گر
(Then) he turned to himself and said, "O mourner
نوحه‌ات را می‌نیرزند آن نفر
those folk are not worth thy mourning."

کژ مخوان ای راست‌خوانندۀ مبین
O thou that readest aright the perspicuous (Book), do not misread it
کیف آسی خلف قوم ظالمین
How should I grieve after (the destruction of) an unjust people?

323

باز اندر چشم و دل او گریه یافت
Again he felt a weeping in his eye and heart:
رحمتی بی‌علتی در وی بتافت
an uncaused (involuntary) compassion shone forth in him.

قطره می‌بارید و حیران گشته بود
He was raining drops of water (shedding tears)
قطره‌ای بی‌علت از دریای جود
and he had become distraught— an uncaused drop from the Ocean of Bounty.

عقل او می‌گفت کین گریه ز چیست
His intellect was saying, "Wherefore is this weeping?
بر چنان افسوسیان شاید گریست
Ought one to weep for such scoffers?

بر چه می‌گریی بگو بر فعلشان
Tell me, what art thou weeping for? For their fraud?
بر سپاه کینه‌توز بد نشان
For the host of (their) ill-omened exactions of vengeance?

بر دل تاریک پر زنگارشان
For their murky hearts full of rust?
بر زبان زهر همچون مارشان
For their venomous snake-like tongues?

بر دم و دندان سگسارانه شان
For their sagsár-like breath and teeth
بر دهان و چشم کژدم خانه‌شان
For their mouths and eyes teeming with scorpions?

بر ستیز و تسخر و افسوسشان
For their wrangling and sneering and scoffing?
شکر کن چون کرد حق محبوسشان
Give thanks, since God has imprisoned (restrained) them.

دستشان کژ پایشان کژ چشم کژ
Their hands are perverse, their feet perverse, their eyes perverse,
مهرشان کژ صلحشان کژ خشم کژ
their love perverse, their peace perverse, their anger perverse.

از پی تقلید و معقولات نقل
For the sake of blind conformity and (for the sake of following) traditional ideas for the standards of tradition,
پا نهاده بر سر این پیر عقل
they set their feet (trampled) on the head of Reason, this venerable guide.

پیرخر نه جمله گشته پیر خر
They were not eager for a guide (pír-khar): they all had become (like) an old donkey
از ریای چشم و گوش همدگر
from paying hypocritical observance to each other's eyes and ears.

از بهشت آورد یزدان بندگان
God brought the (devout) worshippers from Paradise
تا نمایدشان سقر پروردگان
that He might show unto them the nurslings of Hell-fire.

⟨◉⟩⟨◉⟩

در معنی آنک مرج البحرین یلتقیان بینهما برزخ لا یبغیان
On the meaning of "He let the two seas go to meet one another: between them is a barrier which they do not seek

اهل نار و خلد را بین همدکان
Behold the people of (destined for) the Fire and those of Paradise dwelling in the same shop
در میانشان برزخ لایبغیان
(yet) between them is a barrier which they do not seek to cross.

اهل نار و اهل نور آمیخته
He hath mixed the people of the Fire and the people of the Light:
در میانشان کوه قاف انگیخته
between them He hath reared the mountain of Qáf.

همچو در کان خاک و زر کرد اختلاط
He hath mixed (them) like earth and gold in the mine:
در میانشان صد بیابان و رباط
between them are a hundred deserts and caravanserays.

همچنانک عقد در در و شبه
(They are) mixed even as pearls and jet beads in the necklace,
مختلط چون میهمان یک‌شبه
(soon to be parted) like guests of a single night.

بحر را نیمیش شیرین چون شکر
One half of the sea is sweet like sugar:
طعم شیرین رنگ روشن چون قمر
the taste sweet, the colour bright as the moon.

نیم دیگر تلخ همچون زهر مار
The other half is bitter as snake's venom:
طعم تلخ و رنگ مظلم همچو قار
the taste bitter and the colour dark as pitch.

هر دو بر هم می‌زنند از تحت و اوج
Both (halves) dash against one another, from beneath and from the top,
بر مثال آب دریا موج موج
wave on wave like the water of the sea.

صورت بر هم زدن از جسم تنگ
The appearance of collision, (arising) from the narrow body,
اختلاط جانها در صلح و جنگ
is (due to) the spirits' being intermingled in peace or war.

موجهای صلح بر هم می‌زند
The waves of peace dash against each other
کینه‌ها از سینه‌ها بر می‌کند
and root up hatreds from (men's) breasts.

موجهای جنگ بر شکل دگر
In other form do the waves of war
مهرها را می‌کند زیر و زبر
turn (men's) loves upside down (confound and destroy them).

مهر تلخان را به شیرین می‌کشد
Love is drawing the bitter ones to the sweet,
زانک اصل مهرها باشد رشد
because the foundation of (all) loves is righteousness.

قهر شیرین را به تلخی می‌برد
Wrath is carrying away the sweet one to bitterness:
تلخ با شیرین کجا اندر خورد
how should the bitter sort with (be suited to) the sweet?

تلخ و شیرین زین نظر ناید پدید
The bitter and the sweet are not visible to this (ocular) sight,
از دریچهٔ عاقبت دانند دید
(but) they can be seen through the window of the latter end.

چشم آخربین تواند دید راست
The eye that sees the end (ákhir) can see truly;
چشم آخربین غرورست و خطاست
the eye that sees (only) the stable (ákhur) is delusion and error.

ای بسا شیرین که چون شکر بود
Oh, many the one that is sweet as sugar,
لیک زهر اندر شکر مضمر بود
but poison is concealed in the sugar.

آنک زیرکتر ببو بشناسدش
He that is more sagacious (than the rest) will know it by the smell;
و آن دگر چون بر لب و دندان زدش
another (only) when it touches his lips and teeth:

پس لبش ردش کند پیش از گلو
Then his lips will reject it before (it reaches) his throat,
گرچه نعره می‌زند شیطان کلوا
although the Devil is shouting, "Eat ye!"

و آن دگر را در گلو پیدا کند
And to another it will declare (itself) in his throat,
و آن دگر را در بدن رسوا کند
while to another it will unmask in his body;

وان دگر را در حدث سوزش دهد
And to another it will give burning pain in evacuation:
ذوق آن زخم جگردوزش دهد
its outgoing will give him instruction as to its incoming

وان دگر را بعد ایام و شهور
And to another (it will become manifest) after days and months;
وان دگر را بعد مرگ از قعر گور
and to another after death, from the depth of the grave;

ور دهندش مهلت اندر قعر گور
And if he be given a respite in the depth of the grave,
لابد آن پیدا شود یوم النشور
(then) it will inevitably become manifest on the Day of Resurrection.

هر نبات و شکری را در جهان
Every piece of candy and sugar (desirable thing) in the world
مهلتی پیداست از دور زمان
manifestly has a period granted to it from the revolution of Time.

سالها باید که اندر آفتاب
Years are needed in order that the ruby in (exposed to the rays of) the sun
لعل یابد رنگ و رخشانی و تاب
may obtain (the perfect) tint and splendour and brilliance.

باز تره در دو ماه اندر رسد
Vegetables, again, reach maturity in two months,
باز تا سالی گل احمر رسد
while the red rose comes to perfection in a year.

بهر این فرمود حق عز و جل
For this reason the Almighty and Glorious God in the Súratu

سورة الانعام در ذکر اجل
'l-An 'ám has made mention of an appointed term (ajal).

این شنیدی مو بمویت گوش باد
You have heard this (discourse): may the whole of you, hair by hair, be an ear (to receive it)!

آب حیوانست خوردی نوش باد
'Tis the Water of Life: (if) you have drunk, may it do you good!

آب حیوان خوان مخوان این را سخ
Call it the Water of Life, call it not a discourse:

روح نو بین در تن حرف کهن
behold the new spirit in the body of the old letter!

نکتهٔ دیگر تو بشنو ای رفیق
(Now), my friend, hearken to another saying (which is),

همچو جان او سخت پیدا و دقی
ike the soul, very clear (to mystics) and abstruse (to the rest):

در مقامی هست هم این زهر مار
dispositions even this poison and snake (worldliness and sensuality) is (rendered) digestible

از تصاریف خدایی خوش‌گوار
In a certain place (spiritual degree), through Divine

در مقامی زهر و در جایی دوا
In one place (it is) poison and in one place medicine,

در مقامی کفر و در جایی روا
in one place infidelity and in one place approved.

گرچه آنجا او گزند جان بود
Although there it is injurious to the soul,

چون بدینجا در رسد درمان بود
when it arrives here it becomes a remedy.

آب در غوره ترش باشد ولیک
In the young grape (ghúra) the juice is sour,

چون به انگوری رسد شیرین و نیک
but it is sweet and good when the ghúra comes to be an angúr (ripe grape).

باز در خم او شود تلخ و حرام
Again in the wine-jar it becomes bitter and unlawful,

در مقام سرکگی نعم الادام
(but) in the state (form) of vinegar how excellent it is as a seasoning!

در معنی آنک آنچه ولی کند مرید را نشاید گستاخی کردن

Concerning the impropriety of the disciple's (muríd) presuming to do the same things as are done by the saint (walí),

و همان فعل کردن کی حلوا طبیب را زیان ندارد اما بیماران را زیان دارد و سرما و برف انگور را زیان ندارد اما غوره را زیان دارد کی در راهست کی لیغفرلک الله ما تقدم من ذنبک و ما تاخر

inasmuch as sweetmeat does no harm to the physician, but is harmful to the sick, and frost and snow do no harm to the ripe grape, but are injurious to the young fruit; for he (the disciple) is (still) on the way, for he has not (yet) become (the saint to whom are applicable the words in the Qur'án): "That God may forgive thee thy former and latter sins."

گر ولی زهری خورد نوشی شود
If the saint drinks a poison it becomes an antidote,

ور خورد طالب سیه‌هوشی شود
but if the seeker (disciple) drinks it, his mind is darkened.

رب هب لی از سلیمان آمدست
From Solomon have come the words, "O Lord, give me

که مده غیر مرا این ملک دست
that is, "do not give this kingdom and power to any but me.

تو مکن با غیر من این لطف و جود
Do not bestow this grace and bounty on any but me."

این حسد را ماند اما آن نبود
but me." This looks like envy, but it was not that (in reality).

نکتهٔ لا ینبغی می‌خوان بجان
Read with your soul the mystery of "it behoves not,"

سر من بعدی ز بخل او مدان
do not deem the inward meaning of "after me" (to be derived) from his (Solomon's) avarice.

بلک اندر ملک دید او صد خطر
Nay, but in sovereignty he saw a hundred dangers:

موبمو ملک جهان بد بیم سر
kingdom of this world was (has ever been), hair by hair fear for one's head.

بیم سر با بیم سر با بیم دین
Fear for head with fear for heart with fear for religion

امتحانی نیست ما را مثل این
there is no trial for us like this.

پس سلیمان همتی باید که او
Therefore one must needs possess the high aspiration of a Solomon

بگذرد زین صد هزاران رنگ و بو
in order to escape from these myriads of colours and perfumes

با چنان قوت که او را بود هم
Even with such (great) strength (of spirit) as he had,

موج آن ملکش فرو می‌بست دم
the waves of that (worldly) kingdom were stifling his breath

چون برو بنشست زین اندوه گرد
Since dust settled on him from this sorrow,

بر همه شاهان عالم رحم کرد
he had compassion for all the kings of the world.

شد شفیع و گفت این ملک و لوا
Hence he interceded (with God on their behalf) and said, "Give this kingdom

با کمالی ده که دادی مر مرا
with (accompanied by) the (spiritual) perfection which Thou hast given to me.

هرکه را بدهی و بکنی آن کرم
To whomsoever Thou wilt give (it), and (on whomsoever) Thou wilt confer that bounty,

او سلیمانست وانکس هم منم
he (that person) is Solomon, and I also am he.

او نباشد بعدی او باشد معی
He is not 'after me,' he is with me.

خود معی چه بود منم بی‌مدعی
What of 'with me,' indeed? I am without rival."

شرح این فرضست گفتن لیک من
Tis my duty to explain this,

باز می‌گردم به قصهٔ مرد و زن
but (now) I will return to the story of the man and wife.

مخلص ماجرای عرب و جفت او
The moral of the altercation of the Arab and his wife.

ماجرای مرد و زن را مخلصی
for the altercation of the man and wife.

باز می‌جوید درون مخلصی
The heart of one who is sincere is seeking a moral

ماجرای مرد و زن افتاد نقل
The altercation of the man and wife has been related

آن مثال نفس خود می‌دان و عقل
know that it is a parable of your own flesh (nafs) and reason.

این زن و مردی که نفسست و خرد
This man and wife, which are the flesh and the reason,

نیک بایستست بهر نیک و بد
are very necessary for (the manifestation of) good and evil;

وین دو بایسته درین خاکی‌سرا
And this necessary pair in this house of earth

روز و شب در جنگ و اندر ماجرا
(engaged) in strife and altercation day and night.

زن همی‌خواهد حویج خانگاه
The wife is craving requisites for the household,

یعنی آب رو و نان و خوان و جاه
that is to say, reputation and bread and viands and rank

نفس همچون زن پی چاره‌گری
Like the wife, the flesh, in order to contrive the means (of gratifying its desires),

گاه خاکی گاه جوید سروری
is at one time seeking (having recourse to) humility and at another time to domination.

عقل خود زین فکرها آگاه نیست
The reason is really unconscious of these (worldly) thoughts:

در دماغش جز غم الله نیست
in its brain is nothing but love of God.

گرچه سر قصه این دانه ست و دام
Although the inner meaning of the tale is this bait and trap,

صورت قصه شنو اکنون تمام
listen now to the outward form of the tale in its entirety.

گر بیان معنوی کافی شدی
If the spiritual explanation were sufficient,

خلق عالم عاطل و باطل بدی
the creation of the world would have been vain and idle.

گر محبت فکرت و معنیستی
If love were (only spiritual) thought and reality,

صورت روزه و نمازت نیستی
the form of your fasting and prayer would be non-existent

هدیه‌های دوستان با همدگر
The gifts of lovers to one another are,

نیست اندر دوستی الا صور
in respect of love, naught but forms;

تا گواهی داده باشد هدیه‌ها
(But the purpose is) that the gifts may have borne testimony

بر محبتهای مضمر در خفا
to feelings of love which are concealed in secrecy,

زانک احسانهای ظاهر شاهدند
Because outward acts of kindness bear witness to feelings

بر محبتهای سر ای ارجمند
of love in the heart, O dear friend.

شاهدت گه راست باشد گه دروغ
Your witness is sometimes true, sometimes false,

مست گاهی از می و گاهی ز دوغ
sometimes drunken with wine, sometimes with sour curds.

دوغ خورده مستی پیدا کند
He that has drunk sour curds makes a show of intoxication,

های هوی و سرگرانیها کند
shouts ecstatically, and behaves like one whose head is heavy (with the fumes of wine);

آن مرایی در صیام و در صلاست
That hypocrite is (assiduous) in fasting and praying,

تا گمان آید که او مست ولاست
in order that it may be supposed that he is drunken with devotion (to God).

حاصل افعال برونی دیگرست
In short, external acts are different (from internal feelings),

تا نشان باشد بر آنچه مضمرست
(and their purpose is) to indicate that which is hidden.

یا رب این تمییز ده ما را بخواست
O Lord, grant us according to our desire such discernment

تا شناسیم آن نشان کژ ز راست
that we may know the false indication from the true.

حس را تمییز دانی چون شود
Do you know how the sense-perception becomes discerning?

آنک حس ینظر بنور الله بود
In this way, that the sense-perception should be seeing by the light of God.

ور اثر نبود سبب هم مظهرست
And if there be no effect (outward sign), the cause too makes manifest (that which is hidden),

همچو خویشی کز محبت مخبرست
as (for example) kinship gives information concerning love (enables you to infer the presence of love)

نبود آنک نور حقش شد امام
When the light of God comes into the sensorium

مر اثر را یا سببها را غلام
you will not be a slave to effect or cause

یا محبت در درون شعله زند
So that Love will throw a spark within, wax mighty,

زفت گردد وز اثر فارغ کند
and make (the illumined one) independent of effect

حاجتش نبود پی اعلام مهر
He has no need for the signs of love,

چون محبت نور خود زد بر سپهر
since Love has shot its radiance over the sky (of his heart).

هست تفصیلات تا گردد تمام
There are detailed explanations (which I could give) in order to complete this subject;

این سخن لیکن بجو تو والسلام
but seek them (for yourself), and (now) farewell.

گرچه شد معنی درین صورت پدید
And as for him that perceived the inner meaning in this outward form,

صورت از معنی قریبست و بعید
the form is (both) near to the meaning and far (from it).

در دلالت همچو آبند و درخت
In regard to indication, they (the meaning and the form) are like the sap and the tree;

چون بماهیت روی دورند سخت
(but) when you turn to the quiddity, they are very far (removed from each other).

ترک ماهیات و خاصیات گو
(Let me) take leave of quiddities and essential properties,

شرح کن احوال آن دو ماهرو
and relate what happened to those twain with faces like the moon

دل نهادن عرب بر التماس دلبر خویش و سوگند خوردن
How the Arab set his heart on (complying with) his beloved's request and swore

کی درین تسلیم مرا حیلتی و امتحانی نیست
that in thus submitting (to her) he had no (idea of) trickery and making trial (of her).

مرد گفت اکنون گذشتم از خلاف
The man said, "Now I have ceased to oppose (thee):

حکم داری تیغ برکش از غلاف
thou hast authority (to do what thou wilt): draw the sword from the sheath.

هرچه گویی من ترا فرمان برم
Whatsoever thou biddest me do, I will obey:

در بد و نیک آمد آن ننگرم
I will not consider the bad or good result of it.

در وجود تو شوم من منعدم
I will become non-existent in thy existence,

چون محبم حب یعمی و یصم
existence, because I am thy lover: love makes blind and deaf."

گفت زن آهنگ برم می‌کنی
The wife said, "Oh, I wonder if thou art (really) my friend,

یا بحیلت کشف سرم می‌کنی
or whether thou art (bent on) discovering my secret by trickery?"

گفت والله عالم السر الخفی
He said, "(No), by God who knows the thought most deeply hid,

کافرید از خاک آدم را صفی
ho out of dust created Adam pure (chosen above all),

در سه گز قالب که دادش وا نمود
Who, in the body three cubits long which He gave him,

هر چه در الواح و در ارواح بود
displayed everything that was contained in the tablets (of destiny) and the (world of) spirits.

تا ابد هرچه بود او پیش پیش
Through his He (God) taught him (Adam) the Names

درس کرد از علم الاسماء خویش
he at the very first gave instruction concerning everything that shall come to pass unto everlasting

تا ملک بی‌خود شد از تدریس او
So that the angels became beside themselves (in amazement) at his teaching,

قدس دیگر یافت از تقدیس او
and gained from his glorification (of God) a holiness other (than they possessed before).

آن گشادی‌شان کز آدم رو نمود
The revelation that appeared to them from Adam

در گشاد آسمان‌هاشان نبود
was not(contained) in the amplitude of their heavens

در فراخی عرصهٔ آن پاک جان
In comparison with the spaciousness of the range of that pure spirit (Adam),

تنگ آمد عرصهٔ هفت آسمان
the expanse of the seven heavens became narrow.

گفت پیغامبر که حق فرموده است
The Prophet said that God has said,

من نگنجم هیچ در بالا و پست
'I am not contained in the jar of "high" and "low" (spatial dimensions);

در زمین و آسمان و عرش نیز
I am not contained in earth or heaven or even in the empyrean

من نگنجم این یقین دان ای عزیز
know this for certain, O noble one;

در دل مؤمن بگنجم ای عجب
(But) I am contained in the true believer's heart: oh, how wonderful!

گر مرا جویی در آن دلها طلب
He (God) said (also), 'Enter among My servants,

گفت ادخل فی عبادی تلتقی
thou wilt meet with a Paradise (consisting) of vision of Me, O Godfearing one.'

جنة من رویتی یا متقی
when it beheld that (spirit of Adam), was confounded.

عرش با آن نور با پهنای خویش
The empyrean, notwithstanding its wide (far-extending) light,

چون بدید آن را برفت از جای خویش
Truly, the magnitude of the empyrean is very great,

خود بزرگی عرش باشد بس مدید
Truly, the magnitude of the empyrean is very great

لیک صورت کیست چون معنی رسید
but who(what) is form when reality has arrived?

هر ملک می‌گفت ما را پیش ازین
Then the angels were saying (to Adam),

الفتی می‌بود بر روی زمین
Before this (time) we had a friendship (with thee) on the dust of the earth.

تخم خدمت بر زمین می‌کاشتیم
On the earth we were sowing the seed of service(worship):
زان تعلق ما عجب می‌داشتیم
we were marveling at that connexion,

کین تعلق چیست با این خاکمان
Marvelling what connexion we had with that dust,
چون سرشت ما بدست از آسمان
inasmuch as our nature is of heaven.

الف ما انوار با ظلمات چیست
(We said), Why (this) friendship in us, who are light, with darkness?
چون تواند نور با ظلمات زیست
How can light live with darkness?

آدما آن الف از بوی تو بود
O Adam, that friendship was owing to the scent of thee,
زانک جسمت را زمین بد تار و پود
because earth was the woof and warp of thy body.

جسم خاکت را ازینجا بافتند
From this place (the earth) thy earthly body was woven,
نور پاکت را درینجا یافتند
in this place thy pure light was found.

این که جان ما ز روحت یافتست
This (light) that our souls have obtained from thy spirit
پیش پیش از خاک آن می‌تافتست
shone erstwhile from the dust.

در زمین بودیم و غافل از زمین
We were in the earth, and heedless of the earth,
غافل از گنجی که در وی بد دفین
heedless of the treasure that lay buried there.

چون سفر فرمود ما را زان مقام
When He (God) bade us journey from that place of abode our
تلخ شد ما را از آن تحویل کام
palates were soured (we were bitterly grieved) by the change,

تا که حجتها همی گفتیم ما
So that we were arguing (and saying),
که به جای ما کی آید ای خدا
So that we were arguing (and saying),

336

نور این تسبیح و این تهلیل را
we glorify and magnify Thee for babble and palaver?'

می‌فروشی بهر قال و قیل را
Wilt Thou sell the splendour of the praise with which

حکم حق گسترد بهر ما بساط
The decree of God spread for us the carpet

که بگویید ازطریق انبساط
(and He said), 'Speak ye, in the way of boldness

هرچه آید بر زبانتان بی‌حذر
(And) without fear, whatever comes upon your tongues,

همچو طفلان یگانه با پدر
(And) without fear, whatever comes upon your tongues,

زانک این دمها چه گر نالایقست
For what if these words (of yours) are unseemly?

رحمت من بر غضب هم سابقست
My mercy likewise is prior (superior) to My wrath.

از پی اظهار این سبق ای ملک
In order to manifest this priority, O angel,

در تو بنهم داعیهٔ اشکال و شک
I will put in thee incitement to perplexity and doubt,

تا بگویی و نگیرم بر تو من
That thou mayst speak and I not take offence at thee,

منکر حلمم نیارد دم زدن
(so that) none who denies My clemency may dare to utter a word.

صد پدر صد مادر اندر حلم ما
Within My (infinite) clemency (the clemencies of) a hundred fathers and a hundred mothers

هر نفس زاید در افتد در فنا
at every moment are born and vanish.

حلم ایشان کف بحر حلم ماست
Their clemency is (but) the foam of the sea of My clemency:

کف رود آید ولی دریا بجاست
the foam comes and goes, but the sea is (always) there."

خود چه گویم پیش آن در این صدف
What indeed shall I say? Compared with that pearl (Divine clemency) this oyster-shell

نیست الا کف کف کف کف
(human clemency) is naught but the foam of the foam of the foam of foam.

حق آن کف حق آن دریای صاف
By the truth of that foam, by the truth of that pure sea,
کامتحانی نیست این گفت و نه لاف
that these words (of mine) are not (meant to make) trial of thee and are not vain.

از سر مهر و صفا است و خضوع
They are from (inspired by) love and sincerity and humbleness,
حق آنکس که بدو دارم رجوع
and humbleness, (I swear) by the truth of that One to whom I turn.

گر ببیشت امتحانست این هوس
If this affection (which I am showing) seems to thee a trial,
امتحان را امتحان کن یک نفس
do thou for one moment put the (supposed) trial (of thee) to the test.

سر مپوشان تا پدید آید سرم
Do not hide thy secret (but reveal it), in order that mine may be revealed:
امر کن تو هر چه بر وی قادرم
command anything that I am able to do.

دل مپوشان تا پدید آید دلم
Do not hide thy heart (but reveal it),
تا قبول آرم هر آنچه قابلم
in order that mine may be revealed and that I may accept whatever I am capable of

چون کنم در دست من چه چاره است
How shall I do? What remedy is in my power?
درنگر تا جان من چه کاره است
Look what a plight my soul is in."

❖◉❖◉❖

تعیین کردن زن طریق طلب روزی کدخدای خود را و قبول کردن او
How the wife specified to her husband the way to earn daily bread and how he accepted (her proposal).

گفت زن یک آفتابی تافتست
The wife said, "A sun has shone forth,
عالمی زو روشنایی یافتست
a (whole) world has received light from him

نایب رحمان خلیفهٔ کردگار
The Vicar of the Merciful (God), the Khalífa of the Creator:
شهر بغدادست از وی چون بهار
through him the city of Baghdád is (gay and happy) as the season of spring.

گر بپیوندی بدان شه شه شوی
If thou gain access to that King, thou wilt become a king:
سوی هر ادبیر تا کی می‌روی
how long wilt thou go after every (kind of) misfortune?"

همنشینی با شهان چون کیمیاست
Companionship with the fortunate is like the Elixir: indeed,
چون نظرشان کیمیایی خود کجاست
how is an Elixir like (to be compared with) their looks (of favour)?

چشم احمد بر ابوبکری زده
The eye of Ahmad (Mohammed) was cast upon an Abú Bakr:
او ز یک تصدیق صدیق آمده
he by a single act of faith became a Siddíq.

گفت من شه را پذیرا چون شوم
Said the husband, "How should I go to meet the King?
بی بهانه سوی او من چون روم
How should I go to him without a pretext?

نسبتی باید مرا یا حیلتی
I must have some reference or device:
هیچ پیشه راست شد بی آلتی
is any handicraft right (possible) without tools?

همچو مجنونی که بشنید از یکی
As (to mention a similar case) the famous Majnún,
که مرض آمد به لیلی اندکی
when he heard from someone that Laylá was a little unwell,

گفت آوه بی بهانه چون روم
Cried, 'Ah, how shall I go (to her) without a pretext?
ور بمانم از عیادت چون شوم
And if I fail to visit her when she is ill, how (wretched) shall I be!

لیتنی کنت طبیبا حاذقا
Would that I were a skilled physician!
کنت امشی نحو لیلی سابقا
I would have gone on foot to Laylá first of all (before anyone else).'

قل تعالوا گفت حق ما را بدان
God said to us, 'Say, Come ye,'
تا بود شرم‌اشکنی ما را نشان
in order to signify to us the (means of) vanquishing our feeling of shame.

شب پران را گر نظر و آلت بدی

If bats had sight and means (ability to bear the sunshine),

روزشان جولان و خوش حالت بدی

they would fly about and enjoy themselves by day."

گفت چون شاه کرم میدان رود

The wife said, "When the gracious King goes into the field(maydán),

عین هر بی‌آلتی آلت شود

the essence of every lack of means (inability) becomes a means (ability),

زانک آلت دعوی است و هستی است

Because the means (ability) is (involves) pretension and selfexistence:

کار در بی‌آلتی و پستی است

the (pith of the) matter lies in lack of means(inability) and non-existence."

گفت کی بی‌آلتی سودا کنم

"How," said he, "should I do business without means,

تا نه من بی‌آلتی پیدا کنم

unless I make it manifest that I (really) have no means?

پس گواهی بایدم بر مفلسی

Therefore I must needs have attestation of my want of means,

تا مرا رحمی کند شاه غنی

that he (the King) may pity me in want.

تو گواهی غیر گفت و گو و رنگ

Do thou produce some attestation besides talk and show,

وا نما تا رحم آرد شاه شنگ

so that the beauteous King may take pity,

کین گواهی که ز گفت و رنگ بد

For the testimony that consisted of talk

نزد آن قاضی القضاة آن جرح شد

and show was (ever) invalidated before that Supreme Judge.

صدق می‌خواهد گواه حال او

He requires truth (veracity) as witness to his (the indigent man's) state,

تا بتابد نور او بی قال او

so that his (inner) light shall shine forth (and proclaim his indigence) without any words of his."

هدیه بردن عرب سبوی آب باران از میان بادیه
How the Arab carried a jug of rain-water from the midst of the desert as a gift

سوی بغداد به امیرالمؤمنین بر پنداشت آنک آنجا هم قحط آبست
to the Commander of the Faithful at Baghdád, in the belief that in that town also there was a scarcity of water.

گفت زن صدق آن بود کز بود خویش
The wife said, "When people with all their might

پاک برخیزی تو از مجهود خویش
rise up entirely purged of self-existence—that is veracity.

آب بارانست ما را در سبو
We have the rain-water in the jug:

ملکت و سرمایه و اسباب تو
'tis thy property and capital and means.

این سبوی آب را بردار و رو
Take this jug of water and depart,

هدیه ساز و پیش شاهنشاه شو
make it a gift and go into the presence of the King of kings.

گو که ما را غیر این اسباب نیست
Say, 'We have no means except this:

در مفازه هیچ به زین آب نیست
in the desert there is nothing better than this water.

گر خزینه‌ش پر متاع فاخرست
If his treasury is full of gold and jewels,

این چنین آبش نباشد نادرست
(yet) he does not get water like this: 'tis rare."

چیست آن کوزه تن محصور ما
What is that jug? Our confined body:

اندرو آب حواس شور ما
within it is the briny water of our senses.

ای خداوند این خم و کوزهٔ مرا
O Lord, accept this jar and jug of mine

در پذیر از فضل الله اشتری
by the grace of "God hath purchased

کوزه‌ای با پنج لولهٔ پنج حس
('Tis) a jug with five spouts, the five senses:

پاک دار این آب را از هر نجس
keep this water pure (and safe) from every filth,

تا شود زین کوزه منفذ سوی بحر
That there may be from this jug a passage to the sea,
تا بگیرد کوزهٔ من خوی بحر
and that my jug may assume the nature of the sea,

تا چو هدیه پیش سلطانش بری
So that when you carry it as a gift to the King,
پاک بیند باشدش شه مشتری
the King may find it pure and be its purchaser

بی‌نهایت گردد آبش بعد از آن
(And) after that, its water will become without end:
پر شود از کوزهٔ من صد جهان
a hundred worlds will be filled from my jug.

لوله‌ها بر بند و پر دارش ز خم
Stop up its spouts and keep it filled (with water) from the jar
گفت غضوا عن هوا ابصارکم
God said, "Close your eyes to vain desire."

ریش او پر باد کین هدیه کراست
His (the husband's) beard was full of wind (he was puffed up with pride):
لایق چون او شهی اینست راست
Who (thought he) has such a gift as this? This, truly, is worthy of a King like him."

زن نمی‌دانست کآنجا برگذر
The wife did not know that in that place
هست جاری دجله‌ای همچون شکر
on the thoroughfare there is the great stream (of water) sweet as sugar,

در میان شهر چون دریا روان
Flowing like a sea through the city,
پر ز کشتیها و شست ماهیان
full of boats and fishingnets.

رو بر سلطان و کار و بار بین
Go to the Sultan and behold this pomp and state!
حس تجری تحتها الانهار بین
Behold the senses of beneath which the rivers flow!

این چنین حسها و ادراکات ما
Our senses and perceptions, such as they are,
قطره‌ای باشد در آن نهر صفا
are (but) a single drop in those rivers.

در نمد دوختن زن عرب سبوی آب باران را
How the Arab's wife sewed the jug of rain-water in a felt cloth

و مهر نهادن بر وی از غایت اعتقاد عرب
and put a seal on it because of the Arab's utter conviction

مرد گفت آری سبو را سر ببند
"Yes," said the husband, "stop up the mouth of the jug.
هین که این هدیه ست ما را سودمند
Take care, for this is a gift that will bring us profit.

در نمد در دوز تو این کوزه را
Sew this jug in felt, that
تا گشاید شه بهدیه روزه را
King may break his fast with our gift,

کین چنین اندر همه آفاق نیست
For there is no (water) like this in all the world:
جز رحیق و مایهٔ اذواق نیست
no (other) water is so pure as this."

زانک ایشان ز آبهای تلخ و شور
from (drinking) bitter and briny waters.
دایما پر علت‌اند و نیم‌کور
(This he said) because they (people like him) are always full of infirmity and half-blind

مرغ کاب شور باشد مسکنش
The bird whose dwelling-place is the briny water,
او چه داند جای آب روشنش
how should it know where to find in it the clear (and sweet) water?

ای که اندر چشمهٔ شورست جاث
O thou whose abode is in the briny spring,
تو چه دانی شط و جیحون و فرات
how shouldst thou know the Shatt and the Jayhún and the Euphrates?

ای تو نارسته ازین فانی رباط
O thou who hast not escaped from this fleeting caravanseray (the material world),
تو چه دانی محو و سکر و انبساط
how shouldst thou know (the meaning of) "self-extinction" and (mystical) "intoxication" and "expansion"?

ور بدانی نقلت از اب و جدست
And if thou knowest, 'tis (by rote, like the knowledge) handed down to thee from father and grandfather:
پیش تو این نامها چون ابجدست
to thee these names are like abjad.

343

ابجد و هوز چه فاش است و پدید
How plain and evident to all children are abjad and hawwaz,
بر همه طفلان و معنی بس بعید
and (yet) the real meaning is far away (hard to reach).

پس سبو برداشت آن مرد عرب
Then the Arab man took up the jug and set out to journey,
در سفر شد می‌کشیدش روز و شب
carrying it along (with him) day and night.

بر سبو لرزان بد از آفات دهر
He was trembling for the jug, in fear of Fortune's mischiefs:
هم کشیدش از بیابان تا به شهر
all the same, he conveyed it from the desert to the city (Baghdád).

زن مصلا باز کرده از نیاز
His wife unrolled the prayer-rug in supplication;
رب سلم ورد کرده در نماز
she made (the words) Rabbi sallim (Save, O Lord) her litany in prayer,

که نگه‌دار آب ما را از خسان
Crying, "Keep our water safe from scoundrels!
یا رب آن گوهر بدان دریا رسان
O Lord, let that pearl arrive at that sea!

گرچه شویم آگهست و پر فنست
Although my husband is shrewd and artful,
لیک گوهر را هزاران دشمنست
yet the pearl has thousands of enemies.

خود چه باشد گوهر آب کوثرست
Pearl indeed! 'Tis the water of Kawthar:
قطره‌ای زینست کاصل گوهرست
'tis a drop of this that is the origin of the pearl."

از دعاهای زن و زاری او
Through the prayers and lamentation of the wife,
وز غم مرد و گران‌باری او
And through the husband's anxiety and his patience under the heavy burden,

سالم از دزدان و از آسیب سنگ
He bore it without delay, safe from robbers and unhurt by stones,
برد تا دار الخلافه بی‌درنگ
to the seat of the Caliphate (the Caliph's palace).

دید درگاهی پر از انعامها
He saw a bountiful Court,

اهل حاجت گستریده دامها
(where) the needy had spread their nets;

دم بدم هر سوی صاحب حاجتی
Everywhere, moment by moment,

یافته زان در عطا و خلعتی
some petitioner gained (and carried away) from that Court a donation and robe of honour:

بهر گبر و مؤمن و زیبا و زشت
'Twas like sun and rain, nay, like Paradise,

همچو خورشید و مطر نی چون بهشت
for infidel and true believer and good folk and bad.

دید قومی درنظر آراسته
He beheld some people arrayed (with favour) in the sight (of the Caliph),

قوم دیگر منتظر بر خاسته
and others who had risen to their feet (and were) waiting (to receive his commands).

خاص و عامه از سلیمان تا بمور
High and low, from Solomon to the ant,

زنده گشته چون جهان از نفخ صور
they (all) had become quickened with life, like the world at the blast of the trumpet

اهل صورت در جواهر بافته
The followers of Form were woven (entangled) in pearls,

اهل معنی بحر معنی یافته
pearls, the followers of Reality had found the Sea of Reality

آنک بی همت چه با همت شده
Those without aspiration—how aspiring had they become!

وانک با همت چه با نعمت شده
and those of high aspiration—to what felicity had they attained!

◆◉◆◉◆

در بیان آنک چنانک گدا عاشق کرمست

Showing that, as the beggar is in love with bounty

و عاشق کریم کرم کریم هم عاشق گداست اگر گدا را صبر بیش بود کریم بر در او آید و اگر کریم را صبر بیش بود گدا بر در او آید اما صبر گدا کمال گداست و صبر کریم نقصان اوست

and in love with the bountiful giver, so the bounty of the bountiful giver is in love with the beggar: if the beggar have the greater patience, the bountiful giver will come to his door; and if the bountiful giver have the greater patience, the beggar will come to his door; but the beggar's patience is a virtue in the beggar, while the patience of the bountiful giver is in him a defect.

بانگ می‌آمد که ای طالب بیا

A loud call was coming (to his ears): "Come, O seeker!

جود محتاج گدایان چون گدا

Bounty is in need of beggars: (it is needy) like a beggar.

جود می‌جوید گدایان و ضعاف

Bounty is seeking the beggars and the poor,

همچو خوبان کآینه جویند صاف

just as fair ones who seek a clear mirror.

روی خوبان ز آینه زیبا شود

The face of the fair is made beautiful by the mirror,

روی احسان از گدا پیدا شود

the face of Beneficence is made visible by the beggar

پس ازین فرمود حق در والضحی

Therefore on this account God said in the Súra ?a'd-Duh á,

بانگ کم زن ای محمد بر گدا

"O Mohammed, do not shout at (and drive away) the beggar."

چون گدا آیینهٔ جودست هان

Inasmuch as the beggar is the mirror of Bounty, take care!

دم بود بر روی آیینه زیان

Breath is hurtful to the face of the mirror.

آن یکی جودش گدا آرد پدید

In the one case, his (the giver's) bounty makes the beggar manifest (causes him to beg),

و آن دگر بخشد گدایان را مزید

while in the other case he (the giver), (without being asked), bestows on the beggars more

پس گدایان آیت جود حقند

Beggars, then, are the mirror of God's bounty,

وانک با حقند جود مطلقند

and they that are with God are (united with) the Absolute Bounty;

وانک جز این دوست او خود مرده‌ایست
And everyone except those two (types of beggar) is truly a dead man:
او برین در نیست نقش پرده‌ایست
he is not at this door (the Divine Court), he is (lifeless as) a picture (embroidered) on a curtain

◈◉◈◉◈

فرق میان آنک درویش است به خدا و تشنهٔ خدا
The difference between one that is poor for (desirous of) God and thirsting for Him

و میان آنک درویش است از خدا و تشنهٔ غیرست
and one that is poor of (destitute of) God and thirsting for what is other than He.

نقش درویشست او و نه اهل نان
He (that seeks other than God) is the (mere) picture of a dervish,
نقش سگ را تو مینداز استخوان
he is not worthy of bread (Divine bounty): do not throw bread to the picture of a dog!

فقر لقمه دارد او و نه فقر حق
He wants a morsel of food, he does not want God:
پیش نقش مرده‌ای کم نه طبق
do not set dishes before a lifeless picture!

ماهی خاکی بود درویش نان
The dervish that wants bread is a land-fish:
شکل ماهی لیک از دریا رمان
(he has) the form of a fish, but (he is) fleeing from the sea.

مرغ خانه‌ست او و نه سیمرغ هوا
He is a domestic fowl, not the Símurgh of the air:
لوت نوشد او و ننوشد از خدا
he swallows sweet morsels (of food), he does not eat from God.

عاشق حقست او بهر نوال
He loves God for the sake of gain:
نیست جانش عاشق حسن و جمال
his soul is not in love with (God's) excellence and beauty.

گر توهم می‌کند او عشق ذات
If he conceives that he is in love with the Essence (of God),
ذات نبود وهم اسما و صفات
conception of the (Divine) names and attributes is not the Essence.

وهم مخلوقست و مولود آمدست
Conception is begotten of qualities and definition:
حق نزاییده‌ست او لم یولدست
God is not begotten, He is lam yúlad.

عاشق تصویر و وهم خویشتن
How should he that is in love with his own imagination and conception
کی بود از عاشقان ذوالمنن
be one of them that love the Lord of bounties?

عاشق آن وهم اگر صادق بود
If the lover of that (false) conception be sincere,
آن مجاز او حقیقت‌کش شود
that metaphor (unreal judgement) will lead him to the reality.

شرح می‌خواهد بیان این سخن
The exposition of this saying demands a commentary,
لیک می‌ترسم ز افهام کهن
but I am afraid of senile (feeble) minds.

فهم‌های کهنهٔ کوته‌نظر
Senile and short-sighted minds bring a
صد خیال بد در آرد در فکر
a hundred evil fancies into their thoughts.

بر سماع راست هر کس چیر نیست
Not everyone is able to hear rightly:
لقمهٔ هر مرغکی آن چهیر نیست
the fig is not a morsel for every little bird,

خاصه مرغی مرده‌ای پوسیده‌ای
Especially a bird that is dead, putrid;
پرخیالی اعمیی بی‌دیده‌ای
a blind, eyeless (fellow) filled with vain fancy.

نقش ماهی را چه دریا و چه خاک
To the picture of a fish what is the difference between sea and land?
رنگ هندو را چه صابون و چه زاک
To the colour of a Hindoo what is the difference between soap and black vitriol?

نقش اگر غمگین نگاری بر ورق
If you depict the portrait on the paper as sorrowful,
او ندارد از غم و شادی سبق
it has no lesson (learns nothing) of sorrow or joy.

صورتش غمگین و او فارغ از آن
Its appearance is sorrowful, but it is free from that (sorrow);
صورتش خندان و او زان بی‌نشان
(or) its appearance is smiling, but it has no (inward) impression of that (joy).

وین غم و شادی که اندر دل حظیست
And this (worldly) sorrow and joy which are delineated in the heart
پیش آن شادی و غم جز نقش نیست
are naught but a picture in comparison with that (spiritual) joy and sorrow.

صورت خندان نقش از بهر تست
The picture's smiling appearance is for your sake,
تا از آن صورت شود معنی درست
in order that by means of that picture the reality may be established

نقشهایی کاندرین حمامهاست
The pictures (phenomena) which are in these hot baths
از برون جامه‌کن چون جامه‌هاست
from outside the undressing-room (of self-abandonment), are like clothes.

تا برونی جامه‌ها بینی و بس
So long as you are outside, you see only the clothes (phenomena):
جامه بیرون کن درآ ای هم نفس
put off your clothes and enter (the bath of reality), O kindred spirit,

زانک با جامه درون سو راه نیست
Because, with your clothes, there is no way (of getting) inside:
تن ز جان جامه ز تن آگاه نیست
inside: the body is ignorant of the soul, the clothes (are ignorant) of the body.

❖◉❖◉❖

پیش آمدن نقیبان و دربانان خلیفه از بهر اکرام اعرابی و پذیرفتن هدیهٔ او را
How the Caliph's officers and chamberlains came forward to pay their respects to the Bedouin and to receive his gift.

آن عرابی از بیابان بعید
When the Bedouin arrived from the remote desert
بر در دار الخلافه چون رسید
the gate of the Caliph's palace,

پس نقیبان پیش او باز آمدند
The court officers went to meet the Bedouin:
بس گلاب لطف بر جیبش زدند
they sprinkled much rose-water of graciousness on his bosom.

حاجت او فهمشان شد بی مقال
Without speech (on his part) they perceived what he wanted:
کار ایشان بد عطا پیش از سئوال
it was their practice to give before being asked.

پس بدو گفتند یا وجه العرب
Then they said to him, "O chief of the Arabs,
از کجایی چونی از راه و تعب
whence dost thou come? How art thou after the journey and fatigue?"

گفت وجهم گر مرا وجهی دهید
He said, "I am a chief, if ye give me any countenance
بی وجوهم چون پس پشتم نهید
I am without means (of winning respect) when ye put me behind your backs.

ای که در روتان نشان مهتری
O ye in whose faces are the marks of eminence,
فرتان خوشتر ز زر جعفری
O ye whose splendour is more pleasing than the gold of Ja'far,

ای که یک دیدارتان دیدارها
O ye, one sight of whom is (worth many) sights,
ای نثار دینتان دینارها
O ye at the sight of whom pieces of gold are scattered (as largesse),

ای همه ینظر بنور الله شده
O ye, all of whom have become seeing by the light of God,
بهر بخشش از بر شه آمده
who have come from God for the sake of munificence,

تا زنید آن کیمیاهای نظر
That ye may cast the elixir of your looks
بر سر مسهای اشخاص بشر
upon the copper of human individuals,

من غریبم از بیابان آمدم
I am a stranger: I have come from the desert:
بر امید لطف سلطان آمدم
desert: I have come in hope of (gaining) the grace of the Sultan.

بوی لطف او بیابانها گرفت
The scent of his grace covered (took entire possession of) the deserts:
ذره‌های ریگ هم جانها گرفت
even the grains of sand were ensouled (thereby).

تا بدین جا بهر دینار آمدم
I came all the way to this place for the sake of dinars:
چون رسیدم مست دیدار آمدم
as soon as I arrived, I became drunken with sight (contemplation)."

بهر نان شخصی سوی نانبا دوید
A person ran to the baker for bread:
داد جان چون حسن نانبا را بدید
on seeing the beauty of the baker, he gave up the ghost.

بهر فرجه شد یکی تا گلستان
A certain man went to the rose-garden to take his pleasure,
فرجهٔ او شد جمال باغبان
and found it in the beauty of the gardener,

همچو اعرابی که آب از چه کشید
Like the desert Arab who drew water from the well and tasted
آب حیوان از رخ یوسف چشید
the Water of Life from the (lovely) face of Joseph.

رفت موسی کآتش آرد او بدست
Moses went to fetch fire: he beheld such a Fire
آتشی دید او که از آتش برست
that he escaped from (searching after) fire.

جست عیسی تا رهد از دشمنان
Jesus sprang up, to escape from his enemies:
بردش آن جستن به چارم آسمان
enemies: that spring carried him to the Fourth Heaven.

دام آدم خوشهٔ گندم شده
The ear of wheat became a trap for Adam,
تا وجودش خوشهٔ مردم شده
so that his existence became the wheat-ear (seed and origin) of mankind.

باز آید سوی دام از بهر خور
The falcon comes to the snare for food:
ساعد شه یابد و اقبال و فر
it finds the fore-arm(wrist) of the King and fortune and glory

طفل شد مکتب پی کسب هنر
The child went to school to acquire knowledge,
بر امید مرغ با لطف پدر
in hope of (getting) its father's pretty bird (as a prize);

پس ز مکتب آن یکی صدری شده
Then, by (going to) school, that child rose to the top,
ماهگانه داده و بدری شده
paid monthly fees (to his teacher), and became perfect (in knowledge).

آمده عباس حرب از بهر کین
Abbás had come to war for vengeance' sake,
بهر قمع احمد و استیز دین
for the purpose of subduing Ahmad (Mohammed) and opposing the (true) religion:

گشته دین را تا قیامت پشت و رو
He and his descendants in the Caliphate became a back and front
در خلافت او و فرزندان او
(complete support) to the (true) religion until the Resurrection.

من برین در طالب چیز آمدم
"I came to this court in quest of wealth:
صدر گشتم چون به دهلیز آمدم
as soon as I entered the portico I became (a spiritual) chief.

آب آوردم به تحفه بهر نان
I brought water as a gift for the sake of (getting) bread:
بوی نانم برد تا صدر جنان
hope of bread led me to the highest place in Paradise.

نان برون راند آدمی را از بهشت
Bread drove an Adam forth from Paradise:
نان مرا اندر بهشتی در سرشت
bread caused me to mix (made me consort) with those who belong to Paradise.

رستم از آب و ز نان همچون ملک
I have been freed, like the angels, from water and bread(materiality):
بی‌غرض گردم برین در چون فلک
without (any worldly) object of desire I move round this court, like the (revolving) sphere of heaven."

بی‌غرض نبود بگردش در جهان
Nothing in the world is without object
غیر جسم و غیر جان عاشقان
in its movement (activity) except the bodies and the souls of lovers.

◆◉◆◉◆

در بیان آنک عاشق دنیا بر مثال عاشق دیواریست
Showing that the lover of this world is like the lover of a wall

کی بر و تاب آفتاب زند و جهد و جهاد نکرد تا فهم کند کی آن تاب و رونق از دیوار نیست از قرص آفتابست در آسمان چهارم لاجرم کلی دل بر دیوار نهاد چون پرتو آفتاب بفتاب پیوست او محروم ماند ابدا و حیل بینهم و بین ما یشتهون

on which the sunbeams strike, who makes no effort and exertion to perceive that the radiance and splendour do not proceed from the wall, but from the orb of the sun in the Fourth Heaven; consequently he sets his whole heart on the wall, and when the sunbeams rejoin the sun (at sunset), he is left for ever in despair: "and a bar is placed between them and that which they desire."

عاشقان کل نه عشاق جزو
The lovers of the Whole are not those who love the part:
ماند از کل آنک شد مشتاق جزو
he that longed for the part failed to attain unto the Whole.

چونک جزوی عاشق جزوی شود
When a part falls in love with a part,
زود معشوقش بکل خود رود
the object of its love soon goes (returns) to its own whole.

ریش گاو و بندهٔ غیر آمد او
He (the lover of the particular) became the laughing-stock of another's slave:
غرقه شد کف در ضعیفی در زد او
he became (like a man who was) drowning and clung to someone weak (and powerless to help him).

نیست حاکم تا کند تیمار او
He (the loved slave) possesses no authority,
کار خواجهٔ خود کند یا کار او
that he should care for him: shall he do his own master's business or his (the lover's)?

❖❖❖

مثل عرب اذا زنیت فازن بالحرة و اذا سرقت فاسرق الدرة
The Arabic proverb, "If you commit fornication, commit it with a free woman, and if you steal, steal a pearl."

فازن بالحرة بی این شد مثل
Hence (the saying), "Commit fornication with a free woman," became proverbial;
فاسرق الدرة بدین شد منتقل
(and the words) "steal a pearl" were transferred (metaphorically) to this (meaning).

بنده سوی خواجه شد او ماند زار
The slave (the loved one) went away to his master: he (the lover) was left in misery.

بوی گل شد سوی گل او ماند خار
The scent of the rose went (back) to the rose: he remained as the thorn.

او بمانده دور از مطلوب خویش
He was left far from the object of his desire

سعی ضایع رنج باطل پای ریش
}his labour lost, his toil useless, his foot wounded,

همچو صیادی که گیرد سایه‌ای
Like the hunter who catches a shadow

سایه کی گردد ورا سرمایه‌ای
how should the shadow become his property?

سایهٔ مرغی گرفته مرد سخت
The man has grasped tightly the shadow of a bird,

مرغ حیران گشته بر شاخ درخت
the bird on the branch of the tree is fallen into amazement,

کین مدمغ بر کی می‌خندد عجب
(Thinking), "I wonder who this crack-brained fellow is laughing at?

اینت باطل اینت پوسیده سبب
Here's folly for you, here's a rotten cause!

ور تو گویی جزو پیوستهٔ کلست
And if you say that the part is connected with the whole,

خار می‌خور خار مقرون گلست
(then) eat thorns: the thorn is connected with the rose.

جز ز یک رو نیست پیوسته به کل
Except from one point of view, it (the part) is not connected with the whole:

ورنه خود باطل بدی بعث رسل
otherwise, indeed, the mission of the prophets would be vain,

چون رسولان از پی پیوستنند
Inasmuch as the prophets are (sent) in order to connect (the part with the whole):

پس چه پیوندندشان چون یک تنند
how, then, should they (the prophets) connect them when they are (already) one body?

این سخن پایان ندارد ای غلام
This discourse hath no end. O lad,

روز بیگه شد حکایت کن تمام
the day is late: conclude the tale.

354

سپردن عرب هدیه را یعنی سبو را به غلامان خلیفه
How the Arab delivered the gift, that is, the jug to the Caliph's servants

آن سبوی آب را در پیش داشت
He presented the jug of water,
تخم خدمت را در آن حضرت بکاشت
he sowed the seed of homage in that (exalted) court.

گفت این هدیه بدان سلطان برید
"Bear this gift," said he, "to the Sultan,
سایل شه را ز حاجت وا خرید
redeem the King's suitor from indigence.

آب شیرین و سبوی سبز و نو
'Tis sweet water and a new green jug
ز آب بارانی که جمع آمد بگو
some of the rain-water that collected in the ditch."

خنده می‌آمد نقیبان را از آن
The officials smiled at that,
لیک پذرفتند آن را همچو جان
but they accepted it (the jug) as (though it were precious as) life,

زانک لطف شاه خوب با خبر
Because the graciousness of the good and wise King
کرده بود اندر همه ارکان اثر
had made a mark (impressed itself) on all the courtiers.

خوی شاهان در رعیت جا کند
The disposition of kings settles (becomes implanted) in their subjects:
چرخ اخضر خاک را خضرا کند
the green sky makes the earth verdant.

شه چو حوضی دان حشم چون لوله‌ها
Regard the king as a reservoir with pipes in every direction,
آب از لوله روان در گوله‌ها
and water running from all (the pipes) like hoppers (in a mill).

چونک آب جمله از حوضیست پاک
When the water in all (the pipes) is from a pure reservoir,
هر یکی آبی دهد خوش ذوقناک
every single one gives sweet water, pleasant to taste;

ور در آن حوض آب شورست و پلید
But if the water in the reservoir is brackish and dirty,
هر یکی لوله همان آرد پدید
every pipe brings the same to view,

زانک پیوستست هر لوله به حوض
Because every pipe is connected with the reservoir.
خوض کن در معنی این حرف خوض
Dive, dive into (ponder deeply) the meaning of these words.

لطف شاهنشاه جان بی‌وطن
(Consider) how the imperial grace of the homeless Spirit
چون اثر کردست اندر کل تن
has produced effects on the whole body;

لطف عقل خوش‌نهاد خوش نسب
How the grace of Reason, which is of goodly nature,
چون همه تن را در آرد در ادب
nature, of goodly lineage, brings the entire body into discipline;

عشق شنگ بی‌قرار بی سکون
How Love, saucy, uncontrolled, and restless,
چون در آرد کل تن را در جنون
throws the whole body into madness.

لطف آب بحر کو چون کوثرست
The purity of the water of the Sea that is like Kawthar
سنگ ریزه‌ش جمله در و گوهرست
all its pebbles are pearls and gems.

هر هنر که استا بدان معروف شد
For whatever science the master is renowned,
جان شاگردان بدان موصوف شد
the souls of his pupils become endued with the same.

پیش استاد اصولی هم اصول
With the master-theologian the quick and industrious
خواند آن شاگرد چست با حصول
pupil reads (scholastic) theology.

پیش استاد فقیه آن فقه‌خوان
With the master-jurist the student of jurisprudence reads jurisprudence,
فقه خواند نه اصول اندر بیان
when he (the teacher) expounds it, not theology.

پیش استادی که او نحوی بود
Then the master who is a grammarian
جان شاگردش ازو نحوی شود
the soul of his pupil becomes imbued by him with grammar.

باز استادی که او محو رهست
Again, the master who is absorbed in the Way (of Súfism)

جان شاگردش ازو محو شهست
because of him the soul of his pupil is absorbed in the King(God).

زین همه انواع دانش روز مرگ
Of all these various kinds of knowledge,

دانش فقرست ساز راه و برگ
on the day of death the (best) equipment and provision for the road is the knowledge of (spiritual) poverty.

حکایت ماجرای نحوی و کشتیبان
The story of what passed between the grammarian and the boatman.

آن یکی نحوی به کشتی در نشست
A certain grammarian embarked in a boat.

رو به کشتیبان نهاد آن خودپرست
That selfconceited person turned to the boatman

گفت هیچ از نحو خواندی گفت لا
And said, "Have you ever studied grammar?" "No,"

گفت نیم عمر تو شد در فنا
he replied. The other said, "Half your life is gone to naught."

دل‌شکسته گشت کشتیبان ز تاب
The boatman became heart-broken with grief,

لیک آن دم کرد خامش از جواب
but at the time he refrained from answering.

باد کشتی را به گردابی فکند
The wind cast the boat into a whirlpool:

گفت کشتیبان بدان نحوی بلند
the boatman spoke loud (shouted) to the grammarian,

هیچ دانی آشنا کردن بگو
Tell me, do you know how to swim?" "No,"

گفت نی ای خوش جواب خوب رو
said he, "O fairspoken good-looking man!"

گفت کل عمرت ای نحوی فناست
O grammarian," said he, "your whole life is naught,

زانک کشتی غرق این گردابهاست
because the boat is sinking in these whirlpools."

محو می‌باید نه نحو اینجا بدان
Know that here mahw (self-effacement) is needed, not nah?
گر تو محوی بی‌خطر در آب ران
if you are mahw (dead to self), plunge into the sea without peril.

آب دریا مرده را بر سر نهد
The water of the sea places the dead one on its head (causes him to float on the surface);
ور بود زنده ز دریا کی رهد
but if he be living, how shall he escape from the sea?

چون بمردی تو ز اوصاف بشر
Inasmuch as you have died to the attributes of the flesh,
بحر اسرارت نهد بر فرق سر
the Sea of (Divine) consciousness will place you on the crown of its head (will raise you to honour)

ای که خلقان را تو خر می‌خوانده‌ای
(But) O thou who hast called the people asses,
این زمان چون خر برین یخ مانده‌ای
at this time thou art left (floundering), like an ass, upon this ice.

گر تو علامه زمانی در جهان
If in the world thou art the most learned scholar of the time,
نک فنای این جهان بین وین زمان
behold the passing away of this world and this time!

مرد نحوی را از آن در دوختیم
We have stitched in (inserted) the (story of the) grammarian,
تا شما را نحو محو آموختیم
that we might teach you the grammar (nahw) of selfeffacement

فقه فقه و نحو نحو و صرف صرف
the jurisprudence of jurisprudence, the grammar of grammar, and the accidence of accidence.
در کم آمد یابی ای یار شگرف
In self-loss, O venerated friend, thou wilt find

آن سبوی آب دانشهای ماست
That jug of water is (an emblem of) our different sorts of knowledge,
وان خلیفه دجلهٔ علم خداست
and the Caliph is the Tigris of God's knowledge.

ما سبوها پر به دجله می‌بریم
We are carrying jugs full (of water) to the Tigris:
گرنه خر دانیم خود را ما خریم
if we do not know ourselves to be asses, asses we are.

باری اعرابی بدان معذور بود
After all, the Bedouin was excusable,

کو ز دجله غافل و بس دور بود
for he was ignorant of the Tigris and of the (great) river

گر ز دجله با خبر بودی چو ما
If he had been acquainted with the Tigris, as we are,

او نبردی آن سبو را جا بجا
he would not have carried that jug from place to place;

بلک از دجله چو واقف آمدی
Nay, had he been aware of the Tigris,

آن سبو را بر سر سنگی زدی
he would have dashed that jug against a stone.

⟨◉⟩⟨◉⟩

قبول کردن خلیفه هدیه را
How the Caliph accepted the gift

و عطا فرمودن با کمال بی‌نیازی از آن هدیه و از آن سبو
and bestowed largesse, notwithstanding that he was entirely without need of the gift (the water) and the jug.

چون خلیفه دید و احوالش شنید
When the Caliph saw (the gift) and heard his story,

آن سبو را پر ز زر کرد و مزید
he filled the jug with gold and added (other presents).

آن عرب را کرد از فاقه خلاص
He delivered the Arab from penury,

داد بخششها و خلعتهای خاص
he bestowed donations and special robes of honour,

کین سبو پر زر به دست او دهید
Saying, "Give into his hand this jug full of gold.

چونک واگردد سوی دجله‌ش برید
When he returns (home), take him to the Tigris.

از ره خشک آمدست و از سفر
He has come (hither) by way of the desert and by travelling

از ره دجله‌ش بود نزدیکتر
it will be nearer for him (to return) by water."

چون به کشتی در نشست و دجله دید
When he (the Arab) embarked in the boat and beheld the Tigris,
سجده می‌کرد از حیا و می‌خمید
he was prostrating himself in shame and bowing

کای عجب لطف این شه وهاب را
Saying, "Oh, wonderful is the kindness of that bounteous King,
وان عجب تر کو ستد آن آب را
and 'tis (even) more wonderful that he took that water.

چون پذیرفت از من آن دریای جود
How did that Sea of munificence so quickly accept
آنچنان نقد دغل را زود زود
from me such spurious coin as this?"

کل عالم را سبو دان ای پسر
Know, O son, that everything in the universe is a jug
کو بود از علم و خوبی تا بسر
which is (filled) to the brim with wisdom and beauty.

قطره‌ای از دجلهٔ خوبی اوست
It (everything in the universe) is a drop of the Tigris of His beauty,
کان نمی‌گنجد ز پری زیر پوست
which (beauty) because of its fullness is not contained under the skin (that should enclose it).

گنج مخفی بد ز پری چاک کرد
Twas a hidden treasure: because of its fullness it burst forth and made
خاک را تابان‌تر از افلاک کرد
the earth more shining than the heavens.

گنج مخفی بد ز پری جوش کرد
Twas a hidden treasure: because of its fullness it surged up and made
خاک را سلطان اطلس پوش کرد
the earth (like) a sultan robed in satin.

ور بدیدی شاخی از دجلهٔ خدا
And if he (the Arab) had seen a branch of the Divine Tigris,
آن سبو را او فنا کردی فنا
he would have destroyed that jug, destroyed it.

آنک دیدندش همیشه بی خودند
They that saw it are always beside themselves:
بی‌خودانه بر سبو سنگی زدند
like one beside himself, they hurled a stone at the jug

ای ز غیرت بر سبو سنگی زده
O thou who from jealousy hast hurled a stone at the jug,
وان شکستت خود درستی آمده
while the jug has (only) become more perfect through being shattered,

خم شکسته آب ازو ناریخته
The jar is shattered, (but) the water is not spilled from it:
صد درستی زین شکست انگیخته
from this shattering have arisen a hundred soundnesses.

جزو جزو خم برقصست و بحال
Every piece of the jar is in dance and ecstasy,
عقل جزوی را نموده این محال
to the partial (discursive) reason this seems absurd.

نه سبو پیدا درین حالت نه آب
In this state (of ecstasy) neither the jug is manifest nor the water.
خوش ببین والله اعلم بالصواب
Consider well, and God knoweth best what is right.

چون در معنی زنی بازت کنند
When you knock at the door of Reality, it will be opened to you:
پر فکرت زن که شهبازت کنند
beat the pinion of thought, in order that you may be made a king-falcon.

پر فکرت شد گل آلود و گران
The pinion of your thought has become mud-stained
زانک گل‌خواری ترا گل شد چو نان
and heavy because you are a clayeater: clay has become to you as bread.

نان گلست و گوشت کمتر خور ازین
Bread and meat are (originally) clay: eat little thereof,
تا نمانی همچو گل اندر زمین
that you may not remain in the earth, like clay.

چون گرسنه می‌شوی سگ می‌شوی
When you become hungry, you become a dog:
تند و بد پیوند و بدرگ می‌شوی
you become fierce and ill-tempered and ill-natured.

چون شدی تو سیر مرداری شدی
When you have eaten your fill, you have become a carcase
بی‌خبر بی‌پا چو دیواری شدی
you have become devoid of understanding and without feet(inert), like a wall.

پس دمی مردار و دیگر دم سگی
So at one time you are a carcase and at another time a dog:
چون کنی در راه شیران خوش تگی
how will you run well in the road of the lions (follow the saints)?

آلت اشکار خود جز سگ مدان
Know that your only means of hunting is the dog (the animal soul):
کمترک انداز سگ را استخوان
throw bones to the dog but seldom,

زانک سگ چون سیر شد سرکش شود
Because when the dog has eaten its fill, it becomes rebellious:
کی سوی صید و شکار خوش دود
how should it run to the goodly chase and hunt?

آن عرب را بی‌نوایی می‌کشید
Want of food was leading the Arab to that (exalted) court,
تا بدان درگاه و آن دولت رسید
court, and (there) he found his fortune.

در حکایت گفته‌ایم احسان شاه
We have related in the (foregoing) story the kindness shown by the King
در حق آن بی‌نوای بی‌پناه
that needy one who had no refuge.

هر چه گوید مرد عاشق بوی عشق
Whatsoever the man in love (with God) speaks,
از دهانش می‌جهد در کوی عشق
the scent of Love is springing from his mouth into the abode of Love.

گر بگوید فقه فقر آید همه
If he speak (formal) theology, it all turns to (spiritual) poverty:
بوی فقر آید از آن خوش د مدمه
the scent of poverty comes from that man of sweet and beguiling discourse.

ور بگوید کفر دارد بوی دین
And if he speak infidelity, it has the scent of (the true) religion,
آید از گفت شکش بوی یقین
and if he speak doubtfully, his doubt turns to certainty.

کف کژ کز بهر صدق خاستست
The perverse froth that has risen from a sea of sincerity
اصل صاف آن فرع را آراستست
that turbid (froth) has been set out by the pure source.

آن کفش را صافی و محقوق دان
Know that its froth is pure and worthy:
همچو دشنام لب معشوق دان
know that it is like revilement from the lips of the beloved,

گشته آن دشنام نامطلوب او
Whose unsought reproaches have become sweet
خوش ز بهر عارض محبوب او
for the sake of her cheek which he desires.

گر بگوید کژ نماید راستی
If he (the lover of God) speak falsehood, it seems (like) the truth.
ای کژی که راست را آراستی
O (fine) falsehood that would adorn (even) the truth!

از شکر گر شکل نانی می‌پزی
If you cook (a confection) of sugar in the form of a loaf of bread,
طعم قند آید نه نان چون می‌مزی
it will taste of candy, not of bread, while you are sucking it.

ور بیابد مؤمنی زرین وثن
If a true believer find a golden idol,
کی هلد آن را برای هر شمن
how should he leave it(there) for the sake of a worshipper?

بلک گیرد اندر آتش افکند
Nay, he will take it and cast it into the fire:
صورت عاریتش را بشکند
he will break(destroy) its borrowed (unreal) form,

تا نماند بر ذهب شکل وثن
In order that the idol-shape may not remain on the gold,
زانک صورت مانعست و راه‌زن
because Form hinders and waylays (those who seek Reality).

ذات زرش داد ربانیتست
The essence of its gold is the essence of Lordship (Divinity):
نقش بت بر نقد زر عاریتست
the idol-stamp on the sterling gold is borrowed (unreal).

بهر کیکی تو گلیمی را مسوز
Do not burn a blanket on account of a flea,
وز صداع هر مگس مگذار روز
and do not let the day go (to waste) on account of every gnat's headache.

بت‌پرستی چون بمانی در صور
You are an idol-worshipper when you remain in (bondage to) forms:
صورتش بگذار و در معنی نگر
leave its (the idol's) form and look at the reality.

مرد حجی همره حاجی طلب
If you are a man (bound) for the Pilgrimage, seek a pilgrim (as your) companion,
خواه هندو خواه ترک و یا عرب
whether he be a Hindoo or a Turcoman or an Arab.

منگر اندر نقش و اندر رنگ او
Do not look at his figure and colour,
بنگر اندر عزم و در آهنگ او
look at his purpose and intention

گر سیاهست او هم‌آهنگ توست
If he is black, (yet) he is in accord with you: call him white,
تو سپیدش خوان که همرنگ توست
for (spiritually) his complexion is the same as yours.

این حکایت گفته شد زیر و زبر
This story has been told up and down (confusedly),
همچو فکر عاشقان بی پا و سر
like the doings of lovers, without foot (end) or head (beginning).

سر ندارد چون ز ازل بودست پیش
It hath no head, inasmuch as it existed before eternity;
پا ندارد با ابد بودست خویش
it hath no foot: it has (always) been akin to everlastingness.

بلک چون آبست هر قطره از آن
Nay, it is like water: every drop thereof
هم سرست و پا و هم بی هر دوان
is both head and foot, and at the same time without both.

حاش لله این حکایت نیست هین
This is not a story, mark you! God forbid!
نقد حال ما و تست این خوش ببین
This is the ready money of my state and yours. Consider (it) well,

زانک صوفی با کر و با فر بود
Because the Súfí is grand and glorious (in his spiritual vision):
هرچ آن ماضیست لا یذکر بود
whatever is past is not remembered (does not enter his mind).

هم عرب ما هم سبو ما هم ملک
We are both the Arab and the jug and the King;
جمله ما یؤفک عنه من افک
we are all: he that has been turned away from it (the Truth) shall be turned away.

عقل را شو دان و زن این نفس و طمع
Know that the husband is Reason, and the wife is greed and cupidity:
این دو ظلمانی و منکر عقل شمع
these twain are dark and deniers (of Reason); Reason is the (bright) candle.

بشنو اکنون اصل انکار از چه خاست
Now hear the origin of their denial,
زانک کل را گونه گونه جزوهاست
whence it arose: from the fact that the Whole hath various parts.

جزو کل نی جزوها نسبت به کل
The parts of the Whole are not parts in relation to the Whole
نی چو بوی گل که باشد جزو گل
(they are) not like the scent of the rose, which is a part of the rose.

لطف سبزه جزو لطف گل بود
The beauty of (all) green herbs is a part of the Rose's beauty,
بانگ قمری جزو آن بلبل بود
the coo of the turtle-dove is a part of that Nightingale.

گر شوم مشغول اشکال و جواب
If I become occupied with a difficulty (difficult question) and the answer (explanation),
تشنگان را کی توانم داد آب
how shall I be able to give water to the thirsty?

گر تو اشکالی بکلی و حرج
If you are wholly perplexed and in straits,
صبر کن الصبر مفتاح الفرج
have patience: patience is the key to joy.

احتما کن احتما ز اندیشه‌ها
Abstain from (distracting) thoughts, abstain:
فکر شیر و گور و دلها بیشه‌ها
thought is (like) the lion and the wild ass, and (men's) hearts are the thickets

احتماها بر دواها سرورست
Acts of abstinence are superior to medicines,
زانک خاریدن فزونی گرست
because scratching is an increase (aggravation) of the itch.

احتما اصل دوا آمد یقین
Assuredly abstinence is the first principle of medicine:
احتما کن قوت جانت ببین
abstain, and behold the strength of the spirit.

قابل این گفته‌ها شو گوش وار
Receive these words, like the (open) ear,
تا که از زر سازمت من گوش وار
that I may make for you an earring of gold:

حلقه در گوش مه زرگر شوی
(Then) you will become a ring in the ear of (devoted to) the Moon that works in gold,
تا به ماه و تا ثریا بر شوی
you will ascend to the moon and the Pleiades.

اولا بشنو که خلق مختلف
First, hear (and learn) that the diverse created
مختلف جانند تا یا از الف
beings are spiritually different, from yá (Y) to alif (A).

در حروف مختلف شور و شکیست
Amongst the various letters there is a confusion and uncertainty,
گرچه از یک رو ز سر تا پا یکیست
though from one point of view they are (all) one from head (beginning) to foot (end).

از یکی رو ضد و یک رو متحد
From one aspect they are opposites, and from one aspect they are unified;
از یکی رو هزل و از یک روی جد
from one aspect they are jest, and from one aspect they are earnest.

پس قیامت روز عرض اکبرست
Therefore the Resurrection is the day of the supreme inspection:
عرض او خواهد که با زیب و فرست
inspection is desired by him (only) who is glorious and splendid.

هر که چون هندوی بدسوداییست
Whoever is like a fraudulent Hindoo,
روز عرضش نوبت رسواییست
for him the day of inspection is the time of exposure.

چون ندارد روی همچون آفتاب
Inasmuch as he hath not a face like the sun,
او نخواهد جز شبی همچون نقاب
he desires nothing but night (to cover him) like a veil.

برگ یک گل چون ندارد خار او
Since his thorn hath not a single rose-leaf,
شد بهاران دشمن اسرار او
Spring is the enemy of his conscience,

وانک سر تا پا گلست و سوسنست
While to one that is roses and lilies from head to foot
پس بهار او را دو چشم روشنست
Spring is (welcome as) a pair of bright eyes.

خار بی‌معنی خزان خواهد خزان
The unspiritual thorn wishes for autumn,
تا زند پهلوی خود با گلستان
for autumn, in order that it may jostle with (contend as a rival with) the rosegarden,

تا بپوشد حسن آن و ننگ این
And that it (autumn) may hide the beauty of that (the rose) and the shame of this (the thorn),
تا نبینی رنگ آن و زنگ این
so that you may not see the colour of that and the colour of this.

پس خزان او را بهارست و حیات
Therefore autumn is its (the thorn's) Spring and life,
یک نماید سنگ و یاقوت زکات
the (worthless) stone and the pure ruby appear one.

باغبان هم داند آن را در خزان
The Gardener knows that (difference) even in autumn,
لیک دید یک به از دید جهان
but the One's sight is better than the world's sight.

خود جهان آن یک کس است او ابلهست
Truly that One Person is (essentially) the (whole) world: he is unaware of evil
هر ستاره بر فلک جزو مهست
The stars, every one, are all part of the Moon.

پس همی‌گویند هر نقش و نگار
Therefore every fair form and shape (in the world) is crying,
مژده مژده نک همی آید بهار
crying, "Good news! good news! Lo, here comes the Spring."

تا بود تابان شکوفه چون زره
So long as the blossom is shining like a coat of mail,
کی کنند آن میوه‌ها پیدا گره
how should the fruits display their knobs?

چون شکوفه ریخت میوه سر کند
When the blossom is shed, the fruit comes to a head:
چونک تن بشکست جان سر بر زند
head: when the body is shattered, the spirit lifts up its head.

میوه معنی و شکوفه صورتش
The fruit is the reality, the blossom is its form:
آن شکوفه مژده میوه نعمتش
the blossom is the good news, the fruit is the bounty (given as a reward) for it.

چون شکوفه ریخت میوه شد پدید
When the blossom was shed, the fruit became visible:
چونک آن کم شد این اندر مزید
when that diminished this began to increase.

تا که نان نشکست قوت کی دهد
How should bread give strength until it is broken?
نا شکسته خوشه‌ها کی می‌دهد
How should uncrushed clusters (of grapes) yield wine?

تا هلیله نشکند با ادویه
Unless myrobalan is pounded up with medicines,
کی شود خود صحت‌افزا ادویه
how should the medicines by themselves become health-increasing

◈◉◈◉◈

در صفت پیر و مطاوعت وی
Concerning the qualities of the Pír (Spiritual Guide) and (the duty of) obedience to him.

ای ضیاء الحق حسام الدین بگیر
O Splendour of the Truth, Husámu'ddín,
یک دو کاغذ بر فزا در وصف پیر
take one or two sheets of paper and add (them to the poem) in description of the Pír.

گرچه جسم نازکت را زور نیست
Although thy slender body hath no strength,
لیک بی خورشید ما را نور نیست
yet without the sun (of thy spirit) we have no light.

گرچه مصباح و زجاجه گشته‌ای
Although thou hast become the lighted wick and the glass
لیک سرخیل دلی سررشته‌ای
(lamp), yet thou art the heart's leader thou art the end of the thread

چون سر رشته به دست و کام تست
Inasmuch as the end of the thread is in thy hand and will,
درهای عقد دل ز انعام تست
will, the beads (of spiritual knowledge) on the heart's necklace are (derived) from thy bounty

بر نویس احوال پیر راه‌دان
Write down what appertains to the Pír (Guide) who knows the Way:
پیر را بگزین و عین راه دان
Choose the Pír and regard him as the essence of the Way.

پیر تابستان و خلقان تیر ماه
The Pír is (like) summer, and (other) people are (like) the autumn month;
خلق مانند شبند و پیر ماه
(other) people are like night, and the Pír is the moon.

کرده‌ام بخت جوان را نام پیر
I have bestowed on (my) young Fortune (Husámu'ddín) the name of Pír (old),
کو ز حق پیرست نه از ایام پیر
because he is (made) old by the Truth, not (made) old by Time.

او چنان پیرست کش آغاز نیست
So old is he that he hath no beginning:
با چنان در یتیم انباز نیست
there is no rival to such a unique Pearl.

خود قوی‌تر می‌شود خمر کهن
Verily, old wine grows more potent; verily,
خاصه آن خمری که باشد من لدن
old gold is more highly prized.

پیر را بگزین که بی پیر این سفر
Choose a Pír, for without a Pír this journey
هست بس پر آفت و خوف و خطر
is exceeding full of woe and affright and danger

آن رهی که بارها تو رفته‌ای
Without an escort you are bewildered (even) on a road
بی قلاوز اندر آن آشفته‌ای
road you have travelled many times (before):

پس رهی را که ندیدستی تو هیچ
Do not, then, travel alone on a Way that you have not seen at all,
هین مرو تنها ز رهبر سر مپیچ
do not turn your head away from the Guide.

گر نباشد سایهٔ او بر تو گول
Fool, if his shadow (protection) be not over you

پس ترا سرگشته دارد بانگ غول
then the cry of the ghoul will keep you (wandering about) with your head in a whirl.

غولت از ره افکند اندر گزند
The ghoul will (entice you) from the Way (and) cast you into destruction:

از تو داهی‌تر درین ره بس بدند
there have been in this Way many craftier than you (who have perished miserably).

از نبی بشنو ضلال رهروان
Hear (learn) from the Qur'án the perdition of the wayfarers,

که چه شان کرد آن بلیس بدروان
hat the evil-souled Iblís did unto them:

صد هزاران ساله راه از جاده دور
He carried them far—a journey of hundreds of thousands of years

بردشان و کردشان ادبیر و عور
from the Highway, and made them backsliders and naked (devoid of good works).

استخوانهاشان ببین و مویشان
Behold their bones and their hair!

عبرتی گیر و مران خر سویشان
Take warning, and drive not your ass towards them!

گردن خر گیر و سوی راه کش
Seize the neck of your ass (the flesh) and lead him towards the Way

سوی ره بانان و ره دانان خوش
towards the good keepers and knowers of the Way

هین مهل خر را و دست از وی مدار
Beware! do not let your ass go, and do not remove your hand from him

زانک عشق اوست سوی سبزه‌زار
because his love is for the place where green herbs are plentiful.

گر یکی دم تو به غفلت وا هلیش
If you carelessly leave him free for one moment,

او رود فرسنگها سوی حشیش
he will go (many) leagues in the direction of the herbage.

دشمن راهست خر مست علف
The ass is an enemy to the Way, (he is) madly in love with fodder:

ای که بس خر بنده را کرد او تلف
oh, many is the attendant on him that he has brought to ruin

گر ندانی ره هر آنچه خر بخواست
If you know not the Way, whatsoever the ass desires do the contrary thereof:
عکس آن کن خود بود آن راه راست
that, surely, will be the right Way.

شاوروهن و آنگه خالفوا
"Consult them (women), and then oppose (them in what they advise)
ان من لم یعصهن تالف
he that disobeys them not will be ruined."

با هوا و آرزو کم باش دوست
Be not a friend to (sensual) passion and desire
چون یضلک عن سبیل الله اوست
since it leads you astray from the Way of God.

این هوا را نشکند اندر جهان
Nothing in the world will break (mortify)
هیچ چیزی همچو سایهٔ همرهان
this passion like the shadow (protection) of fellow-traveller

❖◉❖◉❖

وصیت کردن رسول صلی الله علیه و سلم مر علی را کرم الله وجهه
How the Prophet, on whom be peace, enjoined 'Alí—may God make his person honoured—saying,

کی چون هر کسی به نوع طاعتی تقرب جوید به حق تو تقرب جوی به صحبت عاقل و بندهٔ خاص تا ازیشان همه پیش‌قدم‌تر باشی
"When everyone seeks to draw nigh to God by means of some kind of devotional act, do thou seek the favour of God by associating with His wise and chosen servant, that thou mayst be the first of all to arrive (to gain access to Him)."

گفت پیغامبر علی را کای علی
The Prophet said to 'Alí, "O 'Alí,
شیر حقی پهلوان پردلی
thou art the Lion of God, thou art a courageous knight,

لیک بر شیری مکن هم اعتماد
But do not even rely upon thy lion-heartedness:
اندر آ در سایهٔ نخل امید
come into the shade of the palm tree of hope.

اندر آ در سایهٔ آن عاقلی
Come into the shade (protection) of the Sage
کش نداند برد از ره ناقلی
whom no conveyer can carry off from the Way.

ظل او اندر زمین چون کوه قاف
His shadow on the earth is like Mount Qáf,
روح او سیمرغ بس عالی‌طواف
his spirit is (like) the Símurgh that circles (soars) exceedingly high

گر بگویم تا قیامت نعت او
If I should tell of his qualities until the Resurrection,
هیچ آن را مقطع و غایت مجو
do not seek (expect) any conclusion and end to them.

در بشر روپوش کردست آفتاب
seek (expect) any conclusion and end to them.
فهم کن والله اعلم بالصواب
apprehend (this mystery), and God knows best what is right.

یا علی از جملهٔ طاعات راه
O 'Alí, above all devotional acts in the Way (of God)
برگزین تو سایهٔ خاص اله
do thou choose the shadow (protection) of the servant of God.

هر کسی در طاعتی بگریختند
Every one took refuge in some act of devotion and
خویشتن را مخلصی انگیختند
discovered for themselves some means of deliverance.

تو برو در سایهٔ عاقل گریز
Go thou, take refuge in the shadow of the Sage,
تا رهی زان دشمن پنهان ستیز
that thou mayst escape from the Enemy that opposes (thee) in secret.

از همه طاعات اینت بهترست
mayst escape from the Enemy that opposes (thee) in secret.
سبق یابی بر هر آن سابق که هست
(thereby) thou wilt gain precedence over every one that has outstripped

چون گرفتت پیر هین تسلیم شو
When the Pír has accepted thee, take heed,
همچو موسی زیر حکم خضر رو
surrender thyself (to him): go, like Moses, under the authority of Khizr

صبر کن بر کار خضری بی نفاق
Bear patiently whatever is done by a Khizr who is without hypocrisy
تا نگوید خضر رو هذا فراق
in order that Khizr may not say, "Begone, this is (our) parting."

372

گرچه کشتی بشکند تو دم مزن
Though he stave in the boat, do not speak a word;
گرچه طفلی را کشد تو مو مکن
though he kill a child, do not tear thy hair.

دست او را حق چو دست خویش خواند
God has declared that his (the Pír's) hand is as His own,
تا ید الله فوق ایدیهم براند
since He gave out (the words) the Hand of God is above their hands.

دست حق میراندش زنده‌ش کند
The Hand of God causes him (the child) to die and (then) brings him to life.
زنده چه بود جان پاینده‌ش کند
What of life? He makes him a spirit everlasting.

هرکه تنها نادرا این ره برید
If anyone, by rare exception, traversed this Way alone(without a Pír),
هم به عون همت پیران رسید
he arrived (at his goal) through the help (and favour) of the hearts of the Pírs.

دست پیر از غایبان کوتاه نیست
The hand of the Pír is not withdrawn from the absent
دست او جز قبضه الله نیست
his hand is naught but the grasp of God.

غایبان را چون چنین خلعت دهند
Inasmuch as they give such a robe of honour to the absent,
حاضران از غایبان لا شک به‌اند
undoubtedly the present are better than the absent.

غایبان را چون نواله می‌دهند
Since they are bestowing (spiritual) food on the absent,
پیش مهمان تا چه نعمتها نهند
see what bounties they must lay before one who is present.

کو کسی کو پیش شه بندد کمر
Where is one that girds himself (for service) before them to
تا کسی کو هست بیرون سوی در
(i.e. how far superior is he to) one that is outside the door?

چون گزیدی پیر نازک دل مباش
When thou hast chosen thy Pír, be not faint-hearted,
سست و ریزیده چو آب و گل مباش
be not weak as water and crumbly as earth.

ور بهر زخمی تو پر کینه شوی
If thou art enraged by every blow,
پس کجا بی‌صیقل آیینه شوی
then how wilt thou become a (clear) mirror without being polished?

❁❁

کبودی زدن قزوینی بر شانه گاه صورت شیر
How the man of Qazwin was tattooing the figure of a lion in blue on his shoulders,
و پشیمان شدن او به سبب زخم سوزن
and (then) repenting because of the (pain of the) needle-pricks.

این حکایت بشنو از صاحب بیان
Hear from the narrator this story
در طریق و عادت قزوینیان
about the way and custom of the people of Qazwin.

بر تن و دست و کتفها بی‌گزند
body and hand and shoulders, so as to suffer no injury.
از سر سوزن کبودیها زنند
They tattoo themselves in blue with the point of a needle on

سوی دلاکی بشد قزوینیی
A certain man of Qazwin went to a barber and said,
که کبودم زن بکن شیرینی
Tattoo me (and) do it charmingly (artistically)."

گفت چه صورت زنم ای پهلوان
O valiant sir," said he, "what figure shall I tattoo?"
گفت بر زن صورت شیر ژیان
He answered, "Prick in the figure of a furious lion.

طالعم شیرست نقش شیر زن
Leo is my ascendant: tattoo the form of a lion.
جهد کن رنگ کبودی سیر زن
Exert yourself, prick in plenty of the blue dye."

گفت بر چه موضعت صورت زنم
On what place," he asked, "shall I tattoo you?"
گفت بر شانه گهم زن آن رقم
Said he, "Prick the design of the beauty on my shoulder-blade."

چونک او سوزن فرو بردن گرفت
As soon as he began to stick in the needle
درد آن در شانه‌گه مسکن گرفت
the pain of it settled in the shoulder,

پهلوان در ناله آمد کای سنی
And the hero fell a-moaning—"O illustrious one,
مر مرا کشتی چه صورت می‌زنی
one, you have killed me: what figure are you tattooing?"

گفت آخر شیر فرمودی مرا
Why," said he, "you bade me do a lion."
گفت از چه عضو کردی ابتدا
What limb (of the lion)," asked the other, "did you begin with?"

گفت از دمگاه آغازیده‌ام
I have begun at the tail," said he.
گفت دم بگذار ای دو دیده‌ام
"O my dear friend," he cried, "leave out the tail!

از دم و دمگاه شیرم دم گرفت
My breath is stopped by the lion's tail and rump:
دمگه او دمگهم محکم گرفت
his rump has tightly closed (choked) my windpipe.

شیر بی‌دم باش گو ای شیرساز
Let the lion be without a tail, O lion-maker,
که دلم سستی گرفت از زخم گاز
for my heart is faint from the blows of the prong (the tattooer's needle)."

جانب دیگر گرفت آن شخص زخم
That person commenced to prick in (the blue) on another part
بی‌محابا و مواسایی و رحم
without fear, without favour, without mercy.

بانگ کرد او کین چه اندامست ازو
He yelled—"Which of his members is this?"
گفت این گوشست ای مرد نکو
"This is his ear, my good man," the barber replied.

گفت تا گوشش نباشد ای حکیم
O Doctor," said he, "let him have no ears:
گوش را بگذار و کوته کن گلیم
omit the ears and cut the frock short."

375

جانب دیگر خلش آغاز کرد
The barber began to insert (his needle) in another part:
باز قزوینی فغان را ساز کرد
once more the man of Qazwīn set out to wail,

کین سوم جانب چه اندامست نیز
Saying, "What is the member (you are pricking in) now on this third spot?"
گفت اینست اشکم شیر ای عزیز
He replied, "This is the lion's belly, my dear sir."

گفت تا اشکم نباشد شیر را
Let the lion have no belly," said he:
گشت افزون درد کم کن زخم ها
"what need of a belly for the picture that is (already) sated?"

خیره شد دلاک و پس حیران بماند
The barber became distraught and remained in great bewilderment:
تا بدیر انگشت در دندان بماند
he stood for a long time with his fingers in his teeth;

بر زمین زد سوزن از خشم اوستاد
Then the master flung the needle to the ground and said,
گفت در عالم کسی را این فتاد
"Has this happened to anyone in the world?

شیر بی‌دم و سر و اشکم کی دید
Who (ever) saw a lion without tail and head and belly?
این‌چنین شیری خدا خود نافرید
God himself did not create a lion like this."

ای برادر صبر کن بر درد نیش
O brother, endure the pain of the lancet,
تا رهی از نیش نفس گبر خویش
that you may escape from the poison of your miscreant self (nafs),

کان گروهی که رهیدند از وجود
To the people who have escaped from self-existence.
چرخ و مهر و ماهشان آرد سجود
(of the man's shoulder) For sky and sun and moon bow in worship to

هر که مرد اندر تن او نفس گبر
Any one in whose body the miscreant self has died,
مر ورا فرمان برد خورشید و ابر
sun and cloud obey his command.

چون دلش آموخت شمع افروختن
Since his heart has learned to light the candle
آفتاب او را نیارد سوختن
(of spiritual knowledge and love), the sun cannot burn him.

گفت حق در آفتاب منتجم
God hath made mention of the rising sun
ذکر تزاور کذی عن کهفهم
God hath made mention of the rising sun

خار جمله لطف چون گل می‌شود
The thorn becomes entirely beautiful, like the rose,
پیش جزوی کو سوی کل می‌رود
in the sight of the particular that is going towards the Universal.

چیست تعظیم خدا افراشتن
What is (the meaning of) to exalt and glorify God?
خویشتن را خوار و خاکی داشتن
To deem yourself despicable and (worthless) as dust.

چیست توحید خدا آموختن
What is (the meaning of) to learn the knowledge of God's unity?
خویشتن را پیش واحد سوختن
To consume yourself in the presence of the One.

گر همی‌خواهی که بفروزی چو روز
If you wish to shine like day,
هستی همچون شب خود را بسوز
burn up your night-like self-existence.

هستیت در هست آن هستی‌نواز
Melt away your existence, as copper (melts away) in the elixir,
همچو مس در کیمیا اندر گداز
in the being of Him who fosters (and sustains) existence.

در من و ما سخت کردستی دو دست
You have fastened both your hands tight on (are determined not to give up) "I" and "we":
هست این جمله خرابی از دو هست
all this (spiritual) ruin is caused by dualism.

رفتن گرگ و روباه در خدمت شیر به شکار
How the wolf and fox went to hunt in attendance on the lion.

شیر و گرگ و رویهی بهر شکار
A lion, wolf, and fox had gone to hunt

رفته بودند از طلب در کوهسار
in the mountains in quest (of food),

ا به پشت همدگر بر صیدها
and fetters (of captivity) on the hunted animals,

سخت بر بندند بار قیدها
That by supporting each other they might tie fast the bonds

هر سه با هم اندر آن صحرای ژرف
And all three together might seize much

صیدها گیرند بسیار و شگرف
and great quarry in that deep wilderness.

گرچه زیشان شیر نر را ننگ بود
Although the fierce lion was ashamed of them (the wolf and fox),

لیک کرد اکرام و همراهی نمود
yet he did them honour and gave them his company on the way.

این چنین شه را ز لشکر زحمتست
To a king like this the (escort of) soldiers are an annoyance,

لیک همره شد جماعت رحمتست
but he accompanied them: a united party is a mercy (from God).

این چنین مه را ز اختر ننگهاست
A moon like this is disgraced by the stars:

او میان اختران بهر سخاست
it is amongst the stars for generosity's sake.

امر شاورهم پیمبر را رسید
The (Divine) command, Consult them, came to the Prophet,

گرچه رایی نیست رایش را ندید
though no counsel is to be compared with his own.

در ترازو جو رفیق زر شدست
In the scales barley has become the companion of gold,

نه از آن که جو چو زر جوهر شدست
(but that is) not because barley has become a substance like gold.

روح قالب را کنون همره شدست
The spirit has now become the body's fellow-traveller:

مدتی سگ حارس درگه شدست
the dog has become for a time the guardian of the palace-gate.

چونک رفتند این جماعت سوی کوه
When this party (the wolf and fox) went to the mountains at the stirrup
در رکاب شیر با فر و شکوه
of the lion majestic and grand,

گاو کوهی و بز و خرگوش زفت
They found a mountain-ox and goat and fat hare,
یافتند و کار ایشان پیش رفت
and their business went forward (prosperously).

هر که باشد در پی شیر حراب
Whoever is on the heels of him that is a lion in combat,
کم نیاید روز و شب او را کباب
roastmeat does not fail him by day or by night.

چون ز که در بیشه آوردندشان
When they brought them (the animals which they had caught) from the mountains to the jungle,
کشته و مجروح و اندر خون کشان
killed and wounded and dragging along in (streams of) blood,

گرگ و روبه را طمع بود اندر آن
The wolf and fox hoped that a division
که رود قسمت به عدل خسروان
would be made according to the justice of emperors.

عکس طمع هر دوشان بر شیر زد
The reflexion of the hope of both of them struck the lion:
شیر دانست آن طمعها را سند
the lion knew (what was) the ground for those hopes.

هر که باشد شیر اسرار و امیر
Any one that is the lion and prince of (spiritual) mysteries,
او بداند هر چه اندیشد ضمیر
he will know all that the conscience thinks.

هین نگه دار ای دل اندیشه خو
Beware! Guard thyself, O heart disposed to thinking,
دل ز اندیشهٔ بدی در پیش او
from any evil thought in his presence.

داند و خر را همی‌راند خموش
He knows and keeps riding on silently:
در رخت خندد برای روی‌پوش
he smiles in thy face in order to mask (his feelings).

شیر چون دانست آن وسواسشان
When the lion perceived their bad ideas,
وا نگفت و داشت آن دم پاسشان
he did not declare (his knowledge), and paid (courteous) regard (to them) at the time,

لیک با خود گفت بنمایم سزا
But he said to himself, "I will show you what
مر شما را ای خسیسان گدا
ye deserve, O beggarly villains!

مر شما را بس نیامد رای من
Was my judgement not enough for you?
ظنتان اینست در اعطای من
Is this your opinion of my bounty,

ای عقول و رایتان از رای من
O ye whose understanding and judgement are (derived) from my judgement
از عطاهای جهان‌آرای من
and from my world-adorning gifts?

نقش با نقاش چه سگالد دگر
What else (but good) should the picture think of the painter,
چون سگالش اوش بخشید و خبر
since he bestowed thought and knowledge upon it?

این چنین ظن خسیسانه بمن
Had ye such a vile opinion of me,
مر شما را بود ننگان زمن
O ye who are a scandal to the world?

ظانین بالله ظن السوء را
If I should not behead them that think ill of God
گر نبرم سر بود عین خطا
it would be the essence of wrong.

وا رهانم چرخ را از ننگتان
I will deliver the Sphere (of Time) from your disgrace,
تا بماند در جهان این داستان
so that this tale shall remain in the world (as a warning).

شیر با این فکر می‌زد خنده فاش
While thus meditating, the lion continued to smile visibly:
بر تبسم‌های شیر ایمن مباش
do not trust the smiles of the lion!

مال دنیا شد تبسمهای حق
Worldly wealth is (like) the smiles of God:
کرد ما را مست و مغرور و خلق
it has made us drunken and vainglorious and threadbare

فقر و رنجوری بهستت ای سند
Poverty and distress are better for thee
کان تبسم دام خود را بر کند
O lord, for (then) that smile will remove its lure.

⁌◉⁌◉⁍

امتحان کردن شیر گرگ را
How the lion made trial of the wolf

وگفتن کی پیش آی ای گرگ بخش کن صیدها را میان ما
and said, "Come forward, O wolf, and divide the prey amongst us."

گفت شیر ای گرگ این را بخش کن
The lion said, "O wolf, divide this (prey):
معدلت را نو کن ای گرگ کهن
The lion said, "O wolf, divide this (prey):

نایب من باش در قسمت گری
Be my deputy in the office of distributor,
تا پدید آید که تو چه گوهری
that it may be seen of what substance thou art."

گفت ای شه گاو وحشی بخش تست
O King," said he, "the wild ox is thy share:
آن بزرگ و تو بزرگ و زفت و چست
he is big, and thou art big and strong and active.

بز مرا که بز میانه ست و وسط
The goat is mine, for the goat is middle and intermediate;
روبها خرگوش بستان بی غلط
do thou, O fox, receive the hare, and no mistake!"

شیر گفت ای گرگ چون گفتی بگو
The lion said, "O wolf, how hast thou spoken?
چونک من باشم تو گویی ما و تو
Say! When I am here, dost thou speak of 'I' and 'thou'?

381

گرگ خود چه سگ بود کو خویش دید
Truly, what a cur the wolf must be, that he regarded himself
پیش چون من شیر بی مثل و ندید
in the presence of a lion like me who am peerless and unrivalled!"

گفت پیش آ ای خری کو خود خرید
(Then) he said, "Come forward, O thou self-esteeming ass!"
پیشش آمد پنجه زد او را درید
He approached him, the lion seized him with his claws and rent him

چون ندیدش مغز و تدبیر رشید
Inasmuch as he (the lion) did not see in him the kernel of right conduct,
در سیاست پوستش از سر کشید
he tore the skin off his head as a punishment.

گفت چون دید منت ز خود نبرد
He said, "Since the sight of me did not transport thee out of thyself,
این چنین جان را بباید زار مرد
a spirit like this (thine) must needs die miserably.

چون نبودی فانی اندر پیش من
Since thou wert not passing away (from thyself) in my presence,
فضل آمد مر ترا گردن زدن
twas an act of grace to smite thy neck (behead thee)."

کل شیء هالک جز وجه او
Everything is perishing except His face:
چون نه‌ای در وجه او هستی مجو
unless thou art in His face (essence), do not seek to exist.

هر که اندر وجه ما باشد فنا
When any one has passed away (from himself) in my face (essence),
کل شیء هالک نبود جزا
(the words) everything is perishing are not applicable (to him),

زانک در الاست او از لا گذشت
Because he is in except, he has transcended not (nonentity):
هر که در الاست او فانی نگشت
whosoever is in except has not passed away (perished).

هر که بر در او من و ما می‌زند
Whosoever is uttering 'I' and 'we' at the door (of the Divine Court),
رد بابست او و بر لا می‌تند
he is turned back from the door and is continuing in not (nonentity).

قصه آنکس کی در یاری بکوفت از درون
The story of the person who knocked at a friend's door:

گفت کیست آن گفت منم گفت چون تو تویی در نمی‌گشایم هیچ کس را از یاران نمی‌شناسم کی او می باشد برو
his friend from within asked who he was: he said, "Tis I," and the friend answered, "Since thou art thou, I will not open the door: I know not any friend that is 'I.'"

آن یکی آمد در یاری بزد
A certain man came and knocked at a friend's door:

گفت یارش کیستی ای معتمد
his friend asked him, "Who art thou, O trusty one?"

گفت من گفتش برو هنگام نیست
He answered, "I." The friend said, "Begone, 'tis not the time

بر چنین خوانی مقام خام نیست
at a table like this there is no place for the raw."

خام را جز آتش هجر و فراق
Save the fire of absence and separation, who (what) will cook the raw one?

کی پزد کی وا رهاند از نفاق
Who (what) will deliver him from hypocrisy?

رفت آن مسکین و سالی در سفر
The wretched man went away,

در فراق دوست سوزید از شرر
and for a year in travel (and) in separation from his friend he was burned with sparks of fire.

پخته گشت آن سوخته پس بازگشت
That burned one was cooked:

بازگرد خانهٔ همباز گشت
then he returned and again paced to and fro beside the house of his comrade.

حلقه زد بر در بصد ترس و ادب
He knocked at the door with a hundred fears and respects,

تا بنجهد بی‌ادب لفظی ز لب
lest any disrespectful word might escape from his lips.

بانگ زد یارش که بر در کیست آن
His friend called to him, "Who is at the door?" He answered,

گفت بر در هم توی ای دلستان
Tis thou art at the door, O charmer of hearts."

گفت اکنون چون منی ای من در آ
Now," said the friend, "since thou art I, come in, O myself:

نیست گنجایی دو من را در سرا
there is not room in the house for two I's.

383

نیست سوزن را سر رشتهٔ دوتا
The double end of thread is not for the needle:
چونک یکتایی درین سوزن در آ
inasmuch as thou art single, come into this needle."

رشته را با سوزن آمد ارتباط
'Tis the thread that is connected with the needle:
نیست در خور با جمل سم الخیاط
the eye of the needle is not suitable for the camel.

کی شود باریک هستی جمل
How should the existence (body) of the camel be fined down
جز بمقراض ریاضات و عمل
save by the shears of ascetic exercises and works?

دست حق باید مر آن را ای فلان
For that, O reader, the hand (power) of God is necessary, for it is the Be,
کو بود بر هر محالی کن فکان
and it was (bringer into existence) of every (seemingly) impossible thing.

هر محال از دست او ممکن شود
By His hand every impossible thing is made possible;
هر حرون از بیم او ساکن شود
by fear of Him every unruly one is made quiet.

اکمه و ابرص چه باشد مرده نیز
What of the man blind from birth and the leper?
زنده گردد از فسون آن عزیز
Even the dead is made living by the spell of the Almighty,

و آن عدم کز مرده مرده‌تر بود
And that non-existence which is more dead than the dead—
در کف ایجاد او مضطر بود
non-existence is compelled (to obey) when He calls it into being.

کل یوم هو فی شان بخوان
Recite (the text), Every day He is (engaged) in some affair:
مر ورا بی کار و بی‌فعلی مدان
do not deem Him idle and inactive.

کمترین کاریش هر روزست آن
His least act, every day, is that He despatches three armies:
کو سه لشکر را کند این سو روان
One army from the loins (of the fathers) towards the mothers,

لشکری ز اصلاب سوی امهات

in order that the plant may grow in the womb;

بهر آن تا در رحم روید نبات

in order that the plant may grow in the womb;

لشکری ز ارحام سوی خاکدان

One army from the wombs to the Earth,

تا ز نر و ماده پر گردد جهان

that the world may be filled with male and female;

لشکری از خاک زان سوی اجل

One army from the Earth (to what is) beyond death,

تا ببیند هر کسی حسن عمل

that every one may behold the beauty of (good) works.

این سخن پایان ندارد هین بتاز

This discourse hath no end.

سوی آن دو یار پاک پاکباز

Come, hasten (back) to those two sincere and devoted friends.

❖◉❖◉❖

صفت توحید
Description of Unification.

گفت یارش کاندر آ ای جمله من

His friend said to him, "Come in, O thou who art entirely myself,

نی مخالف چون گل و خار چمن

not different like the rose and thorn in the garden."

رشته یکتا شد غلط کم شو کنون

The thread has become single. Do not now fall into error

گر دوتا بینی حروف کاف و نون

if thou seest that the letters K and N are two.'

کاف و نون همچون کمند آمد جذوب

K and N are pulling like a noose,

تا کشاند مر عدم را در خطوب

that they may draw nonexistence into great affairs.

پس دوتا باید کمند اندر صور

Hence the noose must be double in (the world of) forms,

گرچه یکتا باشد آن دو در اثر

though those two (letters) are single in effect.

گر دو پا گر چار پا ره را برد
Whether the feet be two or four, they traverse one road,
همچو مقراض دو تا یکتا برد
road, like the double shears (which) makes (but) one cut.

آن دو همبازان گازر را ببین
Look at those two fellow-washermen:
هست در ظاهر خلافی زان و زین
there is apparently a difference between that one and this:

آن یکی کرباس را در آب زد
The one has thrown the cotton garments into the water,
وان دگر همباز خشکش می‌کند
while the other partner is drying them.

باز او آن خشک را تر می‌کند
Again the former makes the dry clothes wet:
گوییا ز استیزه ضد بر می‌تند
'tis as though he were spitefully thwarting his opposite;

لیک این دو ضد استیزه نما
Yet these two opposites, who seem to be at strife,
یک دل و یک کار باشد در رضا
are of one mind and acting together in agreement.

هر نبی و هر ولی را ملکیست
Every prophet and every saint hath a way
لیک تا می برد حق جمله یکیست
but it leads to God: all (the ways) are (really) one.

چونک جمع مستمع را خواب برد
When slumber (heedlessness) overtook the concentration (attention) of the listener,
سنگهای آسیا را آب برد
the water carried the millstones away.

رفتن این آب فوق آسیاست
The course of this water is above the mill:
رفتنش در آسیا بهر شماست
its going into the mill is for your sakes.

چون شما را حاجت طاحون نماند
Since ye had no further need of the mill,
آب را در جوی اصلی باز راند
he (the prophet or saint) made the water flow back into the original stream.

386

ناطقه سوی دهان تعلیم راست
The rational spirit (the Logos) is (coming) to the mouth for the purpose of teaching
ورنه خود آن نطق را جوبی جداست
else (it would not come, for) truly that speech hath a channel apart:

می‌رود بی بانگ و بی تکرارها
It is moving without noise and without repetitions
تحتها الانهار تا گلزارها
to the rose-gardens beneath which are the rivers.

ای خدا جان را تو بنما آن مقام
O God, do Thou reveal to the soul
کاندرو بی‌حرف می‌روید کلام
that place where speech is growing without letters

تا که سازد جان پاک از سر قدم
That the pure soul may make of its head a foot
سوی عرصهٔ دور و پنهای عدم
towards the far stretching expanse of non-existence—

عرصه‌ای بس با گشاد و با فضا
An expanse very ample and spacious;
وین خیال و هست یابد زو نوا
and from it this phantasy and being (of ours) is fed.

تنگ تر آمد خیالات از عدم
(The realm of) phantasies is narrower than nonexistence (potential existence):
زان سبب باشد خیال اسباب غم
on that account phantasy is the cause of pain.

باز هستی تنگ‌تر بود از خیال
existence, again, was (ever) narrower than (the realm of) phantasy:
زان شود در وی قمر همچون هلال
hence in it moons become like the moon that has waned.

باز هستی جهان حس و رنگ
Again, the existence of the world of sense and colour
تنگ‌تر آمد که زندانیست تنگ
is narrower (than this), for 'tis a narrow prison.

علت تنگیست ترکیب و عدد
The cause of narrowness is composition (compoundness) and number (plurality):
جانب ترکیب حسها می‌کشد
the senses are moving towards composition.

زان سوی حس عالم توحید دان
Know that the world of Unification lies beyond sense:
گر یکی خواهی بدان جانب بران
sense: if you want Unity, march in that direction.

امر کن یک فعل بود و نون و کاف
The (Divine) Command KuN (Be) was a single act, and the (two letters) N and K occurred (only) in speech,
در سخن افتاد و معنی بود صاف
while the (inward) meaning was pure (uncompounded).

این سخن پایان ندارد باز گرد
This discourse hath no end. Return,
تا چه شد احوال گرگ اندر نبرد
that (we may see) what happened to the wolf in combat (with the lion).

ادب کردن شیر گرگ را کی در قسمت بی‌ادبی کرده بود
How the lion punished the wolf who had shown disrespect in dividing (the prey).

گرگ را بر کند سر آن سرفراز
That haughty one tore off the head of the wolf,
تا نماند دوسری و امتیاز
in order that two-headedness (dualism) and distinction might not remain (in being).

فانتقمنا منهم است ای گرگ پیر
'Tis (the meaning of) So we took vengeance on them, O old wolf,
چون نبودی مرده در پیش امیر
inasmuch as thou wert not dead in the presence of the Amír.

بعد از آن رو شیر با روباه کرد
After that, the lion turned to the fox and said,
گفت این را بخش کن از بهر خورد
"Divide it (the prey) for breakfast."

سجده کرد و گفت کین گاو سمین
He bowed low and said, "This fat ox
چاشت خوردت باشد ای شاه گزین
will be thy food at breakfast, O excellent King,

وان بز از بهر میان روز را
And this goat will be a portion
یخنی باشد شه پیروز را
reserved for the victorious King at midday,

و آن دگر خرگوش بهر شام هم
And the hare too for supper

شب چرهٔ این شاه با لطف و کرم
the repast at nightfall of the gracious and bountiful King."

گفت ای روبه تو عدل افروختی
Said the lion, "O fox, thou hast made justice shine forth:

این چنین قسمت ز کی آموختی
from whom didst thou learn to divide in such a manner?

از کجا آموختی این ای بزرگ
whom didst thou learn to divide in such a manner?

گفت ای شاه جهان از حال گرگ
O King of the world," he replied, "(I learned it) from the fate of the wolf."

گفت چون در عشق ما گشتی گرو
The lion said, "Inasmuch as thou hast become pledged to love of me,

هر سه را بر گیر و بستان و برو
pick up all the three (animals), and take (them) and depart.

روبها چون جملگی ما را شدی
O fox, since thou hast become entirely mine,

چونت آزاریم چون تو ما شدی
how should I hurt thee when thou hast become myself?

ما ترا و جمله اشکاران ترا
I am thine, and all the beasts of chase are thine:

پای بر گردون هفتم نه بر آ
set thy foot on the Seventh Heaven and mount (beyond)!

چون گرفتی عبرت از گرگ دنی
Since thou hast taken warning from (the fate of) the vile wolf,

پس تو روبه نیستی شیر منی
thou art not a fox: thou art my own lion.

عاقل آن باشد که عبرت گیرد از
The wise man is he that in (the hour of) the shunned

مرگ یاران در بلای محترز
tribulation takes warning from the death of his friends."

روبه آن دم بر زبان صد شکر راند
The fox said (to himself), "A hundred thanks to the lion

که مرا شیر از پی آن گرگ خواند
for having called me up after that wolf.

گر مرا اول بفرمودی که تو
If he had bidden me first, saying, 'Do thou divide this,'
بخش کن این را که بردی جان ازو
would have escaped from him with his life?"

پس سپاس او را که ما را در جهان
Thanks be to Him (God),
کرد پیدا از پس پیشینیان
then, that He caused us to appear (be born) in the world after those of old,

تا شنیدیم آن سیاستهای حق
So that we heard of the chastisements which God
بر قرون ماضیه اندر سبق
inflicted upon the past generations in the preceding time,

تا که ما از حال آن گرگان پیش
That we, like the fox, may keep better watch over
همچو روبه پاس خود داریم بیش
That we, like the fox, may keep better watch over

امت مرحومه زین رو خواندمان
in explanation called us "a people on which God has taken mercy."
آن رسول حق و صادق در بیان
On this account he that is God's prophet and veracious

استخوان و پشم آن گرگان عیان
Behold with clear vision the bones and fur of those wolves,
بنگرید و پند گیرید ای مهان
and take warning, O mighty ones

عاقل از سر بنهد این هستی و باد
The wise man will put off from his head (lay aside) this selfexistence and wind (of vanity),
چون شنید آن چهام فرعونان و عاد
since he heard (what was) the end of the Pharaohs and 'Ád;

ور بننهد دیگران از حال او
And if he do not put it off, others will take warning from
عبرتی گیرند از اضلال او
what befell him in consequence of his being misguided.

❖◉❖◉❖

تهدید کردن نوح علیه‌السلام مر قوم را
How Noah, on whom be peace, threatened his people, saying,

کی با من میپیچید کی من روپوشم با خدای می‌پیچید در میان این بحقیقت ای مخذولان
"Do not struggle with me, for I am (only) a veil: ye are really struggling with God (who is) within this (veil), O God-forsaken men!"

گفت نوح ای سرکشان من من نیم
Noah said, "O ye headstrong ones, I am not I:

من ز جان مردم بجانان می‌زیم
I am dead to the (animal) soul, I am living through the Soul of souls.

چون بمردم از حواس بوالبشر
Inasmuch as I am dead to the senses of the father of mankind

حق مرا شد سمع و ادراک و بصر
God has become my hearing and perception and sight.

چونک من من نیستم این دم ز هوست
Since I am not I, this breath (of mine) is from Him:

پیش این دم هرکه دم زد کافر اوست
in the presence of this breath if any one breathes (a word) he is an infidel."

هست اندر نقش این روباه شیر
In the form of this fox there is the lion:

سوی این روبه نشاید شد دلیر
tis not fitting to advance boldly towards this fox.

گر ز روی صورتش می‌نگروی
Unless thou believe in him from his exterior aspect

غره شیران ازو می‌نشنوی
thou wilt not hear from him the lions' roar.

گر نبودی نوح را از حق یدی
If Noah had not been the Eternal Lion,

پس جهانی را چرا بر هم زدی
why should he have cast a whole world into confusion?

صد هزاران شیر بود او در تنی
He was hundreds of thousands of lions in a single body;

او چو آتش بود و عالم خرمنی
he was like fire, and the world (like) a stack.

چونک خرمن پاس عشر او نداشت
Forasmuch as the stack neglected (to pay) the tithe due to him,

او چنان شعله بر آن خرمن گماشت
he launched such a flame against that stack.

هر که او در پیش این شیر نهان
Whosoever in the presence of this hidden Lion
بی‌ادب چون گرگ بگشاید دهان
opens his mouth disrespectfully, like the wolf,

همچو گرگ آن شیر بر دراندش
That Lion will tear him to pieces, as (he tore) the wolf,
فانتقمنا منهم بر خواندش
and will recite to him (the text) So we took vengeance upon them.

زخم یابد همچو گرگ از دست شیر
He will suffer blows, like the wolf, from the Lion's paw:
پیش شیر ابله بود کو شد دلیر
foolish is he that waxed bold in the presence of the Lion.

کاشکی آن زخم بر تن آمدی
Would that those blows fell upon the body,
تا بدی کایمان و دل سالم بدی
so that it might be that (the sinner's) faith and heart would be safe!

قوتم بگسست چون اینجا رسید
My power is broken (fails me) on reaching this point:
چون توانم کرد این سر را پدید
how can I declare this mystery?

همچو آن روبه کم اشکم کنید
Make little of your bellies, like that fox:
پیش او روباه‌بازی کم کنید
do not play fox's tricks in His presence.

جمله ما و من به پیش او نهید
Lay the whole of your "we" and "I" before Him:
ملک ملک اوست ملک او را دهید
he kingdom is His kingdom: give the kingdom to Him.

چون فقیر آیید اندر راه راست
When ye become poor (selfless) in the right Way,
شیر و صید شیر خود آن شماست
verily the Lion and the Lion's prey are yours,

زانک او پاکست و سبحان وصف اوست
Because He is holy, and Glory is His attribute:
بی نیازست او ز نغز و مغز و پوست
He hath no need of good things and kernel or rind.

هر شکار و هر کراماتی که هست
Every prize and every gift of grace that exists is
از برای بندگان آن شهست
for the sake of the servants of that King (God).

نیست شه را طمع بهر خلق ساخت
The King hath no desire (for anything):
این همه دولت خنک آنکو شناخت
He hath made all this empire for His creatures. Happy is he that knew!

آنک دولت آفرید و دو سرا
be to Him who created (all) empire and the two worlds?
ملک و دولتها چه کار آید ورا
Of what use should the possession of empires

پیش سبحان پس نگه دارید دل
In the presence of His Glory keep close watch over your hearts,
تا نگردید از گمان بد خجل
lest ye be put to shame by thinking evil.

کو ببیند سر و فکر و جست و جو
For He sees conscience and thought and quest
همچو اندر شیر خالص تار مو
as (plainly) as a thread of hair in pure milk.

آنک او بی نقش ساده‌سینه شد
He whose clear breast has become devoid of (any) image(impression) has
نقشهای غیب را آیینه شد
become a mirror for the impressions of the Invisible.

سر ما را بی‌گمان موقن شود
He becomes intuitively and undoubtingly aware of our inmost thought,
زانک مؤمن آینهٔ مؤمن بود
because the true believer is the mirror of the true believer.

چون زند او نقد ما را بر محک
When he rubs our (spiritual) poverty on the touchstone,
پس یقین را باز داند او ز شک
then he knows the difference between faith and doubt.

چون شود جانش محک نقدها
When his soul becomes the touchstone of the coin,
پس ببیند قلب را و قلب را
then he will see (distinguish) the (true) heart and the false money (of hypocrisy).

نشاندن پادشاه صوفیان عارف را پیش روی خویش تا چشمشان بدیشان روشن شود

How kings seat in front of them the Súfís who know God, in order that their eyes may be illumined by (seeing) them.

پادشاهان را چنان عادت بود
Such is the custom of kings:

این شنیده باشی ار یادت بود
you will have heard of this, if you remember.

دست چپشان پهلوانان ایستند
The paladins stand on their left hand,

زانک دل پهلوی چپ باشد ببند
because the heart (the seat of courage) is fixed on the left side (of the body).

مشرف و اهل قلم بر دست راست
On the right hand are the chancellor and the secretaries

زانک علم خط و ثبت آن دست راست
because the science of writing and book-keeping belongs (in practice) to this hand.

صوفیان را پیش رو موضع دهند
They give the Súfís the place in front of their countenance,

کاینۀ جانند و ز آیینه بهند
for they (the Súfís) are a mirror for the soul, and better than a mirror,

سینه صیقلها زده در ذکر و فکر
(Since) they have polished their breasts (hearts) in commemoration (of God) and meditation,

تا پذیرد آینۀ دل نقش بکر
that the heart's mirror may receive the virgin (original) image.

هر که او از صلب فطرت خوب زاد
Whoever is born beautiful from the loins of Creation,

آینه در پیش او باید نهاد
a mirror must be placed before him.

عاشق آیینه باشد روی خوب
The beauteous face is in love with the mirror:

صیقل جان آمد و تقوی القلوب
it (such a face) is a polisher of the soul and (a kindler) of the fear of God in (men's) hearts.

آمدن مهمان پیش یوسف علیه‌السلام
How the guest came to Joseph, on whom be peace,

و تقاضا کردن یوسف علیه‌السلام ازو تحفه و ارمغان
and how Joseph demanded of him a gift and present on his return from abroad.

آمد از آفاق یار مهربان
The loving friend came from the ends of the earth

یوسف صدیق را شد میهمان
and became the guest of Joseph the truthful,

کاشنا بودند وقت کودکی
For they had been well acquainted in childhood,

بر وسادهٔ آشنایی متکی
reclining(together) on the sofa of acquaintance.

یاد دادش جور اخوان و حسد
He spoke to him (Joseph) of the injustice and envy of his brethren: Joseph said,

گفت کان زنجیر بود و ما اسد
"That was (like) a chain, and I was the lion.

عار نبود شیر را از سلسله
The lion is not disgraced by the chain:

نیست ما را از قضای حق گله
I do not complain of God's destiny.

شیر را بر گردن ار زنجیر بود
If the lion had a chain on his neck,

بر همه زنجیرسازان میر بود
(yet) he was prince over all the chain-makers."

گفت چون بودی ز زندان و ز چاه
He asked, "How wert thou in regard to the prison and the well?"

گفت همچون در محاق و کاست ماه
Like the moon," said Joseph, "in the interlunar period (when she is) on the wane."

در محاق ار ماه نو گردد دوتا
If in that period the new moon is bent double,

نی در آخر بدر گردد بر سما
does not she at last become the full moon in the sky?

گرچه دردانه به هاون کوفتند
last become the full moon in the sky?

نور چشم و دل شد و بیند بلند
it becomes the light of eye and heart and looks aloft.

395

گندمی را زیر خاک انداختند
They cast a grain of wheat under earth,
پس ز خاکش خوشه‌ها بر ساختند
then from its earth they raised up ears of corn;
بار دیگر کوفتندش ز آسیا
Once more they crushed it with the mill:
قیمتش افزود و نان شد جان‌فزا
its value increased and it became soul invigorating bread;
باز نان را زیر دندان کوفتند
Again they crushed the bread under their teeth:
گشت عقل و جان و فهم هوشمند
it became the mind and spirit and understanding of one endowed with reason;
باز آن جان چونک محو عشق گشت
Again, when that spirit became lost in Love,
یعجب الزراع آمد بعد کشت
it became (as that which) rejoiceth the sowers after the sowing.
این سخن پایان ندارد بازگرد
This discourse hath no end. Come back,
تا که با یوسف چه گفت آن نیک مرد
that we may see what that good man said to Joseph
بعد قصه گفتنش گفت ای فلان
After he (Joseph) had told him his story, he (Joseph) said,
هین چه آوردی تو ما را ارمغان
"Now, O so-and-so, what traveller's gift hast thou brought for me?"
بر در یاران تهی‌دست آمدن
To come empty-handed to the door of friends
هست بی‌گندم سوی طاحون شدن
is like going without wheat to the mill.
حق تعالی خلق را گوید بحشر
God, exalted is He, will say to the people at the gathering (for Judgement),
ارمغان کو از برای روز نشر
"Where is your present for the Day of Resurrection?
جئتمونا و فرادی بی نوا
Ye have come to Us and alone without provision,
هم بدان سان که خلقناکم کذا
just in the same guise as We created you.

هین چه آوردید دست‌آویز را
Hark, what have ye brought as an offering—
ارمغانی روز رستاخیز را
a gift on homecoming for the Day when ye rise from the dead?

یا امید بازگشتنتان نبود
Or had ye no hope of returning?
وعدهٔ امروز باطلتان نمود
Did the promise of (meeting Me) to-day seem vain to you?"

منکری مهمانیش را از خری
Dost thou (O reader) disbelieve in the promise of being His guest?
پس ز مطبخ خاک و خاکستر بری
Then from the kitchen (of His bounty) thou wilt get (only) dust and ashes.

ور نه‌ای منکر چنین دست تهی
And if thou art not disbelieving, how with such empty hands
در در آن دوست چون پا می‌نهی
rt thou setting foot in the Court of that Friend?

اندکی صرفه بکن از خواب و خور
Refrain thyself a little from sleep and food:
ارمغان بهر ملاقاتش بر
bring the gift for thy meeting with Him.

شو قلیل النوم مما یهجعون
Become scant of sleep (like them that) were slumbering (but a small part of the night);
باش در اسحار از یستغفرون
in the hours of dawn be of (those who) were asking pardon of God.

اندکی جنبش بکن همچون جنین
Stir a little, like the embryo,
تا ببخشندت حواس نوربین
in order that thou mayst be given the senses which behold the Light,

وز جهان چون رحم بیرون روی
And (then) thou art outside of this womb-like world:
از زمین در عرصهٔ واسع شوی
thou goest from the earth into a wide expanse.

آنک ارض الله واسع گفته‌اند
Know that the saying, "God's earth is wide,"
عرصه‌ای دان انبیا را بس بلند
refers to that ample region into which the saints have entered.

397

دل نگردد تنگ زان عرصهٔ فراخ
The heart is not oppressed by that spacious expanse:
نخل تر آنجا نگردد خشک شاخ
there the fresh boughs of the palm-tree do not become dry.

حاملی تو مر حواست را کنون
At present thou art bearing (the burden of) thy senses:
کند و مانده می‌شوی و سرنگون
thou art becoming weary and exhausted and (ready to fall) headlong.

چونک محمولی نه حامل وقت خواب
Since, at the time of sleep, thou art borne (on high), and art not bearing (the burden),
ماندگی رفت و شدی بی رنج و تاب
thy fatigue is gone and thou art free from pain and anguish.

چاشنیی دان تو حال خواب را
Regard the time of sleep as a (mere) taste
پیش محمولی حال اولیا
in comparison with the state in which the saints are borne (on high).

اولیا اصحاب کهفند ای عنود
The saints are (like) the Men of the Cave, O obstinate one:
در قیام و در تقلب هم رقود
they are asleep (even) in rising up and turning to and fro.

می‌کشدشان بی تکلف در فعال
He (God) is drawing them, without their taking trouble to act,
بی‌خبر ذات الیمین ذات الشمال
without consciousness (on their part), to the right hand and to the left.

چیست آن ذات الیمین فعل حسن
What is that right hand? Good deeds.
چیست آن ذات الشکال اشغال تن
What is that left hand? The affairs of the body.

می‌رود این هر دو کار از انبیا
These two (kinds of) actions proceed from the saints,
بی‌خبر زین هر دو ایشان چون صدا
(while) they are unconscious of them both, like the echo:

گر صدایت بشنواند خیر و شر
(while) they are unconscious of them both, like the echo:
ذات که باشد ز هر دو بی‌خبر
evil, the mountain itself is unconscious of either.

گفتن مهمان یوسف علیه‌السلام کی آینه‌ای آوردمت
How the guest said to Joseph, "I have brought thee the gift of a mirror,

کی تا هر باری کی در وی نگری روی خوب خویش را بینی مرا یاد کنی
so that whenever thou lookest in it thou wilt see thine own fair face and remember me."

گفت یوسف هین بیاور ارمغان
Joseph said, "Come, produce the gift."

او ز شرم این تقاضا زد فغان
He (the guest), on account of shame (confusion) at this demand, sobbed aloud.

گفت من چند ارمغان جستم ترا
"How many a gift," said he, "did I seek for thee!

ارمغانی در نظر نامد مرا
No (worthy) gift came into my sight.

حبه‌ای را جانب کان چون برم
How should I bring a grain (of gold) to the mine?

قطره‌ای را سوی عمان چون برم
How should I bring a drop (of water) to the (Sea of) 'Umán?

زیره را من سوی کرمان آورم
I shall (only) bring cumin to Kirmán,

گر به پیش تو دل و جان آورم
if I bring my heart and soul (as a gift) to thee.

نیست تخمی کاندرین انبار نیست
There is no seed that is not in this barn,

غیر حسن تو که آن را یار نیست
except thy beauty which hath no equal.

لایق آن دیدم که من آیینه‌ای
I deemed it fitting that I should bring to thee a mirror

پیش تو آرم چو نور سینه‌ای
like the (inward) light of a (pure) breast,

تا ببینی روی خوب خود در آن
That thou mayst behold thy beauteous face therein,

ای تو چون خورشید شمع آسمان
O thou who, like the sun, art the candle of heaven.

آینه آوردمت ای روشنی
I have brought thee a mirror, O light (of mine eyes),

تا چو بینی روی خود یادم کنی
so that when thou seest thy face thou mayst think of me."

آینه بیرون کشید او از بغل
He drew forth the mirror from beneath his arm:
خوب را آیینه باشد مشتغل
the fair one's business is with a mirror.

آینهٔ هستی چه باشد نیستی
What is the mirror of Being? Not-being.
نیستی بر گر تو ابله نیستی
Bring not-being (as your gift), if you are not a fool.

هستی اندر نیستی بتوان نمود
Being can be seen (only) in not-being:
مال‌داران بر فقیر آرند جود
the rich bestow(exhibit) generosity on the poor.

آینهٔ صافی نان خود گرسنه‌ست
The clear mirror of bread is truly the hungry man; tinder, likewise,
سوخته هم آینهٔ آتش زنه ست
is the mirror of that (the stick or flint) from which fire is struck.

نیستی و نقص هر جایی که خاست
Not-being and defect, wherever they arise (appear),
آینهٔ خوبی جمله پیشه‌هاست
are the mirror which displays the excellence of all crafts.

چونک جامه چست و دوزیده بود
When a garment is neat and well-stitched,
مظهر فرهنگ درزی چون شود
how should it enable the tailor to exhibit his skill?

ناتراشیده همی باید جذوع
Trunks of trees must be unhewn in order
تا دروگر اصل سازد یا فروع
that the woodcutter may fashion the stem or the branches (and thus exercise his craft).

خواجهٔ اشکسته بند آنجا رود
The doctor who sets broken bones goes to
کاندر آنجا پای اشکسته بود
to the place where the person with the fractured leg is.

کی شود چون نیست رنجور نزار
manifest when there is no emaciated invalid?
آن جمال صنعت طب آشکار
How shall the excellence of the art of medicine be made

400

خواری و دونی مسها بر ملا
if the vileness and baseness of coppers is not notorious?

گر نباشد کی نماید کیمیا
How shall the (power of the) Elixir be shown

نقصها آیینهٔ وصف کمال
Defects are the mirror of the quality of perfection,

و آن حقارت آیینهٔ عز و جلال
and that vileness is the mirror of power and glory,

زانک ضد را ضد کند پیدا یقین
Because (every) contrary is certainly made evident by its contrary;

زانک با سرکه پدیدست انگبین
because honey is perceived (to be sweet by contrast) with vinegar.

هر که نقص خویش را دید و شناخت
Whoever has seen and recognised his own deficiency

اندر استکمال خود ده اسپه تاخت
has ridden post-haste (made rapid progress) in perfecting himself.

زان نمی‌پرد به سوی ذوالجلال
The reason why he (any one) is not flying towards the Lord

کو گمانی می‌برد خود را کمال
Lord of glory is that he supposes himself to be perfect.

علتی بتر ز پندار کمال
There is no worse malady in your soul,

نیست اندر جان تو ای ذو دلال
O haughty one, than the conceit of perfection

از دل و از دیده‌ات بس خون رود
Much blood must flow from your heart and eye,

تا ز تو این معجبی بیرون شود
that self-complacency may go out of you.

علت ابلیس انا خیری بدست
The fault of Iblís lay in thinking "I am better (than Adam),"

وین مرض در نفس هر مخلوق هست
and this disease is in the soul of every (human) creature.

گرچه خود را بس شکسته بیند او
Though he regard himself as very broken (in spirit),

آب صافی دان و سرگین زیر جو
know that it is (a case of) clear water (on the surface) and dung under the stream.

چون بشوراند ترا در امتحان
When he (the Devil) stirs you in trial,
آب سرگین رنگ گردد در زمان
immediately the water becomes dung-coloured.

در تگ جو هست سرگین ای فتی
There is dung in the bed of the stream,
گرچه جو صافی نماید مر ترا
my man, though to you the stream appears pure.

هست پیر راهدان پر فطن
'Tis the Pír full of wisdom, well-acquainted with the Way,
باغهای نفس کل را جوی کن
that digs a channel for (draining off) the streams of the flesh and the body.

جوی خود را کی تواند پاک کرد
Can the water of the (polluted) stream clear out the dung?
نافع از علم خدا شد علم مرد
Can man's knowledge sweep away the ignorance of his sensual self?

کی تراشد تیغ دستهٔ خویش را
How shall the sword fashion its own hilt?
رو به جراحی سپار این ریش را
Go, entrust (the cure of) this wound to a surgeon.

بر سر هر ریش جمع آمد مگس
Flies gather on every wound,
تا نبیند قبح ریش خویش کس
so that no one sees the foulness of his wound.

آن مگس اندیشه‌ها وان مال تو
Those flies are your (evil) thoughts and your (love of) possessions:
ریش تو آن ظلمت احوال تو
your wound is the darkness of your (spiritual) states;

ور نهد مرهم بر آن ریش تو پیر
And if the Pír lays a plaster on your wound,
آن زمان ساکن شود درد و نفیر
at once the pain and lamentation are stilled,

تا که پندارد که صحت یافتست
So that you fancy it (the wound) is healed,
پرتو مرهم بر آنجا تافتست
(whereas in reality) the (healing) ray of the plaster has shone upon the (wounded) spot.

هین ز مرهم سر مکش ای پشت ریش
Beware! Do not (scornfully) turn your head away from the plaster, O you who are wounded in the back,
و آن ز پرتو دان مدان از اصل خویش
but recognise that that (healing of the wound) proceeds from the ray: do not regard it as (proceeding) from your own constitution.

◆◉◆◉◆

مرتد شدن کاتب وحی
How the writer of the (Qur'ánic) Revelation fell into apostasy

به سبب آنک پرتو وحی بروز زد آن آیت را پیش از پیغامبر صلی الله علیه و سلم بخواند گفت پس من هم محل وحیم
because (when) the ray of the Revelation shot upon whom be peace, (had dictated it to him); then he said, "So I too am one upon whom Revelation has descended."

پیش از عثمان یکی نساخ بود
Before (the time of) 'Uthmán there was a scribe

کو به نسخ وحی جدی می‌نمود
who used to be diligent in writing down the Revelation.

چون نبی از وحی فرمودی سبق
Whenever the Prophet dictated the Revelation,

او همان را و ا نبشتی بر ورق
he would write out the same (portion) on the leaf.

پرتو آن وحی بر وی تافتی
The beams of that Revelation would shine upon him,

او درون خویش حکمت یافتی
and he would find Wisdom within him.

عین آن حکمت بفرمودی رسول
The substance of that Wisdom was dictated by the Prophet:

زین قدر گمراه شد آن بوالفضول
by this (small) amount (of reflected Wisdom) that meddling fool was led astray,

کآنچه می‌گوید رسول مستنیر
the illumined Prophet is saying."

مر مرا هست آن حقیقت در ضمیر
Thinking, "I have in my conscience the Truth of that which

پرتو اندیشه‌اش زد بر رسول
The ray of his thought struck the Prophet:

قهر حق آورد بر جانش نزول
the wrath of God descended on his (the scribe's) soul.

هم ز نساخی بر آمد هم ز دین
He abandoned both his work as a scribe and the Religion
شد عدو مصطفی و دین بکین
he became the malignant foe of Mustafá(Mohammed) and the Religion.

مصطفی فرمود کای گبر عنود
Mustafá said, "O obstinate miscreant, if the Light was from thee,
چون سیه گشتی اگر نور از تو بود
how shouldst thou have become black (with sin)?

گر تو ینبوع الهی بودیی
If thou hadst been the Divine fountain (whence the Revelation issued),
این چنین آب سیه نگشودیی
thou wouldst not have let out such black water as this."

تا که ناموسش به پیش این و آن
Lest his reputation should be ruined in the sight of all and sundry,
نشکند بر بست او را دهان
this (pride) kept his mouth shut.

اندرون می‌سوختش هم زین سبب
His (a sinner's) heart is being darkened,
توبه کردن می‌نیارست این عجب
hence he is unable to repent: this is wonderful

آه می‌کرد و نبودش آه سود
He (the scribe) was crying "Alas,"
چون در آمد تیغ و سر را در ربود
but "Alas" was of no use to him when the sword came on and took off his head.

کرده حق ناموس را صد من حدید
God has made reputation (to be like) a hundred maunds' weight of iron
ای بسا بسته به بند ناپدید
oh, many a one is bound in the unseen chain!

کبر و کفر آن سان ببست آن راه را
Pride and infidelity have barred that Way (of repentance) in
که نیارد کرد ظاهر آه را
such wise that he (the sinner) cannot utter a sigh.

گفت اغلالا فهم به مقمحون
He (God) said, "(We have put on their necks) shackles (chinhigh),
نیست آن اغلال بر ما از برون
and thereby they are forced to lift up their heads": those shackles are not (put) on us from outside.

خلفهم سدا فاغشیناهم
(And We have put) behind them a barrier, and We have made a covering (of darkness) over them":
می‌نبیند بند را پیش و پس او
the uncle (old sinner) is not seeing the barrier in front (of him) and behind.

رنگ صحرا دارد آن سدی که خاست
The barrier that arose has the appearance of open country:
او نمی‌داند که آن سد قضاست
he does not know that it is the barrier of the Divine destiny.

شاهد تو سد روی شاهدست
Your (earthly) beloved is a barrier to the face of the (Divine) Beloved:
مرشد تو سد گفت مرشدست
your (worldly) guide is a barrier to the words of the (true spiritual) guide.

ای بسا کفار را سودای دین
Oh, many are the infidels that have a passionate longing for the Religion (Islam):
بندشان ناموس و کبر آن و این
his (such a one's) chain (stumblingblock) is reputation and pride and that and this (object of desire).

بند پنهان لیک از آهن بتر
is reputation and pride and that and this (object of desire).
بند آهن را کند پاره تبر
the iron chain is cloven by the axe.

بند آهن را توان کردن جدا
The iron chain can be removed:
بند غیبی را نداند کس دوا
none knows how to cure the invisible chain.

مرد را زنبور اگر نیشی زند
If a man is stung by a wasp,
طبع او آن لحظه بر دفعی تند
he extracts the wasp's sting from his body,

زخم نیش اما چو از هستی تست
But since the stinging wound is from (inflicted by) your self-existence,
غم قوی باشد نگردد درد سست
the pain continues with violence and the anguish is not relieved.

شرح این از سینه بیرون می‌جهد
The (full) explanation of this (matter) is springing forth (seeking to escape) from my breast,
لیک می‌ترسم که نومیدی دهد
but I am afraid it may give (you cause to) despair.

نی مشو نومید و خود را شاد کن
Nay, do not despair: make yourself cheerful,
پیش آن فریادرس فریاد کن
call for help to Him who comes at the call,

کای محب عفو از ما عفو کن
Saying, "Forgive us, O Thou who lovest to forgive,
ای طبیب رنج ناسور کهن
O Thou who hast a medicine for the old gangrenous disease!"

عکس حکمت آن شقی را یاوه کرد
The reflexion of Wisdom led astray that miserable one (the Prophet's scribe):
خود مبین تا بر نیارد از تو گرد
be not self-conceited, lest it (your selfconceit) raise up the dust from you (utterly destroy you).

ای برادر بر تو حکمت جاریه‌ست
O brother, Wisdom is flowing in upon you:
آن ز ابدال‌ست و بر تو عاریه‌ست
it comes from the Abdál, and in you it is (only) a borrowed thing.

گرچه در خود خانه نوری یافته‌ست
Although the house (your heart) has found a light within it,
آن ز همسایهٔ منور تافته‌ست
that (light) has shone forth from a light-giving neighbour.

شکر کن غره مشو بینی مکن
Render thanks, be not beguiled by vanity, do not turn up your nose (in disdain),
گوش دار و هیچ خودبینی مکن
hearken attentively, and do not show any self-conceit.

صد دریغ و درد کین عاریقی
Tis a hundred pities and griefs that this borrowed
امتان را دور کرد از امتی
state (of self-assertion) has put the religious communities far from religious communion.

من غلام آن که او در هر رباط
I am the (devoted) slave of him who does not regard himself in every caravanserai
خویش را واصل نداند بر سماط
(at every stage in his spiritual progress) as having attained to the table

بس رباطی که بباید ترک کرد
Many is the caravanseray that must be quitted,
تا به مسکن در رسد یک روز مرد
in order that one day the man may reach home.

گرچه آهن سرخ شد او سرخ نیست
Though the iron has become red, it is not red
پرتو عاریت آتش زنیست
it (the redness) is a ray borrowed from something that strikes fire.

گر شود پر نور روزن یا سرا
If the window or the house is full of light,
تو مدان روشن مگر خورشید را
do not deem aught luminous except the sun.

هر در و دیوار گوید روشنم
Every door and wall says, "I am luminous:
پرتو غیری ندارم این منم
I do not hold the rays of another, I (myself) am this (light)."

پس بگوید آفتاب ای نارشید
Then the sun says, "O thou who art not right (in thy belief),
چونک من غارب شوم آید پدید
when I set 'twill become evident (thou wilt see what the truth is)."

سبزه‌ها گویند ما سبز از خودیم
The plants say, "We are green of ourselves,
شاد و خندانیم و بس زیبا خدیم
we are gay and smiling (blooming) and we are tall (by nature)."

فصل تابستان بگوید ای امم
The season of summer says (to them),
خویش را بینید چون من بگذرم
"O peoples, behold yourselves when I depart!"

تن همی‌نازد به خوبی و جمال
The body is boasting of its beauty and comeliness,
روح پنهان کرده فر و پر و بال
(while) the spirit, having concealed its glory and pinions and plumes,

گویدش ای مزبله تو کیستی
Says to it, "O dunghill, who art thou?
یک دو روز از پرتو من زیستی
Through my beams thou hast come to life for a day or two.

غنج و نازت می‌نگنجد در جهان
Thy coquetry and prideful airs are not contained in the world
باش تا که من شوم از تو جهان
(go beyond all bounds), (but) wait till I spring up (and escape) from thee!

گرم دارانت ترا گوری کنند
They whose love warmed thee will dig a grave for thee,
طعمهٔ ماران و مورانت کنند
they will make thee a morsel for ants and reptiles.

بینی از گند تو گیرد آن کسی
will hold his nose at thy stench."
کو به پیش تو همی‌مردی بسی
That one who many a time in thy presence was dying

پرتو روحست نطق و چشم و گوش
The beams of the spirit are speech and eye and ear:
پرتو آتش بود در آب جوش
the beam(effect) of fire is the bubbling in the water.

آنچنانک پرتو جان بر تنست
As the beam of the spirit falls on the body,
پرتو ابدال بر جان منست
so fall the beams of the Abdál on my soul.

جان جان چو واکشد پا را ز جان
When the Soul of the soul withdraws from the soul,
جان چنان گردد که بی‌جان تن بدان
the soul becomes even as the soulless (lifeless) body. Know (this for sure)!

سر از آن رو می‌نهم من بر زمین
For that reason I am laying my head (humbly) on the earth,
تا گواه من بود در روز دین
so that she (the earth) may be my witness on the Day of Judgement.

یوم دین که زلزلت زلزالها
On the Day of Judgement, when she shall be made to quake mightily,
این زمین باشد گواه حالها
this earth will bear witness to all that passed (in and from us);

گو تحدث جهرة اخبارها
For she will plainly declare what she knows:
در سخن آید زمین و خاره‌ها
earth and rocks will begin to speak.

فلسفی منکر شود در فکر و ظن
The philosopher, in his (vain) thought and opinion, becomes disbelieving:
گو برو سر را بر آن دیوار زن
bid him go and dash his head against this wall!

نطق آب و نطق خاک و نطق گل
The speech of water, the speech of earth, and the speech of mud
هست محسوس حواس اهل دل
are apprehended by the senses of them that have hearts (the mystics).

فلسفی کو منکر حنانه است
The philosopher who disbelieves in the moaning pillar
از حواس اولیا بیگانه است
is a stranger to the senses of the saints.

گوید او که پرتو سودای خلق
He says that the beam (influence) of melancholia
بس خیالات آورد در رای خلق
brings many phantasies into people's minds.

بلک عکس آن فساد و کفر او
Nay, but the reflexion of his wickedness and infidelity cast
این خیال منکری را زد برو
this idle fancy of scepticism upon him.

فلسفی مر دیو را منکر شود
The philosopher comes to deny the existence of the Devil,
در همان دم سخرۀ دیوی بود
and at the same time he is possessed by a devil.

گر ندیدی دیو را خود را ببین
If thou hast not seen the Devil, behold thyself:
بی جنون نبود کبودی بر جبین
without diabolic possession there is no blueness in the forehead.

هر که را در دل شک و پیچانیست
Whosoever hath doubt and perplexity in his heart,
در جهان او فلسفی پنهانیست
he in this world is a secret philosopher.

مینماید اعتقاد و گاه گاه
He is professing firm belief, but some time or other that
آن رگ فلسف کند رویش سیاه
philosophical vein will blacken his face (bring him to shame).

الحذر ای مؤمنان کان در شماست
philosophical vein will blacken his face (bring him to shame).
در شما بس عالم بی‌منتهاست
in you is many an infinite world.

جمله هفتاد و دو ملت در توست
In thee are all the two-and-seventy sects:

وه که روزی آن بر آرد از تو دست
woe (to thee) if one day they gain the upper hand over thee.

هر که او را برگ آن ایمان بود
From fear of this, everyone who has the fortune (barg) of (holding) this Faith

همچو برگ از بیم این لرزان بود
(Islam) is trembling like a leaf (barg).

بر بلیس و دیو زان خندیده‌ای
Thou hast laughed at Iblís and the devils

که تو خود را نیک مردم دیده‌ای
because thou hast regarded thyself as a good man.

چون کند جان بازگونه پوستین
When the soul shall turn its coat inside out

چند وا ویلی بر آید ز اهل دین
how many a "Woe is me" will it extort from the followers of the (Mohammedan) Religion!

بر دکان هر زرنما خندان شدست
On the counter (of the shop) everything (every gilded coin) that looks like gold is smiling,

زانک سنگ امتحان پنهان شدست
because the touchstone is out of sight.

پرده‌ای ستار از ما بر مگیر
O Coverer (of faults), do not lift up the veil from us,

باش اندر امتحان ما را مجیر
be a protector to us in our test (on the Day of Judgement).

قلب پهلو می‌زند با زر به شب
At night the false coin jostles (in rivalry) with the gold:

انتظار روز می‌دارد ذهب
the gold is waiting for day.

با زبان حال زر گوید که باش
With the tongue of its (inward) state the gold says,

ای مزور تا بر آید روز فاش
Wait, O tinselled one, till day rises clear."

صد هزاران سال ابلیس لعین
Hundreds of thousands of years the accursed Iblís

بود ز ابدال و امیر المؤمنین
was a saint and the prince of true believers;

پنجه زد با آدم از نازی که داشت
On account of the pride which he had,
گشت رسوا همچو سرگین وقت چاشت
he grappled with Adam and was put to shame, like dung at morning tide.

◈◈◈

دعا کردن بلعم با عور
How Bal'am son of Bá'úr prayed (to God), saying,

کی موسی و قومش را از این شهر کی حصار داده‌اند بی مراد باز گردان و مستجاب شدن دعای او
"Cause Moses and his people to turn back, without having gained their desire, from this city which they have besieged."

بلعم با عور را خلق جهان
To Bal'am son of Bá'úr the people of the world became subject,
سغبه شد مانند عیسی زمان
(for he was) like unto the Jesus of the time.

سجدهٔ ناوردند کس را دون او
They bowed (worshipfully) to none but him:
صحت رنجور بود افسون او
his spell was (giving) health to the sick.

پنجه زد با موسی از کبر و کمال
From pride and (conceit of) perfection he grappled with Moses:
آنچنان شد که شنیدستی تو حال
his plight became such as thou hast heard.

صد هزار ابلیس و بلعم در جهان
, a hundred thousand like Iblís and Bal'am.
همچنین بودست پیدا و نهان
Even so there have been in the world manifest or hidden

این دو را مشهور گردانید اله
God caused these twain to be notorious,
تا که باشد این دو بر باقی گواه
that these twain might bear witness against the rest

این دو دزد آویخت از دار بلند
These two thieves He hanged on a high gallows
ورنه اندر قهر بس دزدان بدند
else there were many (other) thieves in (the pale of) His vengeance

411

این دو را پرچم به سوی شهر برد
These twain He dragged by their forelocks to the cit
کشتگان قهر را نتوان شمرد
tis impossible to number (all) the victims of His wrath.

نازنینی تو ولی در حد خویش
You are a favourite (of God), but within your (due) bounds.
الله الله پا منه از حد بیش
(Fear) God, (fear) God, do not set foot beyond (those) bounds.

گر زنی بر نازنین‌تر از خودت
If you combat with one who is a greater favourite than yourself,
در تگ هفتم زمین زیر آردت
'twill bring you down to the lowest depth of the seventh earth

قصهٔ عاد و ثمود از بهر چیست
For what purpose is the tale of 'Ád and Thamúd?
تا بدانی کانبیا را نازکیست
That you may know that the prophets have disdain

این نشان خسف و قذف و صاعقه
These signs the (earth's) swallowing up (sinners), the hurling of stones (upon them),
شد بیان عز نفس ناطقه
and the thunderbolts were evidence of the might of the Rational Soul.

جمله حیوان را پی انسان بکش
Kill all animals for the sake of man,
جمله انسان را بکش از بهر هش
kill all mankind for the sake of Reason.

هش چه باشد عقل کل هوشمند
What is Reason? The Universal Intelligence of the man (prophet or saint) endowed with reason.
هوش جزوی هش بود اما نژند
Partial reason is reason (too), but it is infirm.

جمله حیوانات وحشی ز آدمی
All the animals that are wild (unfriendly) to man
باشد از حیوان انسی در کمی
are inferior to the human animal.

خون آنها خلق را باشد سبیل
Their blood is free to mankind,
زانک وحشی‌اند از عقل جلیل
since they are estranged from the august Reason.

412

عزت وحشی بدین افتاد پست
The honour of the wild animals is fallen low
که مر انسان را مخالف آمدست
because they have grown hostile to man

پس چه عزت باشدت ای نادره
What honour, then, will be thine, O marvel (of folly),
چون شدی تو حمر مستنفره
since thou hast become (like) timorous wild asses?

خر نشاید کشت از بهر صلاح
Because of his usefulness, the (domesticated) ass ought not to be killed;
چون شود وحشی شود خونش مباح
(but) when he turns wild, his blood becomes lawful.

گرچه خر را دانش زاجر نبود
Although the ass had no knowledge to restrain him (from becoming wild)
هیچ معذورش نمی‌دارد ودود
the Loving One is not excusing him at all.

پس چو وحشی شد از آن دم آدمی
How, then, shall man be excused, O noble friend,
کی بود معذور ای یار سمی
when he has become wild (refractory and hostile) to that Word (the voice of Reason)?

لاجرم کفار را شد خون مباح
Of necessity permission was given to shed the blood of the infidels,
همچو وحشی پیش نشاب و رماح
like (that of) a wild beast before the arrows and lances.

جفت و فرزندانشان جمله سبیل
All their wives and children are free spoil,
ژانک بی‌عقلند و مردود و ذلیل
since they are irrational and reprobate and base.

باز عقلی کو رمد از عقل عقل
Once more, a reason that flees from the Reason of reason
کرد از عقلی به حیوانات نقل
(Universal Reason) is transported from rationality to (the grade of) the animals.

◆◉◈◉◆

اعتماد کردن هاروت و ماروت بر عصمت خویش
How Hárút and Márút relied upon their immaculateness

و امیری اهل دنیا خواستن و در فتنه افتادن
and desired to mix with the people of this world and fell into temptation.

همچو هاروت و چو ماروت شهیر
As (for example), because of their arrogance
از بطر خوردند زهرآلود تیر
the celebrated Hárút and Márút were smitten by the poisoned arrow (of Divine wrath).

اعتمادی بودشان بر قدس خویش
They had confidence in their holiness,
چیست بر شیر اعتماد گاومیش
(but) what (use) is it for the buffalo to have confidence in the lion?

گرچه او با شاخ صد چاره کند
Though he make a hundred shifts (to defend himself) with his horn
شاخ شاخش شیر نر پاره کند
the fierce lion will tear him to pieces limb by limb.

گر شود پر شاخ همچون خارپشت
(Even) if he become as full of horns (prickles) as a hedgehog,
شیر خواهد گاو را ناچار کشت
the buffalo will inevitably be killed by the lion

گرچه صرصر پس درختان می‌کند
(But) though the Sarsar wind uproots many trees
با گیاه تر وی احسان می‌کند
it bestows kindness on the wet grass

بر ضعیفی گیاه آن باد تند
That violent wind had pity on the weakness of the grass
رحم کرد ای دل تو از قوت ملند
do not thou, O heart, brag vainly of thy strength.

تیشه را ز انبوهی شاخ درخت
How should the axe be afraid of the thickness of the branches?
کی هراس آید ببرد لخت لخت
It cuts them to pieces.

لیک بر برگی نکوبد خویش را
But it does not beat itself against a leaf,
جز که بر نیشی نکوبد نیش را
it does not beat its edge except against an edge (something hard and solid like itself).

شعله را ز انبوهی هیزم چه غم
What does the flame care for the great quantity of firewood
کی رمد قصاب از خیل غنم
How should the butcher flee in terror from the flock of sheep?

پیش معنی چیست صورت بس زبون
What is form in the presence of (in comparison with) reality? Very feeble.
چرخ را معنیش می‌دارد نگون
'Tis the reality of the sky that keeps it upside down (like an inverted cup).

تو قیاس از چرخ دولابی بگیر
Judge by the analogy of the celestial wheel:
گردشش از کیست از عقل مشیر
from whom does its motion proceed? From directive Reason

گردش این قالب همچون سپر
The motion of this shield-like body
هست از روح مستر ای پسر
is (derived) from the veiled spirit, O son

گردش این باد از معنی اوست
The motion of this wind is from its reality,
همچو چرخی کان اسیر آب جوست
like the wheel that is captive to the water of the stream

جر و مد و دخل و خرج این نفس
The ebb and flow and incoming and outgoing of this breath
از کی باشد جز ز جان پر هوس
from whom does it proceed but from the spirit that is filled with desire?

گاه جیمش می‌کند گه حا و دال
Now it (the spirit) makes it (the breath) jím
گاه صلحش می‌کند گاهی جدال
Now it (the spirit) makes it (the breath) jím, now há and dál

گه یمینش می‌برد گاهی یسار
now it makes it peace, now strife
که گلستانش کند گاهیش خار
now it makes it peace, now strife.

همچنین این باد را یزدان ما
Even so our God had made this (Sarsar) wind
کرده بد بر عاد همچون اژدها
like a (raging) dragon against 'Ád.

415

باز هم آن باد را بر مؤمنان
Again, He had also made that wind

کرده بد صلح و مراعات و امان
peace and regardfulness and safety for the true believers.

گفت المعنی هوالله شیخ دین
The Reality is Allah," said the Shaykh of the (Mohammedan) Religion

بحر معنیهای رب العالمین
(who is) the sea of the spiritual realities of the Lord of created beings.

جمله اطباق زمین و آسمان
All the tiers of earth and heaven

همچو خاشاکی در آن بحر روان
are (but) as straws in that flowing sea.

حمله‌ها و رقص خاشاک اندر آب
The rushing and tossing of the straws in the water

هم ز آب آمد به وقت اضطراب
is produced by the water when it is agitated.

چونک ساکن خواهدش کرد از مرا
When it (the sea of Reality) wishes to make them (the straws) cease from struggling,

سوی ساحل افکند خاشاک را
it casts the straws toward the shore.

چون کشد از ساحلش در موج‌گاه
When it draws them from the shore into the surge

آن کند با او که آتش با گیاه
it does with them that which fire does with grass.

این حدیث آخر ندارد باز ران
This topic is endless. Speed back,

جانب هاروت و ماروت ای جوان
O youth, to (the story of) Hárút and Márút.

باقی قصهٔ هاروت و ماروت
The rest of the story of Hárút and Márút,

و نکال و عقوبت ایشان هم در دنیا بچاه بابل
and how an exemplary punishment was inflicted on them, even in this world, in the pit of Babylon.

چون گناه و فسق خلقان جهان
Inasmuch as the sin and wickedness of the people of the world

می‌شدی بر هر دو روشن آن زمان
was becoming clearly visible to them both at that time,

دست خاییدن گرفتندی ز خشم
They began to gnaw their hands in wrath

لیک عیب خود ندیدندی به چشم
but had no eyes for their own fault.

خویش در آیینه دید آن زشت مرد
The ugly man saw himself in the mirror

رو بگردانید از آن و خشم کرد
he turned his face away from that (spectacle) and was enraged

خویش‌بین چون از کسی جرمی بدید
When the self-conceited person has seen any one commit a sin

آتشی در وی ز دوزخ شد پدید
there appears in him a fire (derived) from Hell

حمیت دین خواند او آن کبر را
He calls that (hellish) pride defence of the Religion

ننگرد در خویش نفس گبر را
he regards not the infidel soul in himself.

حمیت دین را نشانی دیگرست
Defence of the Religion has a different character

که از آن آتش جهانی اخضرست
for from that (religious) fire a (whole) world is green (verdant and flourishing).

گفت حقشان گر شما روشن گرید
God said to them, "If ye are enlightened

در سیه‌کاران مغفل منگرید
(nevertheless) do not look heedlessly (contemptuously) upon the doers of black deeds.

شکر گویید ای سپاه و چاکران
Render thanks, O Host (of Heaven) and Servants (of God)

رسته‌اید از شهوت و از چاکران
Ye are freed from lust and sexual intercourse

گر از آن معنی نهم من بر شما
If I impose that kind of nature on you
مر شما را بیش نپذیرد سما
Heaven will accept you no more.

عصمتی که مر شما را در تنست
The preservation (from sin) which ye have in your bodies
آن ز عکس عصمت و حفظ منست
is from the reflexion of My preservation and care (of you)

آن ز من بینید نه از خود هین و هین
Oh, beware! Regard that as (coming) from Me, not from yourselves
تا نچربد بر شما دیو لعین
lest the accursed Devil prevail against you.

آنچنان که کاتب وحی رسول
As (for example) the writer of the Revelation given to the Prophet
دید حکمت در خود و نور اصول
deemed the Wisdom and the Original Light (to be residing) in himself.

خویش را هم صوت مرغان خدا
He was reckoning himself a fellow-songster of the Birds of God,
می‌شمرد آن بد صفیری چون صدا
(whereas) that (which proceeded from him) was (only) a whistle resembling an echo.

لحن مرغان را اگر واصف شوی
If you become an exponent (imitator) of the song of birds,
بر مراد مرغ کی واقف شوی
how will you become acquainted with the (real) meaning of the bird?

گر بیاموزی صفیر بلبلی
If you learn the note of a nightingale,
تو چه دانی کو چه دارد با گلی
how will you know what (feelings) it has towards a rose?

ور بدانی باشد آن هم از گمان
Or if you do know, 'twill only be from surmise
چون ز لب‌جنبان گمانهای کران
like the conjectures formed by deaf people from those who move their lips.

◆◉◆◉◆

به عیادتِ رفتنِ کر بر همسایهٔ رنجورِ خویش
How the deaf man went to visit his sick neighbour.

آن کری را گفت افزون مایه‌ای
One possessed of much wealth said to a deaf man,
که ترا رنجور شد همسایه‌ای
A neighbour of thine is fallen ill."

گفت با خود کر که با گوشِ گران
The deaf man said to himself, "Being hard of hearing
من چه دریابم ز گفتِ آن جوان
what shall I understand of the words spoken by that youth?

خاصه رنجور و ضعیف آواز شد
Especially (as) he is ill and his voice is weak
لیک باید رفت آنجا نیست بد
but I must go thither, there's no escape

چون ببینم کان لبش جنبان شود
When I see his lips moving
من قیاسی گیرم آن را هم ز خود
I will form a conjecture as to that (movement) from myself.

چون بگویم چونی ای محنت‌کشم
When I say, 'How are you, O my suffering (friend)?' he will reply,
او بخواهد گفت نیکم یا خوشم
'I am fine' or 'I am pretty well.'

ن بگویم شکر چه خوردی ابا
will say, 'Thanks (to God)! What posset have you had to drink
او بگوید شربتی یا ماش با
He will reply, 'Some sherbet' or 'a decoction of kidney-beans.'

من بگویم صحه نوشت کیست آن
(Then) I will say, 'May you enjoy health! Who is the doctor attending you?
از طبیبان پیشِ تو گوید فلان
He will answer, 'So-and-so

من بگویم بس مبارک‌پاست او
He is one who brings great luck with him,' I will remark; 'since he has come,
چونک او آمد شود کارت نکو
things will go well for you.

پای او را آزموده‌ستیم ما
I have experienced (the luck of) his foot:
هر کجا شد می‌شود حاجت روا
wherever he goes, the desired object is attained.'"

این جوابات قیاسی راست کرد
The good man made ready these conjectural answers
پیش آن رنجور شد آن نیک مرد
and went to see the invalid.

گفت چونی گفت مردم گفت شکر
"How are you?" he asked. "I am at the point of death," said he.
شد ازین رنجور پر آزار و نکر
Thanks (to God)!" cried the deaf man. At this, the patient became resentful and indignant,

کین چه شکرست او مگر با ما بدست
Saying (to himself), "What (cause for) thanksgiving is this?
کر قیاسی کرد و آن کژ آمدست
Surely he has always been ill-disposed towards me." The deaf man made a conjecture,
and it has turned out to be wrong.

بعد از آن گفتش چه خوردی گفت زهر
After that, he asked him what he had drunk. "Poison," said he.
گفت نوشت باد افزون گشت قهر
May it do you good!" said the deaf man. His (the invalid's) wrath increased.

بعد از آن گفت از طبیبان کیست او
Then he inquired, "Which of the doctors is it
که همی‌آید به چاره پیش تو
that is coming to attend you?"

گفت عزرائیل می‌آید برو
He replied, "Azrael (the Angel of Death) is coming. Get you gone!"
گفت پایش بس مبارک شاد شو
His foot (arrival)," said the deaf man, "is very blessed: be glad!

کر برون آمد بگفت او شادمان
The deaf man went forth. He said gaily,
شکر کش کردم مراعات این زمان
Thanks (to God) that I paid my respects to him just now."

گفت رنجور این عدو جان ماست
The invalid said, "This is my mortal foe:
ما ندانستیم کو کان جفاست
I did not know he was (such) a mine of iniquity."

خاطر رنجور جویان شد سقط
The mind of the invalid began seeking abusive terms
تا که پیغامش کند از هر نمط
that he might send him a message (filled with abuse) of every description,

چون کسی که خورده باشد آش بد
As, when any one has eaten bad (indigestible) food
می‌بشوراند دلش تا قی کند
it is turning his heart (stomach) until he vomits.

کظم غیظ اینست آن را قی مکن
Suppression of anger is (like) this: do not vomit it
تا بیابی در جزا شیرین سخن
so that you may gain sweet words in recompense.

چون نبودش صبر می‌پیچید او
Since he had no patience, he was tormented.
کین سگ زن روسپی حیز کو
Where," he cried, "is this cur, this infamous cuckold,

تا بریزم بر وی آنچه گفته بود
That I may pour upon him what he said (make a retort in his own style)
کان زمان شیر ضمیرم خفته بود
for at that time the lion of my thought was asleep (I was too weak to contend with him).

چون عیادت بهر دل‌آرامیست
Inasmuch as visiting the sick is for the purpose of (giving them) tranquillity,
این عیادت نیست دشمن کامیست
this is not a visit to the sick: it is the satisfaction of an enemy's wish.

تا ببیند دشمن خود را نزار
that he should see his enemy enfeebled
تا بگیرد خاطر زشتش قرار
and that his wicked heart should be at peace."

بس کسان کایشان ز طاعت گمرهند
Many are they that have gone astray from (true) piety,
دل به رضوان و ثواب آن دهند
(because) they set their hearts on being approved and rewarded for the same.

خود حقیقت معصیت باشد خفی
Tis in truth a lurking sin:
بس کدرگان را تو پنداری صفی
for there is many a foul thing that you think pure,

همچو آن کر که همی پنداشتست
As (in the case of) the deaf man, who fancied that
کو نکویی کرد و آن بر عکس جست
he did a kindness, but it had the opposite result.

او نشسته خوش که خدمت کرده‌ام
He sits down well-pleased, saying, "I have paid my respects
حق همسایه بجا آورده‌ام
I have performed what was due to my neighbour"

بهر خود او آتشی افروختست
(But) he has (only) kindled a fire (of resentment) against himself
در دل رنجور و خود را سوختست
in the invalid's heart and burned himself

فاتقوا النار التی اوقدتم
Beware, then, of the fire that ye have kindled:
انکم فی المعصیه ازددتم
verily ye have increased in sin.

گفت پیغامبر به یک صاحب ریا
The Prophet said to a hypocrite,
صل انک لم تصل یا فتی
"Pray, for indeed thou hast not prayed (aright), my man."

از برای چارهٔ این خوفها
As a means of preventing these dangers,
آمد اندر هر نمازی اهدنا
Guide us" comes in every (ritual) prayer,

کین نمازم را میامیز ای خدا
That is to say, "O God, do not mingle my prayer
با نماز ضالین و اهل ریا
with the prayer of the erring and the hypocrites.

از قیاسی که بکرد آن کر گزین
By the analogical reasoning which the deaf man adopted
صحبت ده‌ساله باطل شد بدین
a ten years' friendship was made vain.

خاصه ای خواجه قیاس حس دون
Especially, O master, (you must avoid) the analogy drawn by the low senses
اندر آن وحی که هست از حد فزون
in regard to the Revelation which is illimitable

گوش حس تو به حرف ار در خورست
If your sensuous ear is fit for (understanding) the letter (of the Revelation)
دان که گوش غیب گیر تو کرست
know that your ear that receives the occult (meaning) is deaf.

422

اول کسی کی در مقابلهٔ نص قیاس آورد ابلیس بود
The first to bring analogical reasoning to bear against the Revealed Text was Iblís.

ول آن کس کین قیاسکها نمود
The first person who produced these paltry analogies

پیش انوار خدا ابلیس بود
in the presence of the Lights of God was Iblís

گفت نار از خاک بی شک بهترست
He said, "Beyond doubt fire is superior to earth

من ز نار و او ز خاک اکدرست
I am of fire, and he (Adam) is of dingy earth.

پس قیاس فرع بر اصلش کنیم
Let us, then, judge by comparing the secondary with its principal:

او ز ظلمت ما ز نور روشنیم
he is of darkness, I of radiant light."

گفت حق نه بلک لا انساب شد
God said, "Nay, but on the contrary there shall be no relationships

زهد و تقوی فضل را محراب شد
asceticism and piety shall be the (sole) avenue to pre-eminence."

این نه میراث جهان فانی است
This is not the heritage of the fleeting world,

که به انسابش بیابی جانی است
so that thou shouldst gain it by ties of relationship: 'tis a spiritual (heritage).

بلک این میراثهای انبیاست
Nay, these things are the heritage of the prophets

وارث این جانهای اتقیاست
the inheritors of these are the spirits of the devout.

پور آن بوجهل شد مؤمن عیان
The son of Bú Jahl became a true believer for all to see;

پور آن نوح نبی از گمرهان
the son of the prophet Noah became one of those who lost the way.

زادهٔ خاکی منور شد چو ماه
The child of earth (Adam) became illumined like the moon

زادهٔ آتش توی رو روسیاه
thou art the child of fire: get thee gone with thy face black (in disgrace)!

این قیاسات و تحری روز ابر
The wise man has made (use of) such reasonings and investigation on a cloudy day

یا بشب مر قبله را کردست حبر
or at night for the sake of (finding) the qibla;

لیک با خورشید و کعبه پیش رو
But with the sun and with the Ka'ba before your face,
این قیاس و این تحری را مجو
do not seek to reason and investigate in this manner

کعبه نادیده مکن رو زو متاب
Do not pretend that you cannot see the Ka'ba,
از قیاس الله اعلم بالصواب
do not avert your face from it because you have reasoned God knows best what is right.

چون صفیری بشنوی از مرغ حق
When you hear a pipe from the Bird of God
ظاهرش را یاد گیری چون سبق
you commit its outward (meaning) to memory, like a lesson,

وانگهی از خود قیاساتی کنی
And then from yourself (out of your own head) you make some analogies
مر خیال محض را ذاتی کنی
you make (what is) mere fancy into a (thing of) substance (reality)

اصطلاحاتیست مر ابدال را
The Abdál have certain mystical expressions
که نباشد زان خبر اقوال را
of which the doctrines (of external religion) are ignorant

منطق الطیری به صوت آموختی
You have learned the birds' language by the sound (alone),
صد قیاس و صد هوس افروختی
you have kindled (invented) a hundred analogies and a hundred caprices.

همچو آن رنجور دلها از تو خست
The hearts (of the saints) are wounded by you, as the invalid (was hurt by the deaf man)
کر پندار اصابت گشته مست
(while) the deaf man became intoxicated (overjoyed) with the vain notion of success.

کاتب آن وحی از آن آواز مرغ
The writer of the Revelation, from (hearing) the Bird's voice,
برده ظنی کو بود همباز مرغ
supposed that he was the Bird's equal:

مرغ پری زد مرورا کور کرد
The Bird flapped a wing and blinded him:
نک فرو بردش به قعر مرگ و درد
it plunged him in the abyss of death and bale.

هین به عکسی یا به ظنی هم شما
Beware! do not ye also, (beguiled) by a reflexion or an opinion
در میفتید از مقامات سما
fall from the dignities of Heaven!

گرچه هاروتید و ماروت و فزون
Although ye are Hárút and Márút and superior to all
از همه بر بام نحن الصافون
(the angels) on the terrace of We are they that stand in ranks,

بر بدیهای بدان رحمت کنید
(Yet) take mercy on the wickednesses of the wicked
بر منی و خویش بین لعنت کنید
execrate egoism and the self-conceited (egoist).

هین مبادا غیرت آید از کمین
Beware, lest (the Divine) jealousy come from ambush
سرنگون افتید در قعر زمین
ye fall headlong to the bottom of the earth.

هر دو گفتند ای خدا فرمان تراست
They both said, "O God, Thine is the command:
بی امان تو امانی خود کجاست
without Thy security (protection) where indeed is any security?

این همی گفتند و دلشان می‌طپید
They were saying this, but their hearts were throbbing (with desire)
بد کجا آید ز ما نعم العبید
How should evil come from us? Good servants (of God) are we!

خار خار دو فرشته هم نهشت
The prick of desire in the two angels did not leave
تا که تخم خویش‌بینی را نکشت
(them) until it sowed the seed of self-conceit.

پس همی گفتند کای ارکانیان
Then they were saying, "O ye that are composed of the (four) elements
بی خبر از پاکی روحانیان
elements (and are) unacquainted with the purity of the spiritual beings,

ما برین گردون تتقها می‌تنیم
We are weaving veils (of worship and glorification of God) over this Heaven
بر زمین آییم و شادروان زنیم
we will come to earth and set up the canopy,

425

عدل توزیم و عبادت آوریم
We will deal justice and perform worship
باز هر شب سوی گردون بر پریم
and every night we will fly up again to Heaven,

تا شویم اعجوبهٔ دور زمان
That we may become the wonder of the world,
تا نهیم اندر زمین امن و امان
that we may establish safety and security on the earth."

آن قیاس حال گردون بر زمین
The analogy between the state of Heaven and (that of) the earth is inexact:
راست ناید فرق دارد در کمین
it has a concealed difference

◈◈

در بیان آنک حال خود و مستی خود پنهان باید داشت از جاهلان
Explaining that one must keep one's own (spiritual) state and (mystical) intoxication hidden from the ignorant

بشنو الفاظ حکیم پرده‌ای
Hearken to the words of the Sage (Hakím) who lived in seclusion,
سر همان‌جا نه که باده خورده‌ای
Lay thy head in the same place where thou hast drunk the wine."

چونک از میخانه مستی ضال شد
When the drunken man has gone astray from a tavern
تسخر و بازیچهٔ اطفال شد
he becomes the children's laughing-stock and plaything.

می‌فتد او به سو بر هر رهی
Whatever way he goes, he is falling in the mud,
در گل و می‌خنددش هر ابلهی
on this side and (now) on that side, and every fool is laughing at him.

او چنین و کودکان اندر پیش
He (goes on) like this, while the children at his heels are
بی‌خبر از مستی و ذوق میش
without knowledge of his intoxication and the taste of his wine.

خلق اطفالند جز مست خدا
All mankind are children except him that is intoxicated with God
نیست بالغ جز رهیده از هوا
none is grownup except him that is freed from sensual desire.

گفت دنیا لعب و لهوست و شما

He (God) said, "This world is a play and pastime,

کودکیت و راست فرماید خدا

and ye are children"; and God speaks truth

از لعب بیرون نرفتی کودکی

If you have not gone forth from (taken leave of) play, you are a child

بی ذکات روح کی باشد ذکی

without purity of spirit how should he (any one) be fully intelligent?

چون جماع طفل دان این شهوتی

Know, O youth, that the lust in which men are indulging here

که همی رانند اینجا ای فتی

is like the sexual intercourse of children.

آن جماع طفل چه بود بازی

What is the child's sexual intercourse? An idle play,

با جماع رستمی و غازی

compared with the sexual intercourse of a Rustam and a brave champion of Islam.

جنگ خلقان همچو جنگ کودکان

The wars of mankind are like children's fights

جمله بی‌معنی و بی‌مغز و مهان

all meaningless, pithless, and contemptible

جمله با شمشیر چوبین جنگشان

All their fights are (fought) with wooden swords

جمله در لا ینفعی آهنگشان

all their purposes are (centred) in futility;

جمله شان گشته سواره بر نی

They all are riding on a reed-cane (hobby-horse), saying,

کین براق ماست یا دلدل پی

"This is our Buráq or mule that goes like Duldul.

حاملند و خود ز جهل افراشته

They are (really) carrying (their hobby-horses), but in their folly they have raised themselves on high

راکب و محمول ره پنداشته

they have fancied themselves to be riders and carried along the road

باش تا روزی که محمولان حق

Wait till the day when those who are borne aloft by God shall pass

اسپ تازان بگذرند از نه طبق

galloping, beyond the nine tiers (of Heaven)!

تعرج الروح اليه و الملک
The spirit and the angels shall ascend to Him
من عروج الروح يهتز الفلک
at the ascension of the spirit Heaven shall tremble.

همچو طفلان جمله تان دامن سوار
Like children, ye all are riding on your skirts
گوشهٔ دامن گرفته اسپ‌وار
ye have taken hold of the corner of your skirt (to serve) as a horse.

از حق ان الظن لا یغنی رسید
From God came (the text), "Verily, opinion doth not enable (you) to dispense
مرکب ظن بر فلکها کی دوید
when did the steed of opinion run (mount) to the Heavens?

اغلب الظنین فی ترجیح ذا
While preferring (in case of doubt) the stronger of the two (alternative) opinions
لا تماری الشمس فی توضیحها
do not doubt whether you see the sun when it is shining!

آنگهی بینید مرکبهای خویش
At that time (when the spirit returns to God) behold your steeds!
مرکبی سازیده‌ایت از پای خویش
Ye have made a steed of your own foot

وهم و فکر و حس و ادراک شما
Come, recognise that your imagination and reflection and sense-perception and apprehension
همچو نی دان مرکب کودک هلا
are like the reed-cane on which children ride.

علمهای اهل دل حمالشان
The sciences of the mystics bear them (aloft);
علمهای اهل تن احمالشان
the sciences of sensual men are burdens to them.

علم چون بر دل زند یاری شود
When knowledge strikes on the heart it becomes a helper
علم چون بر تن زند باری شود
when knowledge strikes on the body it becomes a burden

گفت ایزد یحمل اسفاره
God hath said, "(Like an ass) laden with his books"
بار باشد علم کان نبود ز هو
burdensome is the knowledge that is not from Himself.

علم کان نبود ز هو بی واسطه
The knowledge that is not immediately from Himself does not endure

آن نپاید همچو رنگ ماشطه
(it is) like the tire woman's paint.

لیک چون این بار را نیکو کشی
But when you carry this burden well

بار بر گیرند و بخشندت خوشی
the burden will be removed and you will be given (spiritual) joy

هین مکش بهر هوا آن بار علم
Beware! Do not carry that burden of knowledge for the sake of selfish desire

تا ببینی در درون انبار علم
so that you may behold the barn (store-house) of knowledge within (you)

تا که بر رهوار علم آبی سوار
So that you may mount the smooth-paced steed of knowledge

بعد از آن افتد ترا از دوش بار
afterwards the burden may fall from your shoulder

از هواها کی رهی بی جام هو
How wilt thou be freed from selfish desires without the cup of Hú (Him)

ای ز هو قانع شده با نام هو
O thou who hast become content with no more of Hú than the name of Hú?

از صفت وز نام چه زاید خیال
From attribute and name what comes to birth? Phantasy

و آن خیالش هست دلال وصال
and that phantasy shows the way to union with Him

دیده‌ای دلال بی مدلول هیچ
Hast thou ever seen a subject that shows without (the existence of) an object that is shown:

تا نباشد جاده نبود غول هیچ
unless there is the road, there can never be the ghoul

هیچ نامی بی حقیقت دیده‌ای
Hast thou ever seen a name without the reality (denoted by the name)?

یا ز گاف و لام گل گل چیده‌ای
or hast thou plucked a rose (gul) from the (letters) gáf and lám of (the word) gul?

اسم خواندی رو مسمی را بجو
Thou hast pronounced the name: go, seek the thing named.

مه به بالا دان نه اندر آب جو
Know that the moon is on high, not in the water of the stream

429

گر ز نام و حرف خواهی بگذری
If thou wouldst pass beyond name and letter,
پاک کن خود را ز خود هین یکسری
oh, make thyself wholly purged of self

همچو آهن ز آهنی بی رنگ شو
Like (polished) iron, lose the ferruginous colour
در ریاضت آینهٔ بی زنگ شو
become in thy ascetic discipline (like) a mirror without rust.

خویش را صافی کن از اوصاف خود
Make thyself pure from the attributes of self
تا ببینی ذات پاک صاف خود
that thou mayst behold thine own pure untarnished essence,

بینی اندر دل علوم انبیا
And behold within thy heart (all) the sciences of the prophets
بی کتاب و بی معید و اوستا
without book and without preceptor and master.

گفت پیغامبر که هست از امتم
The Prophet said, "Amongst my people are
کو بود هم گوهر و هم همتم
some who are one with me in nature and aspiration:

مر مرا زان نور بیند جانشان
Their spirits behold me by the same light
که من ایشان را همی‌بینم بدان
by which I am beholding them."

بی صحیحین و احادیث و روات
Without the two Sahîhs and Traditions and Traditionists; nay,
بلک اندر مشرب آب حیات
(they behold him) in the place where they drink the Water of Life.

سر امسینا لکردیا بدان
Know the secret of "In the evening I was a Kurd"
راز اصبحنا عرابیا بخوان
read the mystery of "In the morning I was an Arab.

ور مثالی خواهی از علم نهان
And if you desire a parable of the hidden knowledge
قصه‌گو از رومیان و چینیان
relate the story of the Greeks and the Chinese.

430

قصهٔ مری کردن رومیان و چینیان در علم نقاشی و صورت‌گری
The story of the contention between the Greeks and the Chinese in the art of painting and picturing

چینیان گفتند ما نقاش تر
The Chinese said, "We are the better artists"; the Greeks said,
رومیان گفتند ما را کر و فر
The (superiority in) power and excellence belongs to us."

گفت سلطان امتحان خواهم درین
I will put you to the test in this matter," said the Sultan,
کز شماها کیست در دعوی گزین
(and see) which of you are approved in your claim.

اهل چین و روم چون حاضر شدند
When the Chinese and the Greeks presented themselves
رومیان در علم واقف‌تر بدند
the Greeks were more skilled in the knowledge (of the art of painting).

چینیان گفتند یک خانه به ما
(Then) the Chinese said, "Hand over to us a particular room,
خاص بسپارید و یک آن شما
and (let there be) one for you (as well)."

بود دو خانه مقابل در بدر
There were two rooms with door facing door:
زان یکی چینی ستد رومی دگر
the Chinese took one, the Greeks the other.

چینیان صد رنگ از شه خواستند
The Chinese requested the King to give them a hundred colours
پس خزینه باز کرد آن ارجمند
then that excellent (king) opened the treasury

هر صباحی از خزینه رنگها
Every morning, by (his) bounty, the colours
چینیان را راتبه بود از عطا
were dispensed from the treasury to the Chinese.

رومیان گفتند نه نقش و نه رنگ
The Greeks said, "No tints and pictures are proper for our work
در خور آید کار را جز دفع زنگ
(nothing is needed) except to remove the rust.

در فرو بستند و صیقل می‌زدند
They shut the door and went on burnishing
همچو گردون ساده و صافی شدند
they became clear and pure like the sky.

از دو صد رنگ به بی‌رنگی رهیست
There is a way from many-colouredness to colourlessness
رنگ چون ابرست و بی‌رنگ مهیست
colour is like the clouds, and colourlessness is a moon

هرچه اندر ابر ضو بینی و تاب
Whatsoever light and splendour you see in the clouds
آن ز اختر دان و ماه و آفتاب
know that it comes from the stars and the moon and the sun

چینیان چون از عمل فارغ شدند
When the Chinese had finished their work,
از پی شادی دهل‌ها می‌زدند
they were beating drums for joy.

شه در آمد دید آنجا نقش‌ها
The King entered and saw the pictures there
می‌ربود آن عقل را و فهم را
that (sight) was robbing him of his wits and understanding.

بعد از آن آمد به سوی رومیان
After that, he came towards the Greeks
پرده را بالا کشیدند از میان
they drew up the intervening curtain.

عکس آن تصویر و آن کردارها
The reflexion of those (Chinese) pictures and works
زد برین صافی شده دیوارها
struck upon these walls which had been made pure (from stain).

هر چه آنجا دید اینجا به نمود
All that he had seen there (in the Chinese room) seemed more beautiful here
دیده را از دیده‌خانه می‌ربود
twas snatching the eye from the socket.

رومیان آن صوفیانند ای پدر
The Greeks, O father, are the Súfis:
بی ز تکرار و کتاب و بی هنر
(they are) without (independent of) study and books and erudition

432

لیک صیقل کرده‌اند آن سینه‌ها
But they have burnished their breasts
پاک از آز و حرص و بخل و کینه‌ها
pure from greed and cupidity and avarice and hatreds.

آن صفای آینه وصف دلست
That purity of the mirror is the attribute of the heart
صورت بی منتها را قابلست
receives the infinite form.

صورت بی‌صورت بی حد غیب
That Moses (the perfect saint) holds in his bosom the formless infinite
ز آینهٔ دل تافت بر موسی ز جیب
form of the Unseen (reflected) from the mirror of his heart.

گرچه آن صورت نگنجد در فلک
Although that form is not contained in Heaven
نه بعرش و فرش و دریا و سمک
nor in the empyrean nor the earth nor the sea nor the Fish,

زانک محدودست و معدودست آن
Because (all) those are bounded and numbered
آینهٔ دل را نباشد حد بدان
know that the mirror of the heart hath no bound

عقل اینجا ساکت آمد یا مضل
Here the understanding becomes silent or (else) it leads into error
زانک دل یا اوست یا خود اوست دل
because the heart is with Him (God), or indeed the heart is He.

عکس هر نقشی نتابد تا ابد
The reflexion of every image shines unto everlasting from the heart alone
جز ز دل هم با عدد هم بی عدد
both with plurality and without.

تا ابد هر نقش نو کاید برو
Unto everlasting every new image that falls on it
می‌نماید بی حجابی اندرو
is appearing therein without any veil

اهل صیقل رسته‌اند از بوی و رنگ
They that burnish (their hearts) have escaped from (mere) scent and colour
هر دمی بینند خوبی بی درنگ
they behold Beauty at every moment without tarrying.

نقش و قشر علم را بگذاشتند
They have relinquished the form and husk of knowledge
رایت عین الیقین افراشتند
they have raised the banner of the eye of certainty

رفت فکر و روشنایی یافتند
Thought is gone, and they have gained light
نحر و بحر آشنایی یافتند
they have gained the throat (core and essence) and the sea (ultimate source) of gnosis.

مرگ کین جمله ازو در وحشتند
Death, of which all these (others) are sore afraid
می‌کنند این قوم بر وی ریش‌خند
this people (the perfect Súfís) are holding in derision.

کس نیابد بر دل ایشان ظفر
None gains the victory over their hearts
بر صدف آید ضرر نه بر گهر
the hurt falls on the oyster-shell, not on the pearl.

گرچه نحو و فقه را بگذاشتند
Though they have let go grammar (nahw) and jurisprudence (fiqh),
لیک محو فقر را بر داشتند
yet they have taken up (instead) the (mystical) self-effacement of (spiritual) poverty (faqr)

تا نقوش هشت جنت تافتست
Ever since the forms of the Eight Paradises have shone forth,
لوح دلشان را پذیرا یافتست
they have found the tablets of their (the Súfís') hearts receptive.

برترند از عرش و کرسی و خلا
They who dwell in God's seat of truth are higher than
ساکنان مقعد صدق خدا
the Throne and the Footstool and the Void.

◆◉◆◉◆

پرسیدن پیغمبر صلی الله علیه و سلم مر زید را
How the Prophet, on whom be peace, asked Zayd,

که امروز چونی و چون برخاستی و جواب گفتن او که اصبحت مؤمنا یا رسول الله
"How art thou to-day and in what state hast thou risen?" and how Zayd answered him, saying, "This morning I am a true believer, O Messenger of Allah."

گفت پیغامبر صباحی زید را
One morning the Prophet said to Zayd,

کیف اصبحت ای رفیق با صفا
"How art thou this morning, O sincere comrade?"

گفت عبدا مؤمنا باز اوش گفت
He replied, "(This morning I am) a faithful servant of God."

کو نشان از باغ ایمان گر شکفت
Again he (the Prophet) said to him, "Where is thy token from the garden of Faith, if it has bloomed?"

گفت تشنه بوده‌ام من روزها
He said, "I have been athirst in the daytime,

شب نخفتستم ز عشق و سوزها
at night I have not slept because of love and burning griefs

تا ز روز و شب گذر کردم چنان
So that I passed through (and beyond) day and night,

که ز اسپر بگذرد نوک سنان
as the point of the spear passes through the shield;

که از آن سو جملهٔ ملت یکیست
For beyond (the realm of contraries) all religion is one

صد هزاران سال و یک ساعت یکیست
hundreds of thousands of years are the same as a single hour.

هست ازل را و ابد را اتحاد
Eternity and everlastingness are unified (yonder)

عقل را ره نیست آن سو ز افتقاد
the understanding hath no way thither by means of inquiry."

گفت ازین ره کو ره‌آوردی بیار
The Prophet said, "Where is the traveller's gift (that thou hast brought home) from this journey?

در خور فهم و عقول این دیار
Produce (a gift) suitable to the understanding of (intelligible to) the minds of this country (the phenomenal world)."

گفت خلقان چون ببینند آسمان
Zayd said, "When (other) people see the sky,
من ببینم عرش را با عرشیان
I behold the Throne of God with those who dwell there.

هشت جنت هفت دوزخ پیش من
The Eight Paradises and the Seven Hells
هست پیدا همچو بت پیش شمن
are as visible to me as the idol to the idolater.

یک بیک وا می‌شناسم خلق را
I am distinguishing the people (here), one by one
همچو گندم من ز جو در آسیا
like wheat from barley in the mill

که بهشتی کیست و بیگانه کیست
So that who is for Paradise and who shall be a stranger
پیش من پیدا چو مار و ماهیست
(to Paradise) is as clear to me as (the difference between) snake and fish."

این زمان پیدا شده بر این گروه
At the present time there hath been made manifest to this
یوم تبیض و تسود وجوه
class of men (what shall come to pass) on the Day when faces shall become white or black.

پیش ازین هرچند جان پر عیب بود
Before this (birth), however sinful the spirit was,
در رحم بود و ز خلقان غیب بود
it was in the womb (of the body) and was hidden from the people.

الشقی من شقی فی بطن الام
The damned are they that are damned in the mother's womb:
من سمات الجسم یعرف حالهم
their state is known from the bodily marks.

تن چو مادر طفل جان را حامله
The body, like a mother, is big with the spirit-child:
مرگ درد زادنست و زلزله
death is the pangs and throes of birth

جمله جانهای گذشته منتظر
All the spirits that have passed over (to the next life) are waiting
تا چگونه زاید آن جان بطر
to see in what state that proud spirit shall be born

436

زنگیان گویند خود از ماست او
The Ethiopians (the damned spirits) say, "It belongs to us"
رومیان گویند بس زیباست او
the Anatolians (the blessed spirits) say, "It is very comely.

چون بزاید در جهان جان و جود
As soon as it is born into the world of spirit and (Divine) grace
پس نماند اختلاف بیض و سود
there is no further difference (of opinion) between the whites (the blessed) and the blacks (the damned).

گر بود زنگی برندش زنگیان
If it is an Ethiopian (a damned spirit), the Ethiopians carry it off
روم را رومی برد هم از میان
and if it is an Anatolian (a blessed spirit), the Anatolians lead it away

تا نزاد او مشکلات عالمست
Until it is born (into the next life), it is a riddle for (all) the world:
آنک نازاده شناسد او کمست
few are they that know (the destiny of) the unborn

او مگر ینظر بنور الله بود
Such a one surely is seeing by the light of God
کاندرون پوست او را ره بود
for he has the way (the means of knowing what is hidden) within the skin.

اصل آب نطفه اسپیدست و خوش
Principium aquae seminis candidum est et pulchrum, but the reflexion of the spirit, (whether the spirit be) Anatolian or Ethiopian,
لیک عکس جان رومی و حبش
[The original (nature of) seminal fluid is white and fair, but the reflexion of the spirit, (whether the spirit be) Anatolian or Ethiopian,]

می‌دهد رنگ احسن التقویم را
Is giving colour (glory) to those (the Anatolians) who are most excellent in their (original) constitution
تا به اسفل می‌برد این نیم را
(while) it is bearing this (other) half (i.e. the Ethiopians) down to the lowest depth.

این سخن پایان ندارد باز ران
This discourse hath no end. Hasten back,
تا نمانیم از قطار کاروان
that we may not be left behind by the caravan's file of camels.

یوم تبیض و تسود وجوه
On the Day when faces shall become white or black,
ترک و هندو شهره گردد زان گروه
Turk and Hindi shall become manifest (shall be clearly discerned) from among that company

در رحم پیدا نباشد هند و ترک
In the womb (of this world) Hindoo and Turk are not distinguishable,
چونک زاید بیندش زار و سترگ
(but) when each is born (into the next world) he (the seer) sees that each is miserable or glorious

جمله را چون روز رستاخیز من
I am seeing them all plainly and with ocular vision
فاش میبینم عیان از مرد و زن
as (they shall be) on the Day of Resurrection, men and women

هین بگویم یا فرو بندم نفس
Hark, shall I tell or shall I stop my breath (keep silence)?"
لب گزیدش مصطفی یعنی که بس
Mustafá (Mohammed) bit his (Zayd's) lip, as though to say, "Enough!

یا رسول الله بگویم سر حشر
O Messenger of Allah, shall I tell the mystery of the Gathering (on the Day of Judgement),
در جهان پیدا کنم امروز نشر
shall I make the Resurrection manifest in the world to-day?

هل مرا تا پردهها را بر درم
Let me be, that I may rend the curtains asunder
تا چو خورشیدی بتابد گوهرم
that my (spiritual) substance may shine forth like a sun;

تا کسوف آید ز من خورشید را
That the sun may be eclipsed by me, that I may show
تا نمایم نخل را و بید را
the (fruitful) date-palm and the (barren) willow

وا نمایم راز رستاخیز را
I will show forth the mystery of Resurrection
نقد را و نقد قلبآمیز را
the sterling coin and the coin mixed with alloy,

دستها ببریده اصحاب شمال
The people of the left with their hands cut off
وا نمایم رنگ کفر و رنگ آل
I will show forth the colour of infidelity and the colour of the (Prophet's) folk.

واگشایم هفت سوراخ نفاق
I will lay bare the seven rifts (sins) of hypocrisy
در ضیای ماه بی خسف و محاق
in the light of the moon that suffers no eclipse or waning.

وا نمایم من پلاس اشقیا
I will display the woollen frocks of the damned
بشنوانم طبل و کوس انبیا
I will cause the drums and kettledrums of the prophets to be heard.

دوزخ و جنات و برزخ در میان
Hell and the Gardens (of Paradise) and the intermediate
پیش چشم کافران آرم عیان
state I will bring clearly before the eyes of the infidels.

وا نمایم حوض کوثر را به جوش
I will display the pond of Kawthar heaving (with waves),
کاب بر روشان زند بانگش به گوش
which dashes water on their (the blessed ones') faces, (while) its sound (rings) in their ears;

وان کسان که تشنه بر گردش دوان
And those who have been made to run athirst round it
گشته‌اند این دم نمایم من عیان
I will show clearly at this moment.

می‌بساید دوششان بر دوش من
Their shoulders are rubbing against my shoulder,
نعره‌هاشان می‌رسد در گوش من
their cries are piercing my ears.

اهل جنت پیش چشمم ز اختیار
Before my eyes the people of Paradise,
در کشیده یک‌دگر را در کنار
from free choice, clasp each other to their bosoms,

دست همدیگر زیارت می‌کنند
Visiting one another's high places of honour
از لبان هم بوسه غارت می‌کنند
and snatching kisses from the lips (of the houris).

کر شد این گوشم ز بانگ آه آه
This ear of mine has become deafened by the cries of 'Alas
از خسان و نعرهٔ واحسرتاه
Alas!' (uttered) by the vile wretches (in Hell) and by the screams of 'O sorrow!

این اشارتهاست گویم از نغول
These are (only) hints. I would speak from the depth (of my knowledge)
لیک می‌ترسم ز آزار رسول
but I fear to offend the Messenger (of Allah)."

همچنین می‌گفت سرمست و خراب
He was speaking in this wise, intoxicated and distraught:
داد پیغامبر گریبانش بتاب
the Prophet twitched his collar

گفت هین در کش که اسبت گرم شد
And said, "Beware! Draw (rein), for thy horse has become hot.
عکس حق لا یستحی زد شرم شد
the reflexion of God is not ashamed (to speak the truth) strikes (on the heart), shame is gone.

آینهٔ تو جست بیرون از غلاف
Thy mirror has shot out of the case:
آینه و میزان کجا گوید خلاف
how shall mirror and balance speak falsehood?

آینه و میزان کجا بندد نفس
How shall mirror and balance stop their breath
بهر آزار و حیاء هیچ کس
for fear of hurting and shaming any one?

آینه و میزان محکهای سنی
Mirror and balance are noble touchstones:
گر دو صد سالش تو خدمتها کنی
if thou do service (sue) to them for two hundred years

کز برای من بپوشان راستی
Saying, 'Conceal the truth for my sake,
بر فزون بنما و منما کاستی
display the surplus and do not display the deficiency,'

اوت گوید ریش و سبلت بر مخند
They will say to thee, 'Do not laugh at thy beard and moustache:
آینه و میزان و آنگه ریو و پند
mirror and balance, and then deceit and (hypocritical) advice!

چون خدا ما را برای آن فراخت
Since God has raised us up in order that
که بما بتوان حقیقت را شناخت
by means of us it may be possible to know the truth,

440

این نباشد ما چه ارزیم ای جوان

If this do not happen (if we fail to display the truth), what worth have we,

کی شویم آیین روی نیکوان

O young man? How shall we become a standard for the face of the fair?'

لیک در کش در نمد آیینه را

But (said the Prophet) slip the mirror (back) into the cloth,

کز تجلی کرد سینا سینه را

if (Divine) illumination has made thy breast a Sinai."

گفت آخر هیچ گنجد در بغل

Eternity be contained any wise under the armpit?

آفتاب حق و خورشید ازل

He (Zayd) said, "Why, shall the Sun of the Truth and the Sun of

هم دغل را هم بغل را بر درد

It bursts asunder both imposture (daghal) and armpit (baghal)

نه جنون ماند به پیشش نه خرد

in its presence neither madness nor (soundness of) understanding remains."

گفت یک اصبع چو بر چشمی نهی

He (the Prophet) said, "When thou layest one finger on an eye

بیند از خورشید عالم را تهی

thou seest the world empty of the sun.

یک سر انگشت پردهٔ ماه شد

One finger-tip becomes a veil over the moon

وین نشان ساتری شاه شد

and this is a symbol of the King's covering

تا بپوشاند جهان را نقطه‌ای

So that the (whole) world may be covered (hidden from view) by a single point,

مهر گردد منکسف از سقطه‌ای

and the sun be eclipsed by a splinter.

لب ببند و غور دریایی نگر

Close thy lips and gaze on the depth of the sea (within thee)

بحر را حق کرد محکوم بشر

God made the sea subject to man

همچو چشمهٔ سلسبیل و زنجبیل

Even as the fountains of Salsabíl and Zanjabíl

هست در حکم بهشتی جلیل

are under the control of the exalted ones of Paradise.

چار جوی جنت اندر حکم ماست
The four rivers of Paradise are under our control;
این نه زور ما ز فرمان خداست
this is not (by) our might, 'tis (by) the command of God

هر کجا خواهیم داریمش روان
We keep them flowing wheresoever we will,
همچو سحر اندر مراد ساحران
like magic (which takes its course) according to the

همچو این دو چشمهٔ چشم روان
Just as these two flowing eye-fountains (the two eyes)
هست در حکم دل و فرمان جان
are under the control of the heart and subject to the command of the spirit.

گر بخواهد رفت سوی زهر و مار
If it (the heart) will, they turn towards poison and the snake
ور بخواهد رفت سوی اعتبار
and if it will, they turn to (edifying) consideration.

گر بخواهد سوی محسوسات رفت
If it will, they turn to sensuous things, and if it will,
ور بخواهد سوی ملبوسات رفت
they turn to things clothed (in the forms of thought and phantasy)

گر بخواهد سوی کلیات راند
If it will, they advance towards universals,
ور بخواهد حبس جزویات ماند
and if it will, they remain in bondage to particulars.

همچنین هر پنج حس چون نایزه
Similarly all the five senses are passing
بر مراد و امر دل شد جایزه
according to the will and command of the heart, like the spout.

هر طرف که دل اشارت کردشان
(sweeping along) in whatever direction the heart indicates to them.
می‌رود هر پنج حس دامن‌کشان
All the five senses are moving and trailing their skirts

دست و پا در امر دل اندر ملا
Hand and foot are plainly under command of the heart,
همچو اندر دست موسی آن عصا
like the staff in the hand of Moses.

دل بخواهد پا در آید زو به رقص
If the heart will, at once the foot begins to dance
یا گریزد سوی افزونی ز نقص
or flees from defect towards increase.

دل بخواهد دست آید در حساب
If the heart will, the hand comes to terms
با اصابع تا نویسد او کتاب
with the fingers to write a book

دست در دست نهانی مانده است
The hand remains in (the grasp of) a hidden hand:
او درون تن را برون بنشانده است
it (the hidden hand) within has set the body outside (as its instrument).

گر بخواهد بر عدو ماری شود
If it (the hidden hand) will, it (the external hand) becomes a snake to the enemy;
ور بخواهد بر ولی یاری شود
and if it will, it becomes a helper to the friend;

ور بخواهد کفچه‌ای در خوردنی
And if it will, a spoon in food;
ور بخواهد همچو گرز ده‌منی
and if it will, a mace weighing ten maunds.

دل چه می‌گوید بدیشان ای عجب
I wonder what the heart is saying to them (the members of the body).
طرفه وصلت طرفه پنهانی سبب
'Tis a marvelous connexion, a marvellous hidden link

دل مگر مهر سلیمان یافتست
Surely the heart has gotten the seal of Solomon
که مهار پنج حس بر تافتست
so that it has pulled the reins of (exerted control over) the five senses

پنج حسی از برون میسور او
Five external senses are easy for it to manage,
پنج حسی از درون مامور او
five internal senses (faculties) are under its command.

ده حس است و هفت اندام و دگر
There are ten senses and seven limbs (of the body) et cetera
آنچه اندر گفت ناید می شمر
count over (to yourself) what is not mentioned (here)

443

چون سلیمانی دلا در مهتری
O heart, since thou art a Solomon in empire,
بر پری و دیو زن انگشتری
cast thy seal-ring (powerful spell) upon peri and demon.

گر درین ملکت بری باشی ز ریو
If in this kingdom thou art free from deceit,
خاتم از دست تو نستاند سه دیو
the three demons will not take the seal outmof thy hand;

بعد از آن عالم بگیرد اسم تو
After that, thy name will conquer the world
دو جهان محکوم تو چون جسم تو
the two worlds (will be) ruled by thee like thy body.

ور ز دستت دیو خاتم را ببرد
And if the demon take the seal off thy hand
پادشاهی فوت شد بختت بمرد
thy kingdom is past, thy fortune is dead;

بعد از آن یا حسرتا شد یا عباد
After that, O servants (of God), "O sorrow!
بر شما محتوم تا یوم التناد
is your inevitable doom till the day when ye are gathered together (for Judgement)

مکر خود را گر تو انکار آوری
And if thou art denying thy deceit,
از ترازو و آینه کی جان بری
how wilt thou save thy soul from the scales and the mirror?

❖◉❖◉❖

متهم کردن غلامان و خواجه‌تاشان مر لقمان را
How suspicion was thrown upon Luqmán by the slaves and fellow-servants

کی آن میوه‌های ترونده را که می‌آوردیم او خورده است
who said that he had eaten the fresh fruit which they were bringing (to their master).

بود لقمان پیش خواجهٔ خویشتن
In the eyes of his master, amongst (in comparison with) the (other) slaves

در میان بندگانش خوارتن
Luqmán was despicable on account of his body (outward aspect).

می‌فرستاد او غلامان را به باغ
He (the master) used to send the slaves to the garden

تا که میوه آیدش بهر فراغ
that fruit might come (be brought to him) for his pleasure.

بود لقمان در غلامان چون طفیل
Amongst the slaves Luqmán was (despised) like a parasite;

پر معانی تیره‌صورت همچو لیل
(he was) full of (spiritual) ideas, dark-complexioned as night.

آن غلامان میوه‌های جمع را
Those slaves, being impelled by greed

خوش بخوردند از نهیب طمع را
ate the whole of the fruit with enjoyment,

خواجه را گفتند لقمان خورد آن
And told their master that Luqmán had eaten it

خواجه بر لقمان ترش گشت و گران
(whereupon) the master became bitter and sorely displeased with Luqmán.

چون تفحص کرد لقمان از سبب
When Luqmán inquired (and ascertained) the cause (of this)

در عتاب خواجه‌اش بگشاد لب
he opened his lips to reproach his master

گفت لقمان سیدا پیش خدا
O sire," said Luqmán, "an unfaithful servant

بندهٔ خاین نباشد مرتضی
is not approved in the sight of God

امتحان کن جمله مان را ای کریم
Put us all to the test, O noble sir:

سیرمان در ده تو از آب حمیم
give us our fill of hot water (to drink),

بعد از آن ما را به صحرایی کلان
And afterwards make us run into a great plain
تو سواره ما پیاده می‌دوان
thou being mounted and we on foot

آنگهان بنگر تو بدکردار را
Then behold the evil-doer, (behold) the things
صنعهای کاشف الاسرار را
that are done by Him who revealeth mysteries!"

گشت ساقی خواجه از آب حمیم
The master gave the servants hot water to drink,
مر غلامان را و خوردند آن ز بیم
and they drank it in fear (of him).

بعد از آن می‌راندشان در دشتها
Afterwards he was driving them into the plains
می‌دویدند آن نفر تحت و علا
and those persons were running up and down.

قی در افتادند ایشان از عنا
From distress they began to vomit
آب می‌آورد زیشان میوه‌ها
the (hot) water was bringing up the fruit from them.

چون که لقمان را در آمد قی ز ناف
When Luqmán began to vomit from his navel (belly),
می بر آمد از درونش آب صاف
there was coming up from within him (only) the pure water.

حکمت لقمان چو داند این نمود
Inasmuch as Luqmán's wisdom can show forth this
پس چه باشد حکمت رب الوجود
then what must be the wisdom of the Lord of existence

یوم تبلی والسرائر کلها
On the day when all the inmost thoughts shall be searched out
بان منکم کامن لا یشتهی
there will appear from you something latent, (the appearance of) which is not desired.

چون سقوا ماء حمیما قطعت
When they shall be given hot water to drink
جملة الاستار مما افضعت
all the veils will be cut asunder (torn off) from that which is abhorred

نار زان آمد عذاب کافران
The fire (of Hell) is made the torment of the infidels because
که حجر را نار باشد امتحان
fire is the (proper) test for stones.

آن دل چون سنگ را ما چند چند
How oft, how oft, have we spoken gently to our stony hearts
نرم گفتیم و نمی‌پذرفت پند
and they would not accept the counsel

ریش بد را داروی بد یافت رگ
For a bad wound the vein gets (requires) a bad (severe) remedy
مر سر خر را سر دندان سگ
the teeth of the dog are suitable for the donkey's head

الخبیثات الخبیثین حکمتست
The wicked women to the wicked men is wisdom
زشت را هم زشت جفت و بابتست
the ugly is the mate and fitting (consort) for the ugly.

پس تو هر جفتی که می‌خواهی برو
Whatever, then, you wish to mate with, go
محو و هم‌شکل و صفات او بشو
become absorbed by it, and assume its shape and qualities

نور خواهی مستعد نور شو
If you wish for the light, make yourself ready to receive the light
دور خواهی خویش‌بین و دور شو
if you wish to be far (from God), become self-conceited and far;

ور رهی خواهی ازین سجن خرب
And if you wish (to find) a way out of this ruined prison,
سر مکش از دوست و اسجد واقترب
do not turn your head away from the Beloved, but bow in worship and draw nigh

بقیهٔ قصه زید در جواب رسول صلی الله علیه و سلم
The remainder of the story of Zayd (and what he said) in answer to the Prophet, on whom be peace.

این سخن پایان ندارد خیز زید
This discourse hath no end. "Arise, O Zayd,

بر براق ناطقه بر بند قید
and tie a shackle on the Buráq (steed) of thy rational spirit.

ناطقه چون فاضح آمد عیب را
Since the rational spirit exposes faults

می‌دراند پرده‌های غیب را
it is rending the curtains of concealment.

غیب مطلوب حق آمد چند گا
Concealment is desired by God for awhile

این دهل زن را بر آن بر بند راه
Drive away this drummer, bar the road!

تگ مران درکش عنان مستور به
Do not gallop, draw rein, 'tis better it (the mystery) should be veiled;

هر کس از پندار خود مسرور به
tis better that everyone should be gladdened by his own fancy

حق همی‌خواهد که نومیدان او
God is wishing that even His despairing

زین عبادت هم نگردانند رو
ones should not avert their faces (refrain) from this worship (of Him).

هم باومیدی مشرف می‌شوند
Even on the ground of a hope they become ennobled:

چند روزی در رکابش می‌دوند
for a few days (a short time) they are running at its stirrup (following Divine worship).

خواهد آن رحمت بتابد بر همه
He wishes that that mercy should shine upon all,

بر بد و نیک از عموم مرحمه
on the evil and the good, because of the universality of His mercy.

حق همی‌خواهد که هر میر و اسیر
God is wishing that every prince and captive

با رجا و خوف باشند و حذیر
should be hopeful and fearful and afraid.

این رجا و خوف در پرده بود
This hope and fear are in the veil (separating the seen from the unseen),
تا پس این پرده پرورده شود
that they may be fostered behind this veil.

چون دریدی پرده کو خوف و رجا
When thou hast rent the veil, where are fear and hope?
غیب را شد کر و فری بر ملا
The might and majesty belonging to the Unseen are divulged."

بر لب جو برد ظنی یک فتی
A young man on the bank of a river thought (to himself),
که سلیمانست ماهی‌گیر ما
Our fisherman (here) is Solomon.

گر ویست این از چه فردست و خفیست
(But) if this is he, why is he alone and disguised
ورنه سیمای سلیمانیش چیست
And if not, why has he the aspect of Solomon?"

اندرین اندیشه می‌بود او دو دل
Thus thinking, he remained in two minds
تا سلیمان گشت شاه و مستقل
until Solomon (once more) became king and absolute ruler.

دیو رفت از ملک و تخت او گریخت
The demon departed and fled from his (Solomon's) kingdom and throne
تیغ بختش خون آن شیطان بریخت
the sword of his fortune shed that devil's blood.

کرد در انگشت خود انگشتری
He put the ring upon his finger
جمع آمد لشکر دیو و پری
the hosts of demons and peris assembled.

آمدند از بهر نظاره رجال
The men came to look, amongst them
در میانشان آنک بد صاحب خیال
he who had the fancy (that the fisherman was Solomon in

چون در انگشتش بدید انگشتری
When he saw the ring on his finger,
رفت اندیشه و گمانش یکسری
his perplexity and doubt vanished all at once

وهم آنگاهست کان پوشیده است
Imagination occurs (only) at the time when that (object of desire) is hidden
این تحری از پی نادیده است
this searching is after the unseen.

شد خیال غایب اندر سینه زفت
Whilst he was absent, fancy waxed strong in his breast:
چونک حاضر شد خیال او برفت
as soon as he was present, his fancy departed.

گر سمای نور بی باریده نیست
If the radiant sky is not without rain
هم زمین تار بی بالیده نیست
neither is the dark earth without vegetation.

یومنون بالغیب می‌باید مرا
(God said), "I want (what is signified by the words) they believe in the unseen:
زان ببستم روزن فانی سرا
on that account I have shut the window of the fleeting world

چون شکافم آسمان را در ظهور
When (if) I cleave the sky manifestly, how should I say
چون بگویم هل تری فیها فطور
'Dost thou see any clefts therein?'"

تا درین ظلمت تحری گسترند
In order that in this darkness they may spread (the carpet of) endeavour,
هر کسی رو جانبی می‌آورند
they are turning, every one, their faces in some direction

مدتی معکوس باشد کارها
For a while things are reversed
شحنه را دزد آورد بر دارها
the thief brings the magistrate to the gallows

تا که بس سلطان و عالی‌همتی
So that many a sultan and man of lofty spirit
بندهٔ بندهٔ خود آید مدتی
becomes the slave of his own slave for a while.

بندگی در غیب آید خوب و گش
Service (performed) in absence (through faith in the unseen) is fair and comely; when service is demanded (by God from us),
حفظ غیب آید در استعباد خوش
tis pleasing (to Him) that the absent should be remembered

کو که مدح شاه گوید پیش او
Where (in what position) is one that praises the king in his presence,
تا که در غیبت بود او شرم‌رو
compared with one that is shamefaced in absence (from him)?

قلعه‌داری کز کنار مملکت
The governor of a fortress who, on the border of the kingdom
دور از سلطان و سایهٔ سلطنت
far from the sultan and the shadow (protection) of the sultanate

پاس دارد قلعه را از دشمنان
Guards the fortress from enemies
قلعه نفروشد به مالی بی‌کران
and will not sell it for boundless riches,

غایب از شه در کنار ثغرها
Who, though absent from the king on the outskirt of the frontiers
همچو حاضر او نگه دارد وفا
keeps faith (with him) like one who is present

پیش شه او به بود از دیگران
He in the king's sight is better than the rest who are serving
که به خدمت حاضرند و جان‌فشان
in his presence and ready to devote their lives.

پس بغیبت نیم ذره حفظ کار
Therefore, half an atom of regard to one's duty in absence
به که اندر حاضری زان صد هزار
is better than a hundred thousand fold observance thereof in presence.

طاعت و ایمان کنون محمود شد
Obedience (to God) and faith are praiseworthy now;
بعد مرگ اندر عیان مردود شد
after death, when all is plainly shown, they will be spurned

چونک غیب و غایب و روپوش به
Inasmuch as the unseen and the absent and the veil are better
پس لبان بر بند و لب خاموش به
close thy lips, and the lip is better silent.

ای برادر دست و دار از سخن
O brother, refrain from speech
خود خدا پیدا کند علم لدن
God himself will make manifest the knowledge that is with Him

پس بود خورشید را رویش گواه
Witness enough for the sun is its face
ای شیء اعظم الشاهد اله
what thing is the greatest witness (of all)? God.

نه بگویم چون قرین شد در بیان
of learning are allied in setting forth
هم خدا و هم ملک هم عالمان
Nay, speak I will, since both God and the angels and the men

یشهد الله و الملک و اهل العلوم
God and the angels and those learned in the sciences
انه لا رب الا من یدوم
bear witness that there is no Lord except Him who endureth forever.

چون گواهی داد حق کی بود ملک
Since God hath given testimony, who are the angels
تا شود اندر گواهی مشترک
that they should be associated in the testimony?

زانک شعشاع و حضور آفتاب
the radiance and presence of the Sun,
بر نتابد چشم و دلهای خراب
because unsound (weak) eyes and hearts cannot support

چون خفاشی کو تف خورشید را
Like a bat, which cannot bear
بر نتابد بسکلد اومید را
the glow of the sun and abandons hope.

پس ملایک را چو ما هم یار دان
Know, then, that the angels, as we also, are helpers
جلوه‌گر خورشید را بر آسمان
(co-witnesses) displayers of the sun in heaven

کین ضیا ما ز آفتابی یافتیم
Who say, "We have derived (our) light from a Sun,
چون خلیفه بر ضعیفان تافتیم
we have shone upon the weak, like vicegerents

چون مه نو یا سه روزه یا که بدر
Like the new moon or the moon three days old or the full moon,
هر ملک دارد کمال و نور و قدر
every angel has (a particular) perfection and light and (spiritual) worth.

ز اجنحهٔ نور ثلاث او رباع
Every angel, according to their (different) degrees,
بر مراتب هر ملک را آن شعاع
has (a portion of) that radiance, consisting of three or four (pairs of) luminous wings,

همچو پرهای عقول انسیان
Just as the wings of human intellects
که بسی فرقستشان اندر میان
amongst which there is great difference (in quality).

پس قرین هر بشر در نیک و بد
Hence the associate of every human being in good and evil
آن ملک باشد که مانندش بود
is that angel who resembles him or her.

چشم اعمش چونک خور را بر نتافت
Since the eye of the dim-sighted man could not bear the sunlight
اختر او را شمع شد تا ره بیافت
the star became a candle to him, that he might find the way

❖ ◉ ❖ ◉ ❖

گفتن پیغامبر صلی الله علیه و سلم مر زید را
How the Prophet, on whom be peace, said to Zayd,

کی این سر را فاش‌تر ازین مگو و متابعت نگهدار
"Do not tell this mystery more plainly than this, and take care to comply (with the religious law

گفت پیغامبر که اصحابی نجوم
The Prophet said, "My Companions are (like) the stars
رهروان را شمع و شیطان را رجوم
a candle to travellers (on the Way), and meteors to be cast at the devils.

هر کسی را گر بدی آن چشم و زور
If everyone had the eye and the strength
کو گرفتی ز آفتاب چرخ نور
to receive light from the sun of heaven,

کی ستاره حاجتستی ای ذلیل
O base man, how would the star be needed to
که بدی بر نور خورشید او دلیل
demonstrate the (existence of) sunlight?

453

ماه می‌گوید به خاک و ابر و فی
The Moon (the Prophet) is saying to earth and cloud and shadow,
من بشر بودم ولی یوحی الی
I was a man, but it is revealed to me (that your God is one God)

چون شما تاریک بودم در نهاد
Like you, I was dark in my nature:
وحی خورشیدم چنین نوری بداد
the Sun's revelation gave me such a light as this

ظلمتی دارم به نسبت با شموس
I have a certain darkness in comparison with the (spiritual) suns
نور دارم بهر ظلمات نفوس
(but) I have light for the darknesses of (human) souls.

زان ضعیفم تا تو تابی آوری
I am faint (less bright than the Sun) in order that thou mayst be able to bear (my beams)
که نه مرد آفتاب انوری
, for thou art not the man for (a man who can bear) the most radiant Sun

همچو شهد و سرکه در هم بافتم
I was woven (mingled) together, like honey and vinegar
تا سوی رنج جگر ره یافتم
I might find the way to (cure) sickness of heart.

چون ز علت وا رهیدی ای رهین
Since thou hast recovered from thine illness,
سرکه را بگذار و می‌خور انگبین
O thou (that wert) in thrall (to it), leave the vinegar and continue to eat the honey.

تخت دل معمور شد پاک از هوا
(If) the throne of the heart has become restored to soundness and purged of sensuality,
بین که الرحمن علی العرش استوی
behold how the Merciful God is seated on His Throne.

حکم بر دل بعد ازین بی واسطه
After this, God controls the heart without intermediary,
حق کند چون یافت دل این رابطه
since the heart has attained to this relation

این سخن پایان ندارد زید کو
This discourse hath no end. Where is Zayd
تا دهم پندش که رسوایی مجو
that I may counsel him not to seek notoriety?

رجوع به حکایت زید
The (author's) return to the story of Zayd.

زید را اکنون نیابی کو گریخت
You will not find Zayd now, for he has fled:

جست از صف نعال و نعل ریخت
he has darted away from the shoe-row and dropped his shoes.

تو که باشی زید هم خود را نیافت
Who are you (that you should hope to find him)?

همچو اختر که برو خورشید تافت
Zayd cannot even find himself, (he has vanished) like the star on which the sun shone

نه ازو نقشی بیابی نه نشان
You will find neither mark nor trace of him,

نه کهی یابی به راه کهکشان
you will not find a straw (star) in the straw-strewn Way (the Milky Way)

شد حواس و نطق بابایان ما
Our senses and finite speech (reason) are obliterated

محو نور دانش سلطان ما
in the light of the knowledge of our (Divine) King.

حسها و عقلهاشان در درون
Their (the God-intoxicated mystics') senses and understandings within (them) are (tossed)

موج در موج لدینا محضرون
wave on wave, in (the sea of) they are assembled before Us.

چون بیاید صبح وقت بار شد
When dawn comes, 'tis again the time of (bearing) the burden:

آن چهم پنهان شده بر کار شد
the stars, which had become hidden, go (again) to work

بیهشان را وا دهد حق هوشها
God gives back to the senseless ones their (lost) senses:

حلقه حلقه حلقه‌ها در گوشها
(they return to consciousness) troop after troop, with rings (of mystic knowledge) in their ears,

پای‌کوبان دست‌افشان در ثنا
Dancing, waving their hands in praise (of God),

ناز نازان ربنا احییتنا
triumphing (and crying), "O Lord, Thou hast brought us to life."

آن جلود و آن عظام ریخته
Those crumbled skins and bones have become

فارسان گشته غبار انگیخته
(like) horsemen and have raised the dust:

حمله آرند از عدم سوی وجود
rush along from non-existence towards existence.

در قیامت هم شکور و هم کنود
At Resurrection both the thankful and the ungrateful

سر چه می‌پیچی کنی نادیده‌ای
Why do you turn away your head and pretend not to see? Did you not turn away your head at first,

در عدم ز اول نه سر پیچیده‌ای
Did you not turn away your head at first, in non-existence

در عدم افشرده بودی پای خویش
You had planted your foot (firmly) in non-existence, saying

که مرا کی بر کند از جای خویش
"Who will uproot me from my place?

می‌نبینی صنع ربانیت را
Are not you beholding the action of your Lord,

که کشید او موی پیشانیت را
who dragged you (into existence) by the forelock,

تا کشیدت اندرین انواع حال
Until He drew you into (all) these various states (of being)

که نبودت در گمان و در خیال
which were not in your thought or fancy?

آن عدم او را همواره بنده است
That non-existence is always His slave:

کار کن دیوا سلیمان زنده است
work (in His service), O demon! Solomon is living.

دیو می‌سازد جفان کالجواب
The demon is making large bowls like watering-troughs:

زهره نه تا دفع گوید یا جواب
he dare not say a word in refusal or in retort

خویش را بین چون همی لرزی ز بیم
Look at yourself, how you are trembling with fear (of non-existence):

مر عدم را نیز لرزان دان مقیم
know that nonexistence also is constantly trembling (lest God should bring it into existence).

ور تو دست اندر مناصب می‌زنی
And if you are grasping at (worldly) dignities

هم ز ترس است آن که جانی می‌کنی
'tis from fear too that you are suffering agony of spirit.

هرچه جز عشق خدای احسنست
Except love of the most beauteous God everything,
گر شکرخواریست آن جان کندنست
though (outwardly) it is (pleasant like) eating sugar, is (in truth) agony of spirit.

چیست جان کندن سوی مرگ آمدن
What is agony of spirit? To advance towards death
دست در آب حیاتی نازدن
and not grasp the Water of Life.

خلق را دو دیده در خاک و ممات
People fix both their eyes on earth and death:
صد گمان دارند در آب حیات
they have a hundred doubts concerning the Water of Life.

جهد کن تا صد گمان گردد نود
Strive that the hundred doubts may become ninety (may decrease)
شب برو ور تو بخسپی شب رود
go (towards God) in the night (of this world), for if you slumber, the night will go (from you).

در شب تاریک جوی آن روز را
In the dark night seek that (shining) Day:
پیش کن آن عقل ظلمت سوز را
put in front (follow) the darkness consuming Reason

در شب بدرنگ بس نیکی بود
In the evil-coloured night there is much good
آب حیوان جفت تاریکی بود
the Water of Life is the mate of darkness.

سر ز خفتن کی توان برداشتن
How is it possible to lift up the head from slumber
با چنین صد تخم غفلت کاشتن
whilst you are sowing a hundred such seeds of slothfulness?

خواب مرده لقمه مرده یار شد
Slumber is dead (unlawful) food is dead they are friends
خواجه خفت و دزد شب بر کار شد
the merchant fell asleep and the night-thief got to work

تو نمی‌دانی که خصمانت کیند
Do you not know who your enemies are?
ناریان خصم وجود خاکیند
Those made of fire are enemies to the existence of those made of earth.

نار خصم آب و فرزندان اوست
Fire is the enemy of water and its children
همچنانک آب خصم جان اوست
even as water is an enemy to the life of fire.

آب آتش را کشد زیرا که او
Water kills fire because
خصم فرزندان آبست و عدو
the enemy and foe of the children of water.

بعد از آن این نار نار شهوتست
To proceed, this fire is the fire of lust
کاندرو اصل گناه و زلتست
The external fire may be quenched by some water,

نار بیرونی به آبی بفسرد
(but) the fire of lust is bringing (you) to Hell.
نار شهوت تا به دوزخ می‌برد
The fire of lust is not allayed by water

نار شهوت می‌نیارامد به آب
The fire of lust is not allayed by water
زانک دارد طبع دوزخ در عذاب
because it has the (insatiable) nature of Hell in respect of (inflicting) torment.

نار شهوت را چه چاره نور دین
What is the remedy for the fire of lust? The light of the Religion:
نورکم اطفاء نار الکافرین
your (the Moslems') light is the (means of) extinguishing the fire of the infidels.

چه کشد این نار را نور خدا
What kills this fire? The Light of God.
نور ابراهیم را ساز اوستا
Make the light of Abraham your teacher

تا ز نار نفس چون نمرود تو
That this body of yours, which resembles wood (faggots),
وا رهد این جسم همچون عود تو
may be delivered from the fire of the Nimrod-like flesh (nafs).

شهوت ناری براندن کم نشد
Fiery lust is not diminished by indulging it: it is diminished,
او بماندن کم شود بی هیچ بد
without any escape (inevitably), by leaving it (ungratified).

تا که هیزم می‌نهی بر آتشی
So long as thou art laying faggots on a fire,
کی بمیرد آتش از هیزم‌کشی
how will the fire be extinguished by a carrier of faggots?

چونک هیزم بازگیری نار مرد
When thou withholdest the faggots, the fire dies out
زانک تقوی آب سوی نار برد
because fear of God carries (as it were) water to the fire.

کی سیه گردد ز آتش روی خوب
How should the fire blacken the beauteous face
کو نهد گلگونه از تقوی القلوب
which lays (on itself) rose colour (derived) from the fear of God that is in (men's) hearts?

❖❖❖

آتش افتادن در شهر بایام عمر رضی الله عنه
How a conflagration occurred in the city (Medina) in the days of 'Umar, may God be well-pleased with him.

آتشی افتاد در عهد عمر
A conflagration occurred in the time of 'Umar
همچو چوب خشک می‌خورد او حجر
it was devouring stones as though they were dry wood

در فتاد اندر بنا و خانه‌ها
It fell upon buildings and houses
تا زد اندر پر مرغ و لانه‌ها
until (at last) it darted at the wings and nests of birds.

نیم شهر از شعله‌ها آتش گرفت
Half the city caught fire from the flames:
آب می‌ترسید از آن و می‌شکفت
water was afraid of it (the fire) and amazed.

مشکهای آب و سرکه می‌زدند
throwing skins of water and vinegar on the fire
بر سر آتش کسان هوشمند
Some intelligent persons were

آتش از استیزه افزون می‌شدی
(But) out of spite (obstinacy) the fire was increasing
می‌رسید او را مدد از بی حدی
aid was coming to it from One who is infinite.

خلق آمد جانب عمر شتاب
The people came in haste to 'Umar, saying,
کآتش ما می‌نمیرد هیچ از آب
"Our fire will not be quenched at all by water."

گفت آن آتش ز آیات خداست
He said, "That fire is one of God's signs
شعله‌ای از آتش بخل شماست
'tis a flame from the fire of your avarice.

آب و سرکه چیست نان قسمت کنید
What are water and vinegar? Deal out bread (in charity)
بخل بگذارید اگر آل منید
discard avarice if ye are my people (followers).

خلق گفتندش که در بگشوده‌ایم
The folk said to him, "We have opened our doors
ما سخی و اهل فتوت بوده‌ایم
we have been bountiful and devoted to generosity.

گفت نان در رسم و عادت داده‌اید
He replied, "Ye have given bread by rule and habit,
دست از بهر خدا نگشاده‌اید
ye have not opened your hands for the sake of God

بهر فخر و بهر بوش و بهر ناز
(Only) for glory and for ostentation and for pride,
نه از برای ترس و تقوی و نیاز
not because of fear and piety and supplication."

مال تخمست و بهر شوره منه
Wealth is seed, and do not lay it in every salty ground:
تیغ را در دست هر رهزن مده
do not put a sword in the hand of every highwayman.

اهل دین را باز دان از اهل کین
Distinguish the friends of the Religion (ahl-i Dín) from the enemies of God (ahl-i kín)
همنشین حق بجو با او نشین
seek the man that sits with God, and sit with him.

هر کسی بر قوم خود ایثار کرد
Every one shows favour to his own folk:
کاغه پندارد که او خود کار کرد
the fool (who shows favour to the foolish) thinks he has really done (good and religious) work.

خدو انداختن خصم در روی امیر المؤمنین علی کرم الله وجهه
How an enemy spat in the face of the Prince of the Faithful, Alí, may God honour his person,

و انداختن امیرالمؤمنین علی شمشیر از دست
and how Alí dropped the sword from his hand.

از علی آموز اخلاص عمل
Learn how to act sincerely from 'Alí

شیر حق را دان مطهر از دغل
know that the Lion of God ('Alí) was purged of (all) deceit.

در غزا بر پهلوانی دست یافت
In fighting against the infidels he got the upper hand of (vanquished) a certain knight,

زود شمشیری بر آورد و شتافت
and quickly drew a sword and made haste (to slay him).

او خدو انداخت در روی علی
He spat on the face of 'Alí,

افتخار هر نبی و هر ولی
the pride of every prophet and every saint;

آن خدو زد بر رخی که روی ماه
He spat on the countenance before which the face of the moon

سجده آرد پیش او در سجده‌گاه
bows low in the place of worship.

در زمان انداخت شمشیر آن علی
Alí at once threw his sword away

کرد او اندر غزااش کاهلی
and relaxed (his efforts) in fighting him.

گشت حیران آن مبارز زین عمل
That champion was astounded by this act

وز نمودن عفو و رحمت بی‌محل
And by his showing forgiveness and mercy without occasion

گفت بر من تیغ تیز افراشتی
He said, "You lifted your keen sword against me

از چه افکندی مرا بگذاشتی
why have you flung it aside and spared me?

آن چه دیدی بهتر از پیکار من
What did you see that was better than combat with me,

تا شدی تو سست در اشکار من
so that you have become slack in hunting me down?

آن چه دیدی که چنین خشمت نشست
What did you see, so that such anger as yours abated,
تا چنان برق نمود و باز جست
and so that such a lightning flashed and (then) recoiled?

آن چه دیدی که مرا زان عکس دید
What did you see, that from the reflexion of that vision
در دل و جان شعله‌ای آمد پدید
(of thine) a flame appeared in my heart and soul?

آن چه دیدی برتر از کون و مکان
What did you see, beyond (material) existence and space,
که به از جان بود و بخشیدیم جان
that was better than life? and (so) you gave me life

در شجاعت شیر ربانیستی
In bravery you are the Lion of the Lord
در مروت خود کی داند کیستی
in generosity who indeed knows who (what) you are?

در مروت ابر موسی بتیه
In generosity you are (like) Moses' cloud in the desert
کآمد از وی خوان و نان بی‌شبیه
whence came the dishes of food and bread incomparable."

ابرها گندم دهد کان را بجهد
The clouds give wheat which man with toil
پخته و شیرین کند مردم چو شهد
makes cooked (easy to digest) and sweet as honey.

ابر موسی پر رحمت بر گشاد
Moses' cloud spread the wings of mercy and gave
پخته و شیرین بی زحمت بداد
cooked and sweet food that was (ready to be eaten) without trouble.

از برای پخته‌خواران کرم
For the sake of those (beggars) who partook of its bounty,
رحمتش افراخت در عالم علم
its (the cloud's) mercy raised a banner (displayed itself) in the world.

تا چهل سال آن وظیفه و آن عطا
During forty years that ration and largesse
کم نشد یک روز زان اهل رجا
did not fail the hopeful people (of Israel) for a single day,

تا هم ایشان از خسیسی خاستند
Until they too, because of their vileness,
گندنا و تره و خس خواستند
arose and demanded leeks and green herbs and lettuce

امت احمد که هستید از کرام
O people of Ahmad (Mohammed), who are of the noble,
تا قیامت هست باقی آن طعام
that food is continuing till the Resurrection

چون ابیت عند ربی فاش شد
When (the Prophet's saying), "I pass the night with my Lord," was uttered,
یطعم و یسقی کنایت ز آش شد
"He gives (me) food" and "He gives (me) drink" referred metaphorically to (spiritual) food (and drink)

هیچ بی‌تاویل این را در پذیر
Accept this (saying) without any (perverse) interpretation
تا در آید در گلو چون شهد و شیر
that it may come into your throat (as agreeably) as honey and milk.

زانک تاویلست وا داد عطا
Because interpretation (alteration of the meaning) is a rejection of the gift,
چونک بیند آن حقیقت را خطا
since he (the interpreter) regards that real (original) meaning as faulty.

آن خطا دیدن ز ضعف عقل اوست
The view that it is faulty arises from the weakness of his understanding
عقل کل مغزست و عقل جزو پوست
Universal Reason is the kernel, and the particular reason is (like) the rind

خویش را تاویل کن نه اخبار را
Alter yourself, not the Traditions (of the Prophet):
مغز را بد گوی نه گلزار را
abuse your (dull) brain, not the rose garden (the true sense which you cannot apprehend).

ای علی که جمله عقل و دیده‌ای
O 'Alí, thou who art all mind and eye,
شمه‌ای واگو از آنچه دیده‌ای
relate a little of that which thou hast seen!

تیغ حلمت جان ما را چاک کرد
The sword of thy forbearance hath rent my soul
آب علمت خاک ما را پاک کرد
the water of thy knowledge hath purified my earth.

بازگو دانم که این اسرار هوست
Tell it forth! I know that these are His (God's) mysteries
زانک بی شمشیر کشتن کار اوست
because 'tis His work (way) to kill without sword.

صانع بی آلت و بی جارحه
He that works without tools and without limbs
واهب این هدیه‌های رابحه
He that bestows these profitable gifts,

صد هزاران می چشاند هوش را
Causes the intelligence to taste myriads
که خبر نبود دو چشم و گوش را
of wines in such wise that eyes and ears are unaware.

بازگو ای باز عرش خوش شکار
Tell it forth, O falcon of the empyrean that findest goodly prey
تا چه دیدی این زمان از کردگار
that (I may know) what thou hast seen at this time from the Maker.

چشم تو ادراک غیب آموخته
Thine eye has learned to perceive the Unseen,
چشمهای حاضران بر دوخته
(while) the eyes of bystanders are sealed."

آن یکی ماهی همی‌بیند عیان
One man is beholding a moon plainly
وان یکی تاریک می‌بیند جهان
while another sees the world dark,

وان یکی سه ماه می‌بیند بهم
And another beholds three moons together.
این سه کس بنشسته یک موضع نعم
These three persons (beholders) are seated in one place, yea (verily).

چشم هر سه باز و گوش هر سه تیز
The eyes of all three are open, and the ears of all three are sharp (attentive)
در تو آویزان و از من در گریز
(they are) fastened on thee and in flight from me.

سحر عین است این عجب لطف خفیست
Is this an enchantment of the eye? (Or) is it a marvellous hidden grace
بر تو نقش گرگ و بر من یوسفیست
On thee is the form of the wolf, and on me is the quality (beauty) of Joseph.

عالم ار هجده هزارست و فزون

If the worlds are eighteen thousand and more

هر نظر را نیست این هجده زبون

these eighteen (thousand) are not subject (accessible) to every eye.

راز بگشا ای علی مرتضی

Reveal the mystery, O 'Alí, thou who art approved (by God),

ای پس سؤ القضا حسن القضا

O thou who art goodly ease (comfort and happiness) after evil fate.

یا تو واگو آنچه عقلت یافتست

Either do thou declare that which thy reason hath found,

یا بگویم آنچه برمن تافتست

or I will tell that which hath shone forth on me

از تو بر من تافت چون داری نهان

From thee it shone forth on me: how shouldst thou hide it?

می‌فشانی نور چون مه بی زبان

Without tongue thou art scattering light, like the moon.

لیک اگر در گفت آید قرص ماه

But if the moon's orb come to speech,

شب روان را زودتر آرد به راه

it more quickly leads the night-travellers into the (right) way.

از غلط ایمن شوند و از ذهول

They become safe from error and heedlessness:

بانگ مه غالب شود بر بانگ غول

the voice of the moon prevails over the voice of the ghoul.

ماه بی گفتن چو باشد رهنما

Inasmuch as the moon (even) without speech is showing the way

چون بگوید شد ضیا اندر ضیا

when it speaks it becomes light upon light.

چون تو بابی آن مدینهٔ علم را

Since thou art the gate of the city of Knowledge,

چون شعاعی آفتاب حلم را

since thou art the beams of the sun of Clemency,

باز باش ای باب بر جویای باب

Be open, O Gate, to him that seeks the gate,

تا رسد از تو قشور اندر لباب

so that by means of thee the husks may reach the core

باز باش ای باب رحمت تا ابد
Be open unto everlasting, O Gate of Mercy,
بارگاه ما له کفوا احد
O Entrance-hall to None is like unto Him."

هر هوا و ذره‌ای خود منظریست
Every air and mote is indeed a place for vision (of God),
ناگشاده کی گود کآنجا دریست
(but so long as it is) unopened, who says "Yonder is a door"?

تا بنگشاید دری را دیدبان
Unless the Watcher open a door
در درون هرگز نجنبد این گمان
this idea never stirs within.

چون گشاده شد دری حیران شود
When a door is opened, he (on whom this idea has dawned) becomes amazed,
مرغ اومید و طمع پران شود
the bird of hope and desire begins to fly

غافلی ناگه به ویران گنج یافت
A careless man suddenly found the treasure in the ruin
سوی هر ویران از آن پس می‌شتافت
after that, he was hastening to (search in) every ruin.

تا ز درویشی نیابی تو گهر
Till you gain the pearl from one dervish,
کی گهر جویی ز درویشی دگر
how should you seek the pearl from another dervish?

سالها گر ظن دود با پای خویش
Though opinion run with its own feet for (many) years
نگذرد ز اشکاف بینیهای خویش
it will not pass beyond the cleft of its own nostrils.

تا نبینی نایدت از غیب بو
Until the scent from the Unseen shall come to your nose, say,
غیر بینی هیچ می‌بینی بگو
will you see anything except your nose?

❋◉❋◉❋

سؤال کردن آن کافر از علی کرم الله وجهه
How that infidel asked 'Alí, may God honour his person, saying,

کی بر چون منی مظفر شدی شمشیر از دست چون انداختی
"Since thou wert victorious over such a man as I am, how didst thou drop the sword from thy hand?"

پس بگفت آن نو مسلمان ولی
Then that devoted friend, who had been newly converted to Islam

از سر مستی و لذت با علی
in his enthusiasm and delight said to Ali,

که بفرما یا امیر المؤمنین
Speak, O Prince of the Faithful

تا بجنبد جان بتن در چون جنین
that my soul may stir within my body, like the embryo."

هفت اختر هر جنین را مدتی
O (dear) soul, the seven planets,

می‌کنند ای جان به نوبت خدمتی
(each) in turn, do a (particular) service for a time to every embryo.

چونک وقت آید که جان گیرد جنین
When the time comes for the embryo to receive the (vital) spirit

آفتابش آن زمان گردد معین
at that time the sun becomes its helper.

این جنین در جنبش آید ز آفتاب
This embryo is brought into movement by the sun

کآفتابش جان همی‌بخشد شتاب
for the sun is quickly endowing it with spirit.

از دگر آن چهم به جز نقشی نیافت
From the other stars this embryo received only an impression

این جنین تا آفتابش بر نتافت
until the sun shone upon it.

از کدامین ره تعلق یافت او
By which way did it become connected

در رحم با آفتاب خوب رو
in the womb with the beauteous sun

از ره پنهان که دور از حس ماست
By the hidden way that is remote from our sense-perception

آفتاب چرخ را بس راههاست
The sun in heaven hath many ways:

آن رهی که زر بیابد قوت ازو
The way whereby gold receives nourishment
و آن رهی که سنگ شد یاقوت ازو
and the way whereby the (common) stone is made a jacinth

آن رهی که سرخ سازد لعل را
And the way whereby it makes the ruby red
وان رهی که برق بخشد نعل را
and the way whereby it gives the lightning-flash to the (iron) horse-shoe

آن رهی که پخته سازد میوه را
And the way whereby it ripens the fruit,
و آن رهی که دل دهد کالیوه را
and the way whereby it gives heart to one distraught

بازگو ای باز پر افروخته
Say it forth, O falcon with shining wings who hast learned
با شه و با ساعدش آموخته
(to be familiar) with the King and with his fore-arm.

بازگو ای بار عنقاگیر شاه
Say it forth, O royal falcon that dost catch the 'Anqá
ای سپاه‌اشکن بخود نه با سپاه
O thou that dost vanquish an army by thyself, not with (the aid of) an army.

امت وحدی یکی و صد هزار
Thou alone art the (whole) community, thou art one and a hundred thousand.
بازگو ای بنده بازت را شکار
Say it forth, O thou to whose falcon thy slave has fallen a prey.

در محل قهر این رحمت ز چیست
Wherefore this mercy in the place of vengeance?
اژدها را دست دادن راه کیست
Whose way is it to give the hand to a dragon?"

◆◉◆◆◉◆

جواب گفتن امیر المؤمنین
How the Prince of the Faithful made answer (and explained)

کی سبب افکندن شمشیر از دست چه بوده است در آن حالت
what was the reason of his dropping the sword from his hand on that occasion.

گفت من تیغ از پی حق می‌زنم
He said, "I am wielding the sword for God's sake

بندهٔ حقم نه مأمور تنم
I am the servant of God, I am not under the command of the body.

شیر حقم نیستم شیر هوا
I am the Lion of God, I am not the lion of passion

فعل من بر دین من باشد گوا
my deed bears witness to my religion.

ما رمیت اذ رمیتم در حراب
In war I am (manifesting the truth of) thou didst not throw when thou threwest

من چو تیغم وان زننده آفتاب
I am (but) as the sword, and the wielder is the (Divine) Sun.

رخت خود را من ز ره بر داشتم
I have removed the baggage of self out of the way,

غیر حق را من عدم انگاشتم
I have deemed (what is) other than God to be non-existence

سایه‌ای‌ام کدخدا‌ام آفتاب
I am a shadow, the Sun is my lord; I am the chamberlain,

حاجبم من نیستم او را حجاب
I am not the curtain (which prevents approach) to Him.

من چو تیغم پر گهرهای وصال
I am filled with the pearls of union, like a (jewelled) sword

زنده گردانم نه کشته در قتال
in battle I make (men) living, not slain.

خون نپوشد گوهر تیغ مرا
Blood does not cover the sheen of my sword

باد از جا کی برد میغ مرا
how should the wind sweep away my clouds?

که نیم کوهم ز حلم و صبر و داد
I am not a straw, I am a mountain of forbearance and patience and justice

کوه را کی در رباید تند باد
how should the fierce wind carry off the mountain?

آنک از بادی رود از جا خسیست
That which is removed from its place by a wind is rubbish
زانک باد ناموافق خود بسیست
for indeed the contrary winds are many.

باد خشم و باد شهوت باد آز
The wind of anger and the wind of lust and the wind of greed
برد او را که نبود اهل نماز
swept away him that performed not the (ritual) prayers.

کوهم و هستی من بنیاد اوست
"I am a mountain, and my being is His building;
ور شوم چون کاه بادم یاد اوست
and if I become like a straw, my wind (the wind that moves me) is recollection of Him

جز به باد او نجنبد میل من
My longing is not stirred save by His wind
نیست جز عشق احد سرخیل من
my captain is naught but love of the One.

خشم بر شاهان شه و ما را غلام
Anger is king over kings, and to me it is a slave
خشم را هم بسته ام زیر لگام
even anger I have bound under the bridle.

تیغ حلمم گردن خشمم زدست
The sword of my forbearance hath smitten the neck of my anger
خشم حق بر من چو رحمت آمدست
the anger of God hath come on me like mercy

غرق نورم گرچه سقفم شد خراب
I am plunged in light although my roof is ruined;
روضه گشتم گرچه هستم بوتراب
I have become a garden although I am (styled) Bú Turáb (the father of dust).

چون در آمد علتی اندر غزا
Since a motive (other than God) entered (my heart) in the (holy) war
تیغ را دیدم نهان کردن سزا
I deemed it right to sheathe my sword,

تا احب لله آید نام من
That my name may be he loves for God's sake,
تا که ابغض لله آید کام من
that my desire may be he hates for God's sake,

470

تا که اعطا لله آید جود من
That my generosity may be he gives for God's sake
تا که امسک لله آید بود من
that my being may be he withholds for God's sake

بخل من لله عطا لله و بس
My stinginess is for God's sake, my bounty is for God's sake alone
جمله لله‌ام نیم من آن کس
I belong entirely to God, I do not belong to any one (else);

وآنچه لله می‌کنم تقلید نیست
And that which I am doing for God's sake is not (done in) conformity
نیست تخییل و گمان جز دید نیست
it is not fancy and opinion, it is naught but intuition.

ز اجتهاد و از تحری رسته‌ام
I have been freed from effort and search
آستین بر دامن حق بسته‌ام
I have tied my sleeve to the skirt of God

گر همی‌پرم همی‌بینم مطار
If I am flying, I behold the place to which I soar
ور همی‌گردم همی‌بینم مدار
and if I am circling, I behold the axis on which I revolve;

ور کشم باری بدانم تا کجا
And if I am dragging a burden, I know whither:
ماهم و خورشید پیشم پیشوا
I am the moon, and the Sun is in front of me as the guide."

بیش ازین با خلق گفتن روی نیست
There is no means (possibility) of communicating more than this to the people
بحر را گنجایی اندر جوی نیست
in the river there is no room for the Sea.

پست می‌گویم به اندازهٔ عقول
I speak low according to the measure of (their) understandings:
عیب نبود این بود کار رسول
tis no fault, this is the practice of the Prophet.

از غرض حرم گواهی حر شنو
I am free from self-interest: hear the testimony of a freeman
که گواهی بندگان نه ارزد دو جو
for the testimony of slaves is not worth two barleycorns."

در شریعت مر گواهی بنده را
In the religious law the testimony of a slave

نیست قدری وقت دعوی و قضا
has no value at the time of litigation and judgement.

گر هزاران بنده باشندت گواه
(Even) if thousands of slaves bear witness on thy behalf

بر نسنجد شرع ایشان را به کاه
the law does not assign to them the weight of a straw.

بندهٔ شهوت بتر نزدیک حق
In God's sight the slave of lust is worse than

از غلام و بندگان مسترق
menials and slaves brought into servitude,

کین بیک لفظی شود از خواجه حر
For the latter becomes free at a single word from his master

وان زید شیرین میرد سخت مر
while the former lives sweet but dies exceedingly bitter.

بندهٔ شهوت ندارد خود خلاص
The slave of lust hath no (means of) release at all

جز به فضل ایزد و انعام خاص
all except through the grace of God and His special favour.

در چهی افتاد کان را غور نیست
He has fallen into a pit that has no bottom

وان گناه اوست جبر و جور نیست
and that is his (own) sin: it is not (Divine) compulsion and injustice.

در چهی انداخت او خود را که من
He has cast himself into such a pit

درخور قعرش نمی‌یابم رسن
that I find no rope capable of (reaching) its bottom.

بس کنم گر این سخن افزون شود
I will make an end. If this discourse go further

خود جگر چه بود که خارا خون شود
not only hearts but rocks will bleed

این جگرها خون نشد نه از سختی است
(If) these hearts have not bled, 'tis not because of (their) hardness

غفلت و مشغولی و بدبختی است
'tis (because of) heedlessness and preoccupation and ill-fatedness

خون شود روزی که خونش سود نیست
They will bleed one day when blood is no use to them:
خون شو آن وقتی که خون مردود نیست
do thou bleed at a time when (thy) blood is not rejected

چون گواهی بندگان مقبول نیست
Inasmuch as the testimony of slaves is not accepted,
عدل او باشد که بندهٔ غول نیست
the approved witness is he that is not the slave of the ghoul (of sensuality).

گشت ارسلناک شاهد در نذر
(The words) We have sent thee as a witness came in the Warning (the Qur'án)
زانک بود از کون او حر بن حر
because he (the Prophet) was entirely free from (creaturely) existence.

چونک حرم خشم کی بندد مرا
Since I am free, how should anger bind me?
نیست اینجا جز صفات حق در آ
Nothing is here but Divine qualities. Come in!

اندر آ آزاد کردت فضل حق
Come in, for the grace of God hath made thee free
زانک رحمت داشت بر خشمش سبق
because His mercy had the precedence over His wrath.

اندر آ اکنون که رستی از خطر
Come in now, for thou hast escaped from the peril:
سنگ بودی کیمیا کردت گهر
thou wert a (common) stone, the Elixir hath made thee a jewel.

رسته‌ای از کفر و خارستان او
hou hast been delivered from unbelief and its thorn-thicket
چون گلی بشکف به سروستان هو
blossom like a rose in the cypress-garden of Hú (God).

تو منی و من توم ای محتشم
Thou art I and I am thou, O illustrious one:
تو علی بودی علی را چون کشم
thou wert 'Alí— how should I kill 'Alí?

معصیت کردی به از هر طاعتی
hou hast committed a sin better than any act of piety
آسمان پیموده‌ای در ساعتی
thou hast traversed Heaven in a single moment.

بس خجسته معصیت کان کرد مرد
Very fortunate (was) the sin which the man committed:
نه ز خاری بر دمد اوراق ورد
do not rose-leaves spring from a thorn?

نه گناه عمر و قصد رسول
Was not the sin of 'Umar and his attempt on (the life of) the Prophet
می‌کشیدش تا بدرگاه قبول
leading him to the gate of acceptance?

نه بسحر ساحران فرعونشان
Was not Pharaoh because of the magic of the magicians drawing them (to himself)
می‌کشید و گشت دولت عونشان
and did not (spiritual) fortune come to their aid?

گر نبودی سحرشان و آن جحود
Had it not been for their magic and denial (of Moses)
کی کشیدیشان به فرعون عنود
who would have brought them to rebellious Pharaoh?

کی بدیدندی عصا و معجزات
How would they have seen the rod and the miracles
معصیت طاعت شد ای قوم عصات
Disobedience (to God) became obedience, O disobedient people.

ناامیدی را خدا گردن زدست
God hath smitten the neck of despair,
چون گنه مانند طاعت آمدست
inasmuch as sin has become like obedience.

چون مبدل می‌کند او سیئات
Since He changes evil acts (into good),
طاعتی‌اش می‌کند رغم وشات
He makes it (the disobedience) an act of obedience in despite of slanderers (devils).

زین شود مرجوم شیطان رجیم
By this (mercy of God) the stoned (accursed) Devil is driven away
وز حسد او بطرقد گردد دو نیم
and bursts with envy and is cloven asunder

او بکوشد تا گناهی پرورد
He strives to foster a sin (in us)
زان گنه ما را به چاهی آورد
and by means of that sin bring us into a pit

چون ببیند کان گنه شد طاعتی
When he sees that the sin has become an act of obedience (to God),

گردد او را نامبارک ساعتی
there comes round for him an unblest hour

اندر آ من در گشادم مر ترا
"Come in! I open the door to thee.

تف زدی و تحفه دادم مر ترا
Thou spattest (on me) and I give thee a present.

مر جفاگر را چنینها می‌دهم
Such things I am giving to the doer of iniquity

پیش پای چپ چه سان سر می‌نهم
(thou seest) in what fashion I lay my head before the left foot

پس وفاگر را چه بخشم تو بدان
What then do I bestow on the doer of righteousness? Know thou

گنجها و ملکهای جاودان
I bestow) treasures and kingdoms everlasting.

❖◉❖◉❖

گفتن پیغامبر صلی الله علیه و سلم به گوش رکابدار امیر المومنین علی کرم الله وجهه
How the Prophet, on whom be peace, said in the ear of the stirrup-holder of the Prince of the Faithful ('Alí), may God honour his person,

کی کشتن علی بر دست تو خواهد بودن خبرت کردم
"I tell thee, 'Alí will be slain by thy hand."

من چنان مردم که بر خونی خویش
I am such a man that the honey of my kindness

نوش لطف من نشد در قهر نیش
did not become poison in wrath (even) against my murderer.

گفت پیغامبر به گوش چاکرم
The Prophet said in the ear of my servant

کو برد روزی ز گردن این سرم
that one day he would sever this head of mine from my neck.

کرد آگه آن رسول از وحی دوست
The Prophet, being inspired by the Beloved (God) gave information

که هلاکم عاقبت بر دست اوست
that in the end my destruction would be (wrought) by his hand.

او همی‌گوید بکش پیشین مرا
He (my friend) says, 'Kill me first, in order that
تا نیاید از من این منکر خطا
his hateful crime may not proceed from me.

من همی‌گویم چو مرگ من ز تست
I say, 'Since my death is (to come) from thee
با قضا من چون توانم حیله جست
how can I seek to evade the destiny (of God)?'

او همی‌افتد به پیشم کای کریم
He falls before me, saying, 'O generous man,
مر مرا کن از برای حق دو نیم
for God's sake cleave me in twain,

تا نه آید بر من این آن چهام بد
That this evil end may not come upon me,
تا نسوزد جان من بر جان خود
and that my soul may not burn (with grief) for (thee who art) its (very) life.'

من همی گویم برو جف القلم
I say, 'Go: the Pen (of Divine ordainment) is dry;
زان قلم بس سرنگون گردد علم
by that Pen many a (lofty) landmark is overthrown.

هیچ بغضی نیست در جانم ز تو
There is no hatred of thee in my soul
زانک این را من نمی‌دانم ز تو
because I do not regard this (act) as (proceeding) from thee.

آلت حقی تو فاعل دست حق
Thou art God's instrument, God's hand is the (real) agent
چون زنم بر آلت حق طعن و دق
how should I assail and oppose God's instrument?'

گفت او پس آن قصاص از بهر چیست
He (the knight) said, "For what reason, then, is retaliation (sanctioned)?
گفت هم از حق و آن سر خفیست
'Tis from God, too," said 'Alí, "and that is a hidden mystery.

گر کند بر فعل خود او اعتراض
If He takes offence at His own act,
ز اعتراض خود برویاند ریاض
(yet) He causes gardens (of good) to grow from that taking offence

اعتراض او را رسد بر فعل خود
It beseems Him to take offence at His own act,
زانک در قهرست و در لطف او احد
inasmuch as in vengeance and mercy He is One

اندرین شهر حوادث میر اوست
In this city of phenomena He is the Prince
در ممالک مالک تدبیر اوست
in (all) the realms (of the world) He is the Ruler.

آلت خود را اگر او بشکند
If He breaks His own instrument,
آن شکسته گشته را نیکو کند
He mends that which has become broken.

رمز ننسخ آیة او ننسها
Recognise, O noble sir, the indication of (the text)
نات خیرا در عقب می‌دان مها
(Whatever) verse We shall cancel or cause to be forgotten, followed by We shall bring a better

هر شریعت را که حق منسوخ کرد
Every (religious) law that God has cancelled
او گیا برد و عوض آورد ورد
He has taken away grass and brought roses in exchange

شب کند منسوخ شغل روز را
Night cancels the business of day:
بین جمادی خرد افروز را
behold an inanimateness (inertia) that enlightens the intellect!

باز شب منسوخ شد از نور روز
Again, night is cancelled by the light of day,
تا جمادی سوخت زان آتش‌فروز
so that the inanimateness is consumed by that fire-kindling one.

گرچه ظلمت آمد آن نوم و سبات
Although that sleep and rest are darkness
نه درون ظلمتست آب حیات
is not the Water of Life within the darkness?

نه در آن ظلمت خردها تازه شد
Did not minds become refreshed in that darkness
سکته‌ای سرمایهٔ آوازه شد
Did not a pause (in recitation) become the source of (increased beauty in) the voice?

که ز ضدها ضدها آمد پدید
For contraries are manifested by means of contraries
در سویدا روشنایی آفرید
in the black core (of the heart) He (God) created the light (of love).

جنگ پیغامبر مدار صلح شد
The wars of the Prophet became the pivot (determining cause) of peace
صلح این آخر زمان زان جنگ بد
the peace of this latter age was (produced) from those wars

صد هزاران سر برید آن دلستان
That heart-ravisher cut off hundreds of thousands of heads,
تا امان یابد سر اهل جهان
in order that the heads of the (whole) world's people might win security.

باغبان زان می‌برد شاخ مضر
The gardener lops the harmful bough
تا بیابد نخل قامتها و بر
in order that the date-palm may gain (tallness of) stature and goodness.

می‌کند از باغ دانا آن حشیش
The expert (gardener) digs up the weeds from the garden
تا نماید باغ و میوه خرمیش
in order that his garden and fruit may look flourishing

می‌کند دندان بد را آن طبیب
The physician extracts bad teeth,
تا رهد از درد و بیماری حبیب
in order that the beloved (patient) may be saved from pain and sickness.

پس زیادتها درون نقصهاست
Advantages, then, are (concealed) within defects:
مر شهیدان را حیات اندر فناست
for martyrs there is life in death.

چون بریده گشت حلق رزق‌خوار
When the (martyr's) throat has been cut that swallowed the daily bread,
یرزقون فرحین شد گوار
receiving the (Divine) bounty, rejoicing, shall be delicious (to him).

حلق حیوان چون بریده شد بعدل
When the animal throat is justly cut (i.e. when the sensual capacities and faculties of the soul have
حلق انسان رست و افزونید فضل
there grows (from it) the human throat and its excellence is increased

حلق انسان چون ببرد هین ببین
When a (martyred) man's throat is cut, come, consider what the result will be
تا چه زاید کن قیاس آن برین
Judge of this (case) by the analogy of that (case).

حلق ثالث زاید و تیمار او
A third throat will be born,
شربت حق باشد و انوار او
and care of it will be (taken by) the sherbet of God and His lights.

حلق ببریده خورد شربت ولی
The throat that has been cut drinks (the Divine) sherbet
حلق از لا رسته مرده در بلی
but (only) the throat that has been delivered from Nay and has died in Yea.

بس کن ای دون‌همت کوته بنان
Make an end, O pusillanimous short-fingered (infirm) one
تا کیت باشد حیات جان به نان
How long will the life of thy spirit be (sustained) by bread?

زان نداری میوه‌ای مانند بید
Like the willow, thou hast no fruit,
کب رو بردی پی نان سپید
because thou hast lost thine honour for the sake of white bread.

گر ندارد صبر زین نان جان حس
If the sensual soul cannot refrain from this bread
کیمیا را گیر و زر گردان تو مس
take the elixir and turn thy copper into gold.

جامه شویی کرد خواهی ای فلان
Wouldst thou wash thy garment (clean),
رو مگردان از محلهٔ گازران
O so-and-so, do not avert thy face from the bleachers' quarter

گرچه نان بشکست مر روزهٔ ترا
Although the bread has broken thy fast,
در شکسته بند پیچ و برتر آ
cling to Him that binds what is broken, and ascend!

چون شکسته بند آمد دست او
Inasmuch as His hand binds what is broken
پس رفو باشد یقین اشکست او
it follows that His breaking is assuredly mending.

479

گر تو آن را بشکنی گوید بیا
It thou break it, He will say to thee, "Come, make it whole (again)"
تو درستش کن نداری دست و پا
and thou hast neither hand nor foot (thou art helpless).

پس شکستن حق او باشد که او
Therefore He (alone) has the right to break,
مر شکسته گشته را داند رفو
for He (alone) can mend what has been broken.

آنک داند دوخت او داند درید
He that knows how to sew (together) knows how to tear (asunder)
هر چه را بفروخت نیکوتر خرید
whatsoever He sells, He buys (something) better (in exchange).

خانه را ویران کند زیر و زبر
He lays the house in ruins, upside down
پس بیک ساعت کند معمورتر
then in one moment He makes it more habitable (than it was before).

گر یکی سر را ببرد از بدن
If He sever one head from the body,
صد هزاران سر بر آرد در زمن
He at once raises up hundreds of thousands of heads (for the beheaded person).

گر نفرمودی قصاصی بر جنات
If He had not ordained a retaliation upon the guilty
یا نگفتی فی القصاص آمد حیات
or if He had not said, "In retaliation there is (for you) a life,

خود که را زهره بدی تا او ز خود
Who indeed would have the of himself to wield
بر اسیر حکم حق تیغی زند
a sword against him that is a thrall to the decree of God?

زانک داند هر که چشمش را گشود
Because every one whose eyes He (God) hath opened
کان کشنده سخرهٔ تقدیر بود
would know that the slayer was constrained (to slay) by (Divine) predestination

هر که را آن حکم بر سر آمدی
Any one on whom that decree might come (fall) would strike
بر سر فرزند هم تیغی زدی
a sword-blow even at the head of his (own) child.

رو بترس و طعنه کم زن بر بدان
Go, fear (God) and do not rail at the wicked:
پیش دام حکم عجز خود بدان
know thine own impotence before the snare of the (Divine) decree

⁌◉⁌◉

تعجب کردن آدم علیه‌السلام از ضلالت ابلیس لعین و عجب آوردن
How Adam, on whom be peace, marvelled at the perdition of Iblís and showed vanity.

چشم آدم بر بلیسی کو شقی ست
The eye of Adam looked with contempt
از حقارت وز زیافت بنگریست
and scorn on Iblís who is damned.

خویش‌بینی کرد و آمد خودگزین
He behaved with self-conceit and became self-approving:
خنده زد بر کار ابلیس لعین
he laughed at the plight of accursed Iblís.

بانگ بر زد غیرت حق کای صفی
The jealousy of God cried out (against him)—"O chosen one
تو نمی‌دانی ز اسرار خفی
thou art ignorant of the hidden mysteries (of His providence).

پوستین را بازگونه گر کند
If He should turn the fur inside out,
کوه را از بیخ و از بن برکند
He would tear up from root and bottom (even) the (firmest) mountain (of faith);

پردهٔ صد آدم آن دم بر درد
At that instant He would rend the veil of (put to shame) a hundred Adams
صد بلیس نو مسلمان آورد
and bring (to light) a hundred Devils newly converted to Islam.

گفت آدم توبه کردم زین نظر
Adam said, "I repent of this look;
این چنین گستاخ نندیشم دگر
I will not think so disrespectfully again.

یا غیاث المستغیثین اهدنا
O Help of them that call for help, lead us (aright)
لا افتخار بالعلوم و الغنی
There is no (cause for) pride in knowledge or riches

لا تزغ قلبا هديت بالكرم
Do not let a heart stray that Thou hast guided by Thy grace,
واصرف السؤ الذى خط القلم
and avert the evil which the Pen has written

بگذران از جان ما سؤ القضا
Let the evil of Thy ordainment pass from our souls
وامبر ما را ز اخوان صفا
do not cut us off from those who are sincere

تلخ تر از فرقت تو هیچ نیست
There is naught more bitter than separation from Thee
بی پناهت غیر پیچاپیچ نیست
without Thy protection there is naught but perplexity

رخت ما هم رخت ما را راهزن
Our (worldly) goods waylay (and plunder) our (spiritual) goods
جسم ما مر جان ما را جامه کن
our bodies tear the garment (of spirituality) from our souls

دست ما چون پای ما را می‌خورد
Inasmuch as (the evil wrought by) our hand devours (the good towards which we move) our foot,
بی امان تو کسی جان چون برد
how shall any one save his soul without Thy security?

ور برد جان زین خطرهای عظیم
And (even) if (unaided) he save his soul from these awful dangers,
برده باشد مایهٔ ادبار و بیم
he will (only) have saved a stock of misfortune and fear,

زانک جان چون واصل جانان نبود
Because the soul, when it is not united with the Beloved,
تا ابد با خویش کورست و کبود
is blind and blue (miserable) with itself for ever

چون تو ندهی راه جان خود برده گیر
When Thou wilt not give him admission (to Thy presence) —even suppose he has saved his soul
جان که بی تو زنده باشد مرده گیر
regard as dead the soul that would live without Thee

گر تو طعنه می‌زنی بر بندگان
If Thou art upbraiding Thy slaves, that is suitable to Thee,
مر ترا آن می‌رسد ای کامران
O Thou whose every wish is fulfilled.

ور تو ماه و مهر را گویی جفا
And if Thou utter abuse of the moon and sun
ور تو قد سرو را گویی دوتا
and if Thou say that the (straight) stature of the cypress is (bent) double,

ور تو چرخ و عرش را خوانی حقیر
And if Thou call the sky and the empyrean contemptible,
ور تو کان و بحر را گویی فقیر
and if Thou say that the mine and the sea are poor

آن بنسبت با کمال تو رواست
That is proper in reference to Thy perfection:
ملک اکمال فناها مر تراست
Thine is the power of perfecting (all) mortalities,

که تو پاکی از خطر وز نیستی
For Thou art holy (and free) from danger and from non-existence:
نیستان را موجد و مغنیستی
Thou art He that brings the non-existent ones into being and endows (them with existence).

آنک رویانید داند سوختن
He that made to grow can burn (destroy)
زانک چون بدرید داند دوختن
because when He has torn, He can sew (mend).

می‌بسوزد هر خزان مر باغ را
Every autumn He burns (withers) the garden;
باز رویاند گل صباغ را
He makes to grow again the rose that dyes

کای بسوزیده برون آ تازه شو
Saying, "O thou who wert withered, come forth, be fresh,
بار دیگر خوب و خوب‌آوازه شو
once more be fair and of fair renown!

چشم نرگس کور شد بازش بساخت
The eye of the narcissus became blind He restored it;
حلق نی ببرید و بازش خود نواخت
the throat of the reed was cut: He himself fostered it again (and revived it)

ما چو مصنوعیم و صانع نیستیم
Since we are made (by God) and are not makers
جز زبون و جز که قانع نیستیم
we are not (entitled to be anything) but humble and content

ما همه نفسی و نفسی می‌زنیم
We all are crying "nafsí nafsí" ("save my soul, save my soul!")
گر نخواهی ما همه آهرمنیم
if Thou call us not (to Thyself), we all are Ahrimans (Devils).

زان ز آهرمن رهیدستیم ما
(If) we have been delivered from Ahriman,
که خریدی جان ما را از عمی
(it is only) because Thou hast redeemed our souls from blindness.

تو عصاکش هر کراکه زندگیست
Thou art the Guide of every one that hath life
بی عصا و بی عصاکش کور چیست
what is the blind man without staff and guide?

غیر تو هر چه خوشست و ناخوشست
Excepting Thee (alone), whatsoever is sweet or unsweet
آدمی سوزست و عین آتشست
is man-destroying and the essence of fire.

هر که را آتش پناه و پشت شد
Anyone to whom fire is a refuge and support
هم مجوسی گشت و هم زردشت شد
becomes both a Magian and a Zoroaster.

کل شیء ما خلا الله باطل
Everything except Allah is vain:
ان فضل الله غیم ها طل
verily the grace of Allah is a cloud pouring abundantly and continually.

❖◉❖◉❖

بازگشتن به حکایت علی کرم الله وجهه
Returning to the story of the Prince of the Faithful, 'Alí -may God honour his person!

و مسامحت کردن او با خونی خویش
and how generously he behaved to his murderer.

باز رو سوی علی و خونیش
Go back to 'Alí and his murderer

وان کرم با خونی و افزونیش
and the kindness he showed to the murderer, and his superiority (moral and spiritual excellence).

گفت دشمن را همی‌بینم به چشم
He said, "Day and night I see the enemy with my eyes

روز و شب بر وی ندارم هیچ خشم
(but) I have no anger against him

زانک مرگم همچو من خوش آمدست
Because death has become sweet as manna to me:

مرگ من در بعث چنگ اندر زدست
my death has laid fast hold of resurrection."

مرگ بی مرگی بود ما را حلال
The death of deathlessness is lawful to us,

برگ بی برگی بود ما را نوال
the provision of unprovidedness is a bounty to us.

ظاهرش مرگ و به باطن زندگی
'Tis death outwardly but life inwardly:

ظاهرش ابتر نهان پایندگی
apparently 'tis a cutting-off (decease), in secret (in reality) 'tis permanence (life without end)

در رحم زادن جنین را رفتنست
To the embryo in the womb birth is a going (to another state of existence)

در جهان او را ز نو بشکفتنست
in the world it (the embryo) blossoms anew.

چون مرا سوی اجل عشق و هواست
Since I have intense love and longing for death

نهی لا تلقوا بایدیکم مراست
the prohibition do not cast yourselves (into destruction) is (meant) for me,

زانک نهی از دانهٔ شیرین بود
Because (only) the sweet berry is prohibited;

تلخ را خود نهی حاجت کی شود
(for) how should it become necessary to prohibit the sour one?

دانه‌ای کش تلخ باشد مغز و پوست
The berry that has a sour kernel and rind

تلخی و مکروهیش خود نهی اوست
its very sourness and disagreeableness are (serve as) a prohibition of it.

دانهٔ مردن مرا شیرین شدست
To me the berry of dying has become sweet:

بل هم احیاء بی من آمدست
(the text) nay, they are living has come (from God) on my account.

اقتلونی یا ثقاتی لائما
Slay me, my trusty friends, slay me, vile as I am:

ان فی قتلی حیاتی دائما
verily, in my being slain is my life for evermore.

ان فی موتی حیاتی یا فتی
Verily, in my death is my life,

کم افارق موطنی حتی متی
O youth how long shall I be parted from my home? Until when?

فرقتی لو لم تکن فی ذا السکون
If there were not in my staying (in this world) my separation (from God)

لم یقل انا الیه راجعون
He would not have said, 'Verily, we are returning to Him.'

راجع آن باشد که باز آید به شهر
The returning one is he that comes back to his (native) city,

سوی وحدت آید از تفریق دهر
and (fleeing) from the separation (plurality) of Time approaches the Unity.

افتادن رکابدار هر باری پیش امیر المؤمنین علی کرم الله وجهه
How the stirrup-holder of 'Alí, may God honour his person, came (to him), saying,

کی ای امیر المؤمنین مرا بکش و ازین قضا برهان
"For God's sake, kill me and deliver me from this doom."

باز آمد کای علی کای زودم بکش
"He came back, saying, 'O' Alí, kill me quickly

تا نبینم آن دم و وقت ترش
that I may not see that bitter moment and hour.

من حلالت می‌کنم خونم بریز
Shed my blood, I make it lawful to thee,

تا نبیند چشم من آن رستخیز
so that my eye may not behold that resurrection

گفتم ار هر ذره‌ای خونی شود
I said, 'If every atom should become a murderer and

خنجر اندر کف به قصد تو رود
dagger in hand, go to attack thee,

یک سر مو از تو نتواند برید
None (of them) could cut from thee the tip of a single hair

چون قلم بر تو چنان خطی کشید
since the Pen has written against thee such a line (of doom).

لیک بی غم شو شفیع تو منم
But do not grieve: I am intercessor for thee:

خواجهٔ روحم نه مملوک تنم
I am the spirit's master, I am not the body's slave.

پیش من این تن ندارد قیمتی
This body hath no value in my sight

بی تن خویشم فتی ابن الفتی
without my body I am the noble (in spirit), the son of the noble.

خنجر و شمشیر شد ریحان من
Dagger and sword have become my sweet basil

مرگ من شد بزم و نرگسدان من
my death has become my banquet and narcissus-pot

آنک او تن را بدین سان پی کند
He that hamstrings (mortifies) his body in this fashion,

حرص میری و خلافت کی کند
, how should he covet the Princedom and the Caliphate?

زان به ظاهر کو شد اندر جاه و حکم
Outwardly he strives after power and authority

تا امیران را نماید راه و حکم
(but only) that he may show to princes the (right) way and judgement;

تا امیری را دهد جانی دگر
That he may give another spirit to the Princedom

تا دهد نخل خلافت را ثمر
that he may give fruit to the palm tree of the Caliphate.

◈◉◈◉◈

بیان آنک فتح طلبیدن مصطفی صلی الله علیه و سلم مکه را و غیر مکه را
Explaining that the motive of the Prophet, on whom be peace, in seeking to conquer Mecca and other (places) than Mecca

جهت دوستی ملک دنیا نبود چون فرموده است الدنیا جیفة بلک بامر بود
was not love of worldly dominion, inasmuch as he has said "This world is a carcase," but that on the contrary it was by the command (of God).

جهد پیغامبر بفتح مکه هم
Likewise the Prophet's struggle to conquer Mecca

کی بود در حب دنیا متهم
how can he be suspected of (being inspired by) love of this world?

آنک او از مخزن هفت آسمان
He who on the day of trial shut

چشم و دل بر بست روز امتحان
his eyes and heart to the treasury of the Seven Heavens,

از پی نظارهٔ او حور و جان
houris and genies (who had come) to gaze upon him,

پر شده آفاق هر هفت آسمان
the horizons of all the Seven Heavens were full of

خویشتن آراسته از بهر او
Having arrayed themselves for his sake

خود ورا پروای غیر دوست کو
how indeed should he care for anything except the Beloved?

آنچنان پر گشته از اجلال حق
He had become so filled with magnification of God,

که درو هم ره نیابد آل حق
that even those nearest to God would find no way (of intruding) there.

لا يسع فينا نبى مرسل
In Us (in Our unity) is no room for a prophet sent as an apostle
والملك و الروح ايضا فاعقلوا
nor yet for the Angels or the Spirit. Do ye, therefore, understand!

گفت ما زاغیم همچون زاغ نه
He (also) said, "We are má zágh (that is, Our eye did not rove), we are not like crows (zágh);
مست صباغیم مست باغ نه
We are intoxicated with (enraptured by) the Dyer, we are not intoxicated with the garden

چونک مخزنهای افلاک و عقول
the celestial spheres and intelligences seemed (worthless) as a straw,
چون خسی آمد بر چشم رسول
Inasmuch as to the eye of the Prophet the treasuries of

پس چه باشد مکه و شام و عراق
What, then, would Mecca and Syria and 'Iráq be (worth to him)
که نماید او نبرد و اشتیاق
that he should show fight and longing (to gain possession of them)?

آن گمان بر وی ضمیر بد کند
the evil mind which judges by its own
کو قیاس از جهل و حرص خود کند
ignorance and cupidity will think that of him (impute that motive to him).

آبگینهٔ زرد چون سازی نقاب
When you make yellow glass a veil
زرد بینی جمله نور آفتاب
you see all the sunlight yellow.

بشکن آن شیشهٔ کبود و زرد را
Break those blue and yellow glasses,
تا شناسی گرد را و مرد را
in order that you may know (distinguish) the dust and the man

گرد فارس گرد سر افراشته
The dust (of the body) has lifted up its head (risen) around the (spiritual) horseman:
گرد را تو مرد حق پنداشته
you have fancied the dust to be the man of God.

گرد دید ابلیس و گفت این فرع طین
Iblís saw (only) the dust, and said, and said, "How should this offspring
چون فزاید بر من آتش‌جبین
of clay (Adam) be superior to me of the fiery brow?

تا تو می‌بینی عزیزان را بشر
So long as thou art regarding the holy (prophets and saints) as men
دانک میراث بلیسیست آن نظر
know that that view is an inheritance from Iblís.

گر نه فرزندی بلیسی ای عنید
If thou art not the child of Iblís, O contumacious one
پس به تو میراث آن سگ چون رسید
then how has the inheritance of that cur come to thee?

من نیم سگ شیر حقم حق‌پرست
"I am not a cur, I am the Lion of God, a worshipper of God:
شیر حق آنست کز صورت برست
the lion of God is he that has escaped from (phenomenal) form.

شیر دنیا جوید اشکاری و برگ
The lion of this world seeks a prey and provision
شیر مولی جوید آزادی و مرگ
the lion of the Lord seeks freedom and death.

چونک اندر مرگ بیند صد وجود
Inasmuch as in death he sees a hundred existences,
همچو پروانه بسوزاند وجود
like the moth he burns away (his own) existence.

شد هوای مرگ طوق صادقان
Desire for death became the badge of the sincere
که جهودان را بد این دم امتحان
for this word (declaration) was (made) a test for the Jews.

در نبی فرمود کای قوم یهود
He (God) said in the Qur'án, "O people of the Jews
صادقان را مرگ باشد گنج و سود
death is treasure and gain to the sincere.

همچنانک آرزوی سود هست
Even as there is desire for profit (in the hearts of the worldly),
آرزوی مرگ بردن زان بهست
the desire to win death is better than that (in the eyes of the sincere).

ای جهودان بهر ناموس کسان
O Jews, for the sake of (being held in) honour by men of worth,
بگذرانید این تمنا بر زبان
let this wish be uttered on your tongues.

یک جهودی این قدر زهره نداشت
Not a single Jew had so much courage (as to respond),
چون محمد این علم را بر فراشت
when Mohammed raised this banner (gave this challenge)

گفت اگر رانید این را بر زبان
He said, "If ye utter this on your tongues,
یک یهودی خود نماند در جهان
truly not one Jew will be left in the world."

پس یهودان مال بردند و خراج
Then the Jews brought the property (tribute in kind) and land-tax,
که مکن رسوا تو ما را ای سراج
saying Do not put us to shame, O Lamp

این سخن را نیست پایانی پدید
There is no end in sight to this discourse:
دست با من ده چو چشمت دوست دید
give me thy hand, since thine eye hath seen the Friend.

❖◉❖◉❖

گفتن امیر المؤمنین علی کرم الله وجهه با قرین خود
How the Prince of the Faithful, 'Ali-may God honour his person! said to his antagonist,

کی چون خدو انداختی در روی من نفس من جنبید و اخلاص عمل نماند مانع کشتن تو آن شد
When thou didst spit in my face, my fleshly self was aroused and I could no longer act with entire sincerity (towards God): that hindered me from slaying thee

گفت امیر المؤمنین با آن جوان
The Prince of the Faithful said to that youth,
که به هنگام نبرد ای پهلوان
In the hour of battle, O knight,

چون خدو انداختی در روی من
When thou didst spit in my face
نفس جنبید و تبه شد خوی من
my fleshly self was aroused and my good disposition was corrupted

نیم بهر حق شد و نیمی هوا
Half (of my fighting) came to be for God's sake,
شرکت اندر کار حق نبود روا
and half (for) idle passion: in God's affair partnership' is not allowable.

تو نگاریدهٔ کف مولیستی
Thou art limned by the hand of the Lord
آن حق کردهٔ من نیستی
thou art God's (work), thou art not made by me.

نقش حق را هم به امر حق شکن
reak God's image, (but only) by God's command;
بر زجاجهٔ دوست سنگ دوست زن
cast (a stone) at the Beloved's glass, (but only) the Beloved's stone.

گبر این بشنید و نوری شد پدید
The fire-worshipper heard this, and a light appeared
در دل او تا که زناری برید
in his heart, so that he cut a girdle

گفت من تخم جفا می‌کاشتم
He said, "I was sowing the seed of wrong
من ترا نوعی دگر پنداشتم
I fancied thee (to be) otherwise (than thou art).

تو ترازوی احدخو بوده‌ای
Thou hast (really) been the balance (endued) with the (just) nature of the One (God)
بل زبانهٔ هر ترازو بوده‌ای
nay, thou hast been the tongue of every balance

تو تبار و اصل و خویشم بوده‌ای
Thou hast been my race and stock and kin
تو فروغ شمع کیشم بوده‌ای
thou hast been the radiance of the candle of my religion.

من غلام آن چراغ چشم جو
I am the (devoted) slave of that eye-seeking Lamp
که چراغت روشنی پذرفت ازو
from which thy lamp received splendour.

من غلام موج آن دریای نور
I am the slave of the the billow of that Sea of Light
که چنین گوهر بر آرد در ظهور
which brings a pearl like this into view.

عرضه کن بر من شهادت را که من
Offer me the profession of the (Moslem) Faith
مر ترا دیدم سرافراز زمن
for I regard you as the exalted one of the tim

قرب پنجه کس ز خویش و قوم او
Near fifty persons of his kindred and tribe
عاشقانه سوی دین کردند رو
ovingly turned their faces towards the Religion (of Islam).

او به تیغ حلم چندین حلق را
By the sword of clemency he ('Ali) redeemed so many throats
وا خرید از تیغ و چندین خلق را
and such a multitude from the sword.

تیغ حلم از تیغ آهن تیزتر
The sword of clemency is sharper than the sword of iron
بل ز صد لشکر ظفر انگیزتر
nay, it is more productive of victory than a hundred armies.

ای دریغا لقمه‌ای دو خورده شد
Oh, alas, two mouthfuls were eaten
جوشش فکرت از آن افسرده شد
and thereby the ferment of thought was frozen up

گندمی خورشید آدم را کسوف
A grain of wheat eclipsed the sun of Adam
چون ذنب شعشاع بدری را خسوف
as the descending node is (the cause of) eclipse to the brilliance of the full-moon.

اینت لطف دل که از یک مشت گل
Behold the beauty of the heart,
ماه او چون می‌شود پروین گسل
how its moon scatters the Pleiades (how its light is broken and disordered) by a single handful of clay.

نان چو معنی بود خوردش سود بود
When the bread was spirit, it was beneficial;
چونک صورت گشت انگیزد جحود
since it became form, it produces little good.

همچو خار سبز کاشتر می‌خورد
As (for example) the green thistles which a camel eats
زان خورش صد نفع و لذت می‌برد
and gains from eating them a hundred benefits and pleasures:

چونک آن سبزیش رفت و خشک گشت
When the camel from the desert eats those same thistles,
چون همان را می‌خورد اشتر ز دشت
after their greenness is gone and they have become dry,

می‌دراند کام و لنجش ای دریغ
They rend his palate and cheek— oh
کانچنان ورد مربی گشت تیغ
alas that such a well-nourished rose became a sword

نان چو معنی بود بود آن خار سبز
When the bread was spirit, it was (like) the green thistles;
چونک صورت شد کنون خشکست و گبز
since it became form, it is now dry and gross

تو بدان عادت که او را پیش ازین
According as thou hadst formerly been in the habi
خورده بودی ای وجود نازنین
of eating it, O gracious being,

بر همان بو می‌خوری این خشک را
In the same hope thou (still) are eating this dry stuff
بعد از آن کامیخت معنی با ثری
after the spirit has become mingled with clay.

گشت خاک‌آمیز و خشک و گوشت‌بر
It has become mixed with earth and dry and flesh-cutting
زان گیاه اکنون بپرهیز ای شتر
abstain now from that herbage, O camel!

سخت خاک‌آلود می‌آید سخن
The words are coming (forth) very earth-soiled;
آب تیره شد سر چه بند کن
the water has become turbid: stop up the mouth of the well

تا خدایش باز صاف و خوش کند
That God may again make it pure and sweet,
او که تیره کرد هم صافش کند
that He who made it turbid may likewise make it pure

صبر آرد آرزو را نه شتاب
Patience brings the object of desire, not Haste.
صبر کن والله اعلم بالصواب
Have patience and God knoweth best what is right

مضمون اصلی این کتاب را شرح و تفسیر آیات قرآنی با زبان ساده و شعر در بر می گیرد و اشعاری از عطار و سنائی و دیگر شاعران برجسته، در این گفتار به چشم می‌خورند. قسمت‌های عربی کتاب نشان‌دهنده تسلط کامل مولوی به این زبان و علوم دینی است.

وفات حضرت مولانا

در دوست غیر مردن، کان را دوا نباشد   پس من چگونه گویم، کان در دوا کن
در خواب دوش، پیری در کوی عشق دیدم   با دست اشارتم کرد، که عزم سوی ما کن

سرانجام روح ناآرام زندگی این خداوندگار بلخ و روم در غروب خورشید در پی تبی سوزان در روز یکشنبه پنجم جمادی الاخر سال ۶۷۲ هـ قمری بر اثر بیماری ناگهانی که طبیبان از درمان آن عاجز گشتند با حرکتی سریع و بی وقفه پله پله نردبان نورانی سلوک را یک نفس تا ملاقات خدا طی کرد

آرامگاه مولوی در شهر قونیه، میان دو استان آنکارا و آنتالیا واقع شده است و مکانی بسیار دیدنی برای گردشگران و علاقه مندان شعر و ادب دنیا است. آرامگاه مولانا بر روی تپه ای با ارتفاع ۱۰۱۶متر قرار دارد و در رنگ در بالای قبر او یک گنبد مخروطی شکل فیروزه ای ساخته شده است. در سال ۱۹۲۷میلادی مقبره مولوی را به موزه تبدیل کردند که با نام موزه مولانا شناخته شد. بجز مولانا جلال الدین، بهاءالدین (پدر مولوی)، سلطان ولد (پسر مولوی) و چند تن از اقوام و نزدیکان مولانا نیز در این شهر آرام گرفتند.

۱۷ دسامبر (۲۶ آذر ماه) روز وفات مولاناست. در قونیه هر سال مراسم ویژه بزرگداشت مولانا از ۷ تا ۱۷ دسامبر (۱۶ تا ۲۶ ماه آذر) برگزار می شود. در ترکیه به شب وفات مولانا شب عروسی یا وصلت مولانا نیز گفته می شود. مردم این روز را به علت وصال مولانا با معبود خود جشن می گیرند. در روز هفتم دسامبر جوانانی که لباس لشکریان عثمانی را به تن دارند به تپه کی قباد، محل دیدار شمس و مولانا رفته از این تپه به همراه با ساز و دُهل به سوی آرامگاه مولانا می آیند. در محوطه موزه مولانا به مدت ده شب برنامه های متنوع فرهنگی برای علاقه مندان برگزار می شود. این برنامه ها حاوی سخنرانی، خواندن اشعار مولانا و رقص سماع است و بخش‌های مختلف زندگی مولوی رابه تصویر می‌کشند.

در هفتمین روز از مهرماه هر سال مراسم بزرگداشت دیگری به مناسبت سالروز تولد مولانا در قونیه برپا می شود. از سال ۲۰۰۴ هم به مناسبت زادروز شاعر بزرگ پارسی گوی مولانا فستیوال جهانی موسیقی عرفانی در این شهر اجرا می شود. این فستیوال از ۲۹ شهریور ماه تا ۹ مهر با شرکت گروه های مختلف موسیقی از سرتاسر جهان ادامه دارد. سازمان جهانی یونسکو سال ۲۰۰۷ میلادی را سال جهانی مولانا نام گذاری و مراسم بزرگداشت هشتصدمین سال تولد این عارف برجسته را در ترکیه برگزار کرد.

در کشور ترکیه، مولوی جایگاهی فراتر از شاعر دارد و پیروان زیادی به ستایش او مشغول هستند. «سلطان ولد» فرزند بزرگ مولوی و «اولو عارف چلبی» نوه مولوی هر یک طریقتی متفاوت از اندیشه مولوی پایه گذاری کردند و آن‌ها را «طریقت مولویه» نامیدند.

دفترهای مثنوی معنوی شامل حکایات پند آموز و تعلیمی است و در قالب داستانی و حکایات شیرین به باورهای مختلف دینی، اصول تصوف و مبانی اخلاق می‌پردازد. مولوی، مثنوی را تحت تاثیر الهی نامه حکیم سنایی و مصیبت نامه و منطق الطیر عطار سروده است و در بسیاری از شعرهای مثنوی از این دو شاعر و عارف نام می‌برد و اشعارشان را نقل می‌کند. در بخش‌هایی از این کتاب به داستان‌هایی از کلیله و دمنه نیز اشاره می‌شود. اما اقتباس‌های کتاب مثنوی معنوی از دیگر آثار ادبی پیش از آن، از حافظه مولانا و به‌صورت بداهه بوده و هیچ‌گونه کپی‌برداری انجام نشده است.

مثنوی معنوی مقدمه‌ای عربی نیز دارد که در آن به نام و مضامین کتاب اشاره می‌شود. مهم‌ترین ویژگی مثنوی معنوی سادگی اشعار و داستان‌های آن است به شکلی که همه می‌توانند به‌راحتی مثنوی بخوانند و از حکایاتش لذت ببرند. مثنوی از همان آغاز تألیف در مجالس رقص و سماع خوانده می شد و حتی در دوران حیات مولانا طبقه ای به نام مثنوی خوانان پدید آمدند که مثنوی را با صوتی دلکش می خواندند.

غزلیات: غزلیاتی است که مولانا به نام خود شمس سروده است این بخش از آثار مولانا به کلیات یا دیوان شمس یا «دیوان کبیر» معروف است. دیوان شمس در برگیرنده اشعار پر شور عاشقانه و عارفانه است که در اثر شور و شوق وصف ناپذیر مولانا به عشق و عرفان و در اثر ارتباط با شمس تبریزی شکل گرفته‌اند.

رباعیات: اصل اندیشه‌های مولاناست. معانی و مضامین عرفانی و معنوی در این رباعیها دیده می شود که با روش فکر و عبارت بندی مولانا مناسبت تمام دارد ولی روی هم رفته رباعیات به پایۀ غزلیات و مثنوی نمی رسد.

آثار منثور مولوی:

فیه ما فیه: این کتاب مجموعۀ تقریرات مولانا است که در مجالس خود بیان کرده است. فیه ما فیه مجموعه‌ای از حکایات، تمثیل‌ها، داستان‌ها و روایات و اخباری است که در طول ۳۰ سال توسط سلطان ولد، پسر مولانا و یکی از مریدان او مکتوب شده است. هدف مولوی از گردآوری گفتمان خود در این کتاب، روشنگری برای مریدان و آیندگان بوده است.

مکاتیب: حاصل نامه ها و مکتوبات مولانا به معاصرین خود است. مکتوبات مجموعه‌ای از ۱۵۰ نامه مولوی در زمان‌های مختلف برای افراد متفاوت است که به دست خود مولوی نگاشته شده و سبک نگارش آن مناسب برای مکاتبه با بزرگان، دولت‌مردان، شاگردان و مریدانش است. لحن گفتار این نامه‌ها با دیگر کتاب‌های مولوی تفاوت زیادی دارد و در میان آن‌ها نامه‌هایی با مضامین ساده برای پادشاهان و حاکمان دیده می‌شود. گرچه در بعضی از نامه‌ها که مولوی به نزدیکان و مریدان خود نوشته است، حال و هوای پر شور نثر و نظم مولوی جلب توجه می کند.

مجالس سبعه: مجموعه‌ای از مواعظ و مجالس مولانا یعنی سخنانی که به وجه اندرز و به طریق تذکیر بر سر منبر برای مریدان و شاگردانش بیان فرموده است. این گفتار پیش از دیدار مولانا با شمس در مجالس مختلف بیان شده است و پس از جدایی از شمس، مولوی تنها یک بار به اصرار صلاح الدین زرکوب به منبر رفت و سپس دست از خطابه و موعظه خوانی برداشت. از شور و اشتیاق مثنوی معنوی و دیوان شمس در این کتاب اثری نیست و این خود گواهی دیگر بر تاثیر عمیق شمس تبریزی بر مولانا جلال الدین دارد.

مولانا و شمس تبریزی:

نقطه عطف زندگی مولوی آشنایی و دلدادگی اش با شمس تبریزی است. شمس عارفی وارسته و درویشی دوره گرد که با همه اطرافیان مولانا متفاوت است. او همه معادلات مولوی را به هم می زند. وجود خداوند، عشق و عقل را با نگاهی متفاوت برای مولوی شرح می دهد.

وی همچنانکه گفتیم یک لحظه از تربیت خود غافل نبوده، تاریخ اینچنین می‌نویسد که روزی شمس وارد مجلس مولانا می‌شود. در حالی که مولانا در کنارش چند کتاب وجود داشت. شمس از او می‌پرسد این که اینها چیست؟ مولانا جواب می‌دهد قیل و قال است. شمس می‌گوید و ترا با اینها چه کار است و کتابها را برداشته در داخل حوضی که در آن نزدیکی قرار داشت می‌اندازد. مولانا با ناراحتی می گوید ای درویش چه کار کردی برخی از اینها کتابها از پدرم رسیده بوده و نسخه منحصر بفرد می‌باشد. و دیگر پیدا نمی‌شود؛ شمس تبریزی در این حالت دست به آب برده و کتابها را یک یک از آب بیرون می‌کشد بدون اینکه آثاری از آب در کتابها مانده باشد. مولانا با تعجب می‌پرسد این چه سرّی است؟ شمس جواب می‌دهد این ذوق وحال است که ترا از آن خبری نیست. از این ساعت است که حال مولانا تغییر یافته و به شوریدگی روی می‌نهد و درس و بحث را کناری نهاده و شبانه روز در رکاب شمس تبریزی به خدمت می‌ایستد و "تولدی دوباره" می‌یابد.

شمس اما با در هم شکستن عقاید خشکِ مذهبی در مولانا او را وارد دنیای متفاوتی از شناخت می کند. تاثیر شمس در زندگی مولوی چنان است که از یک فقیه و عالم دینی به عاشقی دل سوخته بدل می شود. مولوی دل به گفته ها و حقایق شمس می بندد.

مولوی به گفته ها و حقایقی که شمس می گوید دل می بندد. از نگاه شمس همه چیز هستی عشق است که هدایت می کند. عشق زیربنای خلقت است. خداوند عاشق بود پس خلق کرد. انسان هم باید عاشق پروردگار باشد به واسطه آیه تحبوا و تحبونهم. البته این طرز فکر در میان همه حلقه های عرفانی وجود داشته و دارد..

شمس خورشیدی بود که زندگی مولانا را روشن کرد و به آن گرما بخشید. چرا که به لحاظ شخصیتی مولوی را دگرگون ساخت. کسی که جز محراب و منبر جایی را نمی ستود به یک باره به رقص و سماع عاشقانه گرایید. شمس وجود هر چه ناخالصی و کدورت است از او دور می کند. نه تنها مکتب فکری مولوی را تغییر داد بلکه او را به وجد و شور درآورد.

آثار منظوم مولوی:

مثنوی: بدون شـک می‌توان مثنوی معنوی را مهم‌ترین و تاثیرگذارترین اثر مولوی نامید که شهرت جهانی دارد. مولوی مجموعه مثنوی معنوی را به خواهش یکی از محبوب‌ترین مریدانش به نام «حسام الدین چلبی» سروده است. کتاب تعلیمی و درسی در زمینهٔ عرفان و اصول تصوف و اخلاق و معارف است. ۱۸ بیت ابتدایی مثنوی که با شعر زیبای «بشنو از نی چون حکایت می‌کند» آغاز می‌شود، توسط مولوی نوشته شده است و بقیه ابیات را پس از سروده شدن توسط مولانا، حسام الدین چلبی مکتوب می‌کرد. این شعر زیبا به مناسبت ذکر نی، «نی نامه» شهرت دارد. نی نامه حاوی تمام معانی و مقاصد مندرج در شش دفتر است به عبارتی همهٔ شش دفتر مثنوی شرحی بر این ۱۸ بیت است.

کرد و به پدر او گفت که این پسر را گرامی بدار، زود باشد که نفس گرم او آتش در سوختگان عالم زند. مولوی این کتاب شیخ عطار را در طول حیات خود همیشه به‌همراه داشت.

از طرفی حمله مغولان به ایران و غارت و کشتار آنان نیز جان علما و ادیبان را تهدید می‌کرد. هم‌زمان با این اتفاقات «علاءالدین کیقباد سلجوقی» در شهر قونیه از بهاءالدین دعوت کرد تا به این شهر برود. در این زمان مولانا تنها ۱۳ سال داشت. پس از گذشتن از شهرهای فراوان، بهاءالدین و خانواده‌اش در قونیه ساکن شدند.

مولوی زیر نظر پدر و سایر استادان و مشایخ علم به تحصیل علوم و فنون متداول آن عصر از ادبیات و فقه و کلام و حدیث و امثال آن اشتغال داشت و در نتیجه ۲۰ سال تحصیل از کار درآمده و سرگرم تدریس و وعظ و تبلیغ معارف مذهبی شده بود.

یک سال پس از وفات پدرش به سال ۶۲۹ بود که سید برهان الدین محقق ترمذی که از مشایخ طریقت و از دوستان و ارادتمندان صمیمی پدرش بهاءالدین ولد بود به قونیه رفت. مولوی در خدمت وی وارد سیر و سلوک عرفانی و طریقه‌ی تصوف گردید و مدت ۹ سال زیر نظر سید محقق مشغول ریاضت و اذکار و وردهای طریقت بود.

مولوی همزمان با تربیت مردم، و علی الظاهر و به تشویق همین استادش برای تکمیل معلوماتش رنج سفر به حلب را برخود آسان نموه و عازم شهر حلب گردید و در شهر حلب علم فقه را از کمال الدین عدیم فرا گرفت.

او پس از مدتی به شهر دمشق رفت و با محی الدین عربی عارف و متفکر زمانش آشنا شد و از معلومات او نیز کمال استفاده‌ها را برده و از آنجا به قونیه سفر کرد و طریق ریاضت را به درخواست سید برهان الدین پیش گرفت. او پس از مرگ استاد طریقتش محقق ترمذی دنباله‌ی ریاضت و مجاهدت را رها نکرد و به مدت ۵ سال علوم دینی را آموزش داد و چهارصد شاگرد را تربیت نمود. مدت ریاضت و جهد و کوشش وی به ۱۴ سال بالغ گردید.

در سال ۶۴۲ هجری که مولوی وارد مرحله‌ی ۳۹ سالگی شد، ملاقات وی با تبریزی دست داد که موجب تحولی عظیم در روح مولوی گردید و به کلی او را منقلب ساخت. این‌جاست که مقامات کرامات و تصرف در نفوس و اشراف بر ضمایر را که در اثر ۱۴ سال ریاضت و رنج و کوشش تحصیل کرده بود یک‌جا به پای عشق شمس می‌ریزد و بی‌ناخن و ناتوان می‌شود.

مدت مصاحبت مولوی با شمس سه چهار سال بیشتر طول نکشید و شمس در سال ۶۴۵ ناپدید شد و اثری از وی نیافتند.

مولوی پس از ناپدیدشدن شمس به حالتی افتاد که در آن جز بر عشاق سر تا پا سوخته‌ی پاکباز میسر نیست. مدت ۷ سال در آتش فراق شمس می‌سوخت و شب و روز در جوش و خروش بود. در این سال مولوی کم کم سرگرم مصاحبت شیخ صلاح‌الدین زرکوب شد که از مریدان و دست‌پروردگان خود مولوی و شمس بود. این مصاحبت ۱۰ سال طول کشید و در سال ۶۶۲ شیخ صلاح الدین هم در گذشت و باز مولوی تنها و بی‌یار و مونس می‌ماند.

اما یک تن دیگر هم از تربیت‌یافتگان آن دستگاه به نام شیخ حسام‌الدین چلپی مولوی را از وحشت تنهایی بیرون آورد و مدت مصاحبت وی با مولوی هم ۱۰ سال طول نکشید که مولوی وفات یافت و پس از وی به فاصله‌ی حدود ۱۲ سال هم حسام‌الدین چلپی در سال ۶۸۳ درگذشت. بهترین اثر جاویدان مولوی که مثنوی باشد، یادگار ۱۰ سال ایام مصاحبت وی با حسام الدین است که خودش نیز در اوایل جلد دوم مثنوی با آغاز ایام مصاحبت و تاریخ شروع مثنوی تصریح کرده است.

آشنایی با زندگی نامه مولانا

گرچه در طول سالیان دراز در ایران شاعران و نویسندگان، آثار مهمی به جا گذاشته‌اند، در این بین کمتر نمونه‌ای مانند آثار مولوی به چشم می‌خورد که در همه جهان، طرفداران و علاقه مندان پر شوری دارد. اشعار مولانا به زبانهای مختلف ترجمه شده‌اند و بارها در دانشگاه‌های مختلف جهان به تفسیر این اشعار پرداخته‌اند.

جلال الدین محمد بلخی، در ششم ربیع الاول سال ۶۰۴ هجری قمری در بلخ که آن زمان از توابع خراسان بود زاده شد. پدر او مولانا محمد بن حسین خطیبی (بهاءالدین ولد) و مادرش مومنه خاتون نام دارند.

نام کامل وی «محمد بن محمد بن حسین حسینی خطیبی بکری بلخی» بوده و در دوران حیات به القاب «جلال‌الدین»، «خداوندگار» و «مولانا خداوندگار» نامیده می شده است. در قرن های بعد (ظاهراً از قرن ۹) که با نام‌هایی «مولوی»، «مولانا»، «مولوی رومی» و «ملای رومی» در جهان شناخته می‌شود و از برخی از اشعارش تخلص او را «خاموش» و «خَموش» و «خامُش» دانسته اند.

زبان مادری وی پارسی و از مشهورترین شاعران ایرانی پارسی‌گوی است. اما برخی از آثارش به زبان‌های عربی نیز نگاشته شده‌اند و در میان آثار به جا مانده از او، جملات محدودی نیز به زبان‌های ترکی و یونانی وجود دارند. این خانواده از مردم خراسان قدیم ساکن ناحیه‌ی بلخ بوده و به نسبت بلخی و خراسانی شهرت داشته‌اند. اما شهرت مولوی به مولانای روم و ملای رومی پس از آن است که از بلخ مهاجرت کرده و در شهر قونیه ساکن شده‌اند که از شهرهای معروف آناطولی و آسیای صغیر و ترکیه‌ی کنونی است و آن را در قدیم کشور روم می گفتند. این شهرت از اوایل قرن هشتم هجری به بعد است برای این که در نوشته‌های نیمه‌ی نخست این قرن از مولوی به عنوان مولانای روم نام برده و اشعاری نقل کرده‌اند.

جلال الدین محمد در هجده سالگی با همسر اول خویش گوهر خاتون دختر خواجه شرف الدین لالای سمرقندی ازدواج نمود که حاصل این ازدواج دو پسر به نام های سلطان ولد و علاءالدین محمد بود.

همسر دوم مولانا خاتون قونوی نام داشت و مولانا از او فرزندانی به نام های مظفرالدین امیر عالم و ملک خاتون داشت. همسر دوم مولانا ۱۹ سال پس از وفات مولانا زنده بود.

بهاءالدین از اکابر صوفیه واعاظم عرفا بود و خرقهٔ او به احمد غزالی می پیوست. وی مردی سخنور بوده، و مردم بلخ علاقه فراوانی بر او داشته اند. ظاهرا همان وابستگی مردم به بهاء ولد سبب ایجاد ترس در محمد خوارزمشاه گردیده است. بهاءولد در جوانی با خانواده برای زیارت کعبه‌ی معظمه و انجام عمل حج در حدود سال ۶۱۶ که گیراگیر حمله‌ی مغول به ایران بود، از بلخ مسافرت کرد. در مسیر حرکت به‌سمت مکه برای انجام مناسک حج، در شهر نیشابور، مولوی همراه پدرش به دیدار «شیخ فریدالدین عطار» عارف و شاعر شتافت. در آن زمان جلال الدین مولانا کوچک بود که عطار نیشابوری او را بسیار ستایش کرد و نسخه‌ای از «اسرار نامه» را به او هدیه داد و برای مولوی به فراست ایمانی آتیه‌ی درخشانی را پیش‌بینی

مثنوی معنوی

جلال الدّین محمد بلخی

با ترجمه انگلیسی: رینولد آلین نیکلسون

گردآوری: حمید اسلامیان

دفتر اول

www.ingramcontent.com/pod-product-compliance
Lightning Source LLC
Chambersburg PA
CBHW081248200825
31409CB00015B/1078